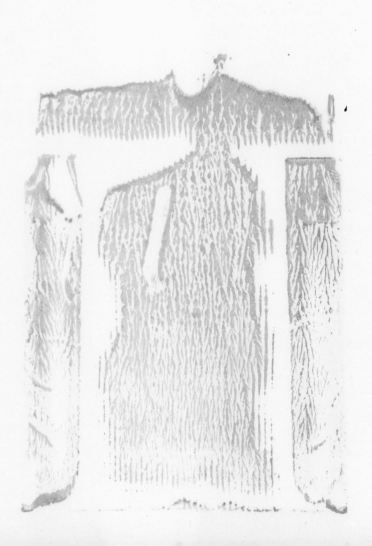

FAMOUS
AMERICAN
BOOKS

FAMOUS AMERICAN BOOKS

ROBERT B. DOWNS

McGRAW-HILL BOOK COMPANY

NEW YORK   ST. LOUIS   SAN FRANCISCO
DÜSSELDORF   JOHANNESBURG   KUALA LUMPUR
LONDON   MEXICO   MONTREAL   NEW DELHI
PANAMA   RIO DE JANEIRO   SINGAPORE
SYDNEY   TORONTO

Library of Congress Catalog Card Number: 72–172256

ISBN: 07–0176655–5

CONTENTS

ACKNOWLEDGMENTS

Particular gratitude should be expressed to three individuals for their aid in bringing the present work into existence. The genesis of the book came from a distinguished librarian, Joseph L. Wheeler, Director Emeritus of the Enoch Pratt Library in Baltimore, who wrote to the author:

> A book is badly needed to show more in detail and from the social viewpoint just what some important books *have done* to change American society. Just what happened when such books came out? It is an exciting story—the reactions of the public, the arguments, the changes in legislation, the general results on American thinking.

In the actual creation of the book, the author feels a deep sense of appreciation to Elizabeth C. Downs, who did much of the preliminary research on each title included, and to Clarabelle Gunning, who prepared the manuscript for publication. Their assistance was indispensable.

ROBERT B. DOWNS
Urbana, Illinois

INTRODUCTION

The present work is the third in a series designed to illustrate and to illuminate the impact of books on history. The first was *Famous Books, Ancient and Medieval,* which began with the Egyptian *Book of the Dead,* several thousand years before Christ, and concluded with Chaucer's *Canterbury Tales;* and the second, *Famous Books Since 1492,* started with Columbus's account of his first voyage to the New World and ended with Sigmund Freud's *Civilization and Its Discontents.* Each was worldwide in scope, though predominantly concerned with works of European and American origin.

Now we move on to a more restricted area—books produced in or relating principally to the United States of America. A number of American or American-oriented titles were dealt with in *Famous Books Since 1492,* and those who miss such old familiars as Franklin's *Autobiography,* Paine's *Common Sense,* Hamilton-Madison-Jay's *The Federalist,* Tocqueville's *Democracy in America,* Emerson's *Essays,* Stowe's *Uncle Tom's Cabin,* Bellamy's *Looking Backward,* Mahan's *Influence of Sea Power,* Dewey's *School and Society,* and Woodrow Wilson's *New Freedom* will find them treated therein.

The chief criterion for selection of the fifty titles presented in *Famous American Books* is influence. In each instance, a book has been examined from the point of view of its effect on our history or way of life. Literary merit is a secondary consideration, though certainly a limited number of the works chosen are literary masterpieces. But far more significant for present purposes is the roles which various books have played in shaping the American world of today. The measurement of influence is, of course, a perplexing question. Books which sell in the tens of millions of copies, for example, the Mickey Spillanes and the Perry Masons, may make little or no impact on popular thought or behavior, while other works, of limited circulation, may shake the world. The crucial test of influence is whether or not the theories, programs, or ideas advanced eventually win wide acceptance, cause disciples, imitators, and rivals to rise, and are gradually incorporated into the lives and thoughts of the people.

The arrangement of *Famous American Books* is strictly chronological, without regard to subject content. From Amerigo Vespucci, at the beginning of the sixteenth century, to Paul Ehrlich in 1968 the order is by date of publication, with the one exception of William Byrd, whose writings did not appear in print until a century or more after their composition. The chronological plan is most useful in illustrating the development of social and scientific thought from generation to generation.

Have some eras been more productive than others in generating books and ideas that have helped to mold the national destiny? The literature of the colonial period offers relatively little to stimulate the mind. Charles Evans's *American Bibliography* lists some thirty thousand titles printed before 1800, but the percentage of dull theological treatises, sermons, and other religious material is excessive, and there were many reprints of English books. The Revolutionary era is rich in writings of historical significance, for example, those by Thomas Jefferson, Benjamin Franklin, Thomas Paine, Alexander Hamilton, James Madison, John Jay, George Washington, and other Founding Fathers. Much intellectual ferment can be observed after 1800; particularly notable was the six-year stretch from 1849 to 1855, which saw the birth of Parkman's *Oregon Trail*, Melville's *Moby Dick*, Thoreau's *Walden*, and Whitman's *Leaves of Grass*, to which could be added Harriet Beecher Stowe's *Uncle Tom's Cabin*, at a lower literary level. The distribution of titles since 1870 is fairly even.

As one reviews the fifty books herein discussed he must be impressed by the multifaceted nature of American culture and civilization, as it has evolved over a period of nearly five centuries. Early in the era came the explorers and discoverers, such as Amerigo Vespucci, Captain John Smith, William Byrd, Crèvecoeur, Audubon, Dana, and Parkman. Our vital concern with the sea around us and America's pioneer contributions to maritime science are illustrated by the works of Nathaniel Bowditch and Matthew Fontaine Maury. The preoccupation of the early settlers with religion and theology emerge in the writings of Cotton Mather and Michael Wigglesworth.

Later came the attempts to interpret our social ideas, government, manners, laws, economic practices, race problems, and history. In this area, which may be broadly defined as the social sciences, fall a large proportion of the fifty titles comprised in the present work. Here, for example, belong the writings of Thoreau, Whitman, Holmes, Bryce, Veblen, Booker T. Washington, W. E. B. DuBois, Tarbell, Sumner, Henry Adams, Bok, Lewis, Gompers, Benedict, Lippmann, Mumford, Steinbeck, Willkie, Kennedy, Mitford, Nader, and Ehrlich, and perhaps Fannie Farmer, Emily Post, Spock, and Kinsey.

It is more difficult to single out individual works in the field of science which have had measurable influence, despite the Americans' almost mystical faith in technology and scientific progress. A trail-blazing book was Benjamin Franklin's *Experiments and Observations on Electricity.* Of enduring importance, too, are Audubon's *Birds of America,* Asa Gray's writing on botany, and William James's *Principles of Psychology.*

The emancipation of women is increasingly evident as one proceeds through the list of fifty titles. The first to appear is Mary Baker Eddy in 1875, but then came Frances Hodgson Burnett, Fannie Farmer, Ida Tarbell, Emily Post, Ruth Benedict, and Jessica Mitford—a reasonable percentage of latter-day writers whose pens have changed our minds, manners, and general culture.

A number of attempts have been made in the past to identify books whose impact on history may be clearly discernible. A unanimous judgment is exceedingly difficult to reach on any given work. Selection is a highly personal and subjective matter. Nevertheless, there is sufficient consensus on the fifty titles chosen for discussion in the present volume to believe that a large majority would rank high in a vote by any knowledgeable and impartial jury.

Comparatively few books, it should be noted, have as much meaning for later generations as for the readers of their own eras. Generally speaking, the times make the book, and a particular work was influential because the time was ripe for it. In some other period, the book would not have been produced at all, or if it had appeared, would have attracted little attention. Exceptions are great literary classics, such as *Walden, Moby Dick,* and *Huckleberry Finn,* which in a sense are timeless.

An unfortunate tendency has spread in recent years to downgrade the importance of books. Denigrators of books, such as the Marshall McLuhan school, would have us believe that books are obsolescent and have been superseded by newer media such as television. Thus they hold that books have had their day, significant and influential in earlier eras, but now on the way to becoming museum pieces. The spuriousness of the argument can be easily shown by citing three books published in the 1960s, all of which have had a direct impact on current events: Rachel Carson's *Silent Spring,* which called dramatic attention to the perils of indiscriminate use of chemical preparations in agriculture and elsewhere; Ralph Nader's *Unsafe at Any Speed,* which forced the automobile industry to produce safer cars; and Jessica Mitford's *American Way of Death,* which has helped to reform funeral practices. A more recent work, Paul Ehrlich's *Population Bomb,* appears to be making a similar impact.

Also significant is the fact that twice as many book titles are being published in the United States as a decade ago. At the same time, book sales have doubled. A leading factor in the "publication explosion" is the paperback book. The number of paperback titles in print has jumped from 4,500 in 1955 to 80,000 in 1970. Despite the competition of other media, the statistics demonstrate that the American people are reading more books, magazines, and newspapers than ever before in their history. And there is no reason to believe that the reading of books is any less influential today than in earlier times.

FAMOUS
AMERICAN
BOOKS

1 | PILOT MAJOR

Amerigo Vespucci's *The Four Voyages of Amerigo Vespucci*, 1505–1506

There is no more controversial figure in American history than a Florentine citizen for whom, in the sixteenth century, two new continents were named. Amerigo Vespucci has been the target of a heavy barrage of character assassination for more than 400 years. Only in recent times have efforts been made to rehabilitate his reputation. A vitriolic statement by Ralph Waldo Emerson has long represented the popular viewpoint:

> Strange that broad America must wear the name of a thief, Amerigo Vespucci, a pickle dealer at Seville, whose highest naval rank was boatswain of an expedition that never sailed, who managed in this lying world to supplant Columbus and baptize half the earth with his dishonest name.

A modern judgment, and a more rational interpretation of facts, comes from historian Garrett Mattingly, who concludes: "Whether or not Amerigo deserved to have two continents named after him, it is certain that he never sought the honor. Possibly he never even heard of it. Nor did he deserve at all the epithets like 'vulgar swindler' and 'ignorant landlubber' with which he was once belabored."

Amerigo Vespucci was born in Florence in 1454 and died in Seville in 1512. He belonged to a family that had been prominent and powerful in the fourteenth century. His early studies emphasized cosmography, astronomy, and mathematics. From 1478 to 1480 he served as secretary to an uncle who was Florentine Ambassador to France. Beginning in 1480, Vespucci was an agent of the Medici family in Florence. Late in 1491 he was sent to Seville to assist in taking care of the Medici shipping interests, and a few years later he signed a contract with the Spanish government "to outfit twelve ships for the next trip of the Admiral Christopher Columbus to the island of Hispaniola."

It was this relationship, apparently, which led Emerson to apply the epithet "pickle dealer," since the provisions that Amerigo supplied usually included barrels of pickles.

Vespucci soon arrived at the decision that outfitting ships for other men's adventures on the high seas was too tame an occupation. Abandoning commercial pursuits, he henceforth devoted himself to the life of a navigator. His qualifications were strengthened by the fact that he had become an expert in maps, charts, and globes, and he was an avid map collector, as well as a better-than-average map maker.

According to Vespucci's own account, now regarded by critics as reasonably authentic, his first long voyage was under Captain Alonso de Ojeda, commissioned by King Ferdinand of Castile. Sailing on May 10, 1497, from Cádiz, the expedition crossed the Atlantic and the Caribbean, making the passage in twenty-four days. It was Vespucci's first experience at sailing, but he learned the science of navigation quickly. In a letter to a friend, Piero Soderini, he reports that there were four boats in the little fleet. Vespucci charted the ships' course along the coast of Africa and by way of the Canary Islands.

The first coast sighted in the 1497 expedition was either Costa Rica or Honduras. If the date is accurate, Vespucci was on the mainland a year before Christopher Columbus, whose third voyage touched the coast of South America in the summer of 1498. Vespucci records that several boats, filled with armed men, went ashore from the fleet. They could "see hordes of naked people running along the shore," but as the boats approached, the natives fled to the nearby hills and refused to respond to the sailors' overtures. There was no protection against rough seas where the ships first anchored, and early next morning they set sail, seeking a safe harbor. After two days, following a northern route, "a place quite suited to our needs" was discovered, and the ships anchored a half-league from the land. There again the voyagers "saw countless hordes of people." At first the natives would not respond to advances, but eventually "they received us kindly, and in fact mingled among us with as complete assurance as if we had often met before."

The customs of the natives and their modes of life are

described in detail by Vespucci—their complete nudity, excellent physical condition, weapons, perpetual wars with neighboring tribes, sexual mores, food, habitations, ornaments, treatment of the ill, and burial customs. Among one tribe, Vespucci noted a strange serpent with huge claws (an iguana) being roasted and eaten. Generally the natives were friendly, but on several occasions the voyagers were attacked by warlike tribes, and once they lost two sailors to cannibals.

Continuing their explorations, the ships sailed around the curve of the Gulf of Mexico, and from Lariab in the Mexican state of Tabasco they probably passed south of Florida. Following the coast northward, the expedition entered what Vespucci describes as "one of the best harbors in the world"—possibly Delaware or Chesapeake Bay. "And since by that time," Vespucci writes, "we had already been thirteen months on our voyage, and since the tackle and rigging were very much the worse for wear and the men were reduced by fatigue, we unanimously agreed to repair our small boats (which were leaking at every point) and to return to Spain." A safe landing was made at Cádiz on October 15, 1498.

The only account that we possess of this first voyage is Vespucci's. Nevertheless, his report is confirmed by the maps drawn immediately following, showing the complete outline of the Gulf of Mexico, the contours of the peninsula of Florida, and the profile of the coast to the north. Cuba appears as an island, instead of a part of the mainland as Columbus had proclaimed it. No other recorded voyage accounts for these new cartographic features, and thus they support the veracity of Vespucci's report.

In May 1499 Vespucci sailed again with Ojeda, landing this time in northeastern South America. During the voyage, pearl fisheries were found near the mouth of the Orinoco River, the coast of Brazil was explored as far as the large bulge which projects into the Atlantic, and the mouth of the Amazon River was explored. On the homeward journey, they visited the northern coast of Brazil, the Guianas, and Venezuela up to Cabo de la Vela in Colombia. Again the native tribes encountered ranged from excessively friendly and hospitable to hostile and warlike. In Venezuela, the travelers saw a settlement built over the sea, with houses constructed of reeds and poles. To this area was given the name *Venezuela,* "Little Venice," which it has retained to the present day.

In the course of the second voyage Vespucci was much occupied with his astronomical researches, and he made an extraordinary discovery concerning the coordinates of latitude. Jesuit Father J. W. Stein, director of the Vatican Observatory, in a study published in 1950, concluded: "Until there is proof to the contrary, we must consider Vespucci as the inventor of the method of lunar distances. He was the first to employ it, measuring the distance between the moon and Mars at midnight of August 23, 1499. He lacked only exact information to have given an exact longitude." In 1501, Vespucci calculated almost precisely the earth's circumference. His figure for the circumference at the equator was 24,852 miles, while modern science places it as 24,902. Columbus's estimate was 6,125 miles short.

Vespucci's most important voyage, and the one most thoroughly documented as to dates and distances, was the third, undertaken at the request of Don Manuel, King of Portugal. The fleet consisted of three ships commanded by Gonzala Coelho. The principal goal was to explore further the coast of Brazil and to seek a passage farther south. Leaving Lisbon on May 13, 1501, the expedition landed on August 7 on the northern coast of Brazil, after a long and dangerous crossing. For most of sixty-seven days, Vespucci reports, "rain, thunder and lightening so darkened the sky that we never saw the sun by day or fair sky by night." The coast was followed east and then south until a point was reached where, in Vespucci's words, "it was no longer possible to see the Small Bear, and the Great Bear was on the line of the horizon," that is, south of the Tropic of Capricorn.

The leaders of the expedition realized that they had reached a line, drawn in 1494, whereby new land discovered was to be divided between Spain and Portugal. After debating whether or not to proceed further, in effect encroaching on Spanish jurisdiction, it was decided to press forward. The weatherbeaten ships penetrated as far south as the ridge of Montevideo, the mouth of the Plata River, and the coast of Patagonia. A terrible storm forced the explorers to turn back before Vespucci could attain his main objective, the search for a water passage to Asia, but he recognized the probability of the route to Asia which was later to be followed by Magellan.

Prior to the third voyage, Vespucci had accepted with little question Columbus's belief that the lands being explored were part of Asia. In a long letter to Lorenzo di Pier Francesco de' Medici in 1503 (later published under the title *Mundus Novus*) it is revealed that Vespucci had come to the conclusion that a new continent had been discovered. "These new regions which we found and explored," he declares, "we may rightly call a new world." Continuing, he writes:

> We knew that land to be a continent and not an island both because it stretches forth in the form of a very long and unbending coast, and because it is replete with infinite inhabitants. For in it we found innumerable tribes and peoples and species of all manner of wild beasts which are found in our lands and others never before seen by us.

The *Mundus Novus*, issued in 1504, became a literary sensation in Europe. It was translated into Latin, and German, Italian, and French versions appeared. The two ideas which caught the popular fancy and brought fame to Vespucci among his contemporaries were, first, that a new continent had been discovered and, second, the antipodes existed and were habitable, refuting long-held beliefs to the contrary. "Without doubt," Amerigo comments of the lands he had visited, "if the Garden of Eden exists anywhere on earth, it is my opinion that it cannot be far from those countries."

Vespucci's fourth voyage, also commanded by Coelho, had as its principal aim a continuation of the earlier discoveries and finding a passage that he believed to exist at the extremity of the continent. But the expedition was a failure and was probably the last to be undertaken by Vespucci. After his return to Spain, he was granted Castilian citizenship by King Ferdinand and appointed to the newly created post of Pilot Major of Spain. In that position, held until his death, Vespucci supervised Spanish pilots and held the responsibility for approving new maps before they were issued. Navigators were expected to report all new discoveries to him.

Vespucci's narratives of travel are generally straightforward, without any inclination to let his imagination run away with him, as other writers of the period frequently had. There are in his accounts, for example, no countries populated by monsters, or kingdoms inhabited only by women, or dog-headed men, or fountains of youth.

A curious series of events led to Amerigo Vespucci's name being permanently attached to the newly discovered continents. The birthplace of the name *America* was in France, in the ancient monastery of Saint-Dié. There the monks had received a copy of Vespucci's *Four Voyages*. At the time, one of the monks, Martin Waldseemüller, was engaged in writing *Cosmographiae Introductio,* "Introduction to Cosmography," an updating of Ptolemy's work. A Latin translation of Vespucci's letters of 1504, under the title *Quattuor Americi Vesputii Navigationes,* was appended to the Waldseemüller geography when it was published in 1507. After discussing the older, better-known parts of the world, Waldseemüller writes:

> Now, these parts of the earth have been more extensively explored and a fourth part has been discovered by Amerigo Vespucci. Inasmuch as both Europe and Asia received their names from women, I see no reason why any one should justly object to calling this part Amerige, i.e., the land of Amerigo, or America, after Amerigo, its discoverer, a man of great ability. Its position and the customs of its inhabitants may be clearly understood from the four voyages of Amerigo, which are subjoined.

Here was the first suggestion that the New World should bear the name of Amerigo Vespucci. Supplementing his geography, Waldseemüller drew a planisphere and a huge map of the world, beautiful works of cartography and design, on which the southern continent of the new hemisphere is labeled "America." Soon the word spread through Europe, and eventually won universal acceptance. The Waldseemüller map showed the general outlines of the northern and southern continents, the Antilles, Cuba as an island, the Gulf of Mexico, and the Yucatan Peninsula, though of course not the Pacific coast, which still remained to be explored. In any event, the naming of the New World had been accomplished, irretrievably. In 1538 Mercator applied the name to the northern continent, also.

But ever since, controversies have raged over the propriety of the name. Perhaps the first and certainly one of the bitterest critics was Bartolomé de Las Casas, Spanish priest and historian, who accompanied Columbus on his fourth voyage to America. An ardent supporter of Columbus, Las Casas's writings damn Vespucci as a sly thief who cunningly robbed Columbus of his rightful glory: "And it is well to give thought here," he asserts in his *Historia de las Indias,* "to the injustice and offense that that Amerigo Vespucci seems to have done the Admiral, or those who first printed his four voyages, attributing to himself, or alluding only to him, the discovery of this mainland."

A well-balanced statement analyzing the respective claims is presented by Frederick J. Pohl in his biography, *Amerigo Vespucci:*

> Columbus was not the discoverer of what Waldseemüller meant by the word "America." He himself had denied it, by insisting to the day of his death that he had reached the mainland of Asia. . . . It was no error and no injustice to name the new continent after the man who discovered that it was a new continent. . . . If by "discover" is meant "to get first sight of," then Columbus was the discoverer of the continent that was named America. . . . Columbus could not bring America to the knowledge of Europe, because he had not faintest conception of what America was or that there was any such thing as a New World. . . . To Columbus, priority; to Vespucci, understanding.

It is significant that Columbus and Vespucci remained firm friends until the former's death in 1506, with never an indication of rivalry. In his letters Columbus speaks highly of Vespucci as a man constant in his devotion, "a true man of his word," and "a man of good will." Neither did Columbus's sons, who were so jealous for their father's fame, voice even the slightest complaint against the Florentine. As Pohl points out,

> Between Columbus and Vespucci there need be no "recriminations in Hades." Columbus destroyed the conception that the western ocean was a vast and impassable barrier. . . . On the other hand, Amerigo Vespucci gave mankind the idea of a hitherto-unknown hemisphere. Which did more to enlarge man's conception of the earth? Here was their only rivalry.

Vespucci was probably the best cosmographer of his day. He was more expert than Columbus in plotting ocean routes. His voyages along the coast of America went far beyond those of any of his predecessors and made it possible to establish the continental nature of America. He prepared the way for Magellan's circumnavigation of South America, and his influence on the cartography of his day was immense. Altogether, the weight of the evidence supports the view that Amerigo Vespucci was a man of whom Americans can be proud—one of the greatest in an age of great seamen, discoverers, and explorers.

2 | THE FIRST AMERICAN

Captain John Smith's *The Generall Historie of Virginia, New-England, and the Summer Isles,* 1624

The first book which can claim specifically to be a history of English territory in the New World is Captain John Smith's *The Generall Historie of Virginia, New-England, and the Summer Isles,* printed in London in 1624. In writing the work, Smith had two objects in view: to promote interest in colonizing the new lands and to apologize and defend his own controversial career in Virginia.

Captain John Smith's veracity has often been questioned. Some historians are inclined to believe almost everything that he wrote; others denounce him as a liar and a braggart. The truth lies somewhere in between. In any event, standards of historical accuracy in Smith's time were considerably less strict than they are today, and the introduction of tall tales in historical narratives is a custom dating back to Herodotus, the father of history.

Smith was born at the height of the Elizabethan era and quickly absorbed the spirit of adventure and the swashbuckling manner characteristic of that age. For a time, indeed, he served on a pirate ship. In his early youth he was attracted to wherever the action was and spent several years in a life of reckless adventure, including a fantastic period of fighting against the Turks, the enemies of Christendom. By the time that he returned to England in 1604, at the age of twenty-four, Smith had visited every country and nearly every city of any importance in Central and Western Europe.

John Smith's opportunity to establish his name and fame came in 1606. The Virginia Company received a royal charter for the discovery and occupation of lands in North America between "New France" (Canada) and the Spanish possessions in Florida and Mexico. Smith was one of the active promoters of the company and was named one of seven members of the council which was to be in charge of the settlement. Arthur Innes, English historian, describes the company of 105 who landed in Virginia in 1607 as "gentlemen, artificers, labourers, loafers and rapscallions. There were good men among them, but they could scarcely be called a select company; they were without training or discipline; all the members of the council were jealous of each other, there was no supreme authority, and few of them had any practical experience." The choice of the site of what was to become Jamestown was fortuitous—the expedition's three ships were driven by a storm into Chesapeake Bay.

The prospects were decidedly inauspicious. The gentlemen had quarreled among themselves during the four-month voyage, and Smith's behavior had been so bumptious that he was accused of mutiny and narrowly escaped hanging. The president of the council, Edward Wingfield, lacked force and the qualities of leadership essential to inspiring or enforcing obedience and discipline. The marshy peninsula in the James River selected for the settlement had obvious drawbacks—it generated malaria —but the land was fertile, and water supplies were ample. Smith's account of the jealousies, follies, bickering, and dissention which came close to wrecking the pioneer settlement is well documented by other sources. As Smith summed up the case some years later, "There is no misery worse than to be conducted by a fool or commanded by a coward."

The story of the first year of the English occupation of Virginia is one of mutual suspicion, distrust, confusion, and anarchy. From the beginning, the fainthearted wished to abandon the colony and return to England's material comforts. Because Wingfield opposed any fortification and insisted on treating the red men as civilized Europeans, the settlement narrowly escaped being wiped out in an Indian massacre. When manpower was urgently needed to build shelters and to cultivate corn and other crops in preparation for winter, the whole colony went mad with gold fever. The London Company had no conception of actual conditions and assumed that Virginia had a year-round summer climate and tropical abundance; hence it neglected to supply the necessities for survival. After the ships' provisions were exhausted, the colonists were to raise their own food. Game and fish were available, but the settlers lacked the Indians' expertise in exploiting the natural resources. Thus, with the supplies left by the departing ships soon exhausted or spoiled, and a trifling acreage of Indian corn having been planted, the settlers were soon reduced to half a pint of barley meal per day, and they were dying of malnutrition. Neither by temperament nor talent were most of the men qualified to make a success of a plantation in the Virginia wilds.

During these perilous early months, John Smith was engaged in his favorite occupation, exploring the Chesapeake Bay area, as well as concerning himself with the practical problems of feeding the adventurers and providing for their safety and defense against the Indians. In the course of his expeditions he learned the Indians' languages, their trading methods, and their social customs. Indeed, Smith showed considerable talent for anthropology, as evidenced by his excellent descriptions of Indian society in all its aspects. He was the one man in the colony who knew how to deal effectively with the savages, for he seems to have had an instinctive understanding of when to trust them and when to be on guard against treachery. Thus he fought them, made treaties of peace and friendship, forced them to trade for corn to feed the starving colonists, and mapped their territory.

In the course of one of Smith's expeditions there occurred one of the most famous episodes in early American history—if we can rely upon the captain's account. While on an exploratory trip in December 1607 Smith was captured by the Indians and taken to the camp of Chief Powhatan, head of the Indians in the Chesapeake area. For about three weeks he was kept prisoner, while the Indians apparently were debating how to dispose of him. The story of his rescue first appeared in print in the *Generall Historie*, seventeen years later. In Captain Smith's words, told in third person,

> Having feasted him [Smith] after their best barbarous manner they could, a long consultation was held, but the conclusion was, two great stones were brought before Powhatan; then as many as could laid hands on him, dragged him to them, and thereon laid his head, and being ready with their clubs to beat out his

brains, Pocahontas, the King's dearest daughter, when no entreaty could prevail, got his head in her arms, and laid her own upon his to save him from death: whereat the Emperor was contented he should live to make him hatchets, and her bells, beads, and copper.

One reason for questioning the veracity of Smith's account is that it was told so long after the event, though the captain claimed that it was included in a letter addressed to Queen Elizabeth eight years earlier. In further substantiation, John Gould Fletcher notes in the biography *John Smith—Also Pocahontas:* "It was the universal practice among Indian tribes to grant the life of a captive, white or red, only at the instance of some favorite squaw; and Pocahontas was notoriously Powhatan's favorite daughter."

Subsequent events lead further credence to the legend. Smith was escorted back to the fort by a dozen of Powhatan's warriors. Afterward, Pocahontas is reported to have often visited the fort, always bringing with her a fresh supply of provisions, thereby helping the colonists to survive. She was perhaps no more than twelve years of age at the time of the celebrated rescue. A satisfying conclusion for the romantic story would have been for John Smith to have married the young heroine, but in fact she wed another Englishman, John Rolfe, and was taken to London, where she died of consumption some ten years later.

In the fall of 1608 Smith was elected president of the council at Jamestown. By this time there were about four hundred Englishmen in Virginia, of whom only thirty were survivors of the original group. Smith's hard work and decisive actions saved the colony from starvation or extermination during the winter of 1608–1609. The Indians were ordered by Powhatan not to trade for corn with the English; Smith changed the chief's mind by threatening war. By a continual show of force, Smith avoided battle and obtained the food needed by the colonists. The captain was an autocratic ruler, however, and his dictatorial methods were resented by the unruly men under him, at least half of whom were unacquainted with hard manual labor and unwilling to do the necessary work of clearing and cultivating the land.

On three occasions the discontented were about to abandon

the colony and return to England. Each time Smith turned the fort's guns on the ships and threatened to sink them. Just as the situation appeared to be improving and a sufficient stock of foodstuffs had been stored to see the settlers through their second winter, it was discovered that the corn had rotted in the poorly constructed granaries. What was unspoiled had been attacked by a plague of rats brought by the ships. For the remainder of the winter, the men had to live off the land, mainly subsisting on fish and wild berries. Nevertheless, Governor Smith brought the colony through with the loss of only seven men—and these from sickness rather than starvation.

One crisis during Smith's administration was created by the return of Captain Christopher Newport, who commanded the original fleet in 1607 and represented the London Company in its dealings with the Jamestown Colony. The company's directors were completely ignorant of the true conditions existing in the area selected for the settlement, but they insisted on some material return for their investment in the enterprise. Captain Newport was directed not to return to England without accomplishing at least one of the following missions: finding a passage to the South Seas, bringing samples from gold mines which he was ordered to discover, or locating survivors of Raleigh's lost colony at Roanoke. Further, Powhatan was to be crowned king, to assure his cooperation and support, and the London investors demanded a return cargo worth at least £2,000 to cover the cost of the voyage. The only part of his instructions which Newport was able to carry out was the crowning of Powhatan in a ridiculous, and what Smith rightly regarded as a futile, ceremony.

Meanwhile, complaints against Smith's authoritarian methods began to reach the officials at home, who were dissatisfied in any case by the lack of immediate profits from their venture, and the Governor was ordered removed from office. At about this time, Smith suffered a serious wound when a bag of gunpowder exploded. In the early fall of 1609, he sailed for England, ill and disappointed over the developments at Jamestown. Smith never returned to Virginia, though his keen interest in the colony's progress was frequently shown during the remaining twenty-two years of his life. That the first permanent English settlement in

America survived its first two years is due almost entirely to the endurance, courage, administrative ability, intelligence, and indomitable will of young Captain John Smith.

Much of the remainder of Smith's career was devoted to the colonization of New England. The name of the region, which first appeared in print in Smith's tract *A Description of New England* (1616) was apparently inspired by Drake's Nova Albion on the Pacific Coast. The first recorded appearance in literature of the name *Massachusetts* is also found in Smith's writings.

In 1614 Smith was given command of a small pioneering expedition to the New England area, with two ships and a crew of about fifty. Under the sponsorship of the Northern Virginia Company, the captain was directed to search for whales, furs, and gold mines, though his own interests were primarily in geographical discovery and colonial settlement. A good deal of the New England coast was explored, and Smith wrote glowing descriptions of the region's natural resources, with its cornfields, extraordinary plenty of fish, fruit, and fowl, good harbors, and healthy, invigorating climate. An eloquent plea was made for colonization for the greater glory of the English nation. Smith's map of the area and his writings made him a kind of press agent for New England and provided essential information for the use, a few years later, of the Pilgrims and the Puritans.

A year after his first voyage, Smith sailed again for New England in a small ship carrying four guns. A series of adventures ended in capture by four French privateers. Following a landing on the French coast, Smith eventually made his way back to England, thus ending the last of his seafaring adventures.

Smith's active efforts to promote the colonization of New England continued after his return home. "I am not so simple to think," he wrote, "that ever any other motive than wealth, will ever erect there a Commonweale; or draw company from their ease and humours at home, to stay in New England." In that assumption Smith was mistaken, for religion was the prime motive for the establishment of five commonwealths in New England. The captain offered his personal services to the Pilgrims, in 1619, to command the emigrating party. The bid was declined, ostensibly "to save charges," but more likely because

Smith was a staunch member of the Church of England. The rebellious Pilgrim Fathers would never have agreed to place themselves under the leadership of one who disliked factions and believed in church unity. Smith recognized that "my books and maps were much better cheap to teach them, than myself," though Smith might have saved both the Pilgrims and the Puritans some of their costly errors in pioneering a new land.

All that Smith ever received for his cooperation and long-time affairs to develop colonies in the region was the worthless title of Admiral of New England. He had the satisfaction before his death, of knowing that his work was bearing fruit, as increasing numbers of emigrants sailed for the English Colonies in North America.

Throughout his colorful and varied career Captain John Smith displayed a liking and talent for writing. An account of his experiences in Virginia was printed in 1608, followed by *A Map of Virginia, with a Description of the Countrey,* in 1612. His final work, *Advertisements for the unexperienced Planters of New-England, or any where,* appeared the year of the author's death, in 1631.

Smith's largest and most ambitious literary production was his *Generall Historie.* A four-page prospectus for the book was printed in 1623. Shortly thereafter a patron, the wealthy countess of Richmond, was found to finance publication. The full title when the large handsome volume came off the press in 1624 read: *The Generall Historie of Virginia, New-England, and the Summer Isles with the names of the Adventurers, Planters, and Governours from their first beginning. Ano: 1584 to this present 1624. With the Proceedings of those Severall Colonies and the Accidents that befell them in all their Journyes and Discoveries. Also the Maps and Descriptions of all those Countryes, their Commodities, people, Government, Customes, and Religion yet knowne.* The work was divided into six parts: The first describes the first settlement of Virginia and the subsequent voyages there to 1605; the second is Smith's description of the country and its English inhabitants; the third relates the occurrences of Smith's voyage and the settlement of Jamestown from December 1606 to 1609; the fourth continues the Virginia history from the planting of Point Comfort in 1609 to 1623; the fifth comprises the history of the Bermudas or Summer Isles (which Smith never visited) from 1593 to 1624; and the sixth and last contains the history of New England from 1614 to 1624.

In the *Generall Historie* Smith aimed to present a complete account of English settlements in America, beginning with the Cabots in 1497 and continuing with the story of the Raleigh settlement at Roanoke, of Jamestown and Plymouth up to 1624, and of Bermuda to 1623. It is in some respects a highly personal narrative, for Smith wrote fully about his own experiences as a settler and explorer, his observations on Indian culture, and his views on the economics of colonizing. A considerable proportion of the book, however, is not original but a collection of travels and voyages. In addition to reprinting his own earlier works in revised form, Smith extracted passages from the writings of some forty-five books and documents by other authors, mainly sixteenth- and early-seventeenth-century works.

In what is probably the best biography of John Smith to date, Bradford Smith's *Captain John Smith: His Life and Legend,* the author observes acutely, "The material Smith likes best to deal with is that which has action in it—exploring new rivers, adventuring into Indian villages, sailing along unexplored coasts, escaping from pirates, hacking homes out of the wilderness, surviving Indian massacres, planting crops, or finding a fortune in ambergris." His writing style has been criticized, because he was a man of action rather than a man of letters, but the narration is clearly expressed, straight forward, and holds one's interest. A perceptive evaluation comes from the pen of Alexis de Tocqueville, who comments:

> That which is most remarkable in Captain Smith is that he mingles with the virtues of his contemporaries qualities which were rare in most of them. His style is simple and clear, his narratives have the seal of truth, his descriptions are not ornate. Upon the state of the Indians in the era of North America's discovery he throws precious light.

Few soldiers of fortune have had careers as full of excitement, adventure, and variety as Captain John Smith—fighting the Turks, serving on pirate ships, escaping Indian captivity, saving

Jamestown from starvation and defeat, exploring new lands, being blown up by gunpowder, quelling mutinies, and innumerable other achievements. Of most long-range importance are his writings and maps which played a significant part in stimulating interest in, and guiding the early stages of, the first English settlements in America.

3 | THE PURITAN MIND RAMPANT

Michael Wigglesworth's *The Day of Doom:*
Or a Poetical Description of the Great and Last
Judgement, 1662

In contemporary renown, Michael Wigglesworth easily outranked all other verse makers of the colonial period. Here was a poet who so perfectly expressed in rhyming meter the religious faith and emotion of Puritan New England that his writings had general distribution throughout the Colonies and exerted a popular influence on a par with the Bible and the Shorter Catechism. Wiggleworth's "blazing and sulphurous poem," *The Day of Doom* (1662), crudely versifies the scriptural Last Judgment with the author's own additions of the harshest sort of Calvinism. The result was the most popular poem ever written in America.

Wigglesworth was born in England, came to New England with his parents at the age of seven, grew up in his father's household in New Haven, and graduated from Harvard College in 1651. For a time he served as a tutor at Harvard, where he worried over the defects, intellectual and moral, of his pupils, criticizing the "spirit of unbridled licentiousness" of the younger generation, especially of a young man who was "heard in the forenoon with ill company playing musick" and of a group who came to ask him if they might stop studying Hebrew. In 1656, Wigglesworth was made pastor of the church at Malden, Massachusetts, and there he remained, as pastor and physician, until his death in 1705. In body he was slight and delicate, described by one of his students, Cotton Mather, as "a feeble little shadow of a man." His health failed, and for some years he was unable to preach. During that trying period, he turned to writing. *The Day of Doom* was composed for God's "dear sake" by one who "wanting other means" would "advantage" Him with his pen.

Ill health did not prevent Wigglesworth from marrying three times and siring a total of eight children.

In his last years, Wigglesworth recovered sufficiently to preach two or three times a week and to give himself, again according to Mather, to "visiting and comforting the afflicted; encouraging the private meetings; catechizing the children of the flock; and managing the government of the church; and attending the sick, not only as a pastor, but as a physician, too; and this not only in his own town, but also in those of the vicinity." Despite his hell-fire-and-brimstone theology, Wigglesworth was spoken of in terms of affection throughout his lifetime, and his character bore no evidence of being harsh or blindly relentless.

The inspiration for *The Day of Doom* came to Michael Wigglesworth some years before the poem's actual composition. One night in October 1653, he had had a dream, of which he writes:

> The latter part of the week I spent in preparing to preach at Charlestown. . . . On the second day at night in my sleep I dreamed of the approach of that great and dreadful day of judgment; and was thereby exceedingly awakened in spirit (as I thought) to follow God with teares and cries until he gave me some hopes of his gracious good will toward me.

The vision may have recurred to Wigglesworth several times. In any case, it absorbed his mind, filling it with fascination and fear, until finally, nine years later, the dream found expression in his epic poem.

The Day of Doom achieved extraordinary success immediately. As the author declared, "It pleased the Lord to give vent for my books and greater acceptance than I could have expected; so that of eighteen hundred there were scarcely any unsold (or but few) at the year's end." A copy of the book was bought for one out of every twenty persons in New England, or one out of every forty-five in the Colonies as a whole. Evidently the entire first edition was worn to shreds, for nothing of it has survived except a single fragment. Popular demand brought about speedy reprinting; there were four American and two London editions before 1701, followed by six editions in the eighteenth century, two in the nineteenth, and one in the twentieth. For over a hundred years, *The Day of Doom* continued to be widely read;

it was printed on broadsides and hawked about the country; and as late as the early years of the nineteenth century elderly persons could still be found able to repeat the whole of it from memory. In a funeral oration at the time of Wigglesworth's death, Mather prophesied that *The Day of Doom* would continue to be read till the last dread day itself—a somewhat optimistic prediction.

The story of *The Day of Doom* is the arrival of Judgment Day and the terrible consternation the cataclysmic event creates among mankind. The sublime and hideous dogmas of New England Puritanism emerge in relentless detail as the narrative unfolds. Wigglesworth looks upon the throngs of men that fill the world as totally depraved. Most of them are doomed in advance by God's eternal decrees to an endless existence of torment. Thus, as Moses Coit Tyler sums up, Wigglesworth "chants with utter frankness, the chant of Christian fatalism, the moan of earthly vanity and sorrow, the physical bliss of the saved, the physical tortures of the damned."

There is no advance warning of the coming of the Last Judgment. On its brink, the scene is thus described in the opening lines of *The Day of Doom:*

> Still was the night, Serene and Bright, when all Men Sleeping Lay;
> Calm was the season, and carnal reason thought so 'twould last for ay.
> Soul, take thine ease, let sorrow cease, much good thou hast in store:
> This was their Song, their Cups among, the Evening before.

But suddenly the peaceful picture changes. With a flash, an explosion, and an all-revealing light, the end of the world arrives, and the millennium is here. All men living and dead are summoned before the throne of Christ. There is no place to hide. As for the abruptly wakened sinners:

> They rush from Beds with giddy heads, and to their windows run,
> Viewing this light, which shines more bright Than doth the Noonday Sun.

At once, in all his appalling splendor appears Christ, the Son of God, to judge both quick and dead:

Before his face the heavens give place, and Skies are rent
   asunder.
With mighty voice, and hideous noise, more terrible than
   Thunder.
No heart so bold, but now grows cold and almost dead with fear.

God's throne is set up, and the sheep and the goats are
separated. The sheep (that is, the saved) are directed to the
right, and the goats (the damned), to the left. Those destined
for eternal bliss are the martyrs for the faith, the physically
afflicted who have kept their faith, the loyal able-bodied, and the
spiritually weak whom God has nevertheless saved. In the last
class are the baptized infants who had not survived to live lives
of sin.

The goats are described as "whining hypocrites," a category
into which are thrown deserters from the faith; those who had
never confessed their faith despite opportunities to do so; worshippers of idols; those who have taken the name of the Lord
in vain; breakers of the Sabbath blue laws; persecutors of the
saints; sex offenders; the "covetous and ravenous"; grossly wicked
children and their parents who have failed to guide them into
paths of righteousness; liars, murderers, witches, and drunkards;
and the heathen who have never heard of God.

The sheep are permitted to sit on thrones around the Lord
while sentences are being passed on their less fortunate brethren.
Christ informs the sheep that it is for them he had suffered
crucifixion, and they are to be rewarded with eternal heavenly
bliss.

When the goats are brought before the bar of judgment, they
must plead their own cause, though the proceedings appear
pointless, for their doom is already sealed. The first group to
approach their Judge have preached and taught orthodox doctrines, but their souls are dead. Among them are those who have
committed blasphemy by partaking of the Lord's Supper without
first clearing their hearts of fault. Closely akin are the pleaders
who have followed the forms of the faith, while knowing that
they are innately sinful and have made no effort to reform, relying
wholly upon Christ for salvation.

Then was brought near a company of "civil honest men,"
respected on earth and guilty of no heinous offenses, but lacking

true faith and piety—men who "thought to scale Heaven's lofty wall by ladders" of their own. They, too, must take their punishment.

The real whiners are those who pretended a want of opportunity to repent. Their intentions were good, but death intervened. Some maintain that they were misled by their superiors; others claim to have misinterpreted the Bible. The cowardly, who have been unwilling to risk their lives and estates to stand up for righteousness, are roundly condemned.

Finally come those who will be granted lighter punishment than the rest. Heathen men plead the want of the written word, and Christ agrees, while holding that they should have followed the light of nature more faithfully. Since they have never heard of Christianity, they will be let off with less painful fires.

The last group to plead were the unbaptized babies:

> Then to the Bar, all they drew near who died in Infancy,
> And never had or good or bad effected personally,
> But from the womb into the tomb were straightway carried.

The infants' claim that they have done no wrong is rejected by the Supreme Judge on the ground that they must be condemned because they have inherited Adam's sin, a fall which made every human being a sinner. Yet the babes are granted a minor reprieve:

> You sinners are, and such a share as sinners may expect,
> Such you shall have; for I do save none but my own elect.
> Yet to compare your sin with their, who lived a longer time,
> I do confess yours is much less, though every sin's a crime.
> A crime it is, therefore in bliss you may not have to dwell;
> But unto you I shall allow the easiest room in Hell.

Thus ends the trial. The saints offer no sympathy or pity for their former friends and relatives about to be sentenced to eternal torment. The Judge proceeds to read the awful doom for those condemned:

> Ye sinful wights, and cursed sprights, that work Iniquity,
> Depart together from me for ever to endless Misery;
> Your portion take in yonder Lake, where Fire and Brimstone
>   flameth;
> Suffer the smart, which your desert as it's due wages claimeth.

The damned wring their hands, gnash their teeth for terror, and cry for anguish. But all to no avail, as Christ commands them:

Depart to Hell, there may you yell, and roar eternally.

Bound hand and foot, the lost are thrown into the burning lake while the saved ascend to heaven "with great joy and melody:"

The Saints behold with courage bold, and thankful wonderment,
To see all those that were their foes thus sent to punishment:
Then do they sing unto their King a Song of endless Praise:
They praise his Name, and do proclaim that just are all his ways.

The 224 stanzas of *The Day of Doom* are composed in the ballad style familiar to and popular with the common folk of its era. Wigglesworth's decision to adopt this meter is explained by a statement in his essay "Eloquence": "He is the best artist who can most clearly and familiarly communicate his thoughts to the meanest capacity." Blank verse or a more sophisticated poetic style, assuming that the author was capable of using them, would have been over the heads of the audience he wished to reach. The ballad measure frequently seems wholly unsuited to a sublime theme, but Wigglesworth's earnest desire to impress sound doctrine on the minds of his readers caused him to sacrifice poetry to theology.

The Day of Doom is orthodox Puritan Calvinism, straight out of the Middle Ages and supporting a medieval concept of heaven and hell. The celestial discoveries of Copernicus were ignored, and Newton's universe would not be revealed for another thirty years. Wigglesworth's epic poem, fed by the apocalyptic passages of the Bible, blazed no new trails but faithfully reflected the theological beliefs of multitudes of Christians of the time. The English playwright Thomas Dekker, a contemporary of Wigglesworth, wrote a poem on the same subject with quite similar language. Kenneth B. Murdock adds:

Anyone who cares to bask in the heat of theological bonfires will find *The Day of Doom* to his taste, but it is well to remember that it has no higher caloric value than, say, some sermons of John Donne, the Anglican poet, some pages of Edwards, the eighteenth century philosopher, or many a forgotten treatise or sermon from days before the Calvinists till days after the Victorians.

Quite conceivably there were some among the Puritans who experienced a morbid satisfaction in reading Wigglesworth's fierce denunciations of sinners, because they were convinced that they themselves were immune from the terrors of the day of doom, and could gaze with complacency on the evil-doers receiving their just punishment. It was not for such as these, however, that Wigglesworth was writing; rather, he wanted to frighten his backsliding congregation into the paths of righteousness.

The mood and temper of *The Day of Doom* were almost certainly influenced by the time of its composition. The year the poem was published, 1662, was a dreadful period for the Puritans in America and in England. The restored Stuart dynasty was "breathing out threatenings and slaughters" against all nonconformists. The colonial charters and liberties of New England were threatened, and the Puritans stood to lose all that they had gained by emigration to the New World. They were also afflicted with epidemics and a great drought, causing increased sickness throughout the colony and a calamitous crop failure. Could these be manifestations of God's wrath against the colony? In any case, the restraining, negative doctrine of punishment was used by the ministers and magistrates to bring any sinful colonists back into the fold.

Wigglesworth's biographer, Richard Crowder, thus concluded an analysis of *The Day of Doom:*

> Its contents, vivid and horrible, were accepted as a matter of course. There is no way to measure its influence. In an era of growing dependence on reason and of exploitation of natural resources for profit and, candidly, for wealth, it no doubt had a restraining effect, at least on the sensitive. Its tremendous popularity most assuredly produced widespread clarification as to the meaning of the theology of the Massachusetts Puritans. Its lines were used to support many a fireside argument, for the problems of divinity and the cosmos were not confined to the conversation of the college-bred.

4 | GOD'S SPOKESMAN

Cotton Mather's *Magnalia Christi Americana:*
Or, The Ecclesiastical History of New England;
From Its First Planting, in the Year 1620,
unto the Year of Our Lord 1698, 1702

When Cotton Mather died in 1728, a memorial to him asserted: "He was perhaps the principal ornament of this country, the greatest scholar that ever was bred in it." Certainly if prolific output is the principal criterion, there could be no argument with the statement. *The Literary History of the United States* records 444 titles from Mather's free-flowing pen, probably the largest total by any American writer, before or after. The great majority of the tremendous production has fallen into merciful oblivion. Virtually the only work of permanent value, historians agree, is the *Magnalia Christi Americana,* a monumental compilation concerned with the early history of American Puritanism.

The Mathers were one of the most remarkable phenomena of the colonial era. The founder of the American branch of the family was Richard Mather, who emigrated to New England in 1635. His son Increase, a noted divine and president of Harvard College from 1685 to 1701, was the father of Cotton Mather, born 1662. Increase was exceeded only by his son in literary productivity; he not only set a rapid pace in the making and publishing of books, but watched over the press to guard against the issue of unauthorized or godless works that might pollute the minds of the people. Increase Mather was a dictator, dominating the press with the same iron hand with which he ruled the pulpit. He and his son Cotton were the last and most unyielding defenders of the ecclesiastical control of government, that is, of theocracy—the principle that political suffrage should be confined to members of the New England churches.

Cotton Mather entered Harvard at the age of twelve and was

graduated at fifteen—one of the youngest graduates in Harvard's history. He preached his first sermon at seventeen and remained associated with the Old North Meeting House of Boston for the remainder of his life. It has been stated of Cotton Mather that he "is unconceivable to one who has not read his diary"—a large two-volume work. He was born and bred in Boston, and in his entire lifetime never traveled more than a few miles from the church over which he and his father reigned for so many years. Vernon L. Parrington's judgment of Cotton Mather is quite harsh:

> Self-centered and self-righteous, the victim of strange asceticisms and morbid spiritual debauches, every circumstance of his life ripened and expanded the colossal egotism of his nature. His vanity was daily fattened by the adulation of silly women and the praise of foolish men, until the insularity of his thought and judgement grew into a disease. His mind was clogged with the strangest miscellany of truth and fiction; he laboured to acquire the possessions of a scholar, but he listened to old wives' tales with an amazing credulity.

Other modern critics have been equally harsh in their appraisals. In H. S. Canby's view, "No better illustration of the ego warped by straining to be virtuous can be found than Cotton Mather . . . he gave the governor advice when he seemed to need it, he bore the sins of his entire community on his own conscience . . . and was one of the most virtuous prigs and well-meaning asses in history." On the other hand, Cotton Mather loved scientific investigation and showed himself courageous and intelligent in such matters as medicine, as Beall and Shryock demonstrate in *Cotton Mather, First Significant Figure in American Medicine.*

Partly because of his own nature and in considerable measure a result of unavoidable circumstances, Cotton Mather's life was unhappy. He was surrounded by fears, bedeviled by illnesses—real and imaginary—and beset by tragedy. He buried two wives and all but two of his fifteen children. He was intensely emotional, high-strung, and nervous, was given to seeing visions; and was haunted by "bodings of a dark cloud hanging over my family" and dread of a personal disaster. His most virulent fears were of "invading devils" who killed his children, persecuted members of his congregation, stole his sermon notes, and committed all manner of mischief in Salem.

Because of his conviction that diabolical influences were at work, Cotton Mather was entirely ready to believe in witchcraft. To demonstrate the reality of the world of evil spirits, he undertook a series of investigations, the results of which were published in his *Memorable Providences, Relating to Witchcrafts and Possessions* (1689), *Wonders of the Invisible World* (1693), and other works. Just before the infamous Salem witchcraft prosecutions began in 1692, Mather warned the judges against using "spectral evidence" and suggested that punishment milder than execution might be imposed. Nevertheless, he urged careful examination of the accused and vigorous prosecution if there were strong proof of guilt. Mather's advice about capital punishment was disregarded, and twenty witches were hanged. While these events were occurring, Mather made no public protest, and in his *Wonders of the Invisible World* he argued for the justice of the verdicts in the trials. Then a strong public reaction set in, following on the panic, and it was generally recognized that great wrongs had been done. The enemies of the Mathers, who were numerous, threw the burden of the tragic blunder on them, the chief pillars of theocracy. Probably more than they deserved, Increase and Cotton Mather have traditionally suffered ever since under this cloud on their reputations. They were, of course, the victims of the popular hysteria and superstitions of their time. In any case, the Mathers lost their influence in the Massachusetts government, and Increase was forced out of the presidency of Harvard.

In about 1693, Cotton Mather conceived the idea of writing a general church history of New England, a plan which culminated four years later in the *Magnalia Christi Americana*, though the book was not actually published until 1702, in London. In his general introduction the author states: "I write the wonders of the Christian Religion, flying from the depravations of Europe, to the American Strand; and . . . report the wonderful displays of His infinite Power, Wisdom, Goodness, and Faithfulness, wherewith His Divine Providence hath irradiated an Indian Wilderness." Mather maintains, "Of all History it must be confessed that the palm is to be given unto Church History, wherein the dignity, the suavity, and the utility of the subject is transcendent." The purpose of the book has been well summed up in Barrett Wendell's *Literary History of America:*

> Its true motive was to excite so enthusiastic a sympathy with the ideals of the Puritan fathers that, whatever fate might befall the civil government, their ancestral seminary of learning should remain true to its colours. . . . The time was come, Cotton Mather thought, when the history of these three generations might be critically examined; if this examination should result in showing that there had lived in New England an unprecedented proportion of men and women and children whose earthly existence had given signs that they were among the elect, then his book might go far to prove that the pristine policy of New England had been especially favoured of the Lord. For surely the Lord would choose His elect most eagerly in places where life was conducted most according to His will.

The *Magnalia* may be regarded as an effort, Wendell notes, at a time when the old order was changing, "to preserve and emphasize all the best things that in the olden time had been thought and said, and done." Thereby perhaps the sons could be inspired to emulate the virtues of the fathers. While writing the book Mather was extremely busy with other matters, and the *Magnalia* bears the earmarks of having been flung together in great haste and under the pressure of pastoral duties, politics, responsibilities to Harvard College, other writings, and assorted related matters. "All the time I have had for my Church History," Mather confesses, "hath been chiefly that which I might have taken else for less profitable recreations; and it hath all been done by *snatches*. I wish I could have enjoyed, entirely for this work, one quarter of the more than two years which have rolled away since I began it."

The *Magnalia* overemphasizes the importance of the events and persons approved by Mather; the rest are neglected or abused. It is therefore both a celebration of the great New England Puritans and a passionate controversial document—all designed to defend the divine right of the New England theocracy. Mather sets out to show of what superlative merit were the men of the heroic age of the settlement of Massachusetts, to what trials they had been subjected, what difficulties they had overcome, with what zeal they had organized their lives and their churches for the greater glory of God, and what remarkable evidences there had been of divine intercession in their affairs— all revelations of a chosen people. As Mather's biographers Ralph and Louise Boas observe, the book "is written from the thoroughly biased point of view of one who saw nothing in the seventy years of Massachusetts that needed defence, who was sublimely unaware that there was another side than he presented." The Boases continued:

> It is clear from the *Magnalia* that the ruling caste of Massachusetts sincerely believed that in establishing the colony they were working for God. He had put upon them the Christian's burden of governing a large majority of very frail souls rendered the more prone to sin by the roughness, privation, monotony, drudgery, and danger of pioneer life; by the presence at their doors of a wild subject race, moody and resentful, which might at any time burst into murderous fury; by the gathering of dissolute and reckless seafarers, adventurers, and traders; and by the emergence from time to time, within the ranks of the faithful, of capable and intelligent heretics whose ideas, were they to receive general acceptance, would completely undermine the authority of the rulers and surrender territory held in trust for God to the control of the very real and very powerful Satan from whom they had wrested it.

The *Magnalia* is divided into seven books. The first, written in epic style, is the story of the beginnings of New England, "reporting the design where-on, the manner where-in, and people where-by the several colonies of New England were planted." It is a well-written, straightforward account which evidently drew freely upon William Bradford's manuscript on the subject. New England was settled solely to plant the gospel, Mather maintains:

> About an hundred and ninety-eight ships were employed in passing the perils of the seas, in the accomplishment of this renowned settlement, whereof, by the way, but one miscarried in those perils. The God of Heaven served as it were a summons upon the spirits of His people in the English nation; stirring up the spirits of thousands with a most unanimous inclination to leave all the pleasant accommodations of their native country, and go over a terrible ocean, into a more terrible desert, for the pure enjoyment of all His ordinances.

The original Plymouth colony was followed by the establishment of other New England colonies which, according to Mather, "have not only enlarged the English empire in some regards more than any other outgoings of our nation, but also afforded a singular prospect of churches erected in an American corner of the world, on purpose to express and pursue the Protestant Reformation." A special chapter relates the history of "the State of Boston, the chief town of New-England, and of the English America."

Book two of the *Magnalia* contains "the lives of the governours, and the names of the magistrates; that have been shields unto the churches of New-England," from the landing of the Pilgrim Fathers to the time of Sir William Phips, or Phipps. Biographical accounts of considerable length deal with William Bradford (whose career is thus summarized: "Men are but flocks: Bradford beheld their need, and long did them at once both rule and feed"), Edward Winslow, Thomas Prince, John Winthrop, Simon Bradstreet, Edward Hopkins, Theophilus Eaton, and William Phips—the last most extensively considered because he had been personally nominated by the Mathers and worked hand in glove with them to maintain political control of the Massachusetts Colony.

Having disposed of the secular aspects of New England colonial history, Mathers turns in his third book to "the lives of many reverend, learned, and holy divines, by whose evangelical ministry the churches of New England have been illuminated." This, the longest section of the two-volume work, fills 400 pages and treats some sixty ministers. The subjects of the most detailed discussions are John Cotton (Cotton Mather's grandfather), John Norton, John Wilson, John Davenport, Thomas Hooker, Francis Higginson, Thomas Shepard, Nathanel Rogers, Richard Mather (Cotton Mather's other grandfather), Charles Chancey, and John Eliot.

Mather is eulogistic in his tribute to John Eliot, missionary to the Indians and translator of the first Indian Bible. In Mather's view, "He was one who lived in heaven while he was on earth, and there is no more than pure justice in our endeavours that he should live on earth after he is in heaven." Mather was lacking, however, in Eliot's sympathy for and understanding of the

Indians. Instead, he held the aboriginal Americans in considerable contempt, seeing them as "abject creatures" cluttering up
the land and unable to make proper use of its rich natural
resources: "Our shiftless Indians were never owners of so much
as a knife till we came among them; their name for an English
man was a knife-man. They live in a country full of the best
ship-timber under heaven; but never saw a ship till some came
from Europe hither." The white colonists were therefore fully
justified in taking the Indians' land away from them.

Closely associated with the church in the eyes of the Mathers
was Harvard. The fourth book is "an account of the University,
from whence the churches of New-England (and many other
churches,) have been illuminated.—Its laws, its benefactors, its
vicissitudes, and a catalogue of such as have been therein educated and graduated. Whereto are added, the lives of some
eminent persons who were plants of renown growing in that
nursery." At the time that Mather was writing, Harvard was
sixty years of age. It was, Mather claimed, a more intelligent and
progressive institution than the English universities. For example,
there was not found at Harvard "such a veneration for Aristotle
as is express'd at Queen's College in Oxford; where they read
Aristotle on their knees, and those who take degrees are sworn
to defend his philosophy." Among Harvard's alumni, Mather
asserts proudly, "it will be found that, besides a supply of
ministers for our churches from this happy seminary, we have
hence had a supply of magistrates, as well as physicians, and
other gentlemen, to serve the commonwealth with their capaci-
ties." Mather includes the lives of ten eminent ministers who
graduated from Harvard.

The three final books deal largely with ecclesiastical matters.
The fifth sets forth the orthodox doctrine and discipline of the
New England churches, as agreed upon in church synods, "with
historical remarks upon all those venerable assemblies, and a
great variety of other church cases." Most astonishing is the
sixth book, a work full of superstitions now incredible, wherein
the author presents "very many illustrious discoveries and demonstrations of the Divine Providence in remarkable mercies and
judgements on many particular persons among the people of
New-England." Among the "remarkable Providences" are ac-

counts of extraordinary rescues from disaster at sea or from warlike Indians, and stories of criminals punished for their crimes. According to Mather, "Molestations from evil spirits have so abounded in this country, that I question whether any one town has been free of sad examples of them." The chapter entitled "Relating the wonders of the invisible world in preternatural occurrences," in particular, reveals Mather's naïve credulity and has severely injured his reputation, but other learned men of his day shared identical or similar beliefs in the miraculous and supernatural.

The *Magnalia* concludes with the seventh book, ". . . relating the afflictive disturbances which the churches of New-England have suffered from their various adversaries: and the wonderful methods and mercies whereby the churches have been delivered out of their difficulties." This section is concerned with "Wars of the Lord." A chapter devoted to Roger Williams is comparatively tolerant, for Mather notes that "there was always a good correspondence held between him and many worthy and pious people in the colony from whence he had been banish'd." The treatment of Anne Hutchinson, however, is harsh; Mather damns her as "the prime seducer of the whole faction which now began to threaten the country." The condemnation of the Quakers is even more violent: "I know not whether the sect which hath appeared in our days under the name of Quakers be not upon many accounts the worst of hereticks, but this I know, they have been the most venemous of all to the churches of America." Mather's special detestation was for "the old Foxian Quakerism, the grossest collection of blasphemies and confusions that ever was heard of." It was not argued by Mather that a magistrate should "take the life of an offender solely for the crime of heresy," but he insisted that the state must resort to strong measures to protect itself against seditious acts and utterance.

In striking contrast to his extremely reactionary opinions on everything of a theological nature, Mather held enlightened views on certain scientific matters. When the new astronomy was being denounced as anti-Biblical, he welcomed it with the comment, "The arguments that prove the stability of the sun and the motion of the earth have now rendered it indisputable." Mather gives a supernatural interpretation of yellow fever and smallpox, believing them to be caused by demons, and of thunder and lightning as warning blasts from God, yet he was the leader in introducing inoculation against smallpox, inoculating his own children in the face of threats and abuse.

Mather brings the *Magnalia* to a pessimistic conclusion: "It is a thing very notorious unto us, that idleness, drunkenness, uncleanness, cheating, lying, prophane swearing, and, above all, that which is the *root* of all, the profanation of the Lord's-day, gains ground upon us. Let all that have any *power* in their hand, unto the utmost of their power endeavour to keep under those enormities." Mather continues gloomily that the whole country was in such a degenerate state "that I have sometimes been discouraged from writing the church-history of the country. God knows what will be the End."

In their biography of Cotton Mather, the Boases appraise the *Magnalia* as follows: "For what it sets out to be it is superb. No single work throws more light upon the ministers and magistrates of the seventeenth-century Massachusetts Commonwealth and their point of view." A leading American historian, Samuel E. Morison, after criticizing Mather's pedantry, inaccuracy, and occasional suppression of the truth, agrees that Mather "does succeed in giving a living picture of the persons he writes about, and he was near enough to the first generation to catch the spirit and flavor of the times." Finally, Barrett Wendell, in *Cotton Mather: The Puritan Priest*, states: "The *Magnalia* has merits which dispose me to rate it among the great works of English literature in the Seventeenth Century. . . . Whatever else Cotton Mather may have been, the *Magnalia* alone, I think, proves him to have been a notable man of letters."

5 | VIRGINIA GENTLEMAN

William Byrd's *Histories of the Dividing Line Betwixt Virginia and North Carolina,* 1728

A leading historian of American literature, Jay B. Hubbell, rates William Byrd of Westover (1674–1744) as "after Benjamin Franklin and perhaps Jonathan Edwards the most important of colonial writers." Another prominent critic, Louis B. Wright, describes Byrd as "one of the most urbane writers of the colonial period in British America." That Byrd's literary reputation grew slowly can be attributed to the tardiness with which his works have been published; even so, as Hubbell notes, "some of our earlier critics and literary historians were inexcusably blind to his merits."

Byrd's most significant work, *The History of the Dividing Line Betwixt Virginia and North Carolina,* received limited circulation in manuscript form during the author's lifetime and after— Thomas Jefferson, for example, was a warm admirer. Not until 1841, however, nearly a century after Byrd's death, was the first edition of the *History* issued, by Edmund Ruffin in Petersburg. Another lengthy period passed before a complementary work, *The Secret History of the Line,* was published in 1929, though Lyman C. Draper had called attention to the manuscript in the library of the American Philosophical Society as early as 1851. Other less well known writings by Byrd, such as *The Journey to the Land of Eden* and *The Progress to the Mines,* are also narratives of business travels through the frontier country, giving invaluable pictures of the places and people he observed, as well as illuminating glimpses of the personality of an extraordinary aristocrat of eighteenth-century Virginia.

William Byrd belonged to one of Virginia's leading families, representative of the colonial society of Virginia at its best. Byrd himself is a brilliant example of the Virginia cavalier. A considerable portion of his life was spent in England, as a student

36

in his younger days and as a colonial politician in later years. Through his efforts, the family's vast estate increased from 26,000 to 180,000 acres. Byrd was a sophisticated gentleman, completely at home in Britain's higher social circles, and somewhat notorious for his many love affairs; but he was also devoted to his native province. At his hospitable Westover mansion he gathered a library of 4,000 volumes—the largest in the colonies —and he was an inveterate reader, even while traveling. It has been remarked of Byrd that he could never resist an old book, a young girl, or a fresh idea. He lived splendidly, conceived large ideas, and was perpetually in debt.

The History of the Dividing Line grew out of Byrd's appointment as one of the commissioners for Virginia in the longstanding dispute over the Virginia–North Carolina border. By prearrangement, the Virginia commissioners met a similar commission appointed by North Carolina and then proceeded to survey the line and to prepare a map plainly showing the border. Byrd's account is a day-by-day journal describing how in 1728 some twenty men went about completing the mission assigned to them. But the *History* is much more than a series of daily entries. In a historical introduction, Byrd reviews some past events, showing how Virginia by successive royal grants had been greatly reduced from its original size—developments which Byrd as a patriotic Virginian viewed with regret. As a member of the commission, he was prepared to resist further encroachments.

The Dividing Line is appropriately titled, metaphorically and literally, for Byrd is obviously a prejudiced witness, repeatedly recording the scorn of the prosperous and efficient Virginia planter and landowner for what he considers the poor white trash of North Carolina. His satirical comments on some of his fellow commissioners from North Carolina and upon North Carolinians generally understandably irked sensitive citizens of that commonwealth. Byrd's amusing but biased views on the Tar Heels' laziness have been often cited:

> Surely there is no place in the world where the inhabitants live with less labor than in North Carolina. It approaches nearer to the description of Lubberland than any other by the great felicity of the climate, the easiness of raising provisions, and the

slothfulness of the people. The men, for their parts, just like the Indians, impose all the work upon the poor women. They make their wives rise out of their beds early in the morning, at the same time that they lie and snore till the sun has risen one-third of his course and dispersed all the unwholesome damps. When the weather is mild, they stand leaning with both their arms upon a cornfield fence and gravely consider whether they had best go and take a small heat at the hoe but generally find reasons to put it off till another time. Thus they loiter away their lives, like Solomon's sluggard, with their arms across and at the winding up of the year scarcely have bread to eat. To speak the truth, 'tis a thorough aversion to labor that makes people file off to North Carolina, where plenty and a warm sun confirm them in their disposition to laziness for their whole lives.

Elsewhere in *The Dividing Line,* further characterizing North Carolinians, Byrd asserts: "One thing may be said for inhabitants of that Province that they are not troubled with any religious fumes, and have the least superstition of any people living. They do not know Sunday from any other day, any more than Robinson Crusoe did, which would give them a great advantage were they given to being industrious." The Carolinians were great pork eaters, Byrd reported, and he attributed certain unfortunate maladies to their monotonous diet. These and similar observations created a distorted picture of North Carolina civilization; they were accepted as authentic by later historians, including Parkman.

Even before the commissioners met, a controversial note had been sounded. The Virginians assumed that they would set standards for the expedition and, therefore, as quoted in Byrd's *Secret History of the Line,* wrote the North Carolina commissioners as follows:

It is very proper to acquaint you in what manner we intend to come provided, that so you gentlemen who are appointed in the same station may, if you please, do the same honor to your government. We shall bring with us about twenty men, furnished with provisions for forty days. We shall have a tent with us and a marquee for the convenience of ourselves and servants. We shall be provided with as much wine and rum as just enable us and our men to drink every night to the success of the following day. And because we understand there are many gentiles on your frontier who never had an opportunity of being baptized, we shall have a chaplain with us to make them Christians.

To this somewhat boastful and patronizing communication the North Carolina commissioners replied with mock humility and not too subtle irony:

> We are at a loss, gentlemen, whether to thank you for the particulars you give us of your tent, stores, and the manner you design to meet us. Had you been silent, we had not wanted an excuse for not meeting you in the same manner; but now you force us to expose the nakedness of our country and tell you we can't possibly meet you in the manner our great respect to you would make us glad to do, whom we are not emulous of out-doing, unless in care and diligence in the affair we came about. So all we can answer to that article is that we will endeavor to provide as well as the circumstances will admit; and what we want in necessaries we hope will be made up in spiritual comfort we expect from your chaplain, of whom we shall give notice as you desire and doubt not of making a great many boundary Christians.

Byrd notes that the reply was "without date, they having no almanacs in North Carolina, but it came about the beginning of January," with the survey scheduled to begin on March 5, 1728

When the commissioners did meet, their work inevitably began with a dispute. The official instructions of the Virginia com-missioners empowered them to carry the survey to a conclusion even if the North Carolina commissioners should delay or refuse to cooperate. The North Carolinians interpreted these instruc-tions as "too lordly and positive." The controversy that the two sides were attempting to settle was long-standing and had exacerbated feelings in both colonies for many years. Virginia and North Carolina each claimed certain territory in the border region, and both governments had tried to collect taxes from the inhabitants of the disputed territory. The charter granted to North Carolina in 1665 had stated that the boundary should run "from the north end of Currituck River or Inlet upon a straight westerly line to Weyanoke Creek, which lies within or about the degrees of 36 and 30′ northern latitude, and so west in a direct line as far as the South Seas." In the ensuing years, Weyanoke Creek had lost its identity. The commissioners finally agreed that Nottoway River was meant, and the survey was run that way, but the agreement was preceded by lengthy and acrimonious arguments.

Across rivers and islands, over creeks and marshes, through wild land and some settled areas, the surveying party proceeded until on March 14 the Dismal Swamp was reached. There lay ahead the most arduous portion of the task. No one knew the size of the swamp and none had penetrated its forbidding interior. After the surveyors entered the Dismal, Byrd reports that they "laid eyes on no living creature: neither bird nor beast, insect nor reptile came in view." His graphic description continues:

> Doubtless the eternal shade that broods over this mighty bog and hinders the sunbeams from blessing the ground makes it an uncomfortabe habitation for anything that has life. Not so much as a Zeeland frog could endure so aguish a situation. It had one beauty, however, that delighted the eye, though at the expense of all the other senses: the moisture of the soil preserves a continual verdure and makes every plant an evergreen; but at the same time the foul damps ascend without ceasing, corrupt the air, and render it unfit for respiration. Not even a turkey buzzard will venture to fly over it, no more than the Italian vultures will fly over the filthy Lake Avernus, or the birds in the Holy Land over the Salt Sea where Sodom and Gomorrah formerly stood.

Two weeks were required for crossing the Dismal, an exhausting undertaking filled with hair-raising adventures. A few days later the survey was suspended for the summer, and then resumed in September. When the Roanoke River was reached, the North Carolina commissioners turned back. The Virginians were determined, however, to continue, which they did until stopped by the advanced season and the challenge of the Appalachian Mountains. In any event, the boundary controversy was resolved and its location settled, though later surveys were needed to correct certain errors.

One of the most valuable features of the Byrd histories is the author's observation on animal and plant life encountered along the border. He was fascinated by the curiosities of nature. When he found some new or interesting specimen, he drew upon his own knowledge and wide reading of ancient authorities, such as Pliny, as a basis for comments. Certain accounts are in the realm of tall tales: alligators swallowed rocks in order to make themselves heavy enough to pull a cow under water and drown her, thereafter spewing up the rocks; Indians captured sturgeon by riding them bareback; squirrels crossed rivers on pieces of bark, using their tails as sails; and a louse guided a settler lost in the Dismal, by pointing north.

But when Byrd relied upon his direct knowledge, his observations were accurate and are still useful to students concerned with the plant and animal ecologies of colonial Virginia and North Carolina. *The History of the Dividing Line* contains excellent descriptions of the elk, opossum, buffalo, bear, turkey, wildcat, polecat, and rattlesnake. Away from the settlements, the woods teemed with deer, bear, and wild turkeys, all of which kept the surveying expedition well fed.

Byrd's acquaintance with plants was even more expert and scientific. His prime interest was in plants potentially useful for *materia medica*. Of all the plants found in the course of the survey, Byrd was most enthusiastic about ginseng, which other American travelers found the Indians drinking as a tea to guarantee a long life. Other favorite medicines were "snakeroot stewed in wine" and ipecac, or ipecacuanha, used as an emetic. Byrd fancied himself a doctor, but some of his stock remedies appear as likely to kill as to cure—for example, sweating, blood letting, vomiting, and swimming in cold water.

As the surveying expedition proceeded, many Indians were encountered, and Byrd's views on the red man are revealing. Despite his cavalier background he was highly tolerant of the Indian civilization and free of race prejudice. In Byrd's judgment, there was "but one way of converting these poor infidels and reclaiming them from barbarity, and that is charitably to intermarry with them, according to the modern policy of the Most Christian King in Canada and Louisiana." Byrd adds:

> It was certainly an unreasonable nicety that prevented the English entering into so good-natured an alliance. All nations of men have the same natural dignity, and we all know that very bright talents may be lodged under a very dark skin. The principal difference between one people and another proceeds only

from the different opportunities of improvement. The Indians by no means want understanding and are in their figure tall and well proportioned. I may safely venture to say, the Indian women would have made altogether as honest wives for the first planters as the damsels they used to purchase from aboard the ships. 'Tis strange, therefore, that any good Christian should have refused a wholesome, straight bedfellow when he might have had so fair a portion with her as the merit of saving her soul.

Byrd and his companions employed Indian hunters to keep them supplied with game, and they visited several Indian villages. As a result of these encounters, Byrd is able to describe the Southern Indian's way of curing deer hides, his superstitions, his marriage customs, his endurance, and his hospitality. On one occasion, Byrd talked at length with Bearskin, his chief hunter, about his religious faith; he discovered that Bearskin believed in a supreme god who had made the world a long time ago and had created many worlds before this, all of which had been destroyed for various reasons.

Byrd's character sketches are lively. The frankest descriptions are in *The Secret History*, where the author's respects were paid both to the North Carolinians and to individual members of the Virginia delegation. John Lavick, one of the North Carolina commissioners, was "a merry, good-humored man," who "had learnt a very decent behavior from Governor Hyde, to whom he had been *valet de chambre*." William Little, another North Carolina commissioner, "had degenerated from a New England preacher, for which his godly parents designed him, to a very wicked but awkward rake." Byrd also spoke his mind freely about two of his Virginia associates, Richard Fitz-William and Alexander Irvine, who on all possible occasions sided with the Carolina commissioners. Southern poor whites first emerge into literature in the *Histories*. A picturesque specimen was a mariner living near the coast:

This man modestly called himself a hermit, though he forfeited that name by suffering a wanton female to cohabit with him. His habitation was a bower, covered with bark after the Indian fashion which in that mild situation protected him pretty well from the weather. Like the ravens, he neither plowed or sowed but subsisted chiefly upon oysters which his handmaiden made a shift to gather from the adjacent rocks. Sometimes, too, for change of diet he sent her to drive up the neighbor's cows to moisten their mouths with a little milk. But as for raiment he depended mostly upon his length of beard, and she upon her length of hair, part of which she decently brought forward, and the rest dangled behind quite down to the rump, like one of Herodotus's east Indian pigmies. Thus did these wretches live in a dirty state of nature and were mere Adamites, innocence only excepted.

The History of the Dividing Line and *The Secret History* are complementary. The first contains a basic account of the surveying mission, including much information not included in *The Secret History*. Its highlights are the sketch of British colonization in America, descriptions of the region traversed by the surveying expedition, including its fauna and flora, the customs of the Indians, and the life of the pioneers, and characterizations of North Carolina and its people. In contrast, *The Secret History* is hardly more than half as long as the *History*, but contains considerable information regarding the expedition not contained in the latter work. The use of fictitious names makes it easy for Byrd to express frank opinions about the leading personalities, though the individuals characterized are easily identifiable. *The Secret History* is much more explicit than the *History* in dealing with the men taking part in the expedition, their quarrels and conflicts of interest, and their attitude toward the women of the frontier. A half-dozen episodes are noted wherein members of the group were guilty of violence toward women met in the course of their travels.

In his excellent introduction to the Dover edition of the *Histories*, Percy G. Adams concludes: "Together they make up a volume that is important for eighteenth-century prose, for early American history, and for travel literature. They reveal the Southeastern American frontier as no other book has. They reveal a witty, observant, intelligent, many-sided Virginia Gentleman . . . and they are entertaining."

6 | ELECTRICAL WIZARD

Benjamin Franklin's *Experiments and Observations on Electricity*, 1751

The Grolier Club's list of *One Hundred Books Famous in Science* includes only five books of American origin, and a single title precedes the 1830s: Benjamin Franklin's *Experiments and Observations on Electricity, Made at Philadelphia in America* (1751), one of the most widely read and discussed books ever written on a scientific subject.

The highly versatile Franklin was both a scientist and an inventor; he created more useful devices than any American prior to Thomas A. Edison. The range of his scientific experimentation and study drew him into many fields—physics, chemistry, oceanography, geology, meteorology, astronomy, aeronautics, geography, and medicine—and to such practical applications as heating stoves, ventilation, treatment of lead poisoning, fertilizers, bifocal glasses, and lightning rods.

But it was in the field of electricity that Franklin conducted his most sensational and original scientific investigations. Though he devoted only a few years to science before his energies were almost completely absorbed by public affairs, Franklin's contributions to the understanding and possible uses of the new branch of knowledge won for him international fame. His imagination and mechanical ingenuity were brought into play at a critical moment in the history of electrical theory. As a side effect, Franklin's prestige in science was an important factor in his rise in politics and subsequently in his notable achievements as a republican diplomat in Paris.

Benjamin Franklin was nearly thirty-seven years of age when he first became aware of the "wonders of electricity." This occurred in a visit to Boston, probably in 1743, when he witnessed demonstrations by Doctor Archibald Spencer, a popular lecturer, who, as Franklin wrote, "was lately arrived from Scotland, and showed me some electrical experiments. These were imperfectly perform'd, as he was not very expert; but being on a subject quite new to me, they equally surpris'd and pleased me."

By this time, Franklin was an established businessman, a successful publisher and journalist, and a prominent citizen of Philadelphia. Earlier in his career, during a sojourn in England, he had become acquainted with a number of English scientists. After returning home he took the lead in forming a discussion club called the "Junto," which later became the American Philosophical Society, the first scientific society in America.

Shortly after Franklin's interest in electricity had been aroused by Spencer's demonstrations, he tried out some experiments on his own account with apparatus sent by Peter Collinson of London to the Library Company of Philadelphia, another organization founded by Franklin. All of Spencer's equipment was purchased by Franklin and added to the items acquired from London. For the next several years he and his friends carried on experiments with electricity, manufacturing for themselves any other equipment needed. Franklin writes, "I eagerly seized the opportunity of repeating what I had seen in Boston: and, by much practice, acquir'd great readiness in performing those also which we had an account of from England, adding a number of new ones."

In a letter to Collinson in March 1747, Franklin reports, "I never was before engaged in any study that so totally engrossed my attention and my time as this has lately done." Franklin promised to report to Collinson, a Fellow of the Royal Society of London, "some particular phenomena that we look upon to be new," though he modestly admitted that it was possible "some one or other has hit on the same observations" in Europe. Collinson turned out to be a valuable friend. He not only provided the first equipment for Franklin's researches but communicated news of the latter's discoveries and theories to English scientists and to the Royal Society. Collinson was also responsible for collecting the reports from Franklin and having them published in book form.

Centuries before Franklin's time men of scientific bent had been tantalized by the question, What is electricity? In the sixth century B.C., Thales of Miletus had found that amber when rubbed would attract such objects as pieces of dry leaves and straw. The Greek word for amber was *elektron*. Later experimenters learned that light objects could also be attracted by sealing wax rubbed with fur and glass rubbed with silk. These two discoveries led to further investigations. A rod of sealing wax rubbed with fur was held near a small pith ball suspended by a silk thread; strangely the pith ball was repelled. The same test was made with a glass rod rubbed with silk; in this instance, the pith ball was attracted. The conclusion was drawn, therefore, that there are two kinds of electricity, one called vitreous (glass) and the other resinous (amber). This was the two-fluid theory of electricity—a theory later rejected by Franklin.

Immediately prior to Franklin's work in the electrical field, important advances had been made in the construction of large glass frictional machines, which could produce strong sparks and electrify various objects. A new device, invented by Pieter van Musschenbroek of Leyden in 1745, proved to be a major contribution for laboratory purposes. This was the Leyden jar, an instrument made of a glass bottle, coated on the outside with metal foil, and filled with metal shot or water into which a wire hook was inserted. The Leyden jar was a primitive condenser, capable of storing a large electric charge from frictional electric glass tubes. Long sparks could be produced by applying a conductor to the two sides of the bottle. Popular entertainers used the marvelous invention to electrocute chickens, roast steaks, set alcohol aflame, blow out flames, transmit shocks across streams, and produce mysterious lights in the dark. People suffering from paralysis were given electric shocks as a possible cure.

Franklin's scientific fame was first solidly established by his analysis of the Leyden jar. He proceeded on the assumption that electricity is a single fluid, not two. Step by step, Franklin discovered that the charge in a Leyden jar is negative on the inside and positive on the outside and that the two charges balance each other; that is, they are always equal. By testing the bottle one element at a time, it was found that the charge was not in the wire, the cork, the water, or the foil, but always in the glass itself. Franklin substituted glass plates for the bottle—thereby inventing the parallel-plate condenser—and showed that the charge resides in the glass because it is a nonconductor. This was a step toward the development of the battery.

The Leyden jar experiments were the origin of a series of electrical terms coined by Franklin, some of which became standard terminology. He was the first to designate the two states of electricity as *positive* and *negative,* and he introduced other, now everyday, words in the field of electricity: *armature, charge, discharge, condenser, conductor, nonconductor, electrical shock,* and *electrician.* As a graphic expression to describe the shock produced by a number of Leyden jars combined, Franklin took over a military term, *battery.* In a report to Collinson on April 29, 1749, he told of making, for the first time in history,

> what we called an electrical battery, consisting of eleven panes of large sash-glass, armed with thin leaden plates pasted on each side, placed vertically and supported at two inches' distance on silk cords, with thick hooks of leaden wire, one from each side, standing upright, distant from each other, and convenient communications of wire and chain from the giving side of one pane to the receiving side of the other; that so the whole might be charged together and with the same labour as one single pane.

Earlier, Franklin had written Collinson that he had "observed some particular phenomena, which we looked upon to be new." "The first," he continued, "is the wonderful effect of pointed bodies, both in drawing off and throwing off the electrical fire." Franklin demonstrated that sharply pointed conductors were more effective than blunt ones in the transmission of electrical charges across gaps. From his experiments with pointed conductors evolved both Franklin's greatest experiment and his most famous invention.

Scientists before Franklin had noted the obvious resemblance between the electric spark and lightning. Franklin proposed by experiment to prove that they are identical. In one of his notebooks, he observes, "Electrical fluid agrees with lightning in these particulars: giving light, color of the light, crooked direction, swift motion, being conducted by metals, crack or noise in exploding, subsisting in water or ice, rending bodies it passes through, destroying animals, melting metals, firing inflammable flames, sulfurous smell." To demonstrate the truth of his theory that the thunderstorm and the artificial spark differ only in intensity, Franklin proposed an experiment. According to his hypothesis or "doctrine of points," lightning or electricity could be attracted from the air during a storm by means of an iron rod shaped like a needle placed at the top of a tall building. There was no spire in Philadelphia at the time high enough to attract the electrical charge, and Franklin was awaiting the construction of a steeple on Christ Church. The Franklin proposal for an experiment was published abroad, and a French scientist, Jean François D'Alibard, put it to a successful test. The identity of lightning and electricity was confirmed.

Meanwhile, back in Philadelphia, Franklin thought of a simpler method of drawing fire from the heavens—by a kite armed with a long point. The plan was to fly a kite as high as possible and by this means to reach an electrified cloud, in order to bring the lightning flash down to earth. The kite was made by stretching a piece of silk over two sticks placed crosswise. A pointed wire was fastened to the top of the kite, and to the lower end of the hempen kite string were tied a metal key and a piece of silk ribbon. As a thunderstorm approached, Franklin and his son William raised the kite, and when the string had become wet enough to conduct electricity, they were able to draw sparks from the key and to charge a Leyden jar from it. No doubt remained that lightning is attracted by metallic points, as are electric sparks.

The perils of the Franklin experiment have often been the subject of comment. If the hemp cord of his kite had been thoroughly wet, he could have been electrocuted. A Swedish physicist, G. W. Richman, visiting the Imperial Academy of Saint Petersburg, was instantly killed trying to repeat the experiment, when a flash of lightning reached him through a wire he was holding in his hand. Franklin used the precaution, however, of holding the kite by the piece of silk ribbon, a nonconductor, and standing inside a shed to keep himself dry while flying the kite.

As one of Franklin's biographers, Ralph L. Ketcham, pointed out:

> When Franklin proved that lightning was a great discharge of static electricity produced by natural movements of air, he placed electricity beside heat, light, and gravity as one of the

primordial forces of the universe. . . . Lightning's dramatic effects, and the superstitions which had long surrounded it, heightened the awe with which its captor was sure to be held.

The practical-minded Franklin, after establishing the nature of lightning, at once began thinking of useful applications of his discovery. Since the experiment had proved successful, he wrote:

> If the fire of electricity and that of lightning be the same . . . may not the knowledge of the power of points be of use to mankind, in preserving houses, churches, ships, etc. from the stroke of lightning, by directing us to fix on the highest parts of those edifices, upright rods of iron made sharp as a needle, and gilt to prevent rusting, and from the foot of those rods a wire down the outside of the building into the ground, or down around one of the shrouds of a ship, and down her side until it reaches the water? Would not these pointed rods probably draw the electricity silently out of a cloud before it came nigh enough to strike, and thereby secure us from that most sudden and terrible mischief?

Here was the concept of the lightning rod invented by Franklin, a device called an "electrical conductor" in the eighteenth century. A well-grounded, pointed metal rod alongside a house, Franklin concluded, can rob the clouds of their dangerous electrical charge before it can do any damage, exactly as under laboratory conditions one can draw off the charge from a metal sphere by a needle held in the hand. Actually, lightning rods do not "steal thunder" from the cloud but attract the actual lightning discharge itself and conduct it safely into the ground.

The lightning rod was the first economically important application of electrical principles. It immediately became the popular symbol of Franklin's fame as an electrical wizard. Many people in Philadelphia were persuaded to use his newest invention, and in the summer of 1752 lightning rods were raised on the academy and statehouse spires. Over his own house, Franklin attached bells to the rod; when electricity from the skies was drawn off into the experimental bottles, the bells would ring. Nevertheless, acceptance of the protective rod was slow because of popular ignorance, superstition, and religious prejudice. Franklin felt vindicated to some degree when the

British government contracted with him to plan a system of lightning rods for arsenals.

As news of the Philadelphia experiments traveled abroad, much interest began to be aroused among Europeans, especially in England and France. Peter Collinson shared the reports received from Franklin with other members of the Royal Society. Franklin's letters were cited in the Society's *Philosophical Transactions,* and they reached a wider public in the *Gentleman's Magazine.* In April 1751, a compilation was printed by Edward Cave in London under the title *Experiments and Observations on Electricity Made at Philadelphia in America, by Mr. Benjamin Franklin, and Communicated in Several Letters to Mr. P. Collinson, of London, F.R.S.* This eighty-six-page pamphlet was the first edition of probably the most famous and influential book to come out of America in the eighteenth century. The wide popularity of the book led to the publication of ten editions before the American Revolution—five in English, three in French, and one each in German and Italian.

Paul J. Conkin in his *Puritans and Pragmatists* concludes that Franklin's reputation in the field of electricity rests on two main achievements. First, during a period of "experimental ferment and theoretical confusion," he "contributed simple theoretical principles that successfully explained or predicted all but one of the existing electrical phenomena." Second, by proving the electrification of clouds, he made electricity a respected branch of natural science.

Franklin's modest approach to the study of electrical matters is revealed in an early statement: "In going on with these Experiments, how many pretty Systems do we build, which we soon find ourselves oblig'd to destroy! If there is no other use discover'd of Electricity, this, however, is something considerable, that it may *help to make a vain man humble.*"

A Nobel Prize winning United States physicist, Robert A. Millikan, sums up Franklin's career as a scientist:

> Franklin lives as a physicist because, dilettante though he is sometimes called, mere qualitative interpreter though he actually was, yet it was he who with altogether amazing insight laid the real foundations on which the whole superstructure of electrical theory and interpretation has been erected.

7 | LAND OF PROMISE

Hector St. John de Crevecoeur's *Letters from an American Farmer*, 1782

Frederick Jackson Turner's theories of the significance of the frontier in the shaping of the American character was foreshadowed more than a century earlier by a Frenchman, Hector St. John de Crèvecoeur, in his *Letters from an American Farmer*, subtitled *Describing Certain Provincial Situations, Manners, and Customs, Not Generally Known; and Conveying Some Idea of the Late and Present Interior Circumstances of the British Colonies in North America* (1782). The author identified himself as "A Farmer in Pennsylvania." His descriptions of life on the frontier are a combination of romanticism and hard-headed realism. By and large, the picture he paints is a happy, optimistic one of a new world untroubled by the ambitions and oppressions of the old—until the outbreak of the Revolution shattered the idyllic dream.

Crèvecoeur was a native of France, born in 1735, who received part of his education in England and then was sent to Canada to serve with Montcalm in the war against the English. After the French defeat, Crèvecoeur emigrated to the English colonies, worked for a time as a surveyor, and eventually acquired a 120-acre farm in Orange County, New York. He became a naturalized American, married Mehetable Tippet of Yonkers, and settled down to become a skillful tiller of the soil and a lover of country life. In his *Letters*, Crèvecoeur tells of the joys of creating a home in the wilderness and of cultivating the virgin soil.

A restless streak in Crèvecoeur's nature, however, took him far afield from his simple farm. He traveled widely as a surveyor and trader through Ohio and the Great Lakes region, to New England, the central Atlantic, as far south as Charleston, and perhaps to Bermuda and Jamaica. Few other Americans knew at first hand and as intimately the English Colonies as a whole.

Moreover, Crèvecoeur could see the Colonies and their settlers against his own European background.

Prior to 1776, Crèvecoeur felt that being a citizen landholder in America was comparable to living in the Garden of Eden. He saw America as a promised land which offered unlimited prospects to European peasants and to other peoples suffering from misery and degradation in their homelands. What more could any man seek than the right to own land, to work, and to have a real voice in the government? Crèvecoeur contemplated his own domain with perfect satisfaction as he saw his fields, herds, flocks, and beehives flourish. Looking into the future, he saw industry and commerce developing—"the avenues of trade are infinite"—and in time the West would be explored and subjugated.

As the thoughtful Frenchman studied the colonial society, he asked himself: How does the American differ from his European ancestors? Crèvecoeur was convinced that a new race was emerging under the potent influence of a new environment. "Men are like plants," he declared; "the goodness and flavor of the fruit proceeds from the peculiar soil and exposition in which they grow. We are nothing but what we derive from the air we breathe, the climate we inhabit, the government we obey, the system of religion we profess, and the mode of our employment."

"The rich stay in Europe," concluded Crèvecoeur; "it is only the middling and the poor that emigrate." Once arrived in the New World, "Every thing tended to regenerate them; new laws, a new mode of living, a new social system; here they are become men: in Europe they were as so many useless plants, wanting vegetable mould, and refreshing showers; they withered and were mowed down by want, hunger, and war; but now by the power of transplantation, like all other plants, they have taken root and flourished!" European society as seen by Crèvecoeur is composed "of great lords who possess everything and of a herd of people who have nothing." In striking contrast, in America "the rich and the poor are not so far separate from each other . . . we are all tillers of the soil, we are all animated with the spirit of an industry which is unfettered and unrestrained because each person works for himself."

Crèvecoeur's definition of an ideal American, the product of the new culture and changed environment, is often quoted:

> *He* is an American, who leaving behind him all his ancient prejudices and manners, receives new ones from the new mode of life he has embraced, the new government he obeys, and the new rank he holds. . . . Here the rewards of his industry follow with equal steps the progress of his labour; his labour is founded on the basis of nature, *self-interest;* can it want a stronger allurement? Wives and children, who before in vain demanded of him a morsel of bread, now, fat and frolicsome, gladly help their father to clear those fields whence exuberant crops are to arise to feed and clothe them all. . . . The American is a new man, who acts upon new principles; he must therefore entertain new ideas and form new opinions. From involuntary idleness, servile dependence, penury, and useless labour, he has passed to toils of a very different nature, rewarded by an ample subsistence.—This is an American.

To make concrete for his readers the opportunities awaiting the poverty-stricken emigrants from the Old World, Crèvecoeur dwells at length on the story of Andrew the Hebridean, illustrating "the progressive steps of a poor man advancing from indigence to ease, from oppression to freedom, from obscurity and contumely to some degree of consequence—not by virtue of any freaks of fortune, but by the gradual operation of sobriety, honesty, and emigration." While on a visit to Philadelphia in 1770 Crèvecoeur meets a family of Scotch emigrants, Andrew and his wife and son from the island of Barra. Crèvecoeur finds jobs for the three of them, and helps to arrange for the purchase of a farm. Andrew clears the land, builds a house, and plants his crops. The family prospers, Andrew becomes a civic leader, and accumulates a sizeable estate—all evidence of "the happy effects which constantly flow in this country from sobriety and industry when united with good land and freedom."

Such a farming community as that in which Crèvecoeur lived was typical of the America of his day. More than 90 percent of the people lived on the soil and were small farmers like himself. The farms were largely self-sufficient and owned by independent families. To Crèvecoeur the rural way of life was ideal.

Crèvecoeur was a lover of nature, and his acute observations

on the world of birds, animals, and insects make fascinating reading. His notes on the struggle for survival are reminiscent of
passages in Charles Darwin's *Origin of Species,* written nearly a
century later:

> I am astonished to see that nothing exists but what has its
> enemy, one species pursue and live upon another: unfortunately
> our kingbirds are the destroyers of those industrious insects
> [the bees]; but on the other hand, these birds preserve our fields
> from the depredations of the crows, which they pursue on the
> wing with great vigilance and astonishing dexterity.

The survival of the fittest is illustrated in Crèvecoeur's anecdote of a fight between wrens and swallows, during which the
tiny wrens attacked the larger, swifter swallows in order to steal
their nests. The wrens were triumphant. Again, a mighty battle,
fought to the death, is described between a great water snake
and a 6-foot black snake, won by the latter, by drowning the
water snake! Other accounts deal with rattlesnakes and copper-
heads, hornets, hummingbirds, passenger pigeons, and ant
colonies.

Bits of natural-history folklore are mixed occasionally with
Crèvecoeur's otherwise realistic descriptions. He repeats, apparently without scepticism, the ancient tale of the snake fangs
imbedded in a pair of boots and killing several wearers. On one
occasion, he reports seeing a kingbird voraciously attacking a
swarm of bees. Crèvecoeur killed the bird, opened its craw, and
found a total of 171 bees. "I laid them all on a blanket in the
sun," the account continued, "and to my great surprise 54
returned to life, licked themselves clean and joyfully went back
to the hive."

A friendship particularly enjoyed by Crèvecoeur was that with
the pioneer Pennsylvania botanist John Bartram, whose farm
he visited on several occasions. Bartram carried on an extensive
correspondence with European botanists and reported to them
on the great variety of plants and trees to be found in America,
insofar as he had opportunities to study them. "The father of
United States botany," as he is called, founded the first botanical
garden in the United States at Philadelphia in 1725. Crèvecoeur
found association with him to be highly stimulating and
rewarding.

Crèvecoeur's wanderings through the colonies took him for extended stays in Nantucket and Martha's Vineyard, to which he devotes five of his twelve chapters, describing at length the manners and customs of the seafaring inhabitants and the lives of the fishermen and whalers. On another expedition he visited Charleston, South Carolina. There he was violently repelled by the institution of slavery as it existed in the American South. Crèvecoeur deplored the way the slaves were treated, "the meanness of their food, the severity of their tasks," and the utter hopelessness of their condition. In one gruesome passage there is described a caged Negro being tortured to death by birds and insects for having killed the overseer of a plantation.

But in general Crèvecoeur has a happy story to tell until the twelfth and final letter, written after the outbreak of the Revolution. The conflict placed him on the horns of a dilemma: "If I attach myself to the Mother Country which is three thousand miles from me, I become what is called an enemy to my own region; if I follow the rest of my countrymen, I become opposed to our ancient masters." Crèvecoeur "wanted nothing more than to live independent and tranquil," not taking sides. Nevertheless, because of his Loyalist sympathies he was forced to abandon his farm and to flee to New York, where he was imprisoned for two months by the British on suspicion of being a spy. Finally, in 1780, he was permitted to sail for Europe, leaving his family behind. His *Letters from an American Farmer* was published in London in 1782, and a French edition appeared two years later. After the war, in 1783, Crèvecoeur returned to the United States as French Consul in New York. In the interim, his wife had died, his children were scattered, and his farmhouse had been burned. In 1790 he returned for the last time to Europe, remaining until his death in 1813.

Both the English and French editions of *Letters from an American Farmer* were immediately popular. Crèvecoeur's glowing descriptions of life in the Colonies persuaded many settlers to come over from Europe, without fully realizing the hardships and difficulties accompanying life on the frontier. The eager emigrants envisioned new opportunities in America, while European romantics, endoctrinated by Rousseau, dreamed of children of nature, noble savages, and backwoods paradises. The

Letters were read and praised by Charles Lamb, Byron, Southey, Coleridge, Hazlitt, and Godwin. The work was also esteemed in America by Washington, Franklin, Jefferson, Madison, and other leaders. As Arthur Hobson Quinn has pointed out, Crève-coeur's book belongs "with a group of colonial works which have special interest because they affected the growth of certain ideas abroad." It is one of the first chapters in the long story of American pioneer progress and tradition.

7 | FATHER OF THE AMERICAN LANGUAGE

Noah Webster's *American Spelling Book*, 1783

The American Colonies' declaration of political independence from Great Britain was followed soon thereafter by a declaration of intellectual independence. The latter was proclaimed by a young Connecticut schoolteacher, Noah Webster. When the first of his efforts toward the creation of a separate American language appeared, the future great American lexicographer was a mere twenty-five years of age. Webster's *American Spelling Book, Containing the Rudiments of the English Language for the United States,* more familiarly known as the "Blue-backed Speller," was first issued in 1783 and was destined to exert a stupendous influence on American life and culture.

The versatility of Noah Webster's career was on a par with Benjamin Franklin's, though—except in the field of education—lacking the latter's immediate impact on events. Beyond his prodigious labors on language, Webster wrote prolifically on political and economic matters, produced a two-volume *History of Epidemics,* edited two newspapers, and led the fight for national copyright legislation.

Webster's ambition, after being granted two degrees from Yale University, was to become a lawyer, but times were hard and money extremely scarce. Legal practice was found unremunerative. Public school teaching was the sole avenue immediately open to Webster for earning a living, and he turned to it. Thereby was saved one of the giants of American educational history.

Webster recognized the extreme inadequacies of the contemporary grammar schools, and he was dissatisfied with the textbooks and teaching methods currently in use. In particular, he objected to the use in the village schools of books that were saturated with English speech, spelling, and ideas.

A cultural reform in America, Webster believed, should be based on a single, uniform language, an American language, a device that would also help to bind the young nation together. "America must be independent in literature as she is in politics," proclaimed Webster. As his own contribution to that end, he projected a tripartite work pompously entitled *A Grammatical Institute of the English Language, Comprising an Easy, Concise and Systematic Method of Education, Designed for the Use of English Schools in America. In Three Parts.* Part 1, the speller, was the first to be published, subsequently followed by a grammar in 1784, and *Lessons in Reading and Speaking in 1785.* About twenty years went by before Webster brought out his *Compendious Dictionary of the English Language* and finally, in 1828, his most monumental work, *The American Dictionary of the English Language.*

Webster's fierce sense of patriotism, as well as his educational philosophy, is stated in the preface to his speller:

> The author wishes to promote the honor and prosperity of the confederated republics of America. . . . This country must in some future time be as distinguished by the superiority of her literary improvements, as she is already by the liberality of her civil and ecclesiastical constitutions. Europe is grown old in folly, corruption and tyranny. For America in her infancy to adopt the maxims of the Old World would be to stamp the wrinkles of decrepit old age upon the bloom of youth, and to plant the seeds of decay in a vigorous constitution. American glory begins to dawn at a favourable period.

Nevertheless, despite his desire to depart from English manners, customs, and models, Webster's speller drew freely upon the most popular English text of the period, Dilworth's *New Guide to the English Tongue,* first issued in London in 1740. Seven years later, an American edition was printed by Benjamin Franklin in Philadelphia, and Dilworth's book remained the standard work in the Colonies until superseded by Webster's. Portions of the Dilworth text, which Webster himself had studied in his boyhood, were lifted verbatim or paraphrased in the "Blue-backed Speller," and Webster borrowed Dilworth's general arrangement, with lists of progressively more difficult words alternating with reading lessons. Some of Dilworth's lists—such as *big, dig, fig, gig, jig, pig, wig,* etc.—were also taken over unchanged.

A second work from which Webster extracted material that he considered suitable for his own compilation was Daniel Fenning's *Universal Spelling Book,* first published in 1756. There is no question, indeed, that much material was lifted by Webster from Dilworth and Fenning, but everything was organized on new principles. Though he had followed a familiar pattern, Webster had produced a basically new book.

The high moral tone of Dilworth and Fenning and of the earlier *New England Primer* permeates the *"Blue-backed Speller."* A characteristic note is sounded in this passage:

> A good child will not lie, swear, nor steal. He will be good at home, and ask to read his book; when he gets up he will wash his hands and face clean; he will comb his hair, and make haste to school; he will not play by the way, as bad boys do.

A moral lesson is taught also in Webster's realistic "Fable of the Boy that Stole Apples:"

> An old man found a rude boy upon one of his trees stealing apples, and desired him to come down; but the young sauce-box told him plainly he would not. Won't you? said the old man, then I will fetch you down; so he pulled up some tufts of grass and threw at him; but this only made the youngster laugh, to think the old man should pretend to beat him down from the tree with grass only.
>
> Well, well, said the old man, if neither words nor grass will do, I must try what virtue there is in stones, which soon made the young chap hasten down from the tree and beg the old man's pardon.
>
> Moral: *If good words and gentle means will not reclaim the wicked, they must be dealt with in a more severe manner.*

Axioms reminiscent of *Poor Richard's Almanac* were strewn through the speller:

> When wine is in, wit is out.
> A good cow may have a bad calf.
> You must not buy a pig in a poke.
> Let not your tongue cut your throat.
> He that lies down with dogs must rise up with fleas.

Without frugality, none can be rich; and with it few would be poor.

Dilworth's book was pervaded by religious material, dwelling, as had much early New England literature, on sin, death, the grave, and eternal damnation. In contrast, Webster's speller was a secular work filled with worldly wisdom, for the author objected to the use of the Bible as a textbook and felt that "nothing has greater tendency to lessen the reverence which mankind ought to have for the Supreme Being than a careless repetition of his name upon every trifling occasion."

The Americanization of the English language was accomplished by Webster in part by what he called "expunging the superfluous letter," such as the *u* in *honour, favour, labour,* and *colour,* and the *k* in *critick* and *musick.* He reversed the imitation French order of letters in *theatre, centre,* and *cheque.* American place names and abbreviations replaced Dilworth's English lists, and there was a chronology of important American dates. Attacking the chaotic matter of syllabication, Webster established logical principles of dividing words to facilitate pronunciation and spelling—rules that are still in effect today. Standards of pronunciation were also developed, based upon "general custom," that is, current speech, especially prevailing New England modes. Footnotes sternly warned children against vulgar and colloquial pronunciations, examples of which were cited.

The disorganized, unsystematic, nonstandardized orthography of Webster's time is almost incredible—practices of which great statesmen were as guilty as the common people. Eighteenth-century America had few rules about how even ordinary words should be spelled. Phonetic spelling led to such monstrosities as *jinerll* for *general, Ffebrewarie* for *February,* and *toune* for *town.* Even stranger-looking forms appeared in the spelling of native American place names.

In time, crude woodcuts illustrating the fables in the Webster speller became an inseparable feature—the boy who stole apples, the country maid and her milk pail, the fox and the swallow, the cat and the rat, the fox and the bramble, the bear and two friends, the two dogs, and the partial judge.

Webster's problems were by no means at an end when he completed the manuscript for *An American Spelling Book.* He searched in vain for a publisher, for no printer would risk the expense. Finally, in June 1783, a contract was arranged with two Connecticut newspaper publishers, Hudson and Goodwin, whereby Webster's note was accepted for the printing bill. An edition of 5,000 copies was produced, to sell at fourteen pence a copy or ten shillings a dozen for a little book of 119 pages. It was an immediate success; the first edition sold out in less than nine months. Second and third editions appeared the next year. Storekeepers began to stock the book as a staple along with such necessities as rum and molasses, needles and cheese. Unable to meet the demand at the Hartford press, sets of the plates were rented for a fee of ½ cent a copy. From Maine to Oregon, sales skyrocketed. No one knows how many copies were sold during the next hundred years. Estimates run as high as 100 million. A conservative guess is 60 to 75 million copies—the best seller of all time, with the exception of the Bible.

Webster's troubles did not end with publication and the achievement of a best-seller, however. Wholesale copyright violations, cheap imitations, dishonest printers, and downright theft of royalties plagued the author for years to come. There was no national copyright until 1790. While promoting the idea of national legislation, Webster set out to gain protection from the individual states. Traveling from state to state over a period of five years, he succeeded in persuading all except Vermont to enact copyright laws.

In presenting his plea for copyright, Webster pointed out that his speller, and later the grammar and reader, would simplify and unify the language, and furthermore they were

calculated to extirpate the improprieties and vulgarisms which were necessarily introduced by settlers from various parts of Europe; to reform the abuses and corruption which, to an unhappy degree, tincture the conversation of the polite part of the Americans; to render the acquisition of the language easy both to American youth and foreigners; and especially to render the pronunciation of it accurate and uniform by demolishing those odious distinctions of provincial dialects which are the subject of reciprocal ridicule in different States.

No less meritorious and praiseworthy in Webster's view were the moral and religious instruction offered by his books and their inculcation of patriotic sentiments in American youth.

In *The American Language*, H. L. Mencken claims that Americans speak more distinctly than Englishmen because their speechways were molded for four generations by Noah Webster's "Blue-backed Speller." "From 1783, when it was first published, until the beginning of the Twentieth Century," continued Mencken," it was the most widely circulated book in the country, and the most influential."

Webster's leading biographer, Harry R. Warfel, concurs: "No other secular book has reached so many minds in America as Webster's Spelling Book, and none has played so shaping a part in our destiny. . . . He [Webster] became our greatest schoolmaster, not by pontificating from a chair in a great university; but by teaching simple fundamentals—in language, morals, economics, politics— to the masses." Because of Webster's teaching, Warfel concludes, a basic pattern of written and spoken English came to prevail in all the states of the Union, among millions of immigrants, as well as the population in general. The speller may justly rate as one of the great unifying forces in American culture.

8 | AMERICAN MYTH MAKER

Mason Locke Weems's *The Life of Washington
the Great,* 1800

Mason Locke Weems has been described as a fiddling parson,
an itinerant bookseller, a sentimentalist and corrupter of history;
but as historian Paul Leicester Ford observed, "No man whose
writings have passed through some two hundred editions, or of
whose productions some two hundred and fifty thousand [a
more recent estimate is in excess of 1 million] copies have sold,
deserves neglect. . . . No history of the American people or their
literature can be complete without noticing the man and his
work." Weems's writings, directed primarily at the uneducated
and the young, were destined to have a permanent impact on
American history.

Weems was born in Anne Arundel County, Maryland, in
1759, the youngest of nineteen children, offspring of a Scotsman,
David Weems. Little is known for certain about the son's early
career, except that in 1784 he was ordained in England as a
priest in the Episcopal Church, and from then until 1790 he was
rector of All Hallows in his native county. In 1791, Weems
launched himself upon a lifetime career as promoter, seller, and
author of books and pamphlets. Though he remained an Episco-
palian minister, he had no permanent clerical connections after
about 1793. At the age of thirty-five, Weems married a colonel's
daughter considerably younger than himself, and the couple
proceeded to produce ten children.

For thirty-one years, Weems wandered over the Southern states
preaching, fiddling, and selling books, mainly following the
Eastern seaboard from New York City to Savannah. His first
book venture was reprinting a series of inspirational and self-
improving works by Robert Russel, Hugh Blair, Hannah More,
Henry Brooke, and others. After 1794 he served as agent for
Mathew Carey, an enterprising Philadelphia publisher, peddling

weighty works by Oliver Goldsmith, John Marshall's five-volume *Life of George Washington,* prayer books, Carey's edition of the Bible, and other general and Biblical literature. Weems's surviving statements evidence a passionate faith in the value of "good books," and he felt that increasing the circulation of such works was as truly doing God's work as preaching from the pulpit. In a letter to Carey in 1796, he wrote:

> This country is large, and numerous are its inhabitants; to culti-vate among these a taste for reading, and by the reflection of proper books to throw far and wide the rays of useful arts and sciences, were at once the work of a true philanthropist and prudent speculator. For I am verily assured that under proper culture, every dollar that you shall scatter on the field of this experiment will yield 30, 60 and 100 fold.

Works edited by or printed for Weems (before he became in-volved in authorship himself on a large scale), and which he added to his selling stock, carried such colorful and alluring titles as *Sure and Certain Methods of Attaining a Long and Healthy Life; An Estimate of the Religion of the Fashionable World; The History of Louisa, the Lovely Orphan; The History of a Reprobate; The American Farmer's Guide; The Death of Abel; The Immortal Mentor: Or Man's Unerring Guide to a Healthy, Wealthy, and Happy Life;* and *An Account of the Pelew Islands.* Several went through multiple editions. At Weems's urging, Carey printed Thomas Paine's *Age of Reason.* Weems was too good a bookseller not to realize the sales pos-sibilities in Paine's controversial work, though he did not want his own name closely linked with it.

Throughout his career, Weems appears to have had an intense desire to write—in good part, no doubt, for mercenary rather than patriotic reasons, because of the commercial possibilities in popular books. He came into his own as an author with the publi-cation in 1800 of a work entitled *The Life and Memorable Actions of George Washington, General and Commander of the Armies of America.* Weems early conceived the idea of a Wash-ington biography, and about six months prior to Washington's death he wrote to Mathew Carey proposing that he print "a piece christened, or to be christened, 'The Beauties of Washing-ton' . . . it will sell like flax seed at a quarter of a dollar." Weems assured Carey: "I could make you a world of pence and popularity by it."

Another letter to Carey, immediately after Washington's death, outlined the general scheme of the book. Weems was certain that "millions are gaping to read something" about the dead hero. With spelling, punctuation, and capitalization modernized, the plan was thus described:

> I give his history, sufficiently minute—I accompany him from his start, through the French and Indian and British or Revolutionary wars, to the President's chair, to the throne in the hearts of 5,000,000 of people. I then go on to show that the unparalleled rise and elevation were owing to his great virtues, his veneration for the Deity or religious principles, his patriotism, his magnanimity, his industry, his temperance and sobriety, his justice, etc. Thus I hold up his great virtues to the imitation of youth. All this I have lined and enlivened with anecdotes apropos interesting and entertaining.

Neither the hardheaded publisher nor the exuberant author could possibly have foreseen the success of the Washington biography nor its permanent effect on the nation's view of its first President. Since its initial appearance, the book has been issued in at least eighty-three editions, the last in 1962, including French and German translations.

The first two editions of the work were anonymous, though the second was "Printed for the Rev. M. L. Weems." Subsequent editions carried Weems's name as author. In the fifth edition (1806)—in most respects the definitive one—Weems revised his little volume, enriching it with many "new and valuable anecdotes," and increased the price to 50 cents. Most of the famous stories of Washington's youth, including the cherry-tree episode, first appeared in this edition. The full title reads: *The Life of Washington the Great, Enriched with a Number of Very Curious Anecdotes, Perfectly in Character, and Equally Honorable to Himself, and Exemplary to His Young Countrymen.*

The legend of George Washington and the cherry tree, one of the best known in American history, has played an instrumental part in fixing the character and image of the "Father of His Country" in the popular mind. The original text is as follows:

When George was about six years old, he was made the wealthy master of a *hatchet!* of which, like most little boys, he was immoderately fond, and was constantly going about chopping every thing that came in his way. One day, in the garden, where he often amused himself hacking his mother's pea-sticks, he unluckily tried the edge of his hatchet on the body of a beautiful young English cherry tree, which he barked so terribly that I don't believe the tree ever got the better of it. The next morning the old gentleman finding out what had befallen his tree, which, by the by, was a great favorite, came into the house, and with much warmth asked for the mischievous author, declaring at the same time, that he would not have *taken five guineas* for his tree. No body could tell him any thing about it. Presently George and his hatchet made their appearance. *George,* said his father, *do you know who killed that beautiful little cherry tree yonder in the garden?* This was a *tough question,* and George staggered under it for a moment; but quickly recovered himself; and looking at his father, with the sweet face of youth brightened with the inexpressible charm of all-conquering truth, he bravely cried out, *"I can't tell a lie, Pa; you know I can't tell a lie. I did cut it with my hatchet."*—*Run to my arms you dearest boy,* cried his father in transports, *run to my arms, glad am I, George, that you ever killed my tree, for you have paid me for it a thousand fold. Such an act of heroism in my son, is more worth than a thousand trees, though blossomed with silver, and their fruits of purest gold.*

Thus George escaped a whipping, a celebrated myth was created, and the process of deification of our first President began. The later inclusion of the cherry-tree yarn in the McGuffey Readers increased its circulation by tens of millions of copies. Close behind the story of the sad fate of the cherry tree in popular esteem came the anecdotes about the cabbage seed (to demonstrate the omnipotence of the Almighty), the heavily laden apple trees (to teach a lesson of unselfishness), and Mary Washington's dream in which she saw her little son George at the age of five extinguish a raging fire about to destroy the family home. To illustrate the belief that Washington bore a charmed life and was destined by fate for greater eminence, there is the story of the Indian warrior, told after General Braddock's disastrous defeat:

A famous Indian warrior, who acted a leading part in that bloody tragedy, was often heard to swear, that *"Washington was not born to be killed by a bullet! For,"* continued he, *"I had seventeen fair fires at him with my rifle, and after all could not bring him to the ground!"* And indeed whoever considers that a good rifle, leveled by a proper marksman, hardly ever misses its aim, will readily enough conclude with this unlettered savage, that there was some invisible hand, which turned aside his bullets.

There is little evidence to support these and similar anecdotes in Weems's account. Indeed, research has revealed that several of the stories have a base in earlier Southern traditions and were simply lifted by Weems for the purpose of moral instruction and to glorify his hero.

But Weems has his defenders. The American literary historian Jay Hubbell observes,

> So much has been written about Weems's historical inaccuracies —which are numerous enough—that his literary powers have been somewhat underrated. He had, as his letters show, an eye for a telling phrase. There is a crude poetic and dramatic power in his descriptive passages; and the speeches which, like the epic poets and the ancient historians, he put into the mouths of his heroes are not lacking in eloquence. His widely read biography helped to perpetuate among the masses down to our own time his conception of Washington. He did his part to create a semi-legendary national hero whose name and fame would help hold together a union of diverse regions.

When Weems wrote his life of Washington, the United States as a nation was only sixteen years old, democracy still had to prove its staying powers, and numerous skeptics doubted that it could or would survive. Threats of secession were in the air and the federal government rested on shaky foundations. "What Weems did," asserts David D. Van Tassel, "was to make national symbols of his subjects, legendary giants of republican virtue and bravery for a hero-starved people, heroes of recent history for a people cut off by their own volition from their heroes of legend."

And who knows? Perhaps there was a grain of truth in Weems's cherry-tree story. In an essay "George Washington and Parson Weems," by Robert W. McLaughlin, written about forty years ago, the author reported that a pottery jug, belonging to the eighteenth century, had been discovered in Germany. On it is an inscription "G. W. 1776." The mug is further adorned with a uniformed figure of an officer in the Continental army. In the foreground is a hacked cherry tree. The assumption is that the tale of the cherry tree was carried back to Germany by a Hessian and thereafter pictured on a mug of German manufacture. It is conceivable, therefore, that Weems did not invent the story, but utilized a piece of prevailing folklore.

Weems was the first to recognize the avid public interest in the colonial and Revolutionary War heroes. Having discovered the gold mine with his biography of Washington, he proceeded to exploit it further with *The Life of Gen. Francis Marion, The Life of Doctor Benjamin Franklin,* and *The Life of William Penn, the Settler of Pennsylvania.* None was as popular as the Washington work, but all went through numerous editions. The biography of Marion rivaled Washington's in color and imagination. The others were less flamboyant and of lesser interest.

Weems's prolific pen was busy also in producing a series of moralizing tracts: *God's Revenge against Murder, God's Revenge against Gambling, The Drunkard's Looking Glass, God's Revenge against Adultery, God's Revenge against Duelling,* and *The Bad Wife's Looking Glass: Or God's Revenge against Cruelty to Husbands.* A political sermon, *The Philanthropist: Or a Good Twenty-five Cents Worth of Political Love Power* (1799), was endorsed in a letter from George Washington. All had large sales.

The reasons for the popularity of Weems's writings are easily apparent. They were aimed at the relatively unlettered farmers, pioneers, and backwoodsmen of the new country. The books made easy, exciting reading; they were cheap; and they appealed to the patriotic instincts of a people only a few years removed from the American Revolution. Americans all over the Union, including Abraham Lincoln, testified to the influence that Weems and his anecdotes exercised over them in their formative years. Weems's most recent biographer and critic, Marcus Cunliffe, offers perceptive explanations for the parson's immense following:

American nationalism was a self-conscious creation, and George Washington was its chief symbol. Traveling widely and continuously, Weems discovered by experiment what Americans wanted to read. They were religiously minded, so they would buy Bibles, sermons, tracts. They were eager for color and excitement, so they would buy novels by the cartload. They were, when stimulated, ferociously patriotic, so they would buy works that ministered to their national pride. What better literary fare than the Weemsian biographies, which satisfied all their wants—religion (or religiosity), romanticism, patriotism—simultaneously? They were stirred by his would-be epic strain, edified by his preachments, tickled by his knockabout fare.

Did it really matter that Weems exercised literary license in creating episodes, dialogue, and fictitious situations? Historical fiction has been an accepted literary genre since the ancient Greeks. Cunliffe suggests that Weems "despite himself may have conveyed valuable truths about George Washington and about the United States. Far from being ruined by his tales, we decide that American history would be thinner without them." Another historian, Michael Kraus, concluded, "It might not be too much to say that generations of historical scholars since his time have been unable to modify seriously the popular picture Weems created of our Revolutionary heroes."

10 | SEAMAN'S BIBLE

Nathaniel Bowditch's *The New American Practical Navigator*, 1802

The natural perils of the sea were vastly increased for early sailors by faulty systems of navigation. Ancient seamen lacked compasses, sextants, chronometers, and of course the electronic devices in common use today. The timid stayed close to shore and sailed only during daylight in fair weather; the more intrepid dared to sail out of sight of land and, using the sun, stars, and winds, managed to reach their destinations without the aid of mechanical devices.

By the sixteenth century, substantial advances had been made. Ferdinand Magellan's expedition to circumnavigate the globe was equipped with sea charts, a terrestrial globe, theodolites, quadrants, compasses, magnetic needles, and hour glasses. Still missing was a vital element: an accurate method of determining longitude. That huge obstacle was overcome two centuries later with the invention of the chronometer. Another basic step was the publication of the first official nautical almanac.

Beginning with the original edition in 1772, John Hamilton Moore's *Practical Navigator* was the leading navigational text until superseded thirty years later by an American work, Nathaniel Bowditch's *New American Practical Navigator* (1802), subtitled *Being an Epitome of Navigation; Containing All the Tables Necessary to Be Used with the Nautical Almanac In Determining the Latitude; and the Longitude By Lunar Observations; And Keeping a Complete Reckoning at Sea: Illustrated by Proper Rules and Examples: The Whole Exemplified In A Journal, Kept From Boston to Madeira: In Which All the Rules Of Navigation Are Introduced: Also The Demonstration of the most useful Rules of Trigonometry: With many useful Problems in Mensuration, Surveying, and Gauging: And a Dictionary of Sea-Terms; with the Manner of Performing the most common Evolutions at Sea. To which Are Added. Some General Instruc-*

tions and Information to Merchants, Masters of Vessels, and others concerned in Navigation, relative to Maritime Laws and Mercantile Customs.

Born in 1773, Nathaniel Bowditch was a native of Salem, Massachusetts. From early youth he was recognized as a brilliant mathematician and linguist, though denied an opportunity for any formal education after age ten, because of family poverty. In the seafaring town of Salem, Bowditch was naturally drawn to the study of navigation. At age thirteen he learned the rudiments of the subject from an old British sailor. A year later he began to study surveying and assisted in a survey of the town of Salem. While still in his early teens, he devised an accurate calendar and constructed a barometer and sundial.

Bowditch's seagoing career began at age twenty-one, when he went on a year-long voyage to the Indian Ocean. Four other trips to sea were made over a period of about nine years, the last as captain and part owner of the three-masted *Putnam* on a thirteen-month voyage to Sumatra and Mauritius.

Accurate time was no more available to the average naval or merchant vessel during this period than it was in earlier centuries. The chronometer had been invented about sixty years earlier, but was too expensive for most shipowners to afford. Ships navigated by a combination of dead reckoning and parallel sailing (a system of sailing north or south to the latitude of the destination and then east or west to the destination).

During his first voyage and afterwards, Bowditch found innumerable errors in Moore's *Practical Navigator*. He began recording the mistakes and undertook, through a Newburyport publisher, Edmund M. Blunt, to issue a revised edition of the work. A total of some ten thousand errors in Moore were corrected in two editions edited by Bowditch. Then he and his publisher decided to bring out their own work, rather than to continue to correct Moore's blunders. They were encouraged in the undertaking by a report of a committee of the East India Marine Society of Salem, which stated:

> After a full examination of the system of Navigation presented to the society by one of its members, (Mr. Nathaniel Bowditch) they find, that he has corrected many thousand errors, existing in the best European works of the kind; especially those in the

Tables for determining the latitude by two altitudes, in those of difference of latitude and departure, of the sun's right ascension, of amplitudes, and many others necessary to the Navigator. Mr. Bowditch has likewise, in many instances, greatly improved the old methods of calculation, and added new ones of his own. That of clearing the apparent distance of the moon, and sun or stars, from the effect of parallax and refraction, is peculiarly adapted to the use of seamen in general. . . . He has much improved the table of latitudes and longitudes of places, and has added those of a number on the American coast hitherto very inaccurately ascertained.

In an advertisment inserted in the beginning of the book, publisher Blunt comments ironically: "While he is tendering his thanks to such as have assisted in the establishment of the work, it would be highly criminal to omit those due to *John Hamilton Moore;* and with the greatest frankness it is acknowledged that he contributed largely to its establishment, as his late editions have been so erroneous that no person would hazard his interest, much less life, in navigating his vessel by the rules there laid down." Bowditch's biographer, Robert E. Berry, notes that some of the errors made by Moore had been fatal to ships—the faulty tables of declination, for example. The year 1800 had been shown as a leap year in the tables, resulting, several masters claimed, in the loss of their ships.

Except in form, *The New American Practical Navigator* incorporated nothing from Moore which Bowditch had not verified at first hand. For instance, in presenting the model of a journal of a sea voyage, Bowditch substituted the record of his own voyage from Boston to Madeira for Moore's log of a voyage between England and the island of Tenerife.

Bowditch's aim was to compile a work which would be intelligible to the average seaman—in effect serving as a text for every member of a crew. In addition to improving methods of determining longitude, *The New American Practical Navigator* gave the ship's officer information on winds, currents, and tides; directions for surveying; statistics on marine insurance; a glossary of sea terms; instruction in mathematics; and numerous tables of navigational data. Berry observes that a diligent student of Bowditch, "learned how to observe an amplitude or azimuth by the compass, to find the moon's declination, to find the time at sea and regulate a watch, to calculate the sun's altitude at any time, and to calculate the altitude of the moon and stars." He could also learn to survey a coast from a ship's deck, survey a harbor from shore, and find the time of high tide.

The first edition of *The New American Practical Navigator* was a large, well-produced book, running to nearly 600 pages in length. The reception of the work was gratifying, making the author known around the world. Copies were soon in the sea chests of every American captain and sailor, and "Bowditch" became standard equipment for seagoing men.

Bowditch's knowledge of navigation was not limited to theory; he was equally skilled in practice. According to one anecdote, on Christmas Day in 1803, returning to Salem from a long voyage on the *Putnam*, he ran into a blizzard. While other ships were standing off shore waiting for the snow to stop, Bowditch headed his ship straight into the rocky harbor and landed safely at night in one of the worst storms on record.

Ten editions of *The New American Practical Navigator* appeared prior to Bowditch's death in 1838, and twenty-five other editions came out through 1867, when the copyright was purchased by the U.S. Navy Hydrographic Office. The title has been changed to the *American Practical Navigator*, but Bowditch's name still appears on the title page. A total of more than 700,000 copies in about seventy editions have been published since 1802.

Bowditch was a prolific writer throughout a long and active career. He prepared and published charts of the Salem, Beverly, and Manchester harbors, and he wrote twenty-three papers for the *Memoirs of the American Academy of Arts and Sciences* on the orbits of comets, meteors, applications of Napier's rules, magnetic variation, eclipses, calculations of tides, and other astronomical and nautical matters. His most monumental achievement, however, was the translation into English of the first four volumes of LaPlace's *Mécanique Céleste* (Paris, 1799–1805), accompanied by a voluminous commentary that considerably more than doubled the size of the original.

Many honors came to Bowditch in recognition of his accomplishments. Offers of professorships, which he refused, were received from Harvard University, the University of Virginia, and West Point. Honorary M.A. and LL.D degrees were conferred on him by Harvard, and he was elected a member of numerous American and European scientific societies.

Major credit belongs to Bowditch for the reputation which Yankee shipmasters achieved for their skill, dexterity, and know-how as navigators. Even before publication of *The New American Practical Navigator*, American ships were engaged in worldwide trade and naval cruises, and their captains were known as able seamen. Bowditch supplied them with the basic scientific and technical knowledge which they had hitherto lacked.

The high esteem in which Bowditch was held by his contemporaries is demonstrated in a eulogy from the Salem Marine Society:

> Not this community, nor our country only, but the whole world, has reason to do honor to his memory. . . . No monument will be needed to keep alive his memory among men; but as long as ships shall sail, the needle point to the north, and the stars go through their wonted course in the heavens, the name of Dr. Bowditch will be revered as of one who helped his fellowmen in a time of need, who was and is a guide to them over the pathless ocean.

11 | FRONTIER ROMANTICIST

James Fenimore Cooper's *Leatherstocking Tales*, 1823–1841

Writing in the *Saturday Review* some years ago, Cleveland Amory posed the question, "Who is the most famous character, the world over, in American fiction?" After suggesting various possible candidates, Amory concluded that the palm should go to Natty Bumppo, otherwise known as "Deerslayer," "Hawkeye," "Pathfinder," "Leatherstocking," or "Long Rifle," the hero of five immensely popular novels by James Fenimore Cooper. For well over a century, readers in all nations where American books have been read at all have regarded this simple but noble master of forest and plains as a supreme characterization in our native literature.

The several volumes of the Leatherstocking Tales, which carry the story of Natty Bumppo from youth to advanced old age, were not written in chronological order. The correct sequence, starting with Hawkeye's youth on the New York frontier in King George's War until his death on the western prairies in Jefferson's administration, should have been: *The Deerslayer, The Last of the Mohicans, The Pathfinder, The Pioneers,* and *The Prairie.* According to their actual appearance in print, the order is *The Pioneers, The Last of the Mohicans, The Prairie, The Pathfinder,* and *The Deerslayer.* Publication dates range from 1823 to 1841.

The elements in each of the Leatherstocking Tales are largely identical: high adventure, untamed nature, frontiersmen and Indians good and bad, and a steady advance westward. In the plots, too, is found a common pattern, characterized by journeys into the wilderness, conflict, Indian captures, pursuit, and rescue, with a generous admixture of romantic interest. Leatherstocking always plays a heroic role, usually in rescuing young women from dire peril. With a few notable exceptions, Indians are murderous savages, but some white characters are equally treacherous and dangerous. Variety is furnished by changing locales; the setting of *The Deerslayer* is Lake Otsego, *The Pathfinder* is in Ontario, *The Last of the Mohicans* is laid in the Lake George area, *The Pioneers* in Cooperstown, New York, at the time of its founding, and *The Prairie* in the trans-Mississippi plains.

The Deerslayer, considered by some critics the best of Cooper's plots, is a narrative of Natty Bumppo's early days as a young hunter brought up among the Delaware Indians, then engaged in warfare against the Hurons. Natty and his closest friend, the heroic Delaware Indian Chingachgook, the Great Serpent, are on an expedition to rescue Chingachgook's beloved, the Indian maiden Hist-oh-Hist or Wah-ta-Wah, who has been abducted by a renegade Delaware and carried off to an enemy tribe, the Mingoes. The main action of the story occurs on the wooded shores of Lake Glimmerglass (Otsego Lake, New York). Following different routes, Deerslayer and his young Indian friend overtake the Huron raiders. On the way, the two youths ally themselves with a couple of white renegades, Hurry Harry March, an ex-pirate and giant of a man, and Tom Hutter, a pioneer settler. The latter's two daughters, Judith—a passionate, tempestuous beauty—and the simple-minded Hetty, accompany them.

Hurry Harry and Tom are morally inferior to the worst of the Indians. Their motives are completely mercenary, and they will go to any lengths to obtain money—even to killing women and children to collect the bounty placed on Indian scalps.

The Deerslayer abounds in dramatic episodes: Hurry's and Hutter's raid on the Indian encampment, where they have been tempted by the bounty for scalps and where they are captured; Hetty's attempt to save the captives from execution by reading her Bible to the savages; the rescue of Hist by Deerslayer and Great Serpent; the scalping of Hutter by the Hurons; the capture and rescue of Deerslayer; Deerslayer's killing of his first Indian (who names him Hawkeye) and the accidental killing of Hetty in the final fight; and finally the timely appearance of a scarlet-coated British regiment, which routs the Huron band.

The romantic interest in *The Deerslayer* is supplied chiefly by Judith, who spurns the advances of Hurry Harry but who falls in love with Deerslayer. However, because she has broken his rigid moral code by previously conferring her favors on a handsome British officer, Natty Bumppo refuses to marry Judith, whereupon she disappears, presumably going to England to become the mistress of her seducer. Like many other frontier heroes, Deerslayer is destined to go through life alone, more or less immune to feminine charms and wiles.

Deerslayer's colorful adventures are continued in *The Last of the Mohicans,* set in the Lake George region some fourteen years later. Here again is presented a striking contrast between good and bad Indians, the former personified by Chingachgook and his stalwart son Uncas, the last of the Iroquois aristocracy, and the latter by barbarous Mingoes. The pattern of chase, escape, and battle is dominant throughout the stirring tale of adventure. All action is enveloped in the immense virgin forest, where Indians are far more at home than are white men. As one critic, Edwin Fussett, observes, "Of all the Leatherstocking Tales, *The Last of the Mohicans* is most unrelentingly bloody, cruel, and savage."

The time is 1757, with war raging between France and England in North America. Montcalm with his Indian allies is marching south to lay siege to Fort William Henry, held by a brave Scotch veteran, Lieutenant Colonel Munro, and his men. Munro's daughters, Cora and Alice, are determined to visit their father, despite the danger. Captain Duncan Heyward, in love with Alice, serves as escort, and the party is guided by a wily Indian scoundrel, Magua, who is prepared to lead them into a trap. Natty Bumppo, now called Hawkeye, accompanied by his two Indian friends Chingachgook and Uncas, comes along in the nick of time and leads the party to the fort, hotly pursued by a band of Indians.

Fort William Henry is soon overwhelmed by Montcalm's vastly superior forces, and his Indian allies massacre the helpless prisoners, including women and children. In the confusion, Cora and Alice Munro are again carried off by Magua. Munro and Heyward, Chingachgook and Uncas pick up the trail which leads to an Indian village. In a series of hair-breadth escapes and through cunning tricks, Alice is rescued, but Cora is slain when she refuses to become Magua's wife; Uncas dies in avenging her. Thus is lost "the last of the Mohicans." A shot from Hawkeye's rifle disposes of the arch villain Magua, as he attempts to flee.

The theme of miscegenation appears in *The Last of the Mohicans* through Uncas's evident love for Cora, who has a slight touch of Negro blood. With the tragic death of both characters the potential romance comes to a sad end.

In *The Pathfinder*, Natty Bumppo's adventures continue. He has now reached the age of forty. In an opening much like that of *The Last of the Mohicans*, Natty and his friends rescue a beautiful girl, Mabel Dunham, in a forest full of Indians. Mabel is on her way to visit her father, an Army sergeant stationed at Fort Oswego, a small outpost on Lake Ontario. An Iroquois traitor named Arrowhead, reminiscent of Magua, leads into ambush the white party that he is guiding. Chingachgook is captured by the Iroquois but escapes, and the group finally reaches the fort. In subsequent action, Sergeant Dunham takes a group of his men out on the lake to attack a French supply boat; in his absence the fort is assaulted by a party of twenty Indians led by the renegade Arrowhead, and a number of the defenders are killed. A relief party headed by Sergeant Dunham is ambushed, and the sergeant is fatally wounded. The survivors, aided by the Pathfinder, Chingachgook, Jasper, and even Mabel, fight off the Indians during the night. One of the whites, Lieutenant Davy Muir, is exposed as a French spy and is stabbed by Arrowhead, who then escapes into the bushes. Arrowhead is followed and scalped by Chingachgook.

In *The Pathfinder*, Natty Bumppo falls in love for the one and only time, with Mabel, whose father actively promotes the match. Mabel and Jasper, however, are in love. When the Pathfinder learns that his love is not reciprocated, he withdraws gracefully, apparently without any great anguish of spirit. It is obvious that the forest is his true mistress, and it would be intolerable for him to settle down to a life of domesticity. The irresistible attraction which the wilderness holds for him comes out again and again in the setting of *The Pathfinder*: the pathless woods north of the Mohawk, the falls of the Oswego, the beauties of the Lake Ontario shore, and the spectacular scenery of the Thousand Islands dotting the St. Lawrence River.

The fourth in the series of Leatherstocking Tales, *The Pioneers*, is set in 1793, during Washington's Presidency. Civilization has begun to catch up with Natty Bumppo, and he has become an old man. The place is again Otsego Lake or "Glimmerglass" where the village of Templeton (Cooperstown) has sprung up. Leatherstocking, as he is now called, lives off the land with his lifetime friend, the old Indian Chief Chingachgook, and young Oliver Edwards. *The Pioneers* is not a tale of high adventure, as the earlier works had been, but consists of a series of loosely connected episodes illustrating life in a frontier community. The animals, birds, fishes, and forests are being recklessly squandered. Among the more dramatic incidents are the arrest and trial of Leatherstocking for killing a deer in violation of a new game law; the accidental shooting of Edwards by a post-Revolution New York landowner, Judge Marmaduke Temple; the rescue of the judge's daughter Elizabeth during a forest fire; another rescue by Leatherstocking, this time from a ferocious panther, of Elizabeth and a friend walking in the forest; the death of the old Indian Chingachgook; the discovery of Edward Effingham— Oliver Edwards's grandfather and an old Loyalist friend of Temple's—living in a cave; and the uniting of Oliver and Elizabeth. In the end, Leatherstocking leaves the settlement and disappears into the woods. "He has gone far towards the setting sun," the author concludes, "the foremost in that band of pioneers who are opening the way for the march of the nation across the continent."

An entirely different locale forms the background for *The Prairie*. Natty, now aged perhaps ninety, too old to earn his living by hunting, is reduced to being a trapper somewhere on the edge of the Great Plains. The plot is complicated and there are many characters. Aside from Leatherstocking, who dominates the tale, the most memorable figures are the old squatter Ishmael Bush, a fugitive from justice, leading an emigrant party west; his wife Esther, who has some of the best and worst characteristics of pioneer womanhood; and the heroine Ellen Wade. Again there are bad Indians and good Indians, the former represented by a branch of the Sioux and a particularly savage villain Mahtoree, the latter by the Pawnees and a brave young warrior Hard-Heart. There are captures by and rescues from the Indians, an Indian battle, a prairie fire, a buffalo stampede (diverted by the braying of a donkey!). In the end the aged Bumppo dies, surrounded by both white and Indian friends, his rifle on his knee, his hound at his feet.

Though Cooper never actually saw the prairie country, his imaginative treatment of it is powerful and highly effective. He captures the spirit of the Great Plains, an area as vast as an ocean, an immensity of grass and sky, stretching in every direction. It is a harsh world, bare and hostile, in striking contrast to the forests, lakes, and rivers of the earlier periods. Ishmael and his unlovely kind are the forerunners of millions who will ultimately conquer and despoil the inhospitable land.

One critic has characterized the Leatherstocking Tales as "the epic of the American Indian," and Cooper has been accused of idealizing the race in the manner of Rousseau's "noble savage." Such a conclusion can hardly be drawn from a careful reading of the Tales. There are heroic and truly admirable Indians— Chingachgook and his son Uncas, Hard-Heart, and the Indian maidens Hist-oh-Hist and Dew-of-June, the wife of Arrowhead— but almost invariably the Indians are villains. Cooper's "good" Indian tribes, the Delawares and the Pawnees, are those who cooperate with the white man, and the "bad" ones, the Mingoes and the Sioux, are those who resist and carry on war against the encroaching whites. There is no doubt in Hawkeye's mind, as Cooper puts words into his mouth, that the two races are fundamentally different, morally and in other vital respects, and the white man is definitely superior.

Another accusation directed at Cooper is that his women are namby-pambies, weakly sentimental and insipid, who faint in every crisis. Again the evidence fails to support the charge. Such incidents as Alice and Cora risking torture rather than joining their Indian captors, Judith pushing an Indian intruder over the edge of the scow into the river, Mabel Dunham helping to defend the blockhouse, and Esther and her two daughters defending their rock citadel against attack show Cooper's female characters cast in the role of true frontier heroines.

Leatherstocking himself has become the symbol of all frontiersmen, an idealized character, essentially Amercan, courageous and with great physical endurance, enterprising, modest, completely loyal and moral, a lover of nature constantly attempting to escape the stultifying effects of civilization. Cooper undoubtedly received inspiration for his creation from real-life frontier heroes—notably Daniel Boone, and to a lesser extent George Rogers Clark, Davy Crockett, Jedidah Smith, Joe Meek, and Kit Carson—but in mind and spirit Leatherstocking is an original.

The influence of Cooper's characters and particularly of Leatherstocking may be clearly perceived down to the present day. The superman tradition has pervaded American popular fiction for the past century and a half. An endless parade of imitative narratives has rolled from the printing presses, each with the attributes of Natty Bumppo, the frontier hero. A comparatively recent manifestation is the Western, beginning in the 1880s, sagas of the cowboys of the Great Plains. Leatherstocking's flight from civilization and his imperviousness to feminine charms are still common features of western folk heroes.

Allan Nevins has ably summarized Cooper's achievement in the Leatherstocking Tales:

> Viewing the five romances as a whole, we are struck by their breadth and grandeur. Their faults, which are many, are faults of detail; their virtues are large and enduring virtues. It was Cooper's felicity to unroll a canvas whose panoramic width matched the shaggy continent; to paint on it the pageant of the primeval Atlantic forests, the Great Lakes, the smaller canoe-threaded waterways, and the rolling prairies; and to fill the foreground with the clangorous action of the era when Indian, Briton, Frenchman, and Spaniard disputed the destiny of the continent. We can go to him in youth for entertainment, and come back to him in maturity for our fullest presentation of the color and magnitude of the American scene in its primitive epoch.

12 | KING OF ORNITHOLOGICAL PAINTERS

John James Audubon's *The Birds of America,*
1827–1838

If Americans were asked to name their favorite naturalist, past or present, the name of John James Audubon would doubtless head the list. Framed reproductions of his paintings hang in innumerable American homes, and his fame is perpetuated through the National Audubon Society, the Canadian Audubon Society, and similar groups dedicated to wildlife conservation and preservation. After examining Audubon's double-elephant-folio edition of *The Birds of America,* his most celebrated achievement, the famous French biologist Georgés Cuvier pronounced it "the greatest monument ever erected by art to Nature"—and so it has remained.

Audubon's artistic temperament shines through in every phase of a long and frequently tempestuous career. His one consuming passion was painting birds and animals as he found them in nature; all else was subordinated to this driving ambition.

Considerable mystery surrounds Audubon's early years. The most authentic evidence supports the belief that he was born in 1785 in Les Cayes, Santo Domingo (now Haiti), the illegitimate son of a French sea captain, Jean Audubon, and a native Creole girl, Mlle. Rabin. After his mother's early death, the four-year-old child was taken to France to be educated. His youth was carefree and somewhat spoiled, spent in rambling through woods and fields, collecting snakes and turtles and birds' eggs, and studying music and drawing, the latter under a well-known teacher, Jacques Louis David. Young Audubon first saw the United States at the age of eighteen, when he was sent to manage his father's estate in Pennsylvania.

Audubon showed no interest in or talent for business, but in a year spent at the "Mill Grove" farm, near Philadephia, he began his study of American birds, devoting much of his time to observing and drawing the avifauna around him. During that period he met, became engaged to, and several years later married a neighbor's daughter, Lucy Green Bakewell, whose loyal support contributed immensely to her husband's subsequent success. The young couple began their life together in Louisville, Kentucky. After several attempts to operate stores, mills, and commission businesses, all of which were failures, Audubon spent an increasing amount of time in the Kentucky wilderness with his gun and sketchbook, making and selling crayon portraits and teaching drawing, music, and dancing. While at Louisville, in 1810, he was visited by Alexander Wilson, then America's foremost ornithologist; a certain degree of rivalry later developed between them, spurred on by friends of both.

Audubon abandoned business altogether after 1819 and henceforth was solely preoccupied with his artistic efforts and attendant publication problems. At this time, apparently, he had fully determined to publish his ornithological studies and paintings. The first of a series of long expeditions took him down the Ohio and Mississippi Rivers to New Orleans, during which he explored the country for birds. Another tour gave him an opportunity to study the bird life of the Lake Ontario and Lake Champlain region. Meanwhile, for the next several years the family's principal support came from his wife's salary as a governess. Near the end of 1822, Audubon received his first instruction in the use of oils from John Stein, an itinerant portrait painter. Later, Thomas Sully, a famous early-American portrait painter, gave Audubon free lessons in oil painting.

The concept of his monumental work, *The Birds of America,* seems to have been in the back of Audubon's mind for a considerable time before it reached maturity. He came to visualize the undertaking as a great portfolio of all the known birds of the North American continent, life-size, perched upon cliffs or tree branches, painted in true colors. Life-size pictures for the largest birds would require pages 3 feet by 2½ feet in size. The artistic side of the project was far simpler than the problem of financing publication and seeing the work through the press.

Visits to Philadelphia and New York in 1824 convinced Audubon that there was no hope of having his paintings published in America. The technical skill was lacking. After a two-year delay to accumulate travel funds, he sailed for England to find a publisher and to raise subscriptions for the huge folio set after it had been produced. Audubon landed at Liverpool on July 21, 1826, and remained abroad nearly three years. Through influential references his drawings were exhibited at the Royal Institution a week after his arrival and were an immediate success.

The original plans for publication of *The Birds of America* provided for the issuance of the drawings in parts of five plates each, at two guineas a part, all to be engraved on copper, life-sized, and colored after Audubon's paintings. The number of parts was estimated at eighty, to be completed in fourteen years. Actually, the finished work consisted of eighty-seven parts of 435 plates, in four volumes, representing more than a thousand individual birds, plus thousands of American trees, shrubs, flowers, insects, and animals of the entire continent. The end was reached in twelve years, from 1827 to 1838.

The specifications for the prodigious enterprise are contained in a prospectus issued in London, after ten numbers had been completed. The details were as follows:

> The Engravings in every instance to be of the exact dimensions of the Drawings, which, without any exception, represent the Birds of their natural size.
>
> The Plates will be coloured, in the most careful manner, from the original Drawings.
>
> The Size of the work will be Double Elephant, and printed on the finest Drawing Paper.
>
> Five plates will constitute a Number; one Plate from one of the largest Drawings, one from one of the second size, and three from the smaller Drawings.
>
> There are 400 Drawings; and it is proposed that they shall comprise Three Volumes, each containing about 133 Plates, to which an Index will be given at the end of each, to be bound up with the Volume.
>
> Five Numbers will come out annually.
>
> The Price of each Number will be Two Guineas; payable on delivery.

The price to each subscriber—£182 14s. in England and $1,000 in America—was enough to give pause to persons of moderate means, and the roll of patrons never reached the level anticipated by Audubon. Actually, the number fluctuated during the twelve years that the work was in process of production. Some of the early subscribers tired of waiting, became dissatisfied, and dropped out, while new customers were picked up along the way. There were 279 names on the original list of patrons who had subscribed to 284 sets. By the time the project was completed the number of names had declined to 161 for 166 copies (84 in Europe and 82 for America). Thus many original subscribers were left with incomplete sets on their hands.

After Audubon had been in England for three months, he journeyed to Edinburgh and there met William Home Lizars, a painter and engraver, who agreed to produce a specimen number of *The Birds of America;* the five plates for the first number were ready early in 1827. By the time that he had finished ten plates, however, Lizars had become discouraged and withdrew from the project. At this state Audubon had the great good fortune to meet and to form a partnership with another engraver, Robert Havell, Jr., then thirty-two years old. It was Havell who carried *The Birds of America* through to completion eleven years later and whose superb technique never faltered. His friendship with Audubon induced him to emigrate to the United States following completion of the long-drawn-out undertaking.

Concerning Havell's contribution to *The Birds of America,* Constance Rourke writes, "He remains one of the greatest artists in the difficult medium of aquatint. He lavished immense skill, conscience, even affection upon this work." The magnitude of the job undertaken by Havell may be better understood if one realizes that every illustration in Audubon's *Birds* was first engraved by hand on a copper plate; that is, each original picture was copied in every detail by etching or cutting lines on a piece of sheet copper. From the engravings, black-and-white reproductions were printed, following which each impression (numbering about 100,000) had to be colored in watercolor paints by hand, as nearly identical to the original painting as possible. The day of modern photoengraving and color printing lay far in the future.

In the course of publication, Audubon returned to America on several occasions to search for additional specimens of bird life. His journeys took him up and down the North and South Atlantic coasts, as far north as Labrador and as far south as Florida, including explorations in New Brunswick, Maine, New Jersey, and South Carolina, supplemented by further expeditions down the Ohio and Mississippi Rivers, and in Louisiana and Texas. These far-flung travels account for the expansion of *The Birds of America* beyond the original estimate of size.

The four enormous volumes of *The Birds of America*, when they finally came from the press, were approximately 3 feet 3 inches high and 2 feet 5 inches wide; each volume was 3 inches thick and weighed between 40 and 45 pounds.

The exact number of complete sets of Audubon's masterpiece presently surviving is unknown. Some volumes have been broken up by dealers and the plates sold separately, for framing. A well-informed estimate is 120 sets extant, a majority in public institutions in the United States and Europe. The last complete set reported sold went for $36,400 in London in 1960, and volume 1 alone brought $16,800 in 1967. A full set in excellent condition would probably be valued at $100,000 in the current rare-book market. Audubon's own set, with added plates, sold at auction for $216,000 in 1970.

Concurrently with *The Birds of America*, Audubon was engaged upon another large and ambitious enterprise, his *Ornithological Biography*, intended to be a complementary work. Preparation of the *Ornithological Biography* began in 1830, with the assistance of William MacGillivray of Edinburgh, and the first volume appeared the following year. The five-volume set, consisting of the life stories of the birds pictured in *The Birds of America*, was completed in 1839, followed immediately by *The Synopsis of the Birds of North America*, a systematic index listing all the birds that Audubon knew, a total of 491.

With the completion of these several major publications, Audubon and his family returned to the United States in the late summer of 1839. Fermenting in his mind were two additional projects. The first was an octavo, or miniature, edition of *The Birds of America*, which began to be issued in parts in 1839 and was in press for four years. The set, published in Philadelphia, grew to seven volumes, illustrated with 500 lithographic, colored plates, picturing seventeen new birds and many new trees and flowers. To Audubon's gratification, the work was an immediate success, attracting a total of 1,198 subscribers.

The second and last of Audubon's American publishing ventures, one which he did not live to complete, was *The Viviparous Quadrupeds of North America*. A large folio edition was issued in two volumes in 1845–1846, and an octavo edition in three volumes appeared during the period from 1846 to 1854. Only the first volume of the latter work was seen by Audubon before his death in 1851.

A century and a half ago, when Audubon was collecting specimens for *The Birds of America* and other writings, the balance of nature in America was relatively undisturbed. The coming of "civilization" in the interim has caused dramatic changes in the environment. Many species and subspecies once numerous are extinct or in imminent peril of becoming extinct. Some species, such as the carrier pigeon, man has slaughtered wholesale. The native habitats of others have been altered so drastically that the birds can no longer exist. To a certain extent, therefore, Audubon has left a record of bird life no longer visible in nature. As Constance Rourke comments in her biography of Audubon:

> The parroquets are no longer a cloud of green among leafless sycamores. The bold ivory-billed woodpecker can be found only in the deep swamps of the far South. The traveler in winter along the Mississippi will not see, as Audubon saw, a flock of trumpeter swans rising with a beating of white wings and a great clangor.

There are evidences, on the other hand, that the American people are awakening to the importance of wildlife preservation, and through the efforts of such conservation organizations as the Audubon Societies and the creation of refuges and sanctuaries the destructive trend is being reversed.

13 | FIRST GREAT AMERICAN BOTANIST

Asa Gray's *Manual of the Botany of the Northern United States*, 1836

What John James Audubon accomplished in identifying and describing the avifauna of America his contemporary Asa Gray did for the botanical kingdom.

When Gray began his labors in the early 1830s, North America, botanically speaking, was virgin territory, and its rich flora was awaiting discovery and scientific study. Because virtually everything was new, the classification of plants—mainly flowering plants—was practically the whole of botany through most of Gray's career. The botanist was preoccupied with forest and field, with outdoor rather than laboratory investigations, as he sought to find hitherto-unknown plants and to accumulate material for research. Aside from amateurish manuals for New England and the middle and southern Atlantic states, botanical literature was extremely limited and largely unreliable. The unsatisfactory state of botanical knowledge was accentuated by the opening of the western territories which were constantly bringing new discoveries to light.

Asa Gray was born in 1810 in upstate New York, the son of a farmer and tanner. His sketchy education in a local grammar school and academy was roughly equivalent to two years in a modern high school. Even with such restricted preparation, he was admitted to a small provincial medical college in Fairfield and graduated with the M.D. degree in 1831.

Several years earlier, however, Gray's lifetime passion for botany had been aroused by reading an article in the *Edinburgh Encyclopedia*, which surveyed the subject comprehensively in 343 double-columned pages, beginning with the ancient Greeks. Gray was also stimulated by a study of Eaton's *Manual of Botany for the Northern States.* As John M. Coulter commented, "This seems to have been like putting a brand to a mass of dry fuel, for his interest became a consuming one, and the fire was never extinguished." The problem was how to earn a living. Botany was a part-time avocation for the clergymen, doctors, lawyers, and teachers concerned with the field. But Gray wanted to spend all his time on plant study. The first seven years after he reached the decision to be a professional botanist were a race with starvation.

Gray's first opportunity came in 1833, through his acquaintance with John Torrey, professor in the New York College of Physicians and Surgeons, at the time the best-known American botanist. In the 1820s, Torrey had published some parts of his *Flora of the Northern United States.* Mutual interest in plants attracted Torrey to the young physician, and he proceeded to offer Gray an appointment as his assistant, to gather new material. Unfortunately, a shortage of funds soon terminated the arrangement. Not long afterward, Gray became curator and librarian of the New York Lyceum of Natural History, an institution which Torrey had helped to establish. Despite a small salary, Gray wrote that "it will be a fine situation for scientific pursuits." His collaboration with Torrey on the *Flora* continued.

The first of Gray's several influential textbooks, *Elements of Botany,* was published in 1836. Succeeding editions of this work, of the *Manual of the Botany of the Northern United States,* and other texts dominated botanical instruction in the United States for the next several generations. Though only twenty-six when the *Elements* appeared, Gray had already developed a smooth, graceful writing style, and his material was logically and systematically arranged. At the beginning, he urged the student to "in the first place direct his attention to the study of plants as organized and living beings, and become familiar with all the ordinary forms of structure." Four chapters were devoted to morphological and physiological subjects, the fifth dealt with flowerless plants, previously generally neglected, and the last with systems of classification.

In *Elements of Botany,* Gray argued vigorously for the natural system of classification, then coming into vogue among European scientists. Previously, Linnaeus's theory of classification of plants based on their sexual system had prevailed. The Linnaean system was founded on the number of stamens and styles as a convenient method of grouping plants. Gray pointed out, on the other hand, that the botanist who simply counted stamens was lost when those parts were missing or when the number varied from species to species. The natural system is based on the form and structure of plants (morphology), establishing their relationships according to various kinds of parts in addition to sexual characteristics.

Following the publication of *Elements of Botany* and joint authorship with Torrey on several parts of the *Flora of North America*, Asa Gray sailed for Europe, in 1838, where he remained for a year, purchasing books for the newly established University of Michigan and traveling and studying widely in Britain and on the Continent. This was the first of six highly rewarding and stimulating European tours taken by Gray over a period of nearly fifty years. His chief purpose was to study original plants in the European herbaria. English travelers in North America had collected plant specimens extensively. In fact, nearly all the earlier collections of North American plants were sent to Europe for description, and Gray had an opportunity to examine in detail the actual plants upon which published descriptions had been based. A knowledge of the plants in European collections, Gray was convinced, was essential to establishing a firm foundation for American botany. His labors abroad involved an immense amount of detailed and exact observation, as well as good judgment and a retentive memory.

A collateral benefit growing out of Gray's European travels was the close personal relations which he established with the leading European botanists. The friendships thus formed continued until his death in 1888. In addition to the herbaria of England and Scotland, Gray visited those of Paris, Lyons, Geneva, Munich, Berlin, Halle, Hamburg, and Vienna.

Shortly after returning from his first European expedition, the president of Harvard University offered Gray the position of Professor of Natural History and Curator of the Botanic Garden. The offer was accepted. As described by William G. Farlow, "On Dr. Gray's accession there was no herbarium, no library, only one insignificant greenhouse, and a garden all in confusion, with few plants of value." When Gray retired, some thirty-one years later, the Harvard herbarium had become the largest and most valuable in America, comparable to the best in Europe, and an excellent library had been formed. The herbarium was a center for the active working botanists of the country and attracted many young men who were subsequently to become leaders in botanical studies throughout the United States.

Gray's travels were not restricted to Europe. He particularly enjoyed field studies and first-hand collecting. Early journeys took him into the southern Appalachians, where he was particularly fascinated with the high-mountain flora of North Carolina. Another collecting mission was to the White Mountains of New Hampshire. The completion of the transcontinental railroad enabled Gray to fulfill a long-held ambition to visit the West Coast, in the summer of 1872. High points of the expedition, from Gray's viewpoint, were the Great Plains, the Utah-Nevada desert, the redwoods and Yosemite valley of California, and the Rockies.

Throughout his long and fruitful career a stream of publications flowed from Gray's pen. For several years following his first voyage to Europe, he continued to collaborate with John Torrey on completion of the *Flora of North America,* subtitled "Containing Abridged Descriptions of All the Known Indigenous and Naturalized Plants Growing North of Mexico, Arranged According to the Natural System." After publication of the second volume in 1843, however, further work was suspended indefinitely because the authors were unable to keep abreast of new material pouring in. A series of great transcontinental surveys had begun, each returning with extensive collections of the plants of various regions of the country. Years later, when the amount of new material being reported had declined, Gray began the preparation of a revised work, the *Synoptical Flora of North America,* two parts of which were published shortly before his death.

Doubtless the most widely used of Gray's many writings was his *Manual of Botany,* a descriptive work including all plant species of the northern United States east of the Mississippi and north of North Carolina and Tennessee. The first edition appeared in 1848, and the second to the fifth during the author's lifetime. Complementing the *Manual* was a series of textbooks, beginning with *Elements of Botany* and continuing with the *Botanical Text-book for Colleges, Schools, and Private Students* (1842), *First Lessons in Botany and Vegetable Physiology* (1857), *How Plants Grow: A Simple Introduction to Structural Botany* (1858), *Forest, Field and Garden Botany* (1868), *How Plants Behave* (1872), and *Structural Botany* (1879). The *Manual* has been republished frequently, with minor modifications, for more than a century, and despite the availability of more modern floras, Gray's *Manual* has remained a standard work. The eighth edition is currently in print.

Of historical significance and human interest are Gray's long association with Charles Darwin. The two men first met in 1838 in London, when Gray was twenty-eight and Darwin a year older. The acquaintance grew into close friendship on subsequent visits. Darwin's theory of the origin of species was foreshadowed in a letter from Gray to another English scientist, Joseph D. Hooker, in 1854, stating: "Scientific systematic botany rests upon species created with almost infinitely various degrees of resemblance among each other." The communication fell into Darwin's hands, and confidential correspondence with Gray followed over the next several years. In 1856 Darwin wrote to Gray as follows:

> Nineteen years ago it occurred to me that whilst otherwise employed on Natural History I might perhaps do good if I noted any sort of facts bearing on the question of the origin of species, and this I have since been doing. Either species have been independently created, or they have descended from other species, like varieties from one species. As an honest man I must tell you that I have come to the heterodox conclusion that there are no such things as independently created species—that species are only strongly defined varieties.

In another letter, September 5, 1857, Darwin sent a detailed account of his theory of evolution to Gray. An advance copy of *The Origin of Species* reached Gray before the publication date. The book became an immediate best-seller and was violently denounced by theological conservatives, as well as by certain scientists, such as Louis Agassiz. Gray, though devoutly religious, became the foremost defender of Darwin's theory of natural selection, in part because he believed that scientific investigation should be free from theological domination and further because he felt that the theory had much merit and did not conflict with religious beliefs. Gray's scattered writings in defense of Darwin were brought together in his *Darwiniana* (1876) and *Natural Science and Religion* (1880). His advocacy of Darwin's unorthodox theories was instrumental in gaining wide acceptance for them in the United States.

Sir Joseph D. Hooker, who in his time was called "the greatest living systematic botantist," summed up Gray's career and attainments in the following comments:

> When the history of the progress of botany during the nineteenth century shall be written, two names will hold high positions: those of Prof. Augustin Pyrame De Candolle and of Prof. Asa Gray. . . . Each devoted half a century of unremitting labor to the investigation and description of the plants of continental areas, and they founded herbaria and libraries, each in his own country, which have become permanent and quasi-national institutions. . . . There is much in their lives and works that recalls the career of Linnaeus, of whom they were worthy disciples, in the comprehensiveness of their labors, the excellence of their methods, their judicious conception of the limits of genera and species, the tenseness and accuracy of their descriptions, and the clearness of their scientific language.

14 | VOICE FROM THE FORECASTLE

Richard Henry Dana, Jr.'s, *Two Years Before the Mast*, 1840

Accounts of sea voyages are a common variety of travel literature from ancient to modern times, from *Sinbad the Sailor* and *The Odyssey* to *Mutiny on the Bounty* and *Kon-Tiki*. Almost invariably, however, the story is told from the point of view of the captain of a ship or of a passenger—seldom, if ever, based on the experiences of a common seaman. Thus it was something of an innovation when Richard Henry Dana, Jr., wrote his minor classic *Two Years Before the Mast* (1840).

Dana could hardly be called a common sailor. His descent was from a long line of Boston blue bloods. His father, Richard Henry Dana, Sr., was an editor and author, and he himself was a Harvard undergraduate. Poor health and weak eyesight, brought on by an attack of measles, lead to Dana's decision to go to sea before the mast, hoping that hard work, plain diet, and the open-air life would restore his health. Young Richard joined the crew of the brig *Pilgrim* in 1836 on her voyage from Boston to San Francisco. The ship sailed two weeks after Dana's nineteenth birthday, and he was gone for more than two years.

Dana sets the scene with the first paragraph of his account: "The fourteenth of August [1834] was the day fixed upon for the sailing of the brig Pilgrim, on her voyage from Boston, round Cape Horn, to the Western coast of North America. As she was to get under way early in the afternoon, I made my appearance on board at twelve o'clock, in full sea-rig, with my chest, containing an outfit for a two or three years' voyage." From there on the story is crowded with action—with man against the sea, not infrequently with man against man, with arduous labors and perilous situations. The ship's mission was to peddle merchandise in California and to bring back hides for the Boston tanneries.

The first section of Dana's book describes the five-month voyage from Boston to Santa Barbara. The routine of life on board a merchant vessel is pictured in minute detail, together with the author's impressions of life at sea and skillful characterization of his shipmates from the brutal Captain Thompson down to his fellow common sailors and the cook. Graphic accounts of a visit to Crusoe's island of San Fernandez and the stormy passage around Cape Horn enliven the story. From a frock-coated, kid-gloved weakling, Dana became a sunburned, vigorous, healthy sailor, able to reef or furl a sail with the best of them. He recalls with satisfaction his first turn at the wheel:

> Inexperienced as I was, I made out to steer to the satisfaction of the officer, and neither Stimson nor I gave up our tricks, all the time that we were off the Cape. This was something to boast of, for it required a good deal of skill and watchfulness to steer a vessel close hauled, in a gale of wind, against a heavy head sea . . . a little carelessness in letting her ship a heavy sea might sweep the decks, or take a mast out of her.

Danger was a constant companion as the sailors scrambled aloft in high seas while gales raged, heavy rains descended, or ice and snow covered the rigging. A slight slip could mean instant death. One such tragic incident is recounted by Dana. A young English sailor, George Ballmer, lost his footing and fell into the sea. Dana observes:

> Death is at all times solemn, but never so much so as at sea. A man dies on shore; his body remains with his friends, and "the mourners go about the streets;" but when a man falls overboard at sea and is lost, there is a suddeness in the event, and a difficulty in realizing it, which give to it an air of awful mystery . . . at sea, the man is near you,—at your side,—you hear his voice, and in an instant he is gone, and nothing but a vacancy shows his loss. Then, too, at sea—to use a homely but expressive phrase—you *miss* a man so much.

A major portion of *Two Years Before the Mast* deals with the sixteen months that Dana and his shipmates spent along the California coast. Cargo brought from Boston was being sold at retail to the natives while the crew was in process of collecting

40,000 hides for the homeward voyage. The business was dull and dreary, but Dana avoids tediousness in the narrative by descriptions of California in the days of the Spanish rancheros and the Mexican hidalgos and of such colorful events as Mexican weddings and dances.

Partly, no doubt, because he did not want to risk offending the Victorian pruderies of the era and in part because of a sense of shame, Dana omitted material that would have made his book even livelier reading. Native girls were free and easy with their favors along the California coast. A shipmate, B. G. Stinson, wrote to Dana in 1841 asking him why he had failed to mention

> *the beautiful Indian lasses,* who so often frequented your humble abode in the *hide house,* and rambled through those *splendid groves* attached thereto or the happy hours experienced rambling over those romantic hills, or sitting at twilight on those majestic rocks, with a lovely Indian girl resting on your knee.

Dana had little respect for the West Coast inhabitants. He termed laziness "the California disease," and concluded: "The Californians are an idle, thriftless people, and can make nothing for themselves."

Soon after the arrival of the *Pilgrim* and her crew there occurred an incident destined to have important later repercussions. Captain Thompson was an evil-tempered bully who ruled the ship with a tyrannical hand. Absolutely no back-talk from subordinates was tolerated. For no good reason, apparently, he took a violent dislike to a sailor named Sam, "a large, heavy-moulded fellow from the Middle States." By the captain's order, the mate placed Sam "against the shrouds, with his wrists made fast to them, his jacket off, and his back exposed." The captain then proceeded to administer a merciless flogging with a thick, strong rope. When another sailor, John the Swede, asked the reason for the beating, the captain ordered him put into irons and subjected him to the same treatment.

These proceedings made young Dana "feel sick and almost faint, angry and excited as I was. A man—a human being, made in God's likeness—fastened up and flogged like a beast." But to resist, as he knew, was mutiny, and to seize the ship was piracy. So, "Disgusted, sick, I turned away," wrote Dana, "and leaned over the rail, and looked down into the water."

It was after this shameful and debasing episode that Dana "vowed that, if God should ever give me the means, I would do something to redress the grievances and relieve the sufferings of that class of beings with whom my lot had so long been cast."

For months on end the *Pilgrim* continued the arduous task of assembling cattle hides for shipment to New England—hides which Dana noted ironically were to be made into shoes and brought back to California to be worn out rounding up more hides. Then word came through that all the hides collected were to be transferred to a larger ship, the *Alert*, and the *Pilgrim* was to remain two more years in California. Dana had previously obtained permission to return home on the *Alert*, and despite Captain Thompson's threats to force him to stay with the *Pilgrim*, he sailed from San Diego on the *Alert*'s homeward voyage, the ship's hold so crammed with hides that her beams creaked.

The return voyage was taken in winter weather, making it a much rougher, more hazardous adventure than had been the outward-bound trip. Dana's memorable account of the storms at sea, rounding Cape Horn, is unsurpassed in maritime literature:

> Rain, sleet, snow, and wind enough to take our breath from us, and make the toughest turn his back to windward! The ship lay nearly over upon her beam-ends; the spars and rigging snapped and cracked; and her top-gallant-masts bent like whip-sticks. . . . The decks were standing at an angle of forty-five degrees, and the ship going like a mad steer through the water, the whole forward part of her in a smother of foam. . . . The violence of the wind, and the hail and sleet, driving nearly horizontally across the ocean, seemed actually to pin us down to the rigging.

The ship was further imperiled by giant icebergs, a collision with which would have ended the voyage. The first one encountered is thus described by Dana:

> And there lay, floating in the ocean, several miles off, an immense, irregular mass, its top and points covered with snow, and its centre of a deep indigo color. This was an iceberg, and of the largest size. As far as the eye could reach, the sea in every direction was of a deep blue color, the waves running high and

fresh, and sparkling in the light, and in the midst lay this immense mountain-island, its cavities and valleys thrown into deep shade, and its points and pinnacles glittering in the sun. . . . But no description can give any idea of the strangeness, splendor, and, really, the sublimity, of the sight. Its great size—for it must have been from two to three miles in circumference, and several hundred feet in height,—its slow motion, as its base rose and sank in the water, and its high points nodded against the clouds; the dashing of the waves upon it . . . ; and the thundering sound of the cracking of the mass, and the breaking and tumbling down of huge pieces; together with its nearness and approach, which added a slight element of fear,—all combined to give to it the character of true sublimity.

Having survived the storm-tossed voyage around the Horn, the remainder of the *Alert*'s passage homeward was comparatively peaceful, with favorable winds and sunny weather. The poetic streak in Dana's nature emerges in his description of those days, when he had time to contemplate the beauties of the scene. Writing of a calm night in tropic waters, he observes: "The sea still as an inland lake; the light tradewind was gently and steadily breathing from astern." A ship with "all her sail upon her" he calls "the most glorious moving object in the world." An inspired passage continues:

So quiet, too, was the sea, and so steady the breeze, that if these sails had been sculptured marble they could not have been more motionless. Not a ripple upon the surface of the canvas; not even a quivering of the extreme edges of the sail, so perfectly were they distended by the breeze. I was so lost in the sight that I forgot the presence of the man who came out with me, until he said (for he, too, rough old man-of-war's-man as he was, had been gazing at the show), half to himself, still looking at the marble sails,—"How quietly they do their work!"

The *Alert* reached Boston on September 22, 1836. Her voyage had taken 137 days, compared to the *Pilgrim*'s 150. Dana re-entered Harvard and graduated from law school. Nearly four years went by before *Two Years Before the Mast* was put on paper and published. Harper's Brothers paid $250 outright for the manuscript, and despite the fact that the book immediately became and remained a best-seller, Dana received nothing more.

The literary influence of *Two Years Before the Mast* was felt at once. Three dozen books with titles resembling Dana's were published between 1840 and 1860. Realistic tales of the sea, notably Herman Melville's early novels, became the vogue.

The direct effect of Dana's book on the lives of common sailors in the merchant marine appears more debatable. A recent biographer, Samuel Shapiro, in his *Richard Henry Dana, Jr., 1815–1882*, questions the long-held belief that Dana "did for the common sailor what Mrs. Stowe was to do for the Negro slave," and concludes: "His book had far more effect on prospective immigrants to California and young boys anxious to go to sea than it did on congressmen who might pass legislation benefiting seamen." On the other hand, Dana's contemporary J. Ross Browne wrote to congratulate him for "putting down quarter-deck tyranny with . . . might and main," and the noted literary critic Van Wyck Brooks maintained that Dana "battled like an avenging angel for seamen's rights." Another critic, John A. Kouwenhoven, asserted: "As propaganda it succeeded; both in England and the United States it led to legislation benefiting seamen."

In any event, *Two Years Before the Mast* was a democratic book, invariably taking the side of the crew, not the captain, and arousing the reader's sympathies for the miserable sailors. After Dana began his law practice, he was a frequent advocate for men before the mast who had been abused and unfairly treated. In a second book, *The Seaman's Friend* (1841), Dana compiled a reference volume of terms, customs, and legal rights of common sailors.

The human element in *Two Years Before the Mast* is as gripping to the reader today as when first written. In addition, the work has assumed first-rate historical importance. Unique in many respects are Dana's accounts of the routine on board the old sailing ships and of trading on the California coast and his description of California before it had been transformed by the gold rush. The book also reveals, though unconsciously on Dana's part, the inevitability of American expansion to the shores of the Pacific Ocean.

15 | HISTORIAN OF THE AMERICAN INDIAN

Francis Parkman's *The Oregon Trail*, 1849

Nearly a half-century had passed since Meriwether Lewis's and George Rogers Clark's trail-blazing expedition to the Pacific, when Francis Parkman retraced their route in part. Vast changes had occurred in the interim. Where Lewis and Clark had found unexplored wilderness, America's march westward was well advanced when Parkman made his "Oregon Trail" trip in the spring and summer of 1846. The old frontier of the Mississippi had disappeared, and a swelling stream of hunters, traders, missionaries, immigrants, and settlers was pushing steadily toward the West Coast. It was a period marked by the annexation of Texas, the Mexican war, the conquest of California and the Spanish Southwest, and the settlement of the Oregon boundary dispute with England.

Mason Wade, Parkman's biographer, notes: "There were only a hundred American men, women, and children in Oregon in 1840; less than a hundred in California; and fewer still in the Southwest. Yet in six years' time these regions became part of the United States, and their American population had increased more than fortyfold." Thus, Parkman's travels were undertaken during a time of transition.

Parkman's first and most famous work, *The Oregon Trail* (1849), is actually a misnomer. The original title was *The California and Oregon Trail*, later changed to *The Oregon Trail*. The closest that Parkman ever got to Fort Hall, in present-day Idaho, where the trail branched off for Oregon, was 500 miles. More accurate was the title used for one early edition, *Prairie and Rocky Mountain Life*, which is precisely the subject matter of the book. Parkman saw thoroughly only the regions now known as Nebraska, Colorado, and Wyoming.

From his early youth, Parkman was obsessed with Indians and

Indian lore. He claimed to have read "everything that had been written about the Indians." His imagination was stirred particularly by James Fenimore Cooper's romantic tales. But he realized that reading was not enough. As he wrote to a friend, the Indians' "character will always remain more or less a mystery to one who does not add practical observations to his studies. In fact I am more than half resolved to devote a few months to visiting the distant tribes." While still a student at Harvard, Parkman began his trips into the wilderness and explored the wildest areas of Maine, New Hampshire, and the Lake George and Lake Champlain country. Later he ranged over the Great Lakes region to Sault Ste. Marie and Mackinac. Added to his subsequent stay among the Plains Indians, Parkman observed at first hand the Indian tribes, or what remained of them, from Maine to the Rockies.

The great adventure narrated in *The Oregon Trail* was undertaken by Parkman in company with his cousin Quincy Adams Shaw. Among the Western tribes, they decided, was the most favorable opportunity to study Indians still living in their native fashion, relatively untouched and unspoiled by the ways of the white men. Parkman explained his aim in these words:

> I wished to satisfy myself with regard to the position of the Indians among the races of men; the vices and virtues that have sprung from their innate character and from their modes of life; their government, their superstitions and their domestic situation. To accomplish my purpose it was necessary to live in the midst of a village, and make myself an inmate of one of their lodges.

When Parkman began his western safari, he was twenty-three years of age, an excellent rider, a good shot, and a natural outdoors man. For reasons which are unclear, however, his health was precarious and remained so until his death nearly fifty years later.

As Lewis and Clark had done earlier, Parkman and Shaw started their expedition at St. Louis. The trip along the Platte River to Fort Laramie, a month with the Indians in southeastern Wyoming, south of the Arkansas River in Colorado, and east across Kansas to Independence lasted five months. Every day was meticulously recorded in Parkman's diaries, from which *The Oregon Trail* was distilled.

Parkman and his cousin Shaw covered the first stage of their long journey by boat as far as Westport, the present Kansas City. There they hired as guide and hunter an experienced "mountain man," Henry Chatillon, who turned out to be a genuine paragon. Also valuable was a half-breed muleteer and campman, Deslauriers. The course set by the explorers took them northwest until they came to the Big Blue River and then up the Little Blue. Turning north, they struck the North Platte, which was followed all the way to Fort Laramie. A circular tour was made through the Medicine Bow Mountains in the Wyoming country.

Parkman's main objective was accomplished when he fell in with a band of Sioux Indians, with whom he lived for some weeks, observing their habits, customs, and ways of thought. He became intimately acquainted with the inhabitants of the lodges and tepees; remained with them in their moving villages; tramped, rode, and hunted buffalo with them; shared their feasts of dog meat; watched the tribes gather for a war of retaliation; and sat around the campfires listening to accounts of the braves' exploits. One murderous savage, Big Crow, claimed he "has killed 14 men; and dwells with great satisfaction on the capture of a Utah whom he took personally; and, with the other Sioux, scalped alive, cut the tendons of his wrist, and flung, still alive, into a great fire."

One of the most memorable characters sketched by Parkman is a formidable young brave, Mahto-Tatonka, who turned out to be the warmest of his Indian friends, constantly vigilant to protect Parkman and Shaw and their property. In Parkman's words:

He never arrayed himself in gaudy blanket and glittering necklaces, but left his statue-like form, limbed like an Apollo of bronze, to win its way to favor. His voice was singularly deep and strong, and sounded from his chest like the deep notes of an organ. . . . See him now in his hour of glory when at sunset the whole village empties itself to behold him, for tomorrow their favorite young partisan goes out against the enemy. His headdress is adorned with a crest of the war-eagle's feathers, rising in a waving ridge above his brow and sweeping far behind him. His round white shield hangs at his breast, with feathers radiating from the centre like a star. His quiver is at his back; his tall lance in his hand, the iron point flashing against the declining sun, while the long scalp-locks of his enemies flutter from the shaft. Thus, gorgeous as a champion in panoply, he rides round and round within the great circle of lodges, balancing with a graceful buoyancy to the free movements of his war-horse, while with a sedate brow he sings his song to the Great Spirit.

Parkman's descriptions of Indian tribes are colorful and revealing, as, for example, in his account of those in the Fort Laramie area:

Looking back, after the expiration of a year, upon Fort Laramie and its inmates, they seem less like a reality than like some fanciful picture of the olden time; so different was the scene from any which this tamer side of the world can present. Tall Indians, enveloped in their white buffalo-robes, were riding across the area or reclining at full length on the low roofs of the buildings which enclosed it. Numerous squaws, gaily bedizened, sat grouped in front of the apartments they occupied; their mongrel offspring, restless and vociferous, rambled in every direction through the fort; and the trappers, traders and *engagés* of the establishment were busy at their labor or their amusements.

The culture of these Western Indians offered a striking contrast to those in the East. The Eastern tribes had been largely decimated by war and disease, their ancient mores corrupted or extinguished by exposure to white society. The Plains Indians, on the other hand, had been touched scarcely at all by the whites, except for an occasional trader or hunter. Those near the settlements, mainly Kaws and Shawnees, had become "irrepressible beggars," lazy and shiftless, but the Sioux "were thorough savages. Neither their manners nor their ideas were in the slightest degree modified by contact with civilization. . . . They were living representatives of the Stone Age." To them, war and aggression were a way of life.

Though obviously fascinated by what he saw of actual Indian life on the Plains, Parkman was repelled by the Indians' sanitary habits, their unreliability, cruelty, and utter savagery, and their promiscuous sexual behavior. The romantic illusions gained from reading Cooper's novels were quickly dispelled. Instead, Parkman concluded that the Indian was a hopelessly barbaric savage. "Ambition, revenge, jealousy, are his ruling passions," asserted Parkman; "a wild love of liberty, an utter intolerance of control, lie at the base of his character." As seen by Parkman and a great majority of white Americans of his time, the Indians were inherently savages, incapable of being absorbed into the white civilization and therefore doomed to vanish from the earth. "Their untractable, unchanging character leaves no other alternative than their gradual extinction," states Parkman, "or the abandonment of the western world to eternal barbarism." These views are stated at length in two later Parkman works: *The History of the Conspiracy of Pontiac* and the novel *Vassal Morton*.

Accompanying Parkman's study of the ways of the savage Indian tribes were his acute and accurate observations of nature. *The Oregon Trail* is rich in descriptions of animals, reptiles, birds, insects, trees, herbs, and blossoming plants spread over the Western prairies and forests.

Through good fortune, Parkman's travels came at a crucial period in Western history. As Mason Wade observes:

> Fate threw Parkman into the company of many of the great men and great movements of the West in that era: of the great Oregon emigration of 1846, of the ill-fated Donner Party which perished in the High Sierras that winter, of the fomenters of the California uprising which brought the flag to the Pacific, of old Pierre Chouteau the co-founder of St. Louis, of Thomas Fitzpatrick, "Broken Hand," the greatest of the mountain men; of Daniel Boone's grandsons, of Louis Vasquez, partner of Jim Bridger and great scout and hunter in his own right; of Colonel Stephen Watts Kearny who led the dragoons of the Army of the West into Mexico that same summer, and in the previous year had marched over most of the route that Parkman followed; of the Mormons seeking a New Jerusalem and a haven from the persecution of the Gentiles; of Paul Dorion, the son of the half-breed voyageur who had accompanied Lewis and Clark's expedition to the Columbia River and the Pacific as far as the South Mandan villages, and who had shared the rigors of Wilson Hunt's journey to found Astoria.

Only an indomitable spirit carried Parkman through the ordeal of his travels to the West. He undertook the expedition in the first place with the hope that the outdoor life would restore his health. In fact, the incredible hardships experienced nearly wrecked his not overly strong constitution. The glare of the sun and the harsh alkali dust of the Plains left him nearly blind; his digestion was ruined by the rough fare supplied by Indians and trappers; he became a lifelong victim of insomnia and was crippled by arthritis. After leaving Fort Laramie, Parkman wrote:

> I had been slightly ill for several weeks, but on the third night after reaching Fort Larmie a violent pain awoke me, and I found myself attacked by the same disorder that occasioned such heavy losses to the army on the Rio Grande. In a day and a half I was reduced to extreme weakness, so that I could not walk without pain and effort. Having within that time taken six grains of opium without the least beneficial effect, and having no medical adviser, nor any choice of diet, I resolved to throw myself upon Providence for recovery, using without regard to the disorder any portion of strength that might remain to me. So on the 20th of June we set out from Fort Laramie to meet the Whirlwind's village. Though aided by the high-bow "Mountain Saddle," I could scarcely keep my seat on horseback.

Because of Parkman's partial blindness after his return home, *The Oregon Trail* had to be a dictated work. Nevertheless, the first chapter appeared in *Knickerbocker Magazine* within four months after the end of the expedition. The original version was written with the help of his trail companion and cousin, Quincy Adams Shaw, and Sara Barlow Shaw, who read aloud Parkman's journal to him and then recorded the sentences that he dictated. Another cousin, Charles Eliot Norton, offered to read proof for the book. The offer, which was accepted, was a fortunate or unfortunate circumstance, depending upon the point of view. Parkman's biographer, Mason Wade, comments: "Still more of the original quality was lost by the editing of Charles Eliot Norton, who revised the *Knickerbocker* version for book publication in accordance with the literary amenities as then understood by right-thinking Bostonians." According to Wade, Norton "carefully bowdlerized much anthropological data and many insights into Western life which seemed too crude to his delicate taste." Another critic, Robert Edson Lee, is inclined to disagree, holding that Norton was not really a censor and that the changes he made in the text—such as the elimination of "adjectival clichés," "moralizing paragraphs," and "undigested rhetoric"—produced a better book.

Despite the always-shaky state of his health, Parkman lived to the age of seventy and went on to become one of America's greatest historians, remembered particularly for his monumental eight-volume study of the English-French struggle for power in the New World—a highly successful combination of historical research and literary color.

Even while writing *The Oregon Trail*, Parkman foresaw that "a time would come when those Plains would be a grazing country, the buffalo give place to tame cattle, farm houses be scattered along the watercourses, and wolves, bears and Indians be numbered among the things that were."

To Parkman we are indebted for bringing the Indian to life, supplanting the romantic concept of the "noble savage." From his vivid tale of adventure, too, we gain glimpses of the great westward movement and of the trail blazers who opened a new continental empire.

16 | SAGA OF THE WHITE WHALE

Herman Melville's *Moby Dick,* 1851

Literary critics differ over whether "the Great American Novel"
has been or is yet to be written. Considerable critical sentiment,
however, supports the view that in *Moby Dick* (1851) Herman
Melville approached and perhaps achieved the creation of such
a masterpiece. In his *Twelve Great American Novels,* Arthur
Mizener appraises *Moby Dick* not only as the greatest of all
Melville's novels, but as "probably the most impressive single
work in American literature."

The appeal of *Moby Dick* is wide-ranging. It can be read as
a tremendous adventure story, planned on an epic scale, filled
with dramatic action and vivid characters, or for its allegorical
and symbolic significance, told with a wealth of imagery and
allusion. The huge canvas which Melville has spread encompasses
the excitement of quest and chase in whale hunting and the
perils confronted by the hunters, together with a long and accurate account of the habits of whales and a superb description
of the whaling industry, once a major factor in New England's
economy. But the greatness of the book undoubtedly derives
from the symbolic representation of man's existence, the conflict
between man and fate, good and evil.

The sea held an endless fascination for Herman Melville. At
age eighteen, he had shipped out of New York to Liverpool as
a cabin boy. A few years later he boarded a whaler at New
Bedford bound for the South Pacific, during which voyage he
picked up the lore for his first two novels: *Typee: A Peep at
Polynesian Life* and *Omoo: A Narrative of Adventure in the
South Seas,* as well as background for *Moby Dick.* A term of
service as a seaman on a United States man-of-war based in
Honolulu also added to his firsthand knowledge of maritime
phenomena.

The opening sentence in *Moby Dick* is "Call me Ishmael."
The story's narrator is Ishmael (assumed to be the voice of

Melville), a schoolteacher, who is seized periodically by spells of restlessness, during which he feels impelled to go to sea. He has decided to sign on a whaling ship, and packing his carpet-bag he leaves Manhattan for New Bedford, where he spends the night near the waterfront. Because of the shortage of room, his bed has to be shared with a savage harpooner, Queequeg, a tattooed cannibal from the South Seas, who in time becomes Ishmael's boon companion. They agree to sign on the same ship.

Ishmael and Queequeg make their way after a few days to Nantucket and there join the crew of the *Pequod*, a whaler, "a rare old craft, long seasoned and weather-stained in the typhoons and calms of all four oceans, apparelled like any barbaric Ethiopian emperor with trophies of whale bone."

The sinister and gigantic figure of Captain Ahab pervades and dominates the vessel. Not until the ship has been at sea for several days does the captain appear on deck. Ishmael is struck by two terrible deformities: a long, thin scar that runs across the captain's face and neck and is lost beneath his collar, as though it extended the entire length of his body, and a mutilated left leg which had been bitten off by a giant white whale and replaced by an ivory leg, made of the polished bone of a sperm whale's jaw. On the quarter deck the captain has bored a shallow hole into which the artificial leg fits; once steadied there, he is practically immovable in the roughest storm.

Scarcely less bizarre are other members of the strange crew assembled for the *Pequod*. The three harpooners are Queequeg, the cannibal, Tashtego, an Indian from Martha's Vineyard, and Daggoo, a huge black Negro from Africa. After many days at sea, Ahab's own boat crew came on deck—strange, silent, secret, black-garbed Malays, fire-worshipping Parsees. The *Pequod's* three mates are Starbuck, a Quaker from Nantucket, perhaps the most rational man on board; Stubb, "fearless as fire, and as mechanical," reckless and jolly on every occasion; and Flask, pugnacious, obstinate, without imagination, contemptous of the whale.

For days the ship continues its southward voyage, in search of whales. Eventually the true purpose of the expedition is revealed: Captain Ahab's insanely obsessive craving to destroy Moby Dick, the terrible, monstrous white whale which had chewed off his leg. On the captain's orders, the entire ship's company is assembed, and Ahab addresses the men: "Whosoever of ye raises me a white-headed whale with a wrinkled brow and a crooked jaw, with three holes punched in his starboard fluke—look ye, whosoever of ye raises me that same white whale, he shall have this Spanish ounce of gold, my boys!" And Captain Ahab nails a golden doubloon to the main mast. His iron determination to revenge himself on the "accursed white whale" is revealed in his speech to the crew: "I'll chase him round Good Hope, and round the Horn, and round the Norway Maelstrom, and round perdition's flames before I give him up. And this is what ye have shipped for, men! to chase that white whale on both sides of land, and over all sides of earth, till he spouts black blood and rolls fin out."

Only Starbuck, the first mate, expresses unhappiness with Ahab's fanatical mission. "I came to hunt whales, not my commander's vengeance," he declares. "Vengeance on a dumb brute that simply smote thee from instinct! Madness! To be enraged with a dumb thing, Captain Ahab, seems blasphemous." But Ahab will not be dissuaded from his single-minded purpose. He sees Moby Dick as evil incarnate.

The *Pequod* cruises across the breadth and length of the Pacific in search of Ahab's prey, meanwhile pursuing the normal business of whale hunting. There are graphic accounts of the sighting and killing of giant whales. After the sudden wild cry of "There she blows" is heard, boats take to the water in pursuit. The harpooner's iron darts into the body of the whale. After the violence of the whale's struggle, in which boats are often overturned and men flung into the sea, the dead body is made fast to the ship. Then follows stripping off the blubber, rendering of the oil, and storing the product in oaken casks below decks. Finally, the monster is decapitated and the carcass set adrift to feed sharks and sea birds. If the catch is a sperm whale, bucketfuls of spermaceti are removed from the head. The teeth, whalebone, and jawbone are also taken from the head.

The struggle for existence in the world of nature becomes a recurring theme, as Ishmael depicts the "sea-vulture" sharks feasting upon the whale's corpse and the "air-shark" vultures overhead which also regard the "funeral" as a gratuitous banquet.

Ishmael comments, "Oh, horrid vulturism of earth! from which not the mightiest whale is free."

From time to time the narrative is interrupted by learned disquisitions on the order of cetaceans, that is, whales, dolphins, porpoises, etc., and the customs of whaling. The different families of whales are classified and described by size; we are told the seasons when they can be found in certain regions, of the ferocity of whales and of their cunning in taking revenge on their tormentors, and much more about the habits of whales in general. What D. H. Lawrence characterized as "perhaps the most stupendous chapter" in *Moby Dick* is the one entitled "The Grand Armada," a dramatic account of a vast host of sperm whales encountered by the *Pequod* as she draws through the Sunda Straits toward Java. In Ishmael's words,

> Broad on both bows, at a distance of two or three miles, and forming a great semicircle, embracing one half of the level horizon, a continuous chain of whale-jets were up-playing and sparkling in the noonday air. . . . But far beneath this wondrous world upon the surface, another and still stranger world met our eyes as we gazed over the side. For, suspended in those watery vaults, floated the forms of the nursing mothers of the whales, and those that by their enormous girth seemed shortly to become mothers.

Also helping to set the atmosphere for the approaching conflict to the death with Moby Dick is an essay on "The Whiteness of the Whale." The ghostlike animal stirs in one a vague, nameless horror. Whiteness signifies death and corruption as well as virginal purity, innocence, and youth. Moby Dick, the rare albino sperm whale, is in his whiteness the most awe-inspiring and most terrifying of nature's creations. The whiteness itself, the absence of color, or the presence of all colors, Melville suggests, brings to our natural instinct thoughts of space and emptiness, annihilation and death itself. "And of all these things, the albino whale was the symbol."

Ahab has plotted a course for his ship which will bring it into the area where Moby Dick is most likely to be found. Whenever another whaling vessel is encountered at sea, Captain Ahab asks for news about the white whale. Reports begin to come in: The *Town-Ho* had lost a mate to the white whale's teeth, as had the *Jeroboam,* whose mate had been drowned when tossed from his boat by the whale; Captain Boomer, of the British ship *Samuel Enderly,* had lost an arm to Moby Dick and is resolved to avoid the monster hereafter; the *Rachel* had met Moby Dick the previous day, and the harpooned whale had run away with one of the boats. The captain of the *Rachel,* a Nantucket man known to Captain Ahab, begs him to join in the search for the lost boat which had held his twelve-year-old son. The fanatical Ahab refuses, thinking only of the time that would be lost in the pursuit of Moby Dick.

Days pass until the *Pequod* has her final encounter with another ship, the *Delight,* which had sighted and attacked Moby Dick, had had one of her whaleboats smashed, and the boat crew lost. The *Delight's* captain declares that "the harpoon is not yet forged" that is capable of destroying the white whale. Disregarding the direful warning, Ahab rushes on.

In one melodramatic scene, Ahab consecrates to his insane vengeance a special harpoon, forged by the ship's blacksmith from the steel of razor blades, intended solely to kill Moby Dick. The harpoon is tempered in blood from the veins of the three savage harpooners on the *Pequod* and blasphemously blessed by Ahab in the name of the devil. The act symbolizes the mad whaleman's defiance of God. It is reminiscent of Ahab's earlier declaration to Starbuck, "Talk not to me of blasphemy, man; I'd strike the sun if it insulted me."

A terrible storm engulfs the ship one night. Lightning hits the masts, and they flame against the blackness, an omen which the crew regard as a warning to abandon their ill-fated mission. But Ahab stands at the foot of the mast, challenges the forces of evil symbolized for him by the fire, and vows his determination to find and kill the white whale.

The chapters which bring *Moby Dick* to its close are appraised by Tyrus Hillman, Melville's biographer, as "among the most vividly written in all the world's literature." They describe the final sighting of Moby Dick and the exciting action, spread over a three-day period, to capture and kill him. The whale is first spotted by Ahab himself, who from his masthead cries out, "There she blows. A hump like a snow-hill! It is Moby Dick!" Boats are lowered and the chase begins, with Captain Ahab's boat in the lead. As he is about to sink his harpoon into the side of the white mountain, the whale suddenly turns, seizes Ahab's whaleboat between his jaws and splinters it into pieces. The men are thrown into the sea and narrowly escape death before the *Pequod* sails directly into Moby Dick to drive him off. The remainder of the day is spent in fruitless pursuit of the whale.

On the second day the men again catch up with the whale and bury three harpoons in his white flanks, but Moby Dick tangles the harpoon lines together, overturns the boats and dashes their crews into the sea among the sharks. Ahab's ivory leg is broken off and the Parsee, Fedallah, is lost.

As the final day of the chase opens, the *Pequod's* boats soon overtake Moby Dick, and the men discover the body of Fedallah bound to the whale's back by the coils of rope from the harpoon ropes. Ahab's harpoon is cast into the whale with all his strength and hate, but the flying rope entangles the whale hunter around the neck and shoots him out of the boat to his death. Now Moby Dick, infuriated by the vicious attacks on him and by the barbed harpoons painfully imbedded in his huge body, glimpses the *Pequod's* black hull and bears down upon it. The solid white buttress of his forehead rams the ship's starboard bow and sinks it with all its crew.

All except Ishmael perish in the catastrophe. A coffin built for Queequeg bobs to the surface as Ishmael struggles in the water. "Buoyed up by that coffin, for almost one whole day and night," he relates, "I floated on a soft and dirge-like main. On the second day, a sail drew near, nearer, and picked me up at last. It was the devious-cruising *Rachel,* that in her retracing search after her missing children, only found another orphan." Thus the famous voyage of the *Pequod* ends in total tragedy because Ahab has refused to submit to human fate.

The symbolism of *Moby Dick* has been read in numerous ways. Lewis Mumford takes Moby Dick as a symbol of evil and Ahab's conflict with him as the conflict of good and evil in which good finally is the loser. Somerset Maugham argues that a contrary interpretation is plausible: "Why should it be assumed that Moby Dick is a symbol of evil? . . . Why should the White Whale not represent goodness rather than evil? Splendid in beauty, vast in size, great in strength, he swims the seas in freedom. Ahab, with his insane pride, is pitiless, harsh, cruel and vindictive; *he* is evil." The "empty malice" of which Mumford writes is a matter of Moby Dick defending himself when attacked.

In any event, theories proliferate. A psychologist, Henry A. Murray, offers three hypotheses: that Ahab is an embodiment of Satan or the satanic principle; that Moby Dick represents a projection of Ahab's Puritan conscience, against which he rebels; and that Ahab-Melville's attitude of aggression was directed chiefly against the social and religious teachings of the nineteenth century. "Ahab's great error," Hillman concludes, "is failure to accept human limitations. In assuming the possibility of learning final truth, he puts himself in effect on a plane of equality with God. Thus he is not only unrealistic but guilty of the fatal sin of pride; for he believes himself above and apart from other men."

"Fortunately," as Maugham points out, "*Moby Dick* may be read, and read with intense interest, without a thought of what allegorical or symbolic significance it may or may not have." Ironically, Melville himself seems to have largely rejected ulterior meanings in the novel. In a letter to Mrs. Nathaniel Hawthorne, a few weeks after the book's appearance, he writes:

> I had some vague idea while writing it, that the whole book was susceptible of an allegorical construction, & also that parts of it were—but the speciality of many of the particular subordinate allegories were first revealed to me after reading Mr. Hawthorne's letter, which, without citing any particular examples, yet intimated the part-&-parcel allegoricalness of the whale.

The epic quality of *Moby Dick* has been remarked upon by numerous critics and other readers. Some suggest a close analogy with *The Iliad, The Odyssey, The Aeneid,* and *Paradise Lost,* and, like those works, regard it more as an epic poem than a novel, despite its form. Alfred Kazin elaborates on the point by his conclusion that whether deliberately or not Melville "drew upon many of the traditional characteristics of epic in order to realize the utterly original kind of novel *he* needed to write in his time"; Kazin notes, in support of his thesis, "the spaciousness of theme and subject, the martial atmosphere, the association of these homely and savage materials with universal myths, the symbolic wanderings of the hero, the indispensable strength of such a hero in Captain Ahab." Another perceptive critic, John Erskine, also describes *Moby Dick* as a poem and states unequivocally that it leads all American novels "in the vastness of the impression it makes. . . . While we read, the ocean, all the oceans seem to spread around us." Citing the inevitable meeting between Captain Ahab and Moby Dick, Erskine adds, "Here perhaps is an image of fate simpler and more awful than we can find in ancient story."

During Melville's lifetime, only a handful of readers recognized the greatness of *Moby Dick*. The novel's reception was generally hostile, though a few critics praised it. Not until some thirty years after the author's death, following World War I, was there a Melville renaissance, at which time *Moby Dick* became firmly established as a supreme masterpiece in the eyes of readers and collectors, at home and abroad.

17 | ESCAPE FROM MATERIALISM

Henry David Thoreau's *Walden,* 1854

E. B. White, in many respects a kindred spirit, characterizes Henry David Thoreau's *Walden* (1854) as "an oddity in American letters"; he continues: "It may very well be the oddest of our distinguished oddities. . . . Many think it a sermon; many set it down as an attempt to rearrange society; some think it an exercise in nature-loving; some find it a rather irritating collection of inspirational puffballs by an eccentric show-off." But to White (and to millions of other readers around the world) *Walden* is none of these, and he concludes: "It still seems to me the best youth's companion yet written by an American, for it carries a solemn warning against the loss of one's valuables, it advances a good argument for traveling light and trying new adventures, it rings with the power of positive adoration, it contains religious feeling without religious images, and it steadfastly refuses to record bad news."

Thoreau spent almost his entire life within a few miles of where he was born, in 1817, at Concord, Massachusetts. His father failed as a merchant, after which he set up a small factory to manufacture pencils. Young Henry was granted a scholarship to attend Harvard, from which he graduated in 1837. In the same year began his association with Ralph Waldo Emerson, who was destined to exert a great influence upon his life. From 1841 to 1843, Thoreau lived in Emerson's home, serving as a glorified handyman in exchange for a room. There he came to know the company of writers and transcendental philosophers surrounding Emerson: Bronson Alcott, Henry W. Longfellow, Oliver Wendell Holmes, James Russell Lowell, Nathaniel Hawthorne, Margaret Fuller, and others.

From his early youth, Thoreau rebelled against the prevailing notion that one should spend his days laboring industriously in order to maintain a high standard of living. To him it seemed a fool's life to pass the years "laying up treasures which moth and rust will corrupt and thieves break through and steal." Thoreau felt the need for solitude and leisure for reflection. His opportunity for both came in 1845.

Emerson had bought a tract of woods on the north shore of Walden Pond, 1½ miles south of Concord. He entered into an agreement with Thoreau whereby the latter would be allowed to build and live in a cabin on the property in return for clearing part of the woods for a garden. Brooks Atkinson theorizes that "if Thoreau had never gone to live alone in a hut at Walden Pond it is possible that he never would have been celebrated. That was the most dramatic thing he ever did; the chronicle of his adventure is a classic."

Late in March 1845 Thoreau borrowed an axe, cut down some white pine timber beside Walden Pond, and began construction of a simple cabin. He bought a laborer's shanty for boards and nails, dug out a cellar, laid the foundation for a chimney, and on July 4 moved into the virtually completed structure. The total cost, carefully recorded item by item, was $28.12½. The hut contained a single room, 10 by 15 feet, a large window, and a brick fireplace. For furniture and equipment Thoreau acquired a bed, a table, a desk, three chairs, a mirror 3 inches in diameter, a pair of tongs and andirons, a kettle, a skillet and frying pan, a dipper, a washbowl, two knives and forks, three plates, one cup, one spoon, a jug for oil, a jug for molasses, and a japanned lamp. He wanted no other possessions, not even a mat on the floor. Thoreau lived in the cabin for two years and two months, supporting himself by raising farm produce for sale and by occasional handyman jobs.

Thoreau's own account of why he decided to live in solitude on the shores of Walden Pond is highly revealing:

I went to the woods because I wished to live deliberately, to front only the essential facts of life, and see if I could not learn what it had to teach, and not, when I came to die, discover that I had not lived. I did not wish to live what was not life, living is so dear; nor did I wish to practice resignation, unless it was quite necessary. I wanted to live deep and suck out all the marrow of life, to live so sturdily and Spartan-like as to put to rout all that was not life, to cut a broad swath and shave close, to drive life into a corner, and, reduce it to its lowest terms, and, if it proved to be mean, why then to get the whole and genuine meanness of it, and publish its meanness to the world; or if it were sublime, to know it by experience, and be able to give a true account of it in my next excursion.

Thoreau's fellow townsmen were curious about the nature of his life in the woods: "Some have asked what I got to eat; if I did not feel lonesome; if I was not afraid; and the like. Others have been curious to learn what portion of my income I devoted to charitable purposes; and some, who have large families, how many poor children I maintained." Responses to such queries are found in the first chapter of *Walden,* entitled "Economy." This is not an essay on economics, however, but on the economic utilization of one's time and energy. "The mass of men," Thoreau believed, "lead lives of quiet desperation," condemning themselves to a ceaseless struggle to increase their material possessions. They realize too late, if ever, that "most of the luxuries, and many of the so-called comforts of life, are not only not indispensable, but positive hindrances to the elevation of mankind."

The essence of Thoreau's message was "simplicity, simplicity, simplicity," and avoidance of "the tyranny of things," that is, going through life with an excess of useless baggage. Food at Walden, other than the crops he raised, cost Thoreau 27 cents a week. By omitting all nonessentials, he could support himself for a year by six weeks' labor. "Possessions are like leg irons," he wrote, and "our life is frittered away by detail." The only commodities required by man are food, shelter, clothing, and fuel, and much of the latter three can be dispensed with.

Thoreau swam in the pond in the early morning before breakfast, after which, barefooted, he hoed his beans. At noon, work ceased, he bathed in the pond again, "and for the afternoon was absolutely free." Strawberries, blackberries, wild grapes, chestnuts, and other uncultivated fruits were available for the picking. A satisfactory sweetening could be obtained from pumpkins and beets, or better still from the sap of the maple trees. On warm evenings Thoreau drifted in his boat on the pond, playing his flute. Housekeeping received minimal attention. The predominant theme of *Walden* is the enjoyment of life, and to that end, it is argued, man needs leisure and energy. In one sense the book is a practical treatise on how to arrange economically the practical side of one's life, to simplify all details in order to allow a generous margin of leisure to explore "reality." "Why should we live with such hurry and waste of life?" asks Thoreau. "We are determined to be starved before we are hungry. Men say that a stitch in time saves nine, and so they take a thousand stitches to-day to save nine to-morrow."

Thoreau was a naturalist by instinct, and his observations on natural history in the vicinity of Walden Pond add immensely to the interest of his narrative. In his chapter "Brute Neighbors," Thoreau describes a colony of mice, "a wild native kind not found in the village," which haunted his house; phoebes, robins, and partridges which nested nearby; and a battle to the death between black and red ants. "It is remarkable," he observes, "how many creatures live wild and free though secret in the woods, and still sustain themselves in the neighborhood of towns, suspected by hunters only." Thus may be found the otter, "four feet long, as big as a small boy"; the raccoon, which comes out at night; the woodcock and the turtle dove; and the red squirrel. In the fall the loon came to moult and bathe in the pond, "making the woods ring with his wild laughter."

"Winter Animals" is the title of a later chapter. A colony of muskrats dwelt in Goose Pond, near Walden, "and raised their cabins high above the ice." Often in winter days and night, Thoreau heard "the forlorn but melodious note of a hooting owl indefinitely far," and the loud honking of geese as they flew overhead. Sometimes he heard foxes "as they ranged over the snow crust, in moonlight nights, in search of a partridge or other game, barking raggedly and demoniacally like forest dogs." Squirrels, rabbits, bluejays, chickadees, and partridges came to the cabin to feed upon the ears of sweet corn which Thoreau threw out for them.

The thoughtless slaughter of wild life was highly repugnant to Thoreau. Even when he was living at Walden Pond, he noted "an increased scarcity of game." He sold his gun before going to the woods, though he sometimes went fishing to add variety to his plain fare. "No humane being, past the thoughtless age of boyhood, will wantonly murder any creature, which holds its life by the same tenure that he does," wrote Thoreau in his chapter "Higher Laws." He found something "essentially unclean" about flesh foods, even fish. "Is it not a reproach that man is a carnivorous animal?" asks Thoreau. "True, he can and does live, in a great measure by preying on other animals; but this is a miserable way."

The austerity of Thoreau's habits is shown further by his preference for drinking water: "For the same reason that I prefer the natural sky to an opium-eater's heaven . . . I believe that water is the only drink for a wise man; wine is not so noble a liquor; and think of dashing the hopes of a morning with a cup of warm coffee, or of an evening with a dish of tea!"

Walden is developed by Thoreau within a logical framework. The story naturally divides itself in three ways: by topics, treating of various aspects of existence at the pond; by the events and occupations of typical days; and by the cycle of the year, describing the changes brought about by the succession of the seasons. The scene is set by "Economy," followed by the chapter "Where I Lived, and What I Lived For," a philosophical discussion of why the author had chosen to withdraw from society and what he hoped to accomplish by his experiment. A period of study and contemplation implied "Reading," chapter three, in which Thoreau praised the riches to be gained by a study of classical writings, "the noblest recorded thoughts of man." The ageless nature of the classics is contrasted with the ephemeral quality of newspapers and popular novels.

From "Reading" Thoreau proceeds to a discussion of "Sounds." At times he sat "rapt in a revery" as he listened to the whistle of a locomotive; the bells of Lincoln, Acton, Bedford, and Concord; lowing cows in far-away pastures; the whippoorwills "chanting their vespers;" the screech owl, with its "dismal scream," and the hooting owl, "the most melancholy sound in nature"; the distant rumbling of wagons over bridges, the baying of dogs, and the croaking of bullfrogs.

In "Solitude" Thoreau dwells further on the complete oneness which he feels with his surroundings. He notes that men frequently said to him, "I should think you would feel lonesome down there, and want to be nearer to folks, rainy and snowy days and nights especially." To which Thoreau was tempted to reply, "This whole earth which we inhabit is but a point in space. How far apart, think you, dwell the two most important inhabitants of yonder star? why should I feel lonely? is not our planet in the Milky Way?" Thoreau continues, "I find it wholesome to be alone the greater part of the time. To be in company, even with the best, is soon wearisome and dissipating. I love to be alone. I never found the companion that was so companionable as solitude. A man thinking or working is always alone, let him be where he will." Humorously he adds, "I have a great deal of company in my house; especially in the morning, when nobody calls."

Actually, Thoreau probably exaggerated the point for effect. He was not a hermit in fact or in taste. His chapter entitled "Visitors" describes his simple provisions for hospitality and the pleasure he took in the visitors, both plain and sophisticated, who came to call on him or whom he encountered in the woods. His frequent trips into Concord offer evidence, too, that he did not wish to cut himself off from human companionship and that he enjoyed people. "I had three chairs in my house," he wrote; "one for solitude, two for friendship, three for society."

After the first six chapters, in which Thoreau is largely concerned with social relations, *Walden* focuses attention on nature and the uncivilized, stressing the cycle of the year in "The Bean-field," "The Ponds," "Brute Neighbors," "House-warming," "Winter Visitors," "Winter Animals," "The Pond in Winter," and "Spring."

Modern conservationists can grieve with Thoreau over the approaching doom of Walden Pond which he describes in "The Ponds":

> Since I left those shores the woodchoppers have still further laid them waste, and now for many a year there will be no more rambling through the aisles of the wood, with occasional vistas through which you see the water. How can you expect the birds to sing when their groves are cut down?

The wood choppers had laid bare first one shore and then another; Thoreau observed, "The Irish have built their sties by it and the railroad has infringed on its border and the ice-men have skimmed it."

Walden concludes with the arrival of spring, when life is reawakening on every side. The thick ice cover on the pond begins to break up; the spring rains come; the earth thaws; the songs of the sparrow, the blue bird, the red-wing, and the robin are heard; green leaves appear on the oaks, hickories, maples, and other trees; and the wild geese make a brief stopover at Walden Pond on their migration northward.

"Thus was my first year's life in the woods completed; and the second year was similar to it," Thoreau concluded. "I finally left Walden September 6th, 1847." Why did he not continue what was for him an idyllic existence? Thoreau replied:

I left the woods for as good a reason as I went there. Perhaps it seemed to me that I had several more lives to live, and could not spare any more time for that one. It is remarkable how easily and insensibly we fall into a particular route, and make a beaten track for ourselves. . . . I learned this, at least, by my experiment; that if one advances confidently in the direction of his dreams, and endeavors to live the life which he has imagined, he will meet with a success unexpected in common hours. . . . In proportion as he simplifies his life, the laws of the universe will appear less complex, and solitude will not be solitude, nor poverty poverty, nor weakness weakness. If you have built castles in the air, your work need not be lost; that is where they should be. Now put the foundations under them.

Thoreau lived only eight years after the publication of *Walden*. The eloquent eulogy delivered by Ralph Waldo Emerson at his funeral is perhaps the most perceptive appraisal ever written of Thoreau's career:

He interrogated every custom, and wished to settle all his practice on an ideal foundation. He was a protestant *a outrance*, and few lives contain so many renunciations. He was bred to no profession; he never married; he lived alone; he never went to church; he never voted; he refused to pay a tax to the State; he ate no flesh, he drank no wine, he never knew the use of tobacco; and, though a naturalist, he used neither trap nor gun. He chose, wisely no doubt for himself, to be the bachelor of thought and nature. He had no talent for wealth, and knew how to be poor without the least hint of squalor or inelegance.

When Thoreau undertook his experiment of living in the woods, he had no intention of abandoning society or of going primitive. He went to nature because there he could lead an uncomplicated, simple life, giving him time to discover eternal verities. As Sherman Paul, a leading Thoreau critic, points out, "He simplified not to economize time but to spend it, to shed the burdens of planting, weaving, and building," thereby providing an opportunity to cultivate the higher faculties. No more striking contrast can be found than that between Thoreau's simple, peaceful life at Walden and the frantic struggle for possessions and prestige which dominates the lives of the majority of mankind.

18 | PATHS OF THE SEA

Matthew Fontaine Maury's *The Physical Geography of the Sea*, 1855

The founder of the modern science of oceanography spent his youth some 450 miles inland from the Atlantic, but from early boyhood the sea held an irresistible fascination for Matthew Fontaine Maury. His inspiration doubtless came from an older brother, who had been marooned in the South Seas, sailed on the *Essex* under Porter against British men-of-war, fought on Lake Champlain, and was flag captain of the squadron that destroyed the pirates of the West Indies.

Maury was born on a farm near Fredericksburg, Virginia, in 1806, and as a five-year-old moved with his family to Franklin, Tennessee, near Nashville. In 1825, as a protégé of Sam Houston, then a congressman from Tennessee, Maury received a midshipman's warrant and reported to the Secretary of the Navy for training. His tour of naval duty included a voyage to France on a ship that carried Lafayette home after his last visit to the United States; circumnavigation of the globe on the *Vincennes*, the first American warship to sail around the world; and sailing master aboard the sloop-of-war *Falmouth* on a cruise around the Horn into the Pacific, to join the American squadron there in patrolling the west coast of South America.

After nine years of almost continuous sea duty, Maury returned home. In the course of his long voyages he had been impressed with the meagerness of the information then available to mariners concerning the ocean's prevailing winds and currents which favor or retard the progress of ships under sail. Maury had learned during his seagoing experience that adverse winds or the drift of currents could force a vessel far off its projected route. He also found that a ship could double its speed by taking advantage of favorable currents. The problem was how to develop a science out of these facts.

During the period when Maury was a young naval officer, a voyage to South America was a leisurely, zigzagging affair. Because of legends that the northeastern extremity of Brazil was swept by dangerous currents, early navigators first sailed to Europe, in order to follow an old and tried route. If their destination was Australia or China, they would cross the Atlantic again to round the Cape of Good Hope.

It cannot be claimed that Maury was the first to recognize the need for reliable information for navigation purposes. The Greek sailors of antiquity had learned how to utilize the etesians—the northerly summer winds of the Aegean Sea—and the monsoons, which, changing their direction twice a year, make the round-trip voyage to India easy sailing. After the fifteenth century, the trade winds of the Atlantic and Pacific began to be understood and used by sailors. The astronomer Halley charted the ocean winds over the intertropical region of the globe in 1688, despite the scanty data then available. Benjamin Franklin produced a usable map of the Gulf Stream in 1770, and from 1809 to 1811 Captain James Horsburgh published full accounts of the winds of the Eastern sea routes. None of these earlier efforts, however, rivaled in completeness, accuracy, and comprehensiveness the sea charts to be prepared by Matthew Fontaine Maury. He was indeed the first great "pathfinder of the seas."

Maury's first scientific article, "On the Navigation of Cape Horn," based on his own experience, described graphically the dangers of the passage of Cape Horn, and gave specific information concerning the winds and the peculiar rising and falling of the barometer in those latitudes. Encouraged by the response to his initial writings, Maury embarked on a larger enterprise, a book on navigation, printed in 1836 under the title *A New Theoretical and Practical Treatise on Navigation*, the first nautical work of science to come from the pen of an American naval officer. Among those who commended the book was Nathaniel Bowditch, of whose *New American Practical Navigator* Maury was a deep student. The Maury work went through several editions, was adopted as a textbook by junior officers in the Navy, and became the basis for the author's later, more famous book, *The Physical Geography of the Sea.*

In a series of anonymous articles appearing in the Richmond *Whig and Public Advertiser* and the *Southern Literary Messenger*, Maury criticized the low quality of education of U.S. Navy midshipmen and called for reorganization and drastic change in other naval matters. The articles urged the establishment of a naval academy similar to the Army's West Point; broader education for naval officers, including foreign languages and international law; higher ranks and better pay for naval officers; and a larger Navy, better harbor defenses, vigorous enforcement of the law against the African slave trade, and greater protection for merchant shipping against the Chinese pirates.

Because of a crippling accident which precluded further sea duty, Maury was placed in charge, in 1842, of the Depot of Charts and Instruments, from which later developed the Hydrographic Office and the Naval Observatory. Still later, the Weather Bureau took over the task of collecting marine weather statistics. Here began Maury's studies in depth of the meteorology of the ocean.

In the old building of the Depot of Charts and Instruments, stored away in cellar, closets, and attic, were bundles of old logbooks covered with dust. The books had been deposited by hundreds of captains after thousands of voyages. They told the stories of the windjammers which had sailed all over the world. Therein were recorded the observations of sea captains who had watched the winds, weather, and currents. The new superintendent at once recognized the mine of information that could be extracted from the primary records. Maury's method of work is described as follows by Harold A. Calahan, naval authority:

If he found that a ship encountered northwest winds in latitude 40° north, longitude 60° west in the month of July, he went through the log of every ship that had sailed near that spot in that month in the 60-odd years of his records to see what winds she had encountered. Presently there began to emerge a picture of the ocean—winds, currents, temperatures, storms, waves, ice, whales, everything. Maury reasoned that if ships found the same conditions in the same seasons in the same parts of the ocean for 60 years, there would be a strong probability that ships in the future would find the same conditions at the same time in the same places.

Altogether, Maury and his assistants catalogued more than 10,000 ships' logs. Slowly they pieced together an imperfect picture of the sea. There were blank spots for which no data were available, but after five years Maury felt sufficiently confident of his facts to publish the first *Wind and Current Chart of the North Atlantic* (1847). Some 5,000 copies were distributed to skippers along the Atlantic seaboard.

To fill gaps in the record, Maury knew that additional, more complete, data were required. A year after the original chart was issued, therefore, he devised and printed thousands of blank charts on which sea captains were asked to mark the tracks of their ships from day to day. As described by Maury's biographer, Charles L. Lewis:

> They were to enter in this log the latitude and longitude every day at noon; the hourly rate of the currents expressed in knots; the variation of the compass; the reading of the thermometer, in both air and water, at nine o'clock each morning; the state of the barometer just before, during, and just after a gale of wind with the changes and time of changes in the direction of the wind during the gale; careful entries as to the direction and force of the winds every eight hours; and other marine phenomena such as whales, flocks of birds, rains and fogs, etc., etc.

By 1851 fully a thousand skippers were cooperating with Maury, sending in logs of winds and weather from far and near on all the oceans. As fast as the information came in, Maury revised his charts and brought out new editions. A long series of charts appeared, accompanied by texts, relating to winds, currents, and other matters of practical interest to sailors, including the average frequency of rain, fog, and thunderstorms in different areas, the temperature of the sea, and the locations of profitable whaling grounds. About 200,000 copies of the charts and 20,000 copies of sailing directions in book form were distributed free to the mariners who cooperated in gathering the information.

The results were spectacular, and quickly converted skeptics among the sea captains who had doubted the value of the charts. The average voyage by a sailing vessel from New York to Rio had been fifty-five days; by following Maury's directions the time was reduced to thirty-five to forty days. Two weeks were cut off the trip to Lisbon, a week saved to Dublin. The average time from New York to San Francisco had been 180 days, and Maury's wind and current charts reduced it to 133 days. Use of the charts by American shipping alone saved owners more than 2 million dollars annually, while Britain gained by 10 million dollars.

On one occasion Maury actually rescued a ship by long-distance methods. The vessel had foundered off Cape Hatteras in a hurricane and was stranded for several weeks. An appeal was made to Maury, who ascertained the position of the ship when struck, then traced on his charts the probable drift of a derelict at sea and marked its course on a map. "If afloat you will find her here," Maury is reported to have said. The ship was recovered in the exact longitude and latitude predicted by Maury.

Another contribution made by Maury was the laying down of lanes for steamers in the North Atlantic, where collisions between ships had been frequent. In 1855 Maury published a chart defining proposed "ocean lanes." Two tracks or lanes, 20 miles wide, were laid down. Steamers westward bound were to follow the northern lane and east-bound ships would stay in the southern lane. The Secretary of the Navy immediately ordered the ships of the Navy to observe the lanes and gradually they were adopted also for commercial shipping. The lanes were designed to keep ships away from icebergs and fog, as far as possible, as well as to avoid collisions. Thereafter, a drastic drop occurred in the accidents which had previously befallen vessels sailing the stormy North Atlantic.

Maury's researches for the laying of the first Atlantic cable were likewise of a pioneering nature. As early as 1848 he had come to the conclusion, in the course of his investigations of winds and currents, that there existed between Newfoundland and Ireland a broad and level plateau at a comparatively moderate depth. In a report to the Secretary of the Navy, February 1854, the results of a series of deep sea soundings were summarized:

> From Newfoundland to Ireland the distance between the nearest points is about 1,600 miles, and the bottom of the sea between the two places is a plateau which seems to have been placed there especially for the purpose of holding the wires of the submarine telegraph, and of keeping them out of harm's way. It

is neither too deep nor too shallow; yet it is so deep that the wires but once landed will remain forever beyond the reach of the anchors of vessels, icebergs, and drifts of any kind, and so shallow that they may be readily lodged upon the bottom.

A topographic map of the North Atlantic ocean floor was constructed by Maury, and he served as adviser to Cyrus W. Field in the actual laying of the first cable. After several failures, the undertaking was finally successfully concluded. At a dinner given in New York in 1858, to celebrate the arrival of the first message across the Atlantic, Field is reported to have said, "I am a man of few words: Maury furnished the brains, England gave the money, and I did the work."

In time, Maury became an international figure. In August 1853 he was the leading spirit at the first International Meteorological Conference, held at Brussels. For seventeen days scientists from nine principal maritime nations discussed the many problems associated with ocean traffic. Steam was gradually replacing sail, but sea charts were as urgently needed as in the past. The conferees agreed on plans to enlist sailors of all nationalities in a vast campaign of nautical and meteorological observations according to Maury's methods. Even in time of war, the records were to be preserved and regarded as inviolate.

A bibliography of forty pages is required to list the titles of Maury's published works. His most famous and popular book was *The Physical Geography of the Sea,* which appeared in 1855 —the first classic work of modern oceanography. Nine American and nineteen English editions and at least a half-dozen translations into European languages were issued. The book was designed for the general reader and written in nontechnical language. In the introduction, the author outlines the work's contents and general scope: "I shall treat of the economy of the sea and its adaptations—of its salts, its waters, its climates, and its inhabitants, and of whatever there may be of general interest in its commercial uses or industrial pursuits, for all such things pertain to its Physical Geography."

The second chapter of *The Physical Geography of the Sea* is devoted to a subject which Maury had studied intensively for years—the Gulf Stream. His opening statement is classical:

There is a river in the ocean: in the severest droughts it never fails, and in the mightiest floods it never overflows; its banks and its bottom are of cold water, while its current is of warm; the Gulf of Mexico is its fountain, and its mouth is in the Arctic Seas. It is the Gulf Stream. There is in the world no other such majestic flow of waters. Its current is more rapid than the Mississippi or the Amazon, and its volume more than a thousand times greater. Its waters, as far out from the Gulf as the Carolina coasts, are of an indigo blue. They are so distinctly marked that their line of junction with the common sea-water may be traced by the eye.

Maury was the world's pioneer investigator on subjects covered by two other chapters—"The Depths of the Ocean" and "The Basin of the Atlantic"—both popular with readers. Practically no aspect of the broad field was neglected, as other divisions dealt with such topics as the atmosphere, rains and rivers, sea currents, salts of the sea, the cloud region and sea fogs, the geological effects of winds, sea routes, monsoons, climates of the sea, tide-rips and sea drift, storms, hurricanes and typhoons, and the Antarctic regions.

Because Maury was an original thinker and investigator and too ready to rush in with theories when factual support was lacking, some of his concepts in later years were found to be erroneous. A number of errors were corrected in subsequent editions. As one Maury biographer, Patricia Jahns, points out, "The book has passages that show that if Maury had had infinite capacity for taking pains that characterizes genius, he would have produced a great work." A detailed analysis of the *Physical Geography* reveals that it is accurate in statements of observed facts concerning ocean phenomena, but is often wrong in assumption and analysis—in part, at least, because of the limitations of knowledge at the time that Maury was writing. Maury was a bold workman who believed that beginnings should be made, even if in time they had to be revised or corrected.

A leading meteorologist, John Leighly, in an introduction to a 1963 reprint of the *Physical Geography*, sums up the case: "There is in fact a great deal of sound information in the book, but the reader now, as a hundred years ago, must weigh each paragraph and sort out its content of objective fact, of material selected to support Maury's interpretations, and of fantasy. The most valuable parts are those in which he describes investigations done under his supervision, such as his account of deep-sea soundings." Leighly concludes that the *Physical Geography* is read today "as the highly personal testament of an energetic and self-assertive man unacquainted with the rigorous methods practiced in the academies, but possessing first-hand knowledge of ships and the sea, boundless self-confidence, and a pen well exercised in persuasive writing."

Maury's later career was an anticlimax. At the outbreak of the Civil War, he resigned from the U.S. Navy to serve as Chief of Sea Coast, River and Harbor Defenses of the Confederacy. For several years following the war he considered himself a refugee, living first in England and then in Mexico. Maury returned to the United States in 1868 and served as professor of meterology in the Virginia Military Institute until his death in 1873.

The permanent significance of Maury's contributions to maritime science is indicated by the inscription placed on the pilot charts issued by the Hydrographic Office (since 1962 the Naval Oceanographic Office) of the Navy Department.

Founded upon the researches made in the early part of the nineteenth century by Matthew Fontaine Maury, while serving as a lieutenant in the United States Navy.

| # POET OF DEMOCRACY

Walt Whitman's *Leaves of Grass,* 1855

The best writing, Walt Whitman once said, has no lace on its sleeves—a precept which guided his own vigorous, earthy poetry and prose style. He boasted, indeed, of a lack of elegance and effeteness, both in himself and in his countrymen, asserting, "The art of art, the glory of expression and the sunshine of the light of letters, is simplicity"; and further, "Men and women, and the earth and all upon it, are to be taken as they are." The transition from the romantic to the realistic tradition in American literature is marked by Whitman's work.

Any softness and overrefinement were missing from Whitman's own beginnings. He was born on a farm on Long Island in 1819, the son of a struggling carpenter. His only formal education was in a Brooklyn elementary school, from which he dropped out before age twelve to learn the printing trade. He was successively printer's devil, compositor, and free-lance writer, and by twenty he was editing his own paper.

Outcroppings of genius are unpredictable, and Walt Whitman's sudden emergence as a major poet, given his unpromising background, is one of the unexplainable miracles of American literature. His early writings have been described as "commonplace, empty of real literary values, imitative, often banal," with no intimation of future greatness. It is known now that, beginning about 1847, Whitman started keeping notebooks, filled with prose and poetry, ideas which he subsequently incorporated into *Leaves of Grass.* Nevertheless, as Henry Seidel Canby, in the *Literary History of the United States,* observes,

> It is impossible to explain by any final analysis this remarkable phenomenon of the unveiling of a genius and prophet in the mind of a busy and successful journalist . . . *Leaves of Grass* seems an incredible achievement for a politician and a journalist only because its long deep roots stretching back into childhood were known only to Whitman himself. This is a reasonable if not

a complete explanation of one of the most surprising outbursts of genius in early middle age known in literary history.

In a few words, a perceptive critic, Robert C. Whittemore, in *Makers of the American Mind*, evaluates Walt Whitman's one great book: "*Leaves of Grass* is the poetic celebration of the common man, the apotheosis of the mind and flesh of the average American, the farmer, laborer, wife and mother, toiler in factory and office, yes, even the bum—as seen and felt by the man who more than anyone else is entitled to be called the poet-philosopher of the American Democracy." The title, *Leaves of Grass*, was chosen by Whitman as a symbol of simplicity. A leaf of grass is the most downtrodden of plants, yet it flourishes everywhere. Grass is "the handkerchief of the Lord," declared Whitman, "a uniform hieroglyphic, and it means, Sprouting alike in broad zones and in narrow, growing among black folks as among white." Whitman wrote, "The insignificant is as big to me as any. I will not have a single person slighted or turned away."

Leaves of Grass in its first edition (1855) bears little resemblance to the ninth, the so-called "Deathbed Edition," published in 1892. The original is a thin folio of ninety-five pages bound in pebbly green cloth stamped with gold. It contains only twelve poems, all untitled, compared with 383 in the last edition to be issued in Whitman's lifetime. One poem, later called "Song of Myself," fills forty-four pages—nearly half the book. There is also a brilliant preface stating a theory of poetry for democracy and for America. The entire volume was designed by the poet, who set about ten pages of the type, supervised the printing (at Rome Brothers' job-printing shop in Brooklyn), corrected the proofs, and acted as salesman for the completed work. The size of the edition has been estimated as not more than 1,000 copies. No author's name appeared on the title page. The frontispiece, however, is a steel-engraved portrait of Whitman in his everyday canvas trousers and workman's shirt, collar open and tieless, black soft hat tilted toward the left ear, knuckles of right hand on hip, a bearded man in his thirties—"the whole pose," as John T. Winterich remarks, "one of dignified swagger."

Few copies of the first edition were sold, but a number of copies were sent out for review to leading American and English critics. The reviews, rather than the book's popularity among readers, served to call attention to the emergence of a dynamic new talent. Only a handful of reviewers liked what they read. As Carl Sandburg, whose own style was profoundly influenced by Whitman's, wrote, *Leaves of Grass* "is the most highly praised and the most deeply damned book that ever came from an American printing press as the work of an American writer; no other book can compete with it in the number of bouquets handed it by distinguished bystanders on one side of the street and in the number of hostile and nasty brickbats flung by equally distinguished bystanders on the other side of the street." In the early years, the brickbats predominated.

For example, the Boston *Intelligencer* suggested that the book had been written by an escaped lunatic, calling it a "heterogeneous mass of bombast, egotism, vulgarity, and nonsense." The London *Critic* was of the opinion that "Walt Whitman is as unacquainted with art, as a hog is with mathematics. His poems—we must call them so for convenience . . . are innocent of rhythm, and resemble nothing so much as the war cry of the Red Indians." The New York *Crayon* characterized *Leaves of Grass* as "barbarous, undisciplined, like the poetry of a half civilized people," and the London *Leader* critic complained that "the poem is written in wild, irregular, unrhymed, almost unmetrical 'lengths' . . . by no means seductive to English ears."

For a time it appears that Whitman was reduced to writing reviews of his own book. Anonymous, and of course favorable, reviews by Whitman appeared in the *United States Review,* the Brooklyn *Times,* and the *American Phrenological Review.* A sample from the *Times:*

> To give judgment on real poems, one needs an account of the poet himself. Very devilish to some, and very divine to some, will appear the poet of these new poems, the "Leaves of Grass;" an attempt, as they are, of a naive, masculine, affectionate, contemplative, sensual, imperious person, to cast into literature not only his own grit and arrogance, but his own flesh and form, undraped, regardless of . . . modesty or law, and ignorant or silently scornful, as at first appears, of all except his own presence and experience, and all outside the fiercely loved land of his birth, and the birth of his parents, and their parents for several generations before him. Politeness this man has none,

and regulation he has none. A rude child of the people!—No imitation—No foreigner—but a growth and idiom of America.

But Whitman did not lack defenders among persons less concerned and less personally interested than himself. Charles Eliot Norton, writing in *Putnam's Monthly Magazine*, praised "this gross yet elevated, this superficial yet profound, this preposterous yet somehow fascinating book . . . a mixture of Yankee transcendentalism and New York rowdyism . . . there is an original perception of nature, a manly brawn, and an epic directness in our new poet." Edward Everitt Hale in the *North American Review* was equally fascinated by the naturalness and vigor of the new poetry.

By far the most influential of any comments, pro or con, on *Leaves of Grass* was a letter from Ralph Waldo Emerson, to whom Whitman had sent a copy. In one of the most famous communications in American literature, Emerson wrote to Whitman from Concord on July 21, 1855:

> Dear Sir, I am not blind to the worth of the wonderful gift of "Leaves of Grass." I find it the most extraordinary piece of wit and wisdom that America has yet contributed. I am very happy in reading it, as great power makes us happy. It meets the demand I am always making of what seemed the sterile and stingy nature, as if too much handiwork, or too much lymph in the temperament, were making our western wits fat and mean. . . . I give you joy of your free and brave thought. I have great joy in it. I find incomparable things said incomparably well, as they must be. I find the courage of treatment which so delights us, and which large perception only can inspire. I greet you at the beginning of a great career, which yet must have had a long foreground somewhere, for such a start.

Whitman was tremendously stimulated by Emerson's warm tribute. The letter restored any self-confidence which he might have lost in reading harsh criticisms and convinced him that his inspiration was indeed genuine. "It was as if God had spoken," Frances Winwar, Whitman's biographer, notes, "for was not Concord the literary Olympus, and Emerson its Jove?" Later Emerson would find Whitman's realism too strong for his delicate New England taste, and he was shocked by what he regarded as the indecency of many poems in the second and third editions, published in 1856 and 1860. But his ringing endorsement of the first edition came at a most psychological moment in Whitman's career.

The preface to the 1855 edition, containing more words than the twelve poems, presents Whitman's conception of the poets and poetry of the future. The greatest poet is seen as the most complete lover of the universe, drawing his materials directly from nature. "The Americans of all nations at any time upon the earth have probably the fullest poetical nature. The United States themselves are essentially the greatest poem. . . . The American poets are to enclose old and new for America is the race of races." The bard's "spirit responds to his country's spirit . . . he incarnates its geography and natural life and rivers and lakes." The greatest poet is a seer and pettiness and triviality are foreign to his nature. The genius of America will be found in a poet of superior vision emerging from the common people. He will be a perfect physical specimen and representative of the national character.

It should be observed that the attributes and qualities which Whitman was seeking in a great national poet were largely to be found in his own personality and character.

The twelve poems contained in the first edition of *Leaves of Grass,* as subsequently titled, were "Song of Myself," "A Song for Occupations," "To Think of Time," "The Sleepers," "I Sing the Body Electric," "Faces," "Song of the Answerer," "Europe," "A Boston Ballad," "There Was a Child Went Forth," "Who Learns My Lesson Complete?" and "Great Are the Myths." One poem, "Song of Myself," placed at the beginning, takes forty-four pages, or nearly one-half the book. It has been called "one of the most self-revealing poems in literature." The opening lines are often quoted:

I celebrate myself, and sing myself,
And what I assume you shall assume,
For every atom belonging to me as good belongs to you.
I loafe and invite my soul,
I learn and loafe at my ease observing a spear of summer grass.

A shorter poem, "One's-Self I Sing," in a group of "Inscriptions," expresses a similar mood:

One's-self I sing, a simple separate person,
Yet utter the word Democratic, the word En-Masse.
Of physiology from top to toe I sing,
Not physiognomy alone nor brain alone is worthy for the Muse,
    I say the Form complete is worthier far,
The Female equally with the Male I sing.
Of Life immense in passion, pulse, and power,
Cheerful, for freest action form'd under the laws divine,
The Modern Man I sing.

In "Song of Myself" Whitman speaks as the voice of democracy, representing the "divine average," emphasizing that every man is part of the eternal time stream, all men are brothers, and life and death are a continuous process. Thus this long and powerful poem reveals the pageant of life: wives, old maids, drivers, farmers, hunters, clam diggers, trappers, runaway slaves, handsome young men bathing and the rich woman hiding behind the window blinds who joins them in fancy, Negro draymen, and many more. Through the voice of the poet are heard prisoners and slaves, the diseased and despairing, the forbidden voices of sex and lust. Whitman sees America whole, in all its vital aspects. In an admirable summing up, Henry Seidel Canby adds:

> It is also a prophetic poem in the Old Testament sense, for Whitman is urging a vigorous country to spiritualize its energy and demanding that a society whose culture is intellectual shall find new sources of power in beautiful blood, in the ardors of sex, in a harmony, like the harmony of animals, with the physical universe. Furthermore, it is a dramatic poem. The author plays a histrionic role, like a revivalist. If he contradicts himself, he says, well, then he contradicts himself. He is large, he contains multitudes. He can and does project a man of this age, great enough to feel with all, to love all, and to point them down the long brown road to self-development. And this is the heart, though not the totality of Whitman's message.

Leaves of Grass was first published when the author was thirty-six, and though Whitman lived to be seventy-three, he never wrote another full-scale book. Instead, he spent the remainder of his life rewriting, retitling, expanding, and rearranging the first edition of *Leaves of Grass*. His art deepened and matured with the passage of time, and out of his later years came some of his most magnificent and memorable poems. The power and charm of Whitman are effectively shown, for example, in two poems, "When Lilacs Last in the Dooryard Bloom'd," the great elegy on the death of Lincoln, and "Out of the Cradle Endlessly Rocking," the cry of a lonely mocking bird along the seashore, symbolizing love, death, and poetic creation. Other acknowledged master-pieces include "Drum-taps," a collection of verse first published separately and then incorporated in *Leaves of Grass*, the greatest body of Civil War poetry, recording the grief and heroism, the tragic companionship, the "large conflicting fluctuations of despair and hope" of the war; the "Passage of India," in which the poet sees the whole of human history as fulfilling a divine plan and urges the union of the human race into one vast family; and "Crossing Brooklyn Bridge," wherein, as Gay Wilson Allen comments, "the crossing becomes a symbolical annihilation of time for Whitman: as he thinks of the people who have crossed this very river on this same ferry before him and will cross the same way after him, he feels his *identity* with them, and they become one."

The sensual quality of Whitman's poetry has intrigued the attention of many critics. The most characteristic examples are in the group of poems titled "Children of Adam," a number of which appeared in the second, the 1856, edition of *Leaves of Grass*, including two of the most famous, "I See the Body Electric" and "A Woman Waits for Me." The extreme sensuousness of Whitman's nature is reflected with complete realism in his songs of love. He saw himself as a "caresser of life" in all its phases and as a believer in the flesh and the appetites. Whitman had nothing except contempt for the "pruriency, sneaking, furtive, mephitic" pervading contemporary literature, "the fashionable delusion of the inherent nastiness of sex," and "feeble and garrulous" modesty. His poems were written with the object of destroying the literary taboo by which the facts of sex in his time were obscured and distorted. In his view, whatever is natural is good and therefore suitable subject matter for poetry.

It is Van Wyck Brooks's conclusion, however, that "Whitman's lovers were primarily parents and he was mainly concerned with sex as conducting to the result of a race of superior men. There was something austere, in point of fact, in Whitman's sexuality, while personally he was rather under- than over-sexed, mildly bisexual and mostly unconscious of the homosexual implications in *Calamus* and other passages in his poems and prose." In any event, Whitman's frank celebration of physical love struck most Americans of his time as not respectable, and perhaps downright indecent.

Numerous passages scattered through *Leaves of Grass* defend the concept of the equality of the sexes. In a fully democratic society, Whitman asserted, women must be as great as men in all departments, entering practical life and politics, "the robust equals, workers":

> The wife, and she is not one jot less than the husband,
> The daughter, and she is just as good as the son,
> The mother, and she is every bit as much as the father.

A shocking and controversial aspect of Whitman's poetry as viewed by his contemporaries was his summary rejection of genteel conventions and literary forms. In complete contrast to the stylized, sentimental poems in rhyme and meter produced by Longfellow, Whittier, Lowell, and Holmes, Whitman abandoned classical poetic forms and imagery. In their place he perfected a new form—long chanting rhythms, free from stylistic conventions. The genteel were offended, too, by Whitman's use of realistic words and images, drawing upon the American idiom, upon slang and colloquialisms—all indispensable constituents of what Whitman referred to as his "barbaric yawp." Lionel Trilling judges "the verse form that he created is, at its best, a triumph of revolutionary invention. It is, of course, not to be thought of as an escape from the difficulties of traditional metrical verse; indeed, cadenced verse is more difficult to use successfully than metrical verse." Whitman scorned what he called "lady-words" and "gloved gentlemen words," and felt a close kinship with "unhemmed latitude, coarseness, directness, live epithets, expletives, words of opprobrium, resistance." His verse is filled, too, with aboriginal Indian names, as he celebrates America, and—to show the great American melting pot—words of foreign origin, especially Spanish and French terms.

Malcolm Cowley remarks that "everything in the poems is common, but touched with the miraculous, and the poems themselves are miracles." In Whitman's glorification of America, there was nothing narrowly chauvinistic. He saw America as a symbol of freedom, expansiveness, and new beginnings, as illustrating the multiplicity and contradictions of life—a mystic vision of what the universe could become. America stood for the new age that Whitman was fighting for, incarnating the great promises of democracy and science. The Whitman viewpoint is eloquently stated by Van Wyck Brooks:

> It was to become not a conquerer nation but rather the grand producing land of nobler men and women, healthy and free, the friendliest nation, the nation of peace, the composite nation, formed from all, and reconciling all as children of an equal brood. It was to be illimitably proud, independent, self-possessed; it was to be generous and gentle; above all, it was to be an example, not an echo.

Whitman's influence on American literature has been profound. His writings, both poetry and prose, had a shattering effect on Puritanical thought, speech, and literary subject matter. He focused attention on all the people and on democratic institutions. His heirs include Edgar Lee Masters, Robinson Jeffers, Edwin Markham, and Carl Sandburg, among the poets, and such novelists as Theodore Dreiser, Sherwood Anderson, John Steinbeck, and Thomas Wolfe—all of whom he inspired to deal with free, vital, and progressive elements in the national culture.

20 | PLUCK AND LUCK

Horatio Alger, Jr.'s, *Ragged Dick*, 1868

In American folklore two concepts are firmly fixed in the national imagination. First, great statesmen are born and reared in log cabins, and second, successful businessmen—through scrupulous honesty, tireless diligence, and unfailing loyalty—have progressed from poverty-stricken youth to wealth and eminence.

The image of Abraham Lincoln is clearly discernible in the first tradition. The other is primarily the creation of a phenomenally popular writer of books for boys in the second half of the nineteenth century. Horatio Alger, Jr., the most successful juvenile author in the whole of American literature, thoroughly indoctrinated millions of young Americans, between the Civil War and World War I, with the belief that virtue and hard work invariably bring financial rewards.

In a highly materialistic sense, though on the lowest literary level, the steady stream of books that flowed from Alger's facile pen portrayed the great American dream. Every immigrant landing on our shores, the poor farm boy remote from large cities, and the ragamuffin on the street were convinced, through reading Alger, that America was the land of opportunity. By pluck and luck they could conquer poverty, defeat any villain, marry the boss's daughter, and live happily ever after. Alger's influence on American youth, at the height of his popularity, has been compared with that exercised on British boyhood by his contemporary George A. Henty, in the latter's extended series of books demonstrating Anglo-Saxon superiority in all eras of history.

No one knows how many books Alger really wrote. His name is found on the title pages of 135, but a number ascribed to him were written after his death in 1899. Also unknown, because of lost publishers' records, is the total number of copies sold. It is the considered judgment of Frank Luther Mott, as stated in his *Golden Multitudes,* that the Alger books sold in excess of 17 million copies, though other estimates range as high as 200 million.

In any event, the circulation was enormous and enough to shape the thoughts and attitudes of at least two generations of American boys.

Horatio Alger was born in 1832 in Revere, Massachusetts, the son of a domineering Unitarian minister who insisted that he, too, should be trained for the ministry. After graduating from Harvard in 1852, Horatio spent most of the next five years teaching and writing, completed a three-year course in the Divinity School at Cambridge, and spent nearly a year in Europe. When he returned home, the Civil War had erupted, but Alger was physically unfit for military service. A few months filling a pulpit in Brewster, Massachusetts, proved his unsuitability for the ministry.

Alger began producing children's books as early as 1856, the first a collection of sentimental tales entitled *Bertha's Christmas Vision*. Not until about a decade later did he discover his true niche. In 1867 Alger's *Ragged Dick: Or, Street Life in New York*, appeared serially in Oliver Optic's magazine, *Student & Schoolmate*, and the following year was brought out in book form. *Ragged Dick* caught the public fancy immediately and became immensely popular. Alger was established as a writer, signed a contract with a Boston publisher, A. K. Loring, for six more books, and was on his way to fame and fortune. By this time, Alger had moved to New York. Most of the remainder of his life was spent in and around the Newsboys' Lodging House, an institution which figures in many of his books. Through a warmhearted, sympathetic nature, Alger won the confidence of the boys, became familiar with details of their lives, and drew upon their experiences, in highly idealized and sentimentalized form, for his stories. His settings were most often in the New York of the latter half of the nineteenth century, and he accurately described the city's streets, hotels, boardinghouses, and restaurants of the period.

Alger had predecessors. Benjamin Franklin was the first and greatest native-born American spokesman for the idea of success. In *Poor Richard's Almanack*, Franklin emphasized that the way to wealth depends on industry and frugality, and the theme is developed at greater length in his famous *Autobiography*. A number of less known authors—Oliver Optic, Mrs. Sarah Stuart

Robbins, Mrs. Madeline Leslie, J. H. Ingraham, A. L. Stimson, the Rev. Elijah Kellog, and others—had produced a flood of children's books dealing with the rise to financial security and social respectability of poor boys. None, however, could compare in popularity and sales with the Alger epics.

Throughout Alger's books runs a common thread: the American faith in personal independence and self-reliance—concepts frequently hammered home earlier by Franklin and Emerson. A typical Alger plot centers around a teen-age boy, nearly always fatherless, who must make his way in a great city against heavy financial and social odds. Often he has to support a widowed mother, whose little home or farm is about to be seized by a ruthless banker or village squire because she has fallen behind on her mortgage payments. Whatever the situation, the boy must rely upon himself to solve the problem and to get ahead in the world. The theme is reflected in such titles as *Sink or Swim, Strive and Succeed, Shifting for Himself, Helping Himself, Facing the World, Do and Dare, Struggling Upward,* and *Risen from the Ranks.* The requisites for success are piety, courage, thrift, alertness, punctuality, morality, hard work, and all the related virtues.

The life stories of numerous individuals during the post–Civil War era lent verisimilitude to the Alger rags-to-riches thesis. It was the age of Rockefeller, Carnegie, Vanderbilt, Guggenheim, Harriman, Gould, Fisk, and other multimillionaires to whom great wealth came suddenly. Carnegie had risen from bobbin-boy to steel king; Buck (James B.) Duke from selling home-grown tobacco on the road to becoming a leading tobacco magnate; Thomas A. Edison from hawking papers on Michigan trains to becoming America's greatest inventor; James A. Farrell from a laboring boy in a wire mill to the presidency of the United States Steel Corporation; Henry Ford from a 2½-dollars-a-week job as a polisher of steam engines to the headship of the huge automotive corporation which still bears his name; Julius Rosenwald from selling chromos from door to door to the presidency of Sears Roebuck; and George Eastman from a 3-dollars-a-week job in an insurance office to the founding of the Eastman Kodak Company.

Who can say how many of these individuals and many others who started low on the ladder and climbed to dizzy heights of success were influenced and inspired by the writings of Horatio Alger, Jr., even if during their ascent they failed frequently to adhere to the elevated code of ethics constantly reiterated by Alger and his heroes? Certainly, all would have acclaimed Alger's laissez faire philosophy for American business. As late as World War I, there were many testimonials regarding Alger's influence, including those of Joyce Kilmer, Christy Mathewson, John Drew, William Wrigley, Jr., John Dewey, and Edward W. Bok.

Alger's heroes followed a formula seldom varied in achieving wealth. The standard plot involves an amazing series of coincidences, several acts of personal heroism and generosity, foiling plots laid by a snobbish boy and his villainous father, and the friendship and patronage of a benevolent merchant. The hero is invariably honest, manly, cheerful, intelligent, self-reliant, ambitious, moral, and frugal, but these admirable traits in themselves are insufficient for attaining riches. Chance and luck are always key elements on the road to riches. Thus the Alger plots depend heavily on good fortune, the lucky break, and being ready to open the door when opportunity knocks. A perceptive essay by Russel B. Nye cites examples:

> Ragged Dick saves his pennies, but when he rescues a child from the river her father turns out to be a rich banker who gives Dick a job. Phil the Fiddler, ground under the padrone system, falls exhausted in a snowstorm at the door of a wealthy old physician who has lost a son of Phil's age. Tom Thatcher catches a runaway horse, and in the buggy is the golden-haired daughter of a wealthy Wall Street broker. Sam, in *Sam's Chance*, finds a gold nugget approximately the size of a basketball; the hero of *Bound to Rise* befriends a lonely old man who gives him a sizable packet of downtown Tacoma real estate. Frank the Cash Boy, saves his meager salary, but is really set on his way to wealth by capturing a thief.

In other strokes of fortune, the dead father's seemingly worthless speculation in mining stock suddenly becomes a bonanza; the strongbox which the hero saves from thieves turns out to belong to an eccentric and wealthy old man who rewards the hero; or the upward climb is expedited by other chance occurrences. Alger remarks, "It is precisely to such lucky chances that men are often indebted for their advancement."

It should be noted, however, that luck alone does not account for the success of Alger's heroes. They earn their good fortune by such virtues as industry, fidelity, and good manners, and by possessing qualities of character and intellect which make them desirable members of society. The boy heroes do not smoke or drink, keep late hours, or attend theaters or other places of amusement. They learn to dress neatly and modestly, to refrain from the use of slang and colloquialisms in their speech, and are always good to their mothers. Rychard Fink, in his introduction to a recent reissue of *Ragged Dick*, pointed out that "Alger did far more than push success upon his poor and honest heroes. He gave them dignity and planted it in their natures in such a way that it had the status of a natural right."

No less admirable in Alger's eyes than his young heroes are the rich bankers, merchants, and stockbrokers who were once poor boys themselves, but who seized their chances to rise in the world. These were the men whom Alger's boys hope to emulate. Clear distinctions are made by Alger, however, among rich men. Not all are honorable and wise. There are greedy, antisocial, despicable characters who foreclose mortgages, dispossess widows, and threaten young men with ruin, and there are useless rich men, snobbish, idle parasites. The good rich men in Alger are consistently kind, generous, and virtuous, providing models for the young to follow. In their business dealings they are honest and upright, scorning all but the most elevated commercial practices.

Villains abound in the Alger books. Typical among the adults are a mean stepfather, a grasping uncle or cousin who is the hero's legal guardian, and a cruel, miserly squire who holds a mortgage on the family property. In whatever guise the villain appears, he attempts to assert his tyrannical authority over the hero and comes out the loser.

Perhaps even meaner and more contemptible is the youthful villain as depicted by Alger. One son of the rich, for example, is described as "a boy of sixteen, of slender form and sallow complexion, dressed with more pretension than taste. His mean and insignificant features were far from rendering him attractive." Another character is thus described:

Mark Manning was slender and dark, with a soft voice and rather effeminate ways. He didn't care for the rough sports in which most boys delight; he never played baseball or took part in athletic exercises, but liked to walk about sprucely dressed, and had even been seen on the campus on a Saturday afternoon with his hands incased in kid gloves.

Such young prigs are always snobbish and full of airs, lazy, ignorant, and unwilling to work, and contemptuous of the poor boy whom they regard as beneath them in social status. The rich boys try every dirty trick to gain their ends, fly into temper tantrums when they lose, and in the end are punished for their arrogance by a sudden descent into poverty.

The spirit of democratic equality pervades the Alger tales. The Alger hero is never snobbish or condescending. He is democratic in his tastes, he befriends other poor boys, and never lacks courtesy, modesty, and dignity in dealing with people of all classes. An Alger lad, as described by the author, "was a bright-looking boy, with brown hair, a ruddy complexion, and dark-blue eyes, who looked, and was, frank and manly"; or he might have "a face not handsome, but frank and good-humored, and an expression indicating an energetic and hopeful temperament"; or he could possess "a bright, attractive face, strong and resolute." The Alger hero always defends himself as a free-born American who is as good as any other man. He is generally impoverished by the death of his father, a member of the middle class, and temporarily down on his luck.

Alger's assumption, emerging again and again in his plots, that rural origins increased one's chances for success in a large city is of dubious validity, according to most critics. For example, H. L. Mencken commented, "The notion that yokels always succeed in the cities is a great delusion. The overwhelming majority of our rich men are city-born and city-bred. And the overwhelming majority of our elderly motormen, forlorn corner grocerymen, neighborhood carpenters, and such other blank cartridges are country-bred."

Various attempts have been made to analyze Alger's secret of success in writing books for boys. Parents may have encouraged their children to read the novels because they preached the virtues of hard work, economy, integrity, and family loyalty. But parental recommendations would not have been sufficient without Alger's lively plots, all-black and all-white characters, and exciting locales. The author glorified financial success, and this too must have hit a sympathetic chord, for many of his young readers dreamed of the day when they would be rich enough to buy the things they craved. Furthermore, as John G. Cawelti suggests, in his *Apostles of the Self-made Man,* "Alger has a simple and unsophisticated sense of justice, which punishes the enemies of boyhood. The snobs, the bullies, the uncles and spinster aunts who do not like boys get their comeuppances in ways that must have appealed to a juvenile audience." Cawelti adds a Freudian interpretation: "The late nineteenth century was an era of relatively strict paternal discipline and control," and "the Alger hero's victory over the villainous father-figure" was doubtless a popular touch among the young who felt themselves dominated by overstern parents.

Contrary to the general notion, Alger did not, in his stories, urge the accumulation of great wealth as a worthy ambition. He saw America, instead, according to Henry A. Wallace's diagnosis, "not as a nation of propertyless workers but rather an America where all can become members of what has been called the 'middle class,' where all can share in the benefits which that class has enjoyed in the past." And Rychard Fink concludes, "Alger was a major pump station on the pipe line that carried the American dream. There was not an idea in anything he wrote that was not already in the thought and feelings of Americans. But Alger affirmed the obvious in his claptrap prose with such conviction and energy that the big ideas he transmitted became even more credible."

21 | MENTAL HEALER

Mary Baker Eddy's *Science and Health,* 1875

America has given the world two major religions—the Church of Jesus Christ of Latter-day Saints, or Mormonism, and the Church of Christ, Scientist, or Christian Science. The latter has the distinction of being the only religion founded by a woman.

Throughout the nineteenth century, during which both the Mormon and Christian Science churches were established, occult philosophies flourished. Nonconformist and utopian movements attracted numerous adherents. Particularly appealing in the latter part of the century were such Oriental faiths as Vedanta, Baha'ism, Rosicrucianism, Theosophy, and Yoga, and there were churches of Divine Science, Religious Science, the Science of Mind, and New Thought.

In this highly charged atmosphere, so preoccupied with the supernatural and theological disputation, a new faith was born, Christian Science, destined for a permanence, vitality, and wide acceptance denied a majority of other sects of the era.

The founder of the Christian Science movement, Mary Baker Eddy, was a controversial figure for a major portion of her nearly ninety years of life and remained so after her death. From infancy she was an odd child, given to "fits," temper tantrums, and hysteria. Because of delicate health, she remained out of school for long periods, and thus most of what she learned was absorbed from books at home. Her mind was filled with religion at an unusually early age, and she could hear voices calling her name. At the age of twenty-two, Mary acquired the first of three husbands. None of the marriages was happy or successful, and Mary's poor health continued. When her spells of depression were most profound, and morphine failed to relieve pain, the family called in a local mesmerist, "Boston John" Clark. Mary, who was peculiarly suggestible, became fascinated with mesmerism—an omen of things to come—developed a habit of falling into trances, and began to receive messages from the dead.

The turning point in Mary Baker Eddy's life came at the age of forty, when she heard of Phineas P. Quimby, of Portland, Maine, a man who was reputed to effect miraculous cures through the use of hypnotism or mesmerism, rather than through orthodox medicine. Mary resolved at once to visit the new wonder worker, and secretly and alone she set off for Maine. Three weeks later, in a letter to the local Portland newspaper, she declared that through the great principle discovered by Dr. Quimby, who "speaks as never man spoke and heals as never man healed since Christ," she was well on the way to complete recovery of her health. Thereafter for the next several years she was an ardent disciple of Quimby. She read all his writings and continued to write letters to the newspapers extolling his work. The Quimby method, Mrs. Eddy insisted, did not resort to "animal magnetism," "electro-magnetism," or hypnotism, but was based on a "science not understood." "I can see dimly the great principle which underlies Dr. Quimby's faith and works," she wrote, "the truth which he opposed to the error of giving intelligence to matter."

The essence of Quimby's teaching was to deny all evil and to affirm the reality and possession of all good. His system of mental suggestion is in accord with modern psychiatry. Quimby's fundamental premise was that suggestion would cure disease, and further, that all states of either health or disease were created solely by the mind. Carrying the idea further, it was held that a person would be affected physically by his own mind or by other minds; that is, that one mind could affect the life of another even from a remote distance. Finally, the theory is advanced that the mind creates all objective reality.

In later years violent controversy was to rage concerning Mrs. Eddy's debt to her teacher. At first she remained deeply loyal to Quimby and made extensive use in her own teaching of a Quimby manuscript entitled "The Science of Man." Gradually she lost her sense of dependence upon her tutor and convinced herself that the doctrines developed by him were original with herself. Most non–Christian Science writers believe that Mrs. Eddy derived at least the beginnings of her system of healing from Quimby, though all agree that she added significantly to his thought and even modified it substantially. The official Christian Science view, however, is that Quimby was merely a hypnotist, a mesmerist, making use of animal magnetism, and perhaps something of a charlatan, to whom Mrs. Eddy gave more than she received. If this were true, it is hardly probable that when Quimby died in 1866 Mary Baker Eddy would have written a commemorative poem, "Lines on the Death of Dr. P. P. Quimby, Who Healed with the Truth that Christ Taught in Contradistinction to All Isms."

Another turning point in Mrs. Eddy's career came a few weeks after Quimby's death. The event, generally recognized as marking the actual beginning of Christian Science, is thus described in the Lynn (Massachusetts) *Reporter:*

> Mrs. Mary Patterson [later Mrs. Eddy], fell upon the ice near the corner of Market and Oxford Streets on Thursday evening and was severely injured. She was taken up in an insensible condition and carried into the residence of S. M. Bubier, Esq., near by, where she was kindly cared for during the night. Dr. Cushing who was called, found her injuries to be internal and of a severe nature, inducing spasms and internal suffering. She was removed to her home in Swampscott yesterday afternoon, though in a very critical condition.

The attending physician believed that his patient would never walk again, and possibly her injuries would prove fatal. It was then, Mrs. Eddy wrote, that "I discovered the science of divine metaphysical healing, which I named Christian Science." Opening a Bible by her bedside, her eyes chanced to fall upon an account of the healing of the palsied man by Jesus. The passage became a revelation to her, she arose from her bed, dressed, and walked into the parlor, to the astonishment of a group of friends gathered there. The marvelous experience of healing herself, of recovering from "an injury that neither medicine nor surgery could reach," according to Mrs. Eddy's autobiography published twenty-five years afterward, "was the falling apple that led me to the discovery how to be well myself and how to make others so." "During twenty years prior to my discovery," she continued, "I had been trying to trace all physical effects to a mental cause; and . . . I gained the scientific certainty that all causation was Mind, and every effect a mental phenomenon."

Mrs. Eddy was in her fiftieth year when the first draft was

completed of the book which was to bring her fame and fortune. Three more years were spent in revisions before the volume appeared in print in 1875, a 456-page work. Quimby had called his method the "Science of Health;" Mrs. Eddy entitled her book *Science and Health,* later adding a subtitle, *With Key to the Scriptures.* Two devoted students agreed to provide a subsidy of 1,500 dollars demanded by the publisher.

The first edition of *Science and Health* consisted of 1,000 copies, cheaply bound, crudely printed, and full of typographical errors. Today it is one of the rarest books in the world, for only a handful of copies survive; the remainder have been systematically destroyed. In his *Mental Healers,* Stefan Zweig suggests that "this almost unobtainable version, the only one that was exclusively Mary Baker's work and was untouched by any editorial hand, is essential to the psychological understanding of the book and its author, for none of the very numerous subsequent editions have more than a trace of the primitive and barbaric charm of the original. In later editions many of the wildest tilts against reason, many of the crudest historical and philosophical blunders, have been expunged by better-educated advisers." The text was completely reworked by a retired minister, James Henry Wiggin, who turned out to be an excellent editor.

Successive editions of *Science and Health* were subjected by Mrs. Eddy to rearrangements of chapters, partly in a search for some logical order in the text and in part for financial reasons, since members of the church were expected to purchase the latest edition. The headings in the first edition read as follows: "Natural Science," "Imposition and Demonstration," "Spirit and Matter," "Creation," "Prayer and Atonement," "Marriage," "Physiology," and "Healing the Sick." The last edition is arranged under these chapter titles: "Prayer," "Atonement and Eucharist," "Marriage," "Christian Science versus Spiritualism," "Animal Magnetism Unmasked," "Science," "Theology," "Medicine," "Physiology," "Footsteps of Truth," "Creation," "Science of Being," Some Objections Answered," "Christian Science Practice," "Teaching Christian Science," and "Recapitulation." Two Eddy biographers, Bates and Dittemore, conclude that after all Mrs. Eddy's efforts, "the arrangement of chapters in the last edition is less logical than that of the first," since in its original form the book began with an exposition of general metaphysical principles, followed later by specific application, whereas the final version scatters the discussion of general principles among a number of chapters near the end.

Christian Science as a system of healing had one great improvement over Quimby's doctrine—it was a theology, not merely a method of healing. As stated by Mrs. Eddy's biographer, Dakin,

> The main thesis of *Science and Health*, stripped of its con- tradictions, develops the conviction that Christ came to redeem men not merely from sin but also from sickness and death; that his methods are applicable to a modern age; that all men can heal both themselves and others if they develop the correct Christ consciousness, and this long lost Christ-art was again revealed to mankind in the instruction from Mary Baker Eddy.

The one basic thought is the "unity of God and unreality of evil." In brief, nothing exists but God, and if God is good there can be no evil. Therefore pain and illness may appear to exist, but in reality are due entirely to the "error" of the human senses.

In further elucidation of the doctrine, Mrs. Eddy declares, "The chief stones in the temple of Christian Science are to be found in the following postulates: that Life is God, good, and not evil; that Soul is sinless, not to be found in the body; that Spirit is not, and cannot be, materialized; that life is not subject to death; that the spiritual real man has no birth, no material life, and no death." In making theology serve as a therapy, Mrs. Eddy was convinced that she had discovered and revealed a hitherto-unknown means of divine healing. Man can be troubled by illness, old age, and infirmity only so long as he remains under the delusion that illness and old age exist. The idea that man may be attacked by physical infirmities is rejected by Mrs. Eddy with the declaration that "God never made a man sick."

Mrs. Eddy's adamant belief in the unreality of matter is dif- ficult for those not philosophically inclined to grasp. In this concept, she departed radically from such predecessors as Mesmer and Quimby, who accepted the fact that they were treating material human bodies and attempted to relieve the suffering of their patients by animal magnetism, hypnosis, mental suggestion, or similar devices. But Mrs. Eddy insisted that "man is not matter, he is the composed idea of God"; we merely dream that we have bodies, and man's earthly existence is nothing more than a "dream of life in matter." Though there seems to be no evidence that she was a student of Hinduism or ever read the basic Hindu sacred texts, the whole idea of the unreality of matter could have been taken directly from those sources. As Charles S. Braden, in *These Also Believe,* observes:

> The closest approximation to the thought of Mrs. Eddy is to be found in the Hindu concept of the one Real, and the illusory character of all else. So, also, her fundamental denial of the reality of evil and suffering is an almost exact restatement of one phase of Hindu thought.

The prevention and cure of illness are only one side of Christian Science, but they are the aspect that looms largest in public consciousness. How authentic are the claims of the Christian Science practitioners to having been responsible for innumerable miraculous recoveries? Braden, a nonmember, concedes: "There can be no doubt that myriads of people have been healed and have stayed well, thanks to the help of Christian Science." Mrs. Eddy herself maintained that she had cured consumption, cancer, and diptheria, restored sight to the blind, hearing to the deaf, speech to the dumb, made the lame walk, and caused an eighty-five-year-old woman to grow new teeth. In an appendix to the version of *Science and Health* in current use, entitled "Fruitage," 100 pages are devoted to letters testifying to cures wrought through Christian Science for rheumatism, hernia, tumors, cataracts, heart disease, cancer, Bright's disease, dyspepsia, deafness, rupture, dropsy, kidney disease, eczema, asthma, and a variety of other ailments.

In few instances where remarkable cures have been claimed were there any expert diagnoses of the diseases or objective reports on the results of the treatments. It is also certain that delays among Christian Scientists in seeking medical advice in the early stages of diseases have not infrequently proved fatal. But in situations where applicable, the combination of religious emotionalism and applied psychology in Christian Science have achieved near miracles, especially in mentally disturbed patients. As Dakin points out in his biography of Mrs. Eddy:

> Human experience has tended to indicate, over a long period of years, that the force called suggestion is particularly effective when a state of high religious exaltation can be induced in the subject. Healing through suggestion has been associated with religious ecstasy as far back as there is a record of human history; and modern psychologists and psychiatrists have not been slow to recognize evidence of some important relationship between these two forces.

Christian Scientists are quick to deny, however, that their doctrine is based on mental healing, as practiced by others. "On the contrary," in Mrs. Eddy's words, "the physical healing of Christian Science results now, as in Jesus' time, from the operation of divine Principle, before which sin and disease lose their reality in human consciousness and disappear as naturally and as necessarily as darkness gives place to light and sin to reformation."

In *The Doctors' Dilemmas*, Louis Lasagna reports on a twenty-year study of deaths of Christian Scientists in the Pacific Northwest area. The average age at death was found to be slightly below the average for the state of Washington; no deaths from homicide or suicide occurred; the incidence of pneumonia did not differ from non-Christian Scientists, but malignant disease was much more common among Christian Scientists; diabetes as a cause of death in Christian Scientists was in excess of the national average, and the incidence of tuberculosis was significantly higher; deaths from automobile accidents and accidental falls, however, were almost nonexistent in the Christian Science group.

A phase of Christian Science not mentioned in the first edition of *Science and Health,* but featured forcefully in the second and later versions, was a belief in mental malpractice, identified as "malicious animal magnetism," a mental influence which evil-minded persons could exert, to produce disease or misfortune in others. Such absent mesmerism could make another person sick, if the mesmerist so desired. Mrs. Eddy attributed the ills and difficulties in her own career to "M.A.M.," or the mental malpractice of some of her enemies, and in her writings and in several lawsuits she repeatedly demanded that the courts take cognizance of the crime of mesmeric influence. The death of her third husband in 1882 was blamed by Mrs. Eddy on malicious magnetism. To counteract this baleful influence a method of treatment was devised whereby a group of Mrs. Eddy's friends would gather around and set their minds to warding off the evil feared or anticipated.

The first organization to support the new faith, established in 1876 by an informal group of students, was "The Christian Scientists' Association." Three years later a charter was obtained for "The Church of Christ, Scientist." It is contrary to the church's rules to publish statistics of membership, though in 1901 Mrs. Eddy challenged a critic of her work to match a record which "could start thirty years without a Christian Scientist on earth, and in this interval number one million." On the other hand, writing as late as 1949, Braden concluded that "the total world membership would be certainly not more than 375,000." According to the most recent statistics available, there are more than 3,200 branches of the Mother Church in Boston in some forty-five countries, as well as 278 Christian Science organizations at colleges and universities. In any case, the doctrine that traces physical effect to a mental cause and asserts that the power of prayer and belief will deliver one from sickness has had an influence out of all proportion to the church's actual membership. The whole field of medicine and surgery has felt its impact, as the mental factor in disease receives increased attention from medical schools and practitioners.

An excellent summation of Mary Baker Eddy's extraordinary career appears in Zweig's *Mental Healers*:

> In twenty years out of a maze of metaphysical confusion she created a new method of healing; established a doctrine counting its adherents by the myriad, with colleges and periodicals of its own, and promulgated in textbooks credited with inspiration; established a Church and built numerous churches; appointed a sanhedrim of preachers and priests; and won for herself private wealth amounting to three million dollars. Over and above all this, by her very exaggerations she gave contemporary psychology a vigorous forward thrust, and ensured for herself a special page in the history of mental science.

22 | THE GREAT DISSENTER

Oliver Wendell Holmes, Jr.'s, *The Common Law*, 1881

Oliver Wendell Holmes, the younger, had a theory that every man would demonstrate whatever greatness he possessed by the age of forty. Holmes was barely forty when he published a notable work of legal scholarship, literature, and philosophy, *The Common Law* (1881), a book destined to reshape American jurisprudence. The treatise is a faithful reflection, too, of the credo which subsequently guided Holmes's long judicial career. An American historian, Henry Steele Commager, asserts that "Holmes was indubitably the greatest jurist that the English-speaking world produced in two generations, but he was, for all his dedication to the law, more than a jurist, and his greatness in the law was a product of greatness of mind and of spirit that encompassed more than law."

Holmes's career as a jurist spanned a fifty-year period, from 1882 to 1932; the first twenty years he sat on the bench of the Supreme Judicial Court of Massachusetts, and for the next thirty years he was an associate justice of the U.S. Supreme Court. In commenting on Holmes's extended tenure on the U.S. Supreme Court, Felix Frankfurter, another eminent associate justice, noted that "the Court, during his whole thirty years, was sucked into political controversies more continuous and of more immediate popular concern than at any other time in its history."

The Common Law grew out of a number of articles written by Holmes for the *American Law Review*, of which he was co-editor in the 1870s. As a result of the reputation gained from his work for the journal, Holmes was honored by being invited to deliver a series of lectures at the Lowell Institute in Boston. The eleven lectures presented in *The Common Law* gave the author an opportunity to systematize his ideas into what he described as "a connected treatise."

In *The Common Law,* Holmes deals with the origins of law, particularly the common law, with the history of tort, crime, property, and contract. But Holmes was no mere antiquarian; he was concerned with reasons and with present-day relevance. "It is revolting," he wrote, "to have no better reason for a rule of law than that so it was laid down in the time of Henry IV. It is still more revolting if the grounds upon which it was laid down have vanished long since, and the rule simply persists from blind imitation of the past."

In the opening passage of his first lecture, Holmes states the basic tenet of his philosophy of legal history:

> The life of the law has not been logic: it has been experience. The felt necessities of the time, the prevalent moral and political theories, intuitions of public policy, avowed or unconscious, even the prejudices which judges share with their fellow-men, have had a good deal more to do than the syllogism in determining the rules by which men should be governed. The law embodies the story of a nation's development through many centuries, and it cannot be dealt with as if it contained only the axioms and corollaries of a book of mathematics. In order to know what it is, we must know what it has been, and what it tends to become.

Law, Holmes felt, was as in a constant state of change, reflecting the ebb and flow of life. "The truth is," Holmes declares, "that the law is always approaching, and never reaching, consistency. It is forever adopting new principles from life at one end, and it always retains old ones from history at the other, which have not yet been absorbed or sloughed off. It will become entirely consistent only when it ceases to grow." These are reasons why the legal world must be eternally conscious of history and of historical precedents. Holmes's passion for exploring the past derived also from finding a solution to a problem of his own: to "give some reasonable meaning" to law, and to discover indeed whether the study of law was "worthy of the interest of an intelligent man."

In Holmes's opening lecture, "Early Forms of Liability," the origins of three contemporary rules of law were traced. The first rule holds the owner of an animal of "known ferocious habits" liable for damage which the animal may do to the owner's neighbor. The second rule reads: "A baker's man, while driving his master's cart to deliver hot rolls of a morning, runs another man down. The master has to pay for it." The third rule, enacted into law by Congress in 1851, permits the owner of a vessel which does injury in certain circumstances to limit the amount of his liability to the value of the offending ship. Holmes follows each of the three rules back to its origin in primitive societies—Jewish, Greek, Teutonic, and Roman—and notes how different were the reasons leading to its original adoption from its modern applications.

The second Holmes lecture, "The Criminal Law," demonstrates that the roots of criminal law were planted in the desire for vengeance and that this passion was accompanied by the assumption that the offender, whether thing or person, was guilty of moral blame. The chief purpose of the lecture was to defend the preventive theory of punishment. Public law is meant to discourage acts of private vengeance. "If people would gratify the passion for revenge outside of the law, if the law did not help them," Holmes writes, "the law has no choice but to satisfy the craving itself, and thus avoid the greater evil of private retribution."

In two lectures on torts, Holmes analyzes in depth two extremes of legal thought, one, with ancient English antecedents, that a man is civilly responsible for all damage flowing directly from his acts, however blameless he may have been; the second, that in actions involving negligence, fraud, intent, and malice, only a personally culpable defendant could be charged. Holmes sought for a general principle to reconcile the two doctrines. Here and in other chapters of *The Common Law*, the aim was to break down the walls of formalism and empty traditionalism which had grown up around the law, in America and England. Holmes was convinced that many of the rules, "like the clavicle in the cat," had once served a purpose but had become obsolete. Consequently, "the result of following them must often be failure and confusion from the merely logical point of view."

In his seven succeeding lectures, Holmes dealt with legal history and theory relating to possession and ownership, the law of contracts in all its phases, and finally successions before and after death. There is obvious throughout *The Common Law* a search for objectivity in legal standards, whether the author is discussing crime, tort, contract, or other aspects of the law. Holmes was aware that the era of individualism in interpretation of the law was passing. He had a pragmatic preference for concreteness and specificity in law, accompanied by a mistrust for metaphysical abstractions.

What Holmes stated so emphatically in *The Common Law,* he continued to say for the next fifty years in his legal opinions. Prior to an examination of the practical applications of his philosophical beliefs, however, it would be appropriate, for background purposes, to place Holmes in his historical setting.

There is justification for the view expressed by Max Lerner that "The Supreme Court, when Holmes joined it, was one of the worst in our history. The two great antagonists who had given it, in the eighties, some measure of greatness—Justices Miller and Field—were gone. With the exception of Harlan and White, the men on it were mediocre minds." The dominant economic and political philosophy was laissez faire. Before Holmes came to the Court, and in fact during most of his tenure, the justices were enforcing a limited theory of American democracy. They held that the federal government had highly restricted powers. As late as 1905, the Court ruled that it was unconstitutional to limit working hours, no income tax could be levied on individuals without an amendment to the Constitution, the interstate shipment of goods made by child labor could not be banned, nor could monopolistic practices in manufacturing industries be controlled. Property rights were virtually sacred, minimum wages could not be fixed or maximum prices regulated in peace time, and employers were free to discriminate against union labor. The "due process" clauses of the Fifth and Fourteenth Amendments to the Constitution were frequently cited to block legislative attempts to subject economic power to social responsibility.

In an essay entitled "The Legal and Social Philosophy of Mr. Justice Holmes," James H. Tufts presents a brilliant analysis of the national problems and forces which became Holmes's primary concern:

> In the interval between the Civil War and the Great War, the great legislative movements of interest to political and social

philosophy were of three general groups: (1) the efforts to resist the menace of big business through such legislation as the Sherman Act or the Granger legislation; (2) legislation designed to help the underdog whether the Negro, the laborer or the child; (3) to secure a juster distribution of burdens, such as the Sixteenth Amendment. The reasons were obvious: the great business organization had come to have power of taxation and thereby of control . . . far greater than the taxing powers of the government. It could legislate practically without appeal upon the daily household expenses of every family in the country. It could build up or tear down communities. It could decree employment or unemployment. It could and in several cases did control legislatures and courts.

Holmes immediately found himself in conflict with a majority of the Supreme Court in his conception of the Constitution and its limitations. In one opinion he stressed that "the provisions of the Constitution are not mathematical formulas having their essence in their form; they are organic living institutions transplanted from English soil. Their significance is vital not formal; it is to be gathered not simply by taking the words and a dictionary, but by considering their origin and the line of their growth." In their reactionary decisions, Holmes suggested that the justices were reading their own views into the Constitution and usurping legislative functions.

The power of judges to review legislation was a matter of vital significance to Holmes. A forceful expression of his point of view concerned a case that came up on appeal from New York:

I think the proper course is to recognize that a state legislature can do whatever it sees fit to do unless it is restrained by some express prohibition in the Constitution of the United States or of the state, and that courts should be careful not to extend such prohibitions beyond their obvious meaning by reading into them conceptions of public policy that the particular court may happen to entertain.

Holmes could discover nothing in the Constitution forbidding Congress or the states to experiment with social legislation.

Not that Holmes was an economic or social liberal. Actually, his own philosophy was very conservative. He had no use for social nostrums and regarded socialism and Karl Marx as humbugs; believed that the Sherman Act was based upon "economic

ignorance and incompetence"; distrusted attempts to improve
society by what he deemed futile if not mischievous economic
tinkering; and held illiberal race theories, based on his study of
Malthus and the Darwinian concepts of the struggle for existence
and the survival of the fittest.

And yet Holmes made a clear distinction between private beliefs and public decisions, tolerating legislation which he thought
was folly and experiments that he held to be futile. If the people
wished to make fools of themselves, he is quoted as remarking,
it was not the duty of the courts to prevent them. As Walton
Hale Hamilton points out, Holmes "believes in the right of each
individual—and each community—to choose for himself his own
primrose way to the everlasting bonfire. He is, in short, 'the adult
jurist,' much too well acquainted with the annals of mankind to
be intolerant, much too sophisticated to read his own likes and
dislikes into the Constitution."

Holding the views which he did on the constitutional freedom
for social experiments, Holmes, in his judicial decisions, fought
for equal bargaining power for workers, against yellow-dog contracts, for congressional power to ban interstate shipments of
"the products of the ruined lives" of children, for workmen's
compensation laws, against labor injunctions, for minimum wage
and hour laws, for laws guaranteeing bank deposits and regulating chain stores and trucking, for federal control of slaughtering
and meat-packing, for adequate tax programs, for strong governmental powers both in peace and in war, and for freedom of
speech and thought, especially "for the thought that we hate."
In an eloquent defense of freedom of speech, an issue on which
he felt most strongly, Holmes stated:

> When men have realized that time has upset many fighting
> faiths, they may come to believe even more than they believe
> the very foundations of their own conduct that the ultimate good
> desired is better reached by free trade in ideas—that the best
> test of truth is the power of the thought to get itself accepted
> in the competition of the market, and that truth is the only ground
> upon which their wishes safely can be carried out. That at any
> rate is the theory of our Constitution. It is an experiment, as
> all life is an experiment.

Inevitably, Holmes's conception of the judicial function brought him into conflict with more conservative and less tolerant colleagues on the Supreme Court, as a result of which Holmes in time acquired the title of "the great dissenter." On such important issues as social legislation regulating the hours of work, the minimum wage, child labor, injunctions, open shop, and the right to express opinions hateful to the majority or hostile to the government, almost all of Holmes's opinions dissented from the Court's majority. He recognized the reasons for the Court's decisions, which were designed to protect the interests of the moneyed classes. "The comfortable classes of the community," as Holmes called them, were frightened by socialism and radical proposals, leading "people who no longer hope to control the legislatures to look to the courts as expounders of the Constitutions, and in some courts new principles have been discovered outside the bodies of those instruments, which may be generalized into acceptance of the economic doctrines which prevailed about fifty years ago, and a wholesale prohibition of what a tribunal of lawyers does not think about right." On another occasion, Holmes noted that judges are elderly men and are likely to hate at sight any analysis to which they are not accustomed and which disturbs peace of mind.

As Holmes saw the actions of his fellow justices, they were sworn to defend the Constitution, but in fact were constantly violating it in practice. His dissents, which were stated in affirmative, not negative, terms almost invariably endorsed and supported some positive power in government. Henry Steele Commager observed, "Where Holmes dissented from the majority, it was the majority who usually dissented from the Constitution. Almost all of his dissents came in time to be accepted as good law."

Time has vindicated Holmes, as Commager stated, and his dissenting opinions have been gradually accepted by a majority of the Supreme Court. Four examples may be cited: (1) In 1914, with Holmes dissenting, the Court ruled that an employer had the right to discharge a man who refused to give up union membership; in 1937 the Court upheld the Wagner Act. (2) In 1917 a law banning child-labor products from interstate commerce was declared unconstitutional, despite Holmes's scathing remark that all civilized men denounce "the evil of premature and excessive child labor;" in 1941, the Court upheld the Wage and Hours Act of 1938, one section of which bans child-labor products in interstate commerce. (3) In 1919 the Court declared that the salaries of federal judges were not subject to the income tax; in 1939 the Court reversed the ruling and agreed with Holmes that federal judges should pay income taxes. (4) In 1923 the Court decided that legislation establishing minimum wages for the protection of women was unconstitutional because it violated liberty of contract; in 1937 the Court came around to accept Holmes's dissenting opinion, upholding minimum wage laws for women.

Henry R. Luce, who was basically unsympathetic to Holmes's ideas and principles, conceded that

> Holmes was the elder prophet of that school of American legal realism which brought our nineteenth-century jurisprudence back into touch with the facts of life. He and his friends forced the legal profession to admit that other disciplines, such as Mr. Brandeis' sociology, had something to contribute to the perennial quest for justice; that the distribution of property, especially in a democracy, has some bearing on the right to it; and that even judges may be subject to bias and indigestion.

Holmes's successor on the Supreme Court bench, Benjamin N. Cardozo, appraised his famous predecessor as an outstanding historian and technician and added: "He is today for all students of the law and for all students of human society the philosopher and the seer, the greatest of our age in the domain of jurisprudence, and one of the greatest of the ages."

Equally discerning is a judgment expressed by Arthur D. Little:

> Justice Holmes's greatest contribution both to his profession and his state and country has been his personality. His name will survive because he has been a great human figure more than by reason of the legal questions in the decisions of which he has been a part. . . . Justice Holmes's greatest service as a lawyer was that he showed to all men that the law need not be a dreary competition of sordid interests and that "a man may live greatly in the law as well as elsewhere."

23 | AMERICAN EPIC

Mark Twain's *The Adventures of Huckleberry Finn,* 1884

In a preamble to his greatest and most popular book, *The Adventures of Huckleberry Finn,* Mark Twain wrote, in characteristic style: "Persons attempting to find a motive in this narrative will be prosecuted; persons attempting to find a moral in it will be banished; persons attempting to find a plot in it will be shot." Despite the author's warning, scores of scholars, annotators, critics, and literary historians have explored *Huckleberry Finn's* motive, moral, and plot, chiefly within the past thirty-five years, and the number increases.

Huckleberry Finn has been a best-seller since it was first published in 1884, and translations into foreign languages are more numerous than for any other American literary work. No fewer than 10 million copies have been sold. Furthermore, the audience for the book has always been unrestricted in age or degree of literacy. How can one explain the universal appeal of this story of a fourteen-year-old boy, essentially a social outcast, and his adventures in the pre–Civil War South? The phenomenon cannot be accounted for in simple terms. Bernard DeVoto described the novel quite perceptively as "a faring-forth with inexhaustible delight through the variety of America, the heritage of a nation not unjustly symbolized by the river's flow." Explanations may be found also in the book's dramatic setting along 1,000 miles of the Mississippi; the rich characterizations, most notably of Huckleberry Finn and Nigger Jim; the naïve but profound humor; a succession of exciting events; and a deep understanding of the frailties of human nature. The book has an immense vitality, for Mark Twain poured into it his memories of people and places observed during his childhood in Hannibal, Missouri, in the 1840s and his years on the Mississippi as a steamboat pilot in the 1850s.

Huckleberry Finn is a first-person narrative, told in Huck's own words—a colorful dialect completely true to the period and place, without exaggeration of grammar, spelling, or speech, recorded by an author with a perfect ear for the nuances of folk talk. The story takes up where *The Adventures of Tom Sawyer* ended. After receiving a reward of 6,000 dollars for the recovery of stolen money, as recorded in the earlier book, Huck goes on to report:

> The Widow Douglas she took me for her son, and allowed she would sivilize me; but it was rough living in the house all the time, considering how dismal regular and decent the widow was in all her ways; and so when I couldn't stand it no longer I lit out. I got into my old rags and my sugar-hogshead again, and was free and satisfied. But Tom Sawyer he hunted me up and said he was going to start a band of robbers, and I might join if I would go back to the widow and be respectable. So I went back.

But the well-meant intentions of the good people of St. Petersburg to rescue Huck from the freedom of a tramp's life are in vain. The civilizing process is too painful. A short while later, Huck is kidnapped and carried off to a cabin across the river by his drunken, thoroughly disreputable father, who is after Huck's 6,000 dollars. Whenever "Pap" can get his hands on any money for whiskey, he drinks himself into a dangerous fit. For a time, Huck enjoys the lazy, free-and-easy life, fishing and hunting. Eventually, however, he gets tired of his father's frequent beatings and even begins to fear for his own life. On one occasion, Huck sits up all night in the hut on the island, with his father's gun in hand, fearing it might be necessary to blow his father's brains out. When Pap awakes next morning and asks what he is doing with the gun, Huck invents an elaborate lie about a thief who tried to break in during the night. In order to escape Pap's violence, Huck finally stages a mock murder of himself and flees in an empty canoe that has come floating down the river at high tide.

Huck's first stop is Jackson's Island, about 2½ miles downstream. A few days later he discovers the island has another camper, Nigger Jim, who has run away from Miss Watson because she was about to separate him from his family and sell him down the river for 800 dollars. For a time, Huck and Jim live in comfort in a cave, but then a reward is offered for the black man's capture. It is thought that Jim had killed Huck, and a posse is ready to begin a search of Jackson's Island. The two refugees catch a raft as it is floating by and go on down the river toward Cairo. If Jim can land in Illinois and go north up the Ohio, he will be free. The life of indolent ease afloat on the great river is described by Huck:

> We would watch the lonesomeness of the river, and kind of lazy along and by and by lazy off to sleep. Wake up by and by, and look to see what done it and maybe see a steamboat coughing along up-stream, so far off towards the other side you couldn't tell nothing about her only whether she was a stern-wheel or a side-wheel; then for about an hour there wouldn't be nothing to hear nor nothing to see—just solid lonesomeness. . . . So we would put in the day—lazying around, listening to the stillness.

A succession of bizarre adventures await Huck and Jim. After a thunderstorm a house floats by on the flood, and they go aboard to find a murdered man, who is revealed later to be Pap, though Jim covers his face before Huck has a chance to see the body.

Every night Huck slips ashore at some little village and buys a few cents' worth of meal or bacon; sometimes he "lifted a chicken that warn't roosting comfortable, and took him along. Pap always said, take a chicken when you get a chance, because if you don't want him yourself you can easy find somebody that does, and a good deed ain't ever forgot." Early mornings, before daylight, Huck "slipped into cornfields and borrowed a watermelon, or a mushmelon, or a punkin, or some new corn, or things of that kind. Pap always said it warn't no harm to borrow things, if you was meaning to pay them back some time."

One night in a thick fog, Jim on the raft and Huck in the canoe become separated and spend hours searching for each other. When Huck finally catches up with the raft, he finds Jim asleep from exhaustion and plays a practical joke on him, trying to convince Jim that the fog and other events of the wild night had been simply a dream. But the trick backfires; at first, the bewildered Jim believes Huck's made-up story. Then he realized there had been no dream, and that Huck is trying to make fun of him. In one of the most touching scenes in the book, Jim says:

When I got all wore out wid work, en wid de callin' for you, en went to sleep, my heart wuz mos' broke bekase you wuz los', en I didn' k'yer no mo' what become er me en de raf'. En when I woke up en fine you back agin', all safe en soun', de tears come en I could a got down on my knees en kiss yo' foot I's so thankful. En all you wuz thinkin' 'bout wuz you could make a fool uv ole Jim wid a lie.

Then Jim gets up and walks away without saying anything more, making Huck "feel so mean I could almost kissed *his* foot to get him to take it back." Huck continues, "It was fifteen minutes before I could work myself up to go and humble myself to a nigger—but I done it, and I warn't sorry for it afterwards, neither. I didn't do him no more mean tricks, and I wouldn't done that one if I'd a knowed it would make him feel that way."

The nearer they approached Cairo, the more Huck's conscience troubles him for aiding and abetting Jim's escape from his "rightful" owner. Huck's conscience says to him, "What has poor Miss Watson done to you, that you could see her nigger go off right under your eyes and never say one single word? What did that poor old woman do to you, that you could treat her so mean?" Huck starts to go ashore in the canoe to inform on Jim, but on the way meets two white men with guns looking for escaped slaves. Huck keeps them from going out to search the raft by convincing them that its lone inhabitant is down with smallpox.

On a dark night when "you can't see no distance," Huck and Jim miss Cairo, and shortly afterward their raft is hit by a steamboat. Jim goes overboard on one side and Huck on the other. In the darkness they become separated. Huck grabs a plank and strikes out for shore, 2 miles away. When he lands, he meets the Grangerford family, living in "a big old-fashioned double log house." The Grangerfords are involved in a vicious, meaningless feud with a neighboring family, the Shepherdsons. The two families meet only at church, where

the men took their guns . . . and kept them between their knees or stood them handy against the wall. The Shepherdsons done the same. It was pretty ornery preaching—all about brotherly love, and such-like tiresomeness; but everybody said it was a good sermon, and they all talked it over going home.

In the afternoon Huck returns to the church, and finds "there warn't anybody at the church, except maybe a hog or two, for there weren't any lock on the door, and hogs like a puncheon floor in summer-time because its cool. If you notice, most folks don't go to church only when they've got to; but a hog is different."

The next day the feud is resumed and the final battle breaks out. Buck, the Grangerford's young son, about the same age as Huck, is shot, and Huck, sickened by the wanton slaughter, flees to the raft and the river, where he is reunited with Jim. Only the lovers, the Grangerford daughter and the Shepherdson son, true to feuding tradition and romance, manage to escape their murderous families by eloping.

Shortly after the voyage on the raft is resumed, Huck and Jim are thrown into the company of a pair of rogues, known as the Duke and the Dauphin. One claims to be the Duke of Bilgewater in disguise, and the other says he is the lost Dauphin of France, by rights a king. Actually they are drifters and human scum, living by their wits. The Duke sells medicine, poses as a Shakespearean actor and lecturer, teaches singing-geography schools, and practices mesmerism and phrenology. The King can tell fortunes, cure cancer or paralysis by the laying on of hands, but preaching, missionarying, and temperance revivals are his favorite occupations. Huck is revolted by the King's hypocrisy. "I never see anything so disgusting" is his comment after listening to one of the King's sermons, "all full of tears and flapdoodle." At a camp meeting, the Dauphin passes himself off as a reformed pirate and collects $87.75 and a stolen jug of whiskey from the gullible audience. The precious pair force Huck and Jim to accompany them from village to village, to assist them in their frauds. The climax comes when the adventurers attempt to pose as English brothers of a wealthy villager who has just died, in order to rob his three daughters. Clever work on Huck's part thwarts the plot, and the scoundrels escape just ahead of a lynching mob, but again make Huck and Jim accompany them on down the river.

Now financially pinched, the King and Duke begin to dream up new frauds to perpetrate. At one stop, the King sells Jim for 40 dollars as a runaway slave. Huck is shocked and grief-stricken, to know that anyone "could have the heart to serve Jim such a trick as that, and make him a slave again all his life, and amongst strangers, too, for forty dirty dollars." Conscience-smitten again, Huck proceeds to write a letter to Miss Watson:

> Miss Watson your runaway nigger Jim is down here two mile below Pikesville and Mr. Phelps has got him and he will give him up for the reward if you send.   Huck Finn.

But after agonizing over the matter for a while and recalling all that Jim had done for him and the warm friendship that has developed between them, Huck tears up the letter, even if it meant that he would "go to hell" for his sinful behavior. Having made that decision, the next step is to try to rescue Jim.

When Huck shows up at the Phelps's place, where Jim is imprisoned, it seems that they are expecting a visit from their nephew Tom Sawyer and mistake Huck for Tom. When Tom actually arrives, Huck manages to intercept him and tell him the state of affairs, after which the latter pretends to be his own brother, Sid Sawyer.

The remainder of the book, according to the nearly unanimous verdict of critics and other readers, is anticlimactic. Tom organizes an elaborate "adventure" for freeing Jim, incorporating all the conventional features of hairbreadth escapes in romantic novels. The log cabin where Jim is confined becomes a dungeon, and there is a pretense of a moat and high walls to cross and valiant guards to overcome. As it happens, Miss Watson has died and as a final action had given Jim his freedom—a fact known to Tom, but Tom cannot resist carrying through the extravagant mock rescue of Nigger Jim. So the burlesque liberation of the already-freed slave proceeds with near disastrous consequences; Jim is "rescued" by Huck and Tom, but Tom gets a bullet in the leg from a pursuing posse, and Jim is recaptured.

In the end all is well. Jim is free and Tom is recovering from his wound. Everyone is happy except Huck Finn, who is in effect back where he was at the opening of the story, with the one difference, that Pap is dead. He cannot endure such a civilized situation, and in the last words in the book he says: "I reckon I got to light out for the territory ahead of the rest, because Aunt

Sally she's going to adopt me and sivilize me, and I can't stand it. I been there before."

Vernon L. Parrington, in his *Main Currents in American Thought* calls *Huckleberry Finn* "the one great picaresque tale of the frontier . . . a drama of the struggle between the individual and the village *mores*, set in a loose picturesque framework." Parrington's characterization continues:

Huck Finn is a child of nature who has lived close to the simple facts of life, unperverted by the tyrannies of the village that would make a good boy of him. He had got his schooling from the unfenced woods, from the great river that swept past him as he idly fished, from the folk-tales of negroes and poor whites, from queer adventures with Tom Sawyer; and from such experiences he had got a code of natural ethics.

Soon after its publication, *Huckleberry Finn* was barred from certain schools and libraries for its immoral tone. The censors of the time condemned the book because of Huck's proclivity for lying (always to save himself or a friend), the ridicule of respectability and religion, the profane words, and the bad grammar. Louisa May Alcott is reported to have remarked, "If Mr. Clemens cannot think of something better to tell our pure-minded lads and lassies, he had best stop writing for them." A leading Twain authority, Lionel Trilling, concedes that

in point of fact *Huckleberry Finn* is indeed a subversive book— no one who reads thoughtfully the dialectic of Huck's great moral crisis [whether or not to betray Jim back into slavery] will ever again be wholly able to accept without question and some irony the assumptions of the respectable morality by which he lives, nor will ever again be certain that what he considers the clear dictates of moral reason are not merely the engrained customary beliefs of his time and place.

Huckleberry Finn was of course written and published after the Civil War. John Erskine suggests that "if *Huckleberry Finn* had been written early enough to serve the purpose, it would have been more subtly convincing than Mrs. Stowe's *Uncle Tom's Cabin*, for the dramatic method, without preaching of any kind, here stirs the emotions deeply."

Through *Huckleberry Finn*, Mark Twain was attacking the moral values of the nineteenth century which he thought shabby,

mean, violent, cruel, and hypocritical. Miss Watson, always talking of Providential mercy and who had promised never to sell
Jim away from his wife and children, cannot resist the sight of
800 dollars and agrees to sell him down the river. When Huck
goes to church with the Grangerfords, the minister preaches a
sermon on brotherly love while the armed feudists wait to kill
one another. The King pretends to be infused with divine grace
in order to con the camp meeting. Slavery is only one part of the
social order which Huck has decided to repudiate completely.
In the end, therefore, Huck turns his back on the corruption of
society.

A creation hardly less memorable than Huck Finn is Jim. From
the moment he first appears in the story, a "big nigger" standing
in the kitchen door with the light behind him, Jim is a figure of
dignity. His reasoning ability is slow but highly intelligent, and
his love of the river and natural beauty is comparable to Huck's.
In a way, Jim becomes Huck's spiritual father, protecting Huck
through his folk wisdom, knowledge of weather phenomena, and
the vagaries of the river. Jim's capacity for affection shown in
his feelings for Huck is revealed in even more poignant form
when he speaks of his family:

> He was thinking about his wife and his children, away up
> yonder, and he was low and homesick; because he hadn't ever
> been away from home before in his life; and I do believe he
> cared just as much for his people as white folks does for
> their'n. It don't seem natural but I reckon it's so.

Jim is a treasure of folklore and superstitions. *Huckleberry
Finn* is filled with omens and taboos, mostly of a negative nature:
Don't look at the moon over the left shoulder; to shake the table-
cloth after sundown or to handle a snakeskin invites bad luck;
seeing young birds skip along means rain; don't count the things
you cook for dinner; tell the bees in their hives when their owner
dies, or they will weaken and perish.

"From one point of view," in Clifton Fadiman's opinion, "its
language is the most important thing about *Huckleberry Finn*,
more important than its humor, its characters, the story. . . . It
has in it the casual drawl of the frontier, the irreverent intona-
tion of the democratic idea, and an innocent disregard of all the

traditions of European writing." Lionel Trilling calls the style "a new discovery in the English language." The flavor of the book is shown in such passages as these:

> All kings is mostly rapscallions. . . . The funeral sermon was very good, but pison long and tiresome. . . . When the place was packed full the undertaker he slid around in his black gloves with his softly soothering ways, and making no more sound than a cat, and there warn't no more smile to him than there is to a ham. . . . Hain't we got all the fools in town on our side? And ain't that a big enough majority in any town? . . . The sky was darking up, and the lightning beginning to wink and flitter, and the wind swished and swushed along, and the lightning came brisker and brisker, and the thunder boomed.

Mark Twain's love of nature, and of the great Mississippi in particular, shines through in numerous passages. The river is the story's unifying force. Trilling maintains that "the River makes the book a great book. As with Conrad, we are continually reminded of the power and terror of Nature, and the isolation and feebleness of Man." The broad and ever-changing river, the starry nights, the dense fogs, and fearful storms form a background against which mere man can only appear minuscule. Huck's spirit responds to the quiet stretches: "It was kind of solemn, drifting down the big, still river, looking up at the stars, and we didn't ever feel like talking aloud, and it warn't often we laughed."

Basic insights into the meaning of *Huckleberry Finn* for the modern world are found in an eloquent summing up by Clifton Fadiman:

> Here in this rambling tale about the unimportant adventures of a boy who will probably not amount to much when he grows up (except that he will never grow older) are the matters, the myths, the deep conflicts of the American people: the influence of the frontier, the unresolved problem of the Negro, the revolt against city-convention, the fascinated absorption in deeds of violence, the immense sense of a continent cut in two by a vast river, the type-figure of the self-sufficient frontiersman, the passion for exploration, the love of the hoax, the exaggeration, and the practical joke, the notion of basic social equality, the enskying of youth.

24 | MOTHER'S DARLING

Frances Hodgson Burnett's *Little Lord
Fauntleroy*, 1886

It would be difficult, if not impossible, to name any literary character who has been beloved or loathed by more people than Frances Hodgson Burnett's most successful creation, Little Lord Fauntleroy. Millions read the book immortalizing this juvenile paragon, while millions of others viewed him on stage and screen. The influence of the character on an entire generation of young males was little short of traumatic. A sentimental age, with some taste for snobbery even in democratic America, found perfect expression in the story of an American boy who falls heir to an English earldom.

The author of *Little Lord Fauntleroy*, Frances Hodgson Burnett, was as extraordinary a personality as any in the forty novels and ten children's books which poured from her pen. She was born in Manchester, England, but was brought to America at an early age. Her son Vivian (the prototype of Little Lord Fauntleroy) in a biography of his mother, *The Romantick Lady*, attempts to present her as a wholly charming person. On the other hand, in the view of one severe critic, "Mrs. Burnett emerges from his pages aggressively domineering, offensively whimsical and abominably self-centred and conceited." She wed and shed two husbands (living with the second for some years before marriage), smoked constantly (nibbling a cream peppermint after each puff), and was addicted to bizarre dress, running heavily to ribbons and lace. However eccentric her behavior may have been, Mrs. Burnett became one of the most popular and wealthy writers of her era. Her first stories were sold at age sixteen, and it has been stated that not a word she wrote was ever refused by a publisher.

The initial inspiration for *Little Lord Fauntleroy* came from Vivian, a youngster of eight, who suggested to his mother that she "write some books that little boys would like to read." Until then, she had written only for grown-ups. Almost immediately the plot of a story began to take shape in Mrs. Burnett's mind—with Vivian as the hero. In her words:

> I will write a story about him. I will put him in a world quite new to him and see what he will do. How shall I bring a small American boy into close relationship with an English nobleman—irascible, conservative, disagreeable? He must live with him, talk to him, show him his small, unconscious republican mind. He will be more effective if I make him a child who has lived in the simplest possible way. Eureka! Son of younger son, separated from ill-tempered noble father because he has married a young American beauty. Young father dead, elder brothers dead, boy comes into title! How it would amaze him and bewilder him! Yes, there it is, and Vivian shall he be—just Vivian with his curls and his eyes, and his friendly, kind, little soul. Little Lord Something-or-other . . . and a day later it was Little Lord Fauntleroy.

And so it was. *Little Lord Fauntleroy* began to appear serially in *St. Nicholas Magazine* in 1885, and the following year it was brought out in book form.

The scenario is simple. The Earl of Dorincourt had three sons. He was a hard, bitter, irascible old nobleman, who detested his two older sons, both of whom were dissipated, hard-living young men who died in their prime. The youngest son was an admirable character, but in a fit of temper the father had sent him to America. There he married a beautiful, though penniless, American girl, causing the earl to disown him. A son, Cedric Errol, the future Lord Fauntleroy, is born to the young couple. After the father's death, Cedric and his mother live on in humble circumstances in New York City. Cedric's closest friends are Mr. Hobbs, the corner grocer, Dick the bootblack, and Bridget the washerwoman.

The big change came with the arrival of an emissary from the earl, the lawyer Mr. Havisham, to announce that Cedric was heir to his grandfather's title and fortune. The boy was to accompany Mr. Havisham to England to be properly trained for his new station in life. The earl wanted nothing to do with his daughter-in-law, but provided a house nearby where her seven-year-old son could visit her daily. The earl anticipated with aversion, if not dread, the arrival of his heir, expecting to find an ill-mannered cub, the natural offspring of a loud-voiced, pushing, underbred American mother.

The account of the first meeting between the grandfather and grandson is dramatic:

> And then the Earl looked up. What Cedric saw was a large old man with shaggy white hair and eyebrows, and a nose like an eagle's beak between his deep, fierce eyes. What the Earl saw was a graceful childish figure in a black velvet suit, with a lace collar, and with lovelocks waving about the handsome, manly little face whose eyes met his with a look of innocent good-fellowship . . . there was a sudden glow of triumph and exultation in the fiery old Earl's heart as he saw what a strong beautiful boy his grandson was, and how unhesitatingly he looked up as he stood with his hand on the big dog's neck. It pleased the grim old nobleman that the child should show no shyness or fear, either of the dog or of himself.

Thenceforth the House of Dorincourt is transformed. Fauntleroy wins the devotion of the gouty old earl by his affection, by his belief in his grandfather's generosity, his unbelievably angelic manners, and his precise academic English speech. The earl is persuaded to undertake charitable projects and to improve his tenants' living conditions. Finally, he decides to give a great dinner at the castle for the purpose of showing off the new heir of whom he is so proud.

In the midst of the festivities, Mr. Havisham arrived with devastating news. A woman had come to him that morning claiming that the earl's second son had married her six years earlier, and she had a five-year-old son who was the real Lord Fauntleroy and the heir to the Earldom of Dorincourt. The earl was thunderstruck, but of course Cedric turns out to be the genuine Lord Fauntleroy after all. The spuriousness of the rival's claims is exposed by Cedric's friend Dick the bootblack, who recognized the woman from a newspaper picture as the runaway wife of his brother Ben. The shock of these events brought about the reconciliation of the earl with Fauntleroy's mother, and thereafter the three live happily at Dorincourt.

From the first, *Little Lord Fauntleroy* was a resounding hit. In novel form hundreds of thousands of copies were sold in

English, and the book was translated into French, Italian, German, and other languages. Innumerable later editions were printed. The story's stage career was even more spectacular. The original London company ran for 680 performances. Soon after a New York production opened, 400 companies were touring the United States.

Strangely, except for the author, the lives of nearly everyone associated with the book and the play were blighted by the experience. The original model for Fauntleroy, Mrs. Burnett's son Vivian, became a track star at Harvard and continually heard shouts from the grandstand "Fauntleroy—Mama's boy." When he died at the age of sixty-one, heroically rescuing some drowning yachtsmen, the newspaper headlines read "Little Lord Fauntleroy Dies." Reginald Birch, whose drawings illustrated the original story and who was instrumental in creating the popular image of Fauntleroy—dressed in velvet suit, lace collar, cuffs and sash, and wearing long curly locks, a slim-legged little figure—remarked bitterly a few years before his death, "Oh God, they will still insist on talking about Fauntleroy. All my work of better quality has been pushed in the background."

The young actors who achieved fame for their Fauntleroy characterizations were thereafter forever typed. No matter how well they played their subsequent theatrical roles, all the public seemed to remember was their Fauntleroy performances. On many occasions the role of Fauntleroy was played by girls (Mary Pickford starred in the first movie version), and they were likely to suffer the same fate. One such actress was Elsie Leslie who lived to regret bitterly her own part in the popular play. Over and over she complained that critics and directors did not give her a fair chance, because the memory of her impersonation of Little Lord Fauntleroy lingered on.

But the "Fauntleroy Plague," as it has been called, affected a far larger number of individuals outside the theatrical world. The book and the play instantly created a vogue for long curls, velvet jacket and pants, lace collar and cuffs, and velvet tam-o'-shanter inflicted upon thousands of helpless small boys in the United States. Clothing manufacturers and merchants flooded the market with costumes designed after the stage Fauntleroys. Other manufacturers produced decks of playing cards carrying pictures of the characters in the play; perfumes were named after Little Lord Fauntleroy; a song was composed about him; statuettes in metal, plaster, and chocolate were sold; and toys galore cashed in on the mania.

Mothers all over America found in *Little Lord Fauntleroy* a perfect answer on how to rear boys. Matrons dressed their unwilling sons in the manner of Master Cedric and then fondly exhibited them as though they were in a style show. Naturally, red-blooded American boys were humiliated, hating the clothes and the curls, and rebelled in every way open to them. Neighborhood gangs delighted in throwing mud, snowballs, old eggs, lemons, and stones at the plague victims.

Though the Fauntleroy pestilence spread to practically every community in America, the effects were most noticeable in the large cities, such as Boston, New York, and Chicago. The Chicago World's Fair of 1893 helped to spread the contagion. Women from smaller towns saw the thousands of city youngsters dressed in Fauntleroy costume and proceeded to purchase similar garments for their own sons.

An anecdote about the American novelist Stephen Crane relates that he had a heart full of sympathy for lads who suffered the ignominy of wearing black velvet and lace. Out walking one day, he met two boys attired in the detested garments and with long flaxen hair falling to their shoulders. They were obviously unhappy and tears stood in their eyes. Other boys were playing in old clothes in a vacant lot. Crane gave the two afflicted youngsters money and directed them to the nearest barbershop, where their locks were shorn with clippers. When the boys returned home, one mother fainted at the sight, and the other had hysterics; but one of the fathers sent Crane a box of cigars with an anonymous note inscribed, "From a grateful public."

Another incident was told by Louis Wolheim, who played the title role in *The Hairy Ape*. On a dull hot summer day in New York City a group of boys were leaning against an empty building on Lexington Avenue, wishing for something to relieve the tedium. Relief came from the appearance of a rich boy from Gramercy Park—a perfect replica of Little Lord Fauntleroy. His face was flushed, he looked neither to the right or left, marching straight ahead. The catcalls began: "Pipe them shoes!" "Look at that lid!" "Get on to the shirt front!" To all this the victim made no reply. His fists were clenched, his lips tightly closed, and he kept moving onward. Finally one of the gang yelled: "Hey, who cut your hair?" And then the rich boy turned, and said through set teeth: "My mother, *God damn her!*"

The English writer Marghanita Laski comments on *Little Lord Fauntleroy:* "The usual verdict of adults to-day is that it is a repellent book." That is doubtless an unfair verdict, for as Miss Laski goes on to point out, "It is, in fact, the best version of the Cinderella story in modern idiom that exists." Also, it is a highly moral book, teaching the basic lesson of the value of good character to generations of children.

25 | BRITISH VIEW OF AMERICAN DEMOCRACY

James Bryce's *The American Commonwealth,* 1888

Fifty years after Alexis de Tocqueville came to the United States from France—out of which stay came his classic *Democracy in America*—a British visitor landed on our shores, also for the purpose of studying the nation's political institutions. James Bryce's subsequent two-volume work, *The American Commonwealth* (1888), ranks second only to *Democracy in America* in its deep understanding of American political philosophy, and probably it is second to none as a systematic analysis and interpretation of American government. For decades, the book has served as a basic text for the study of political science as applied in America.

Bryce was a native of Belfast, Ireland, educated at Glasgow, Oxford, and Heidelberg. For about fifteen years, from 1867 to 1882, he practiced law, and from 1870 to 1893 he served as professor of civil law at Oxford. His reputation for erudition was established early; at the age of twenty-four he published an outstanding work of scholarship, *The Holy Roman Empire*. British politics occupied much of Bryce's career from 1880 to 1906, during which period he served as a member of Parliament and successively held the offices of Under-secretary of State for Foreign Affairs, Chancellor of the Duchy of Lancaster, President of the Board of Trade, and Chief Secretary for Ireland. In 1907 he was appointed Ambassador to the United States and held that post until 1913. He was created viscount a few years before his death.

Thus, as Woodrow Wilson pointed out in reviewing the first edition of *The American Commonwealth,* Bryce brought extraordinary qualifications to his task of studying the complexities of American government. "He has breathed the air of practical politics in the country from which we get our habits of political action," Wilson wrote, "and he is so familiar with the machinery of government at home as to be able to perceive at once the most characteristic differences as well as the real resemblances, between political arrangements in England and in the United States." Bryce was also schooled in ancient Roman law and English legal practice and possessed a broad knowledge of comparative politics. To these qualities he added an intimate acquaintance with American affairs based on extended visits and study and was warmly sympathetic to American ways of life.

The American Commonwealth is divided into six parts. The least original part of the work, because it has been dealt with by numerous commentators, is entitled "The National Government." Fresh insight is provided by Bryce, however, as he examines both legal theory and interpretation and the practical aspects and operation of the federal machinery. Congress, the presidency, and the federal courts are discussed from practically every conceivable point of view. The most striking difference between the American and all other governments of the world, Bryce found, is the separation of the executive and legislative functions. Everywhere else the legislature is provided with ministerial leadership or cabinet government in some form. The third element in the system of checks and balances created by the founding fathers is of course an independent judiciary.

The uniqueness of the American Constitution is stressed by Bryce in his opening sentence: "The acceptance of the Constitution made the American people a nation"; and further, "the subjection of all the ordinary authorities and organs of government to a supreme instrument expressing the will of the sovereign people, and capable of being altered by them only, has been usually deemed the most remarkable novelty of the American system."

Bryce questions whether America always chooses its ablest men for the presidency:

> Europeans often ask, and Americans do not always explain, how it happens that the office of President of the United States, the greatest in the world . . . is not more frequently filled by great and striking men. In America, which is beyond all other countries, the country of a "career open to talents," a country, more-

over, in which political life is unusually keen and political ambition widely diffused, it might be expected that the highest place would always be won by a man of brilliant gifts.

The explanations offered by Bryce are that the proportion of first-rate ability drawn into politics is smaller in America than in most European countries (Tocqueville likewise pointed out the difficulties in recruiting men of superior ability for public office); the methods and habits of Congress and of political life generally give fewer opportunities for personal distinction; and eminent men make more enemies than do obscure individuals. Certainly Bryce was mistaken in any blanket condemnation of the quality of men who have attained the White House, but unquestionably a high proportion of mediocrities have occupied the office.

Bryce expressed himself on two frequently debated issues relating to the presidency. He questions the wisdom of an election by popular vote: "To have left the choice of the chief magistrate to a direct popular vote over the whole country would have raised a dangerous excitement, and would have given too much encouragement to candidates of merely popular gifts." The perils of the casual method by which vice presidents are usually selected are criticized, for "if the president happens to die, a man of small account may step into the chief magistracy of the nation." In actual practice Bryce concedes that the electoral college system is ordinarily an election of the president by a majority of the popular vote, even though indirect, but the system may occasionally result in the president's being elected by a minority of popular votes.

The control over foreign policy exercised by the Senate has both advantages and disadvantages, in Bryce's view. The Senate "may deal with foreign policy in a narrow, sectional, electioneering spirit indifferent to foreign affairs," but the system "has tended, by discouraging the executive from schemes which may prove resultless, to diminish the taste for foreign enterprises, and to save the country from being entangled with alliances, protectorates, responsibilities of all sorts beyond its own frontiers"—a conclusion of doubtful validity in the light of recent history.

The senatorial function of confirming nominations submitted by the president is often abused in practice, in Bryce's opinion, as "Senators have used their right of confirmation to secure for themselves a huge mass of federal patronage . . . by means of this right, a majority hostile to the president can thwart and annoy him."

Concerning the House of Representatives, Bryce sees serious drawbacks in the frequent elections and high rate of turnover in its membership. "Uneasy lies the head of an ambitious Congressman," he observes, "for the chances are about even that he will lose his seat at the next election. Anyone can see how much influence this constant change in the composition of the American House must have upon its legislative efficiency."

In a series of chapters, largely descriptive, but sometimes critical and interpretive, Bryce considers in detail the Senate as an executive and judicial body, the work and committees of the House, congressional legislation and finance, the relations of the two houses, and the relation of Congress to the president. Next in order for review are the federal courts, including the Supreme Court, the circuit and district courts, and their relationships to the state courts.

"This complex system of two jurisdictions (Federal and State) over the whole country," Bryce found "after a hundred and twenty years of experience, despite the wonder of foreigners, works smoothly." The lack of conflict results from the principle that federal law must prevail wherever applicable. The Supreme Court, as "the living voice of the Constitution," is admired by Bryce. He notes its responsiveness to the will of the people: "The Supreme Court feels the touch of public opinion. Opinion is stronger in America than anywhere else in the world, and judges are only men. To yield a little may be prudent, for the tree that cannot bend to the blast may be broken." Another characteristic is that the Court's temper and tendencies have varied "according to the political proclivities of the men who composed it," though the changes are slow.

In the light of Franklin Delano Roosevelt's attempt years later to enlarge the Court, it is of interest to recall Bryce's comments. He observes that the number of judges in the Supreme Court is unspecified. "Here was a weak point, a joint in the Court's armor through which a weapon might some day penetrate. As the Constitution does not prescribe the number of justices, a statute may increase or diminish the number as Congress thinks fit, and it is possible the court might be 'packed' for a purpose."

Bryce was the first major writer on political science to treat comprehensively the history, nature, course of development, and operations of state and local government. Earlier commentators had concentrated on the federal system. Bryce considers the state constitutions to be "a mine of instruction for the natural history of democratic institutions," for they are more frequently amended, generally longer, and more filled with minute matters than is the federal Constitution. As Woodrow Wilson remarked, "The states have been laboratories in which English habits, English law, English political principles have been put to the most varied, and sometimes to the most curious, tests; and it is by the variations of institutions under differing circumstances that the nature and laws of institutional growth are to be learned."

With a few exceptions, Bryce was struck by the lack of power of state governors, though in older states and in crises they still had great influence. Most governmental authority is seen to reside in the state legislatures, which Bryce was convinced were even more deficient than the Congress in able and high-minded men among their members. In general, it was his conclusion that "the dignity and magnitude of state politics have declined" as the power of the national government has expanded.

Reminiscent of Lincoln Steffens's muckraking work, *The Shame of the Cities,* is Bryce's criticism of municipal government:

> There is no denying that the government of cities is the one conspicuous failure of the United States. The deficiencies of the national government tell but little for evil on the welfare of the people. The faults of the State governments are insignificant compared with the extravagance, corruption, and mismanagement which mark the administrations of most of the great cities. For these evils are not confined to one or two cities. . . . Even in cities of the third rank similar phenomena may occasionally be discerned.

The plight of municipal government has become more aggravated rather than diminished since Bryce's day, of course, though corruption is probably much less prevalent. Pessimists have even concluded that the largest cities are ungovernable from a practical standpoint and their complex problems virtually insoluble.

"The Party System," the third major part of *The American Commonwealth*, is analyzed in systematic detail. Bryce describes the political "machine" and the political "bosses" and the methods of "practical politics"; sketches party history and the main characteristics of the leading parties; and discusses the conditions of public life which tend to keep the best men out of politics and to produce certain distinctively American types of politicians. The inner workings of nominating conventions are also studied in depth; this mechanism has grown up, according to Bryce, as

> an effort of nature to fill the void left in America by the absence of the European parliamentary or cabinet system, under which an executive is called into being out of the legislature by the majority of the legislature. In the European system no single act of nomination is necessary, because the leader of the majority comes gradually to the top in virtue of his own strength.

The highly significant role of public opinion in American politics and public affairs in general impressed Bryce. "Of all the experiments which America has made," he declares, "public opinion is that which best deserves study, for she has shown more boldness in trusting it, in recognizing and giving effect to it, than has yet been shown elsewhere." This is true, Bryce observes, despite the fact that the Founding Fathers who invented the machinery of checks and balances in government "were anxious not so much to develop public opinion as to resist and build up breakwaters against it," because "they were penetrated by a sense of the dangers incident to democracy." Also of great importance in Bryce's view is that public opinion in the United States "is the opinion of the whole nation, with little distinction of social classes."

In his final section, "Social Institutions," Bryce deals with railroads, Wall Street, the bench, the bar, the universities, the influence of religion, the position of women, the influence of democracy on thought and on creative intellectual power, American oratory, etc., and concludes with some forecasts of the political, social, and economic future of the United States.

Bryce shares many of Tocqueville's views regarding the strength and weaknesses of American democracy. He admires the national acceptance of law and legal methods, restrictions on official authority, and the people's faith in liberty and in their own institutions. In describing the weaknesses, he again follows Tocqueville in a number of important aspects. The chief criticisms concern the general level of political life in America, the low intellectual standard of leadership, and the inefficiency of government. Bryce finds a lack of dignity among the people's representatives, who "behave as ordinary men," and a lack of knowledge and judgment in legislative and administrative affairs. The best talent is not attracted to public life, as a consequence of which all branches of government function below the level to be expected in a great nation.

Two defects of American democracy less observable when Tocqueville was writing in the 1830s are pointed out by Bryce: the corrupt and unethical practices prevalent in party politics and in city governments and the tremendous power of wealth in America. The political machines, rings, and bosses are condemned as "the ugliest feature" in American politics. Civil service reform and better ballot and election laws, Bryce thought, would help to correct the weaknesses which had grown up over a period of years.

Bryce was convinced that American democracy was strong enough to overcome any forces of evil which might menace it. Near the end of his life (he died in 1922) he wrote:

No Englishman who remembers American politics as they were half a century ago, and who, having lived in the United States, has formed an affection as well as an admiration for its people will fail to rejoice at the many signs that the sense of public duty has grown stronger, that the standards of public life are steadily rising, that democracy is more and more showing itself a force making for ordered progress, true to the principles of Liberty and Equality from which it sprang.

26 | FOUNDER OF AMERICAN PSYCHOLOGY

William James's *The Principles of Psychology,* 1890

Until the coming of William James in the last quarter of the nineteenth century, modern psychology was a science yet unborn. Previously, the approach to the field had been philosophical, with emphasis on its ethical and moral aspects. It was James who played a pioneer role in creating a "new" psychology allied with the natural sciences and combining, as Ralph Barton Perry noted, "the methods of observation with those of speculation and reflection."

William James was born in New York City, the son of a theologian, Henry James, and the brother of the novelist Henry James. His background provided ideal preparation for a reexamination of psychology as a science. After a period of study in England, France, Switzerland, and Germany, James entered the Lawrence Scientific School at Harvard in 1861 and in the ensuing years studied chemistry, anatomy, physiology, and medicine, receiving the M.D. degree from Harvard in 1869. From 1872 to 1907, James was a member of the Harvard University faculty, beginning as an instructor in anatomy and physiology, and then serving successively as professor of psychology and professor of philosophy. In 1876, he was the leading spirit in founding at Harvard the first laboratory for psychological research in the United States. James also had the advantage of being well acquainted with accomplishments in psychology in England, France, and Germany, doing much to reshape into lively and understandable language the complicated, overly technical writings of the European psychologists.

Charles Darwin's theory of biological evolution deeply influenced James, and the system of psychology which the latter developed was a comprehensive attempt to explain mind in terms of evolution. After his work in anatomy, physiology, and medicine, James found unacceptable a psychology that stressed the soul and ignored the body. The psychological aspects of life, he held, could be explained satisfactorily only in terms harmonizing with the general theory of evolution. "A real science of man," James wrote in 1875, "is now being built up out of the theory of evolution and the facts of archaeology, the nervous system and the senses." In a letter to the president of Harvard University, the same year, James expressed the view that "psychology cannot be taught as a living science by anyone who has not a first-hand acquaintance with the facts of nervous physiology." As a medical student and teacher of physiology James had acquired all that was currently known about the nervous system, how it received stimuli through the sense organs and transmitted the impulses to the brain.

The climax of James's career as a psychologist was the publication in 1890 of his *Principles of Psychology,* a two-volume work 1,400 pages in length, on which he had labored for twelve years. The publication of the *Principles* was hailed at home and abroad as an event of first importance in the psychological world. It was not only a comprehensive survey of an essentially new subject, synthesizing the facts of psychology, but a major contribution to the field. The book treated psychology as a natural science, with emphasis on the biological aspects. A recent writer, John J. McDermott, calls the *Principles* "actually a running commentary on the total human experience as well as a rich expression of much of its untold psychic activity. To this day, the chapter on 'Habit' is the classic statement on that aspect of human life. No detail is too slight to be given a full and complete hearing in the mèlange of sensations which is open to James's analysis."

As a biologist, James saw the mental processes as inseparable from the activities of living creatures—processes, indeed, which are essential to survival in the world of nature. The American school of psychology known as functionalism grew out of this theory. Further, James stresses throughout the *Principles* the irrational side of human nature and demonstrates that man is a creature of emotion and action as well as of knowledge and reason. The intellect is governed by definite physiological conditions, James was convinced, and belief is determined by emotion and will. The earlier concept of man as a rational being is largely rejected.

One of the most influential doctrines presented in the *Principles* is the "stream of consciousness," a stream of thoughts from which a functioning brain makes selections. The process of selection is synonymous with the mind, and thinking or intelligence may be defined as the ability to select. As summarized by Gay Wilson Allen, James's biographer, James maintained that "the mind or consciousness is never empty, even in sleep; something is always in it, and the content is always changing, accumulating new images, points of attention, or 'thoughts' in the process, so that, like a river, it seems to flow in one direction. Even when the mind attempts to retrace its course, it is never the same course because the contents have changed in many subtle ways."

The British philosopher John Locke had divided ideas into simple and complex categories, arguing that the mind takes simple ideas and combines them into complex structures in any process of logical reasoning. James rejected such a classification and also the doctrine of "association of ideas" which had previously prevailed. So-called reasoning, he held, is usually nothing more than rationalizing, in an attempt at self-justification or to satisfy emotional needs. Thus all thought is shaped by the individual thinker's needs, likes, dislikes, and peculiarities. According to James, the primary mental fact is that thinking of some kind goes on, but he insisted that "no one ever had a simple sensation by itself. Consciousness, from our natal day, is of a teeming multiplicity of objects and relations, and what we call simple sensations are results of discriminative attention, pushed often to a very high degree."

Another concept with which James's name is closely associated is his celebrated theory of the emotions, sometimes referred to as the James-Lange theory, since the Danish physiologist Carl George Lange presented a similar idea almost simultaneously. The essence of the theory is that the causes of emotion are entirely physiological; bodily changes follow perception of the stimulus, and the subjective feeling of these changes, such as quickened heart beats, shallow breathing, and trembling, as they occur, constitutes the emotion. As James expresses the hypothesis,

"We feel sorry because we cry, angry because we strike, afraid because we tremble, and not that we cry, strike, or tremble, because we are sorry, angry, or fearful, as the case may be." Interpreting the meaning of his theory of emotions in its psychological applications, James continues:

> It makes us realize more deeply than ever how much our mental life is knit up with our corporeal frame, in the strictest sense of the term. Rapture, love, ambition, indignation, and pride, considered as feelings, are fruits of the same soil with the grossest bodily sensations of pleasure and pain.

In developing the theory of emotions, James was influenced by Darwin's ideas, which inclined him to link the emotions with the instincts. A recent critic of James's psychological teaching, Margaret Knight, questions the theory. She does not deny that emotions have physical causes, adding, "but modern research has shown that they are caused primarily by processes in the thalamic region of the brain . . . which give rise (via the autonomic nervous system) to the involuntary physical changes by which the emotion is accompanied."

Closely associated with James's theory of consciousness was his doctrine of the will. A basic question is whether human beings are largely automatons whose behavior is determined by their environment and heredity, or whether it is possible for them, through exertions of will, to act otherwise. No system of ethics, for example, is possible without free will. Individual differences, of course, are inevitable, as James points out:

> When a dreadful object is presented, or when life as a whole turns up its dark abysses to our view, then the worthless ones among us lose their hold on the situation altogether, and either escape from its difficulties by averting their attention, or if they cannot do that, collapse into yielding masses of plaintiveness and fear. . . . But the heroic mind does differently. To it, too, the objects are sinister and dreadful, unwelcome, incompatible with wished-for things. But it can face them if necessary, without for that losing its hold upon the rest of life.

The latter type of mind can maintain some control over its destiny and learn to play the game of life to its own advantage. A person with such a mind becomes a master of life, able to direct his own experience and to influence the lives of others, for, James asserted, "we draw new life from the heroic example."

Perhaps the most famous of all James's chapters is "Habit." The benign effect of routine and the cumulative significance of little acts are summed up by James in the statement: "Sow an action, and you reap a habit; sow a habit and you reap a character; sow a character and you reap a destiny." The importance of *first experience* in shaping future experiences was emphasized by James, who noted that once a neural path has been established by habit, it will be traveled again and again unless some stronger force breaks a new path. The effects of the "law of habit" are described as follows:

> The great thing, then, in all education, is *to make our nervous system our ally instead of our enemy.* It is to fund and capitalize our acquisitions, and live at ease upon the interest of the fund. The more of the details of our daily life we can hand over to the effortless custody of automatism, the more our higher powers of mind will be set free for their own proper work. There is no more miserable human being than one in whom nothing is habitual but indecision. Full half the time of such a man goes to the deciding, or regretting, of matters which ought to be so ingrained in him as practically not to exist for his consciousness at all.

Good habits, James maintains, are a great boon to man and should be carefully cultivated; by taking advantage of the "plasticity of the living matter in our nervous system" they make the difficult easy. Beginning as early in life as possible, useful actions should be made automatic and habitual. By adulthood, the good and bad habits which man has formed effectively suppress most natural impulses. In the adult, James says, "nine hundred and ninety-nine thousandths of our activity is purely automatic and habitual." It is thus clear that in forming habits man is shaping his own future self. As a method of forming good habits, James suggests four rules:

> We must take care to *launch ourselves with as strong and decided initiative as possible. . . . Never suffer an exception to occur till the new habit is securely rooted in your life. . . . Seize the very first possible opportunity to act on every resolution you make, and on every emotional prompting you may experience in*

the direction of the habits you aspire to gain. . . . Keep the faculty of effort alive in you by a little gratuitous exercise every day.

Reflecting his medical training, James emphasized "exceptional mental states" in his writings, thus pioneering in the study and development of abnormal psychology and psychopathology. He drew freely on the researches of three French psychologists and neurologists, Jean Martin Charcot, Pierre Janet, and Alfred Binet, who had undertaken the first important investigations of the phenomena of disassociation. Such matters as multiple consciousness, subconsciousness, hallucination, the hypnotic trance, and various aspects of hysteria were extensively treated by James. He was fascinated by unusual psychical phenomena, devoted years of thought and research to reports of occult phenomena, and served as president of the Society for Psychical Research. These activities were condemned by most contemporary psychologists, on the ground that they were unscientific. But their disapproval in no way deterred James, who was a nonconformist by nature, hospitable to the examination of all doctrines, even those of the "faith healers" and "mental healers," no matter how much despised by the orthodox. His keen interest in mental illness and citation of numerous case histories drawn from clinical psychology anticipated psychoanalysis and psychiatry. James was among the first proponents of a theory of the subconscious mind.

After publication of the *Principles,* James expressed frankly his views on the state of psychology in his time. As a science, he wrote, "Psychology is the condition of physics before Galileo and the laws of motion, of chemistry before Lavoisier and the notion that mass is preserved in all reactions. The Galileo and the Lavoisier of psychology will be famous men indeed when they come, as come they some day surely will, or past successes are no index to the future." James regarded his own monumental treatise as exploratory and provisional. Eventually, he hoped, laws would be discovered that would make possible the prediction and control of mental life.

In summing up the impact of James's work, Lloyd Morris, in his *William James: The Message of a Modern Mind,* concludes:

The Principles appears to be one of the major watersheds of twentieth-century thought. Directly or indirectly, its influence has penetrated politics, jurisprudence, sociology, education and the arts. In the domain of psychology, it has foreshadowed nearly all subsequent developments of primary importance. Viewed retrospectively, the permanent significance of *The Principles* was incentive. It explored possibilities and indicated directions.

Largely because of James, American psychology made a smooth transition from mental philosophy to a science. Henceforth, the distinction between philosophical matters, such as the problems of the soul and the psychological aspects of life, could be established with reasonable exactitude. In James's time, psychology lacked the hard facts essential to the creation of a mature science, but he showed that such facts must be obtained on the basis of experience and of experimental verification. As Knight states, the *Principles*, "though it is inevitably out of date on points of detail, is almost startlingly modern in its general approach. Most of the unsolved problems with which James was preoccupied—such as the relation between brain-processes and consciousness, or the physiology of the learning process—are still unsolved, and still burning questions, to-day." Unquestionably, James was years ahead of his time in his view that psychology should be more closely allied with biology and physiology than with philosophy. James's recognition that psychology was in a state of infancy when he was writing is evidenced by a passage in his last chapter:

> Even in the clearest parts of psychology our insight is insignificant enough. And the more sincerely one seeks to trace the actual course of *psychogenesis,* the steps by which as a race we may have come by the peculiar mental attributes which we possess, the more clearly one perceives "the slowly gathering twilight close in utter night."

27 | MOTHER OF LEVEL MEASUREMENTS

Fannie Farmer's *The Boston Cooking-School Cook Book*, 1896

Until such Johnny-come-latelies as the *Better Homes and Gardens Cookbook*, Betty Crocker's *New Picture Cookbook*, and Elizabeth Woody's *Pocket Cook Book* spurted ahead of it, Fannie Farmer's *Boston Cooking-School Cook Book* had been the champion best-seller of all time in its field. Even in the midst of such lively competition, Hackett, in her *Seventy Years of Best Sellers*, reports that the Farmer classic was sixth in sales among all hard-bound American books from 1859 to 1965.

Fanny Farmer's original cookbook, published in 1896, was a plain-looking volume of 557 pages selling for 2 dollars. The publisher, Little, Brown & Company of Boston, had so little faith in it that the first edition was limited to 3,000 copies—printed at the author's expense. But as sales mounted and edition after edition appeared, the skeptics were quickly converted. The eleventh edition was issued in 1965, and track has been lost of the number of printings.

Miss Farmer selected an appropriate quotation from John Ruskin to preface her book:

> Cookery means the knowledge of Medea and of Circe and of Helen and of the Queen of Sheba. It means the knowledge of all herbs and fruits and balms and spices, and all that is healing and sweet in the fields and groves and savory in meats. It means carefulness and inventiveness and willingness and readiness of appliances. It means the economy of your grandmothers and the science of the modern chemist; it means much testing and no wasting; it means English thoroughness and French art and Arabian hospitality; and, in fine, it means that you are to be perfectly and always, ladies—loaf givers.

The Boston Cooking-School Cook Book appeared at a time highly propitious for its success. The amateur or professional cook could choose between such pamphlets as *Fifteen-cent Dinners for Families of Six*, with their very imprecise directions, or enormous tomes by professional chefs of Paris or Delmonico's, whose instructions presupposed huge kitchens, richly stocked pantries, and large staffs. In contrast, Fannie Farmer's book was simple, comprehensive, and aimed at an average-sized family of six, with not more than one servant.

That Boston should be the birthplace of a work which was to become the standard guide for the setting of American tables was in itself a curious anomaly. The Puritans had once preached hell-fire to those who took pleasure in eating. Shortly before the book came out, one of the Concord sages, Bronson Alcott, had been proclaiming the virtues of high thinking and plain living—mostly on apples and vegetables. Fannie Farmer was undeterred by such austere traditions.

The original edition of *The Boston Cooking-School Cook Book*, along with recipes and menus, gave elaborate instructions for building fires with such fuels as kerosene, gas, wood, charcoal, coal, coke, and alcohol. In harmony with the custom for bounteous meals which prevailed in the 1890s, the menus recommended would shock modern calorie counters. Breakfast might end up with a generous wedge of apple pie or a piece of strawberry shortcake. A full-course dinner consisted of ten to a dozen courses, including, for example, clams or oysters, soup, *rissoles* or *bouchées*, fish, venison, beef or mutton, a meat entree or light fish, one vegetable, cheese or punch, game with salad, cold dessert with fancy cakes, bonbons, crackers and cheese, and *café noir*.

Miss Farmer did not discuss such new-fangled subjects as calories and vitamins, but that she was aware of scientific research in the field is shown by her brief preface to the first edition:

> With the progress of knowledge the needs of the human body have not been forgotten. During the last decade much time has been given by scientists to the study of foods and their dietetic value, and it is a subject which rightfully should demand much consideration from all. I certainly feel that the time is not far

distant when a knowledge of the principles of diet will be an essential part of one's education. Then mankind will eat to live, will be able to do better mental and physical work, and disease will be less frequent.

Recent editions of the *Cook Book* recognize only gas and electricity as fuels for cooking, and a variety of information is offered on vitamins, calories, and menu planning. Life for the cook and chef has been immensely simplified by refrigerators, deep freezes, electric blenders, and pressure cookers—all unavailable in 1896.

The most important principle introduced into cooking by Fannie Farmer was uniform, accurate measurements. The cookbooks of her day contained only the vaguest of rules: "add flour to thicken," or "a pinch of lard," or "butter size of an egg" (pullet's or ostrich's?), or "scant cupful," or "rounded teaspoon," or "heaping spoonful." After Fannie Farmer, "the Mother of Level Measurements," it would never be necessary for housewives to wonder about the size of the egg or how heaping a tablespoon should be. Her tablespoons were never heaping, scant, or generous, but always level. Cups and teaspoons were level, too. The cup or spoon was to be dipped into the flour or sugar, a knife used to cut off the top, and what was left fitted exactly into the utensil used for measuring, the surface even with the top of the cup or the edges of the spoon. And so Fannie Farmer's system of level measurements, as elementary as the decimal system, changed cooking from a guessing game to a near science.

"Correct measurements are absolutely necessary to obtain the best results," stated Miss Farmer's *Cook Book*. "Good judgment, with experience, has taught some to measure by sight, but the majority need definite guides. . . . A cupful of liquid is all the cup will hold. A tea or tablespoonful is all the spoon will hold."

Also elementary were some of Aunt Fannie's other pointers for the novice in the kitchen: "To bake," in case anyone was in doubt, "is to cook in an oven"; "To boil is to cook in boiling water (212° F. at sea level)."

The main object of the Farmer book was to cover what is known in America as "good home cooking," without exploring too deeply the matter of glamorous gourmet and foreign dishes. For those with expansive ideas there was a sunshine cake requiring ten eggs; but for the economical minded, a recipe for a one-egg cake was included. To her meat and fish recipes, Miss Farmer added warmed-over dishes—croquettes, hash, and casseroles— all designed to be prepared in the most appetizing fashion. Thus, from "Baked Ham with Champagne Sauce" to "Poor Man's Pudding" (rice) few well-known dishes were missed.

Presented for the first time in Fannie Farmer's *Cook Book* was a complete soup-to-nuts collection of formulas so easy to follow that anyone could go into the kitchen and learn to cook by them. Though more emphasis was placed on eating for health than for enjoyment, the recipes obviously were aimed also at achieving delicious flavors.

When first published, *The Boston Cooking-School Cook Book* contained many recipes calling for wine and brandy. Such recipes were removed when prohibition went into effect, but they have been restored in recent editions. During her lifetime, Fannie Farmer was continually devising new recipes, thoroughly testing each one before putting it in her book.

The origin and development of this most famous of cookbooks can perhaps be best understood and appreciated by reviewing the author's background. Fannie Farmer was born in 1857, the daughter of a printer and ex-newspaperman. When seventeen years of age, she was stricken with a mysterious "paralysis" which crippled her for life. The misfortune forced the cancellation of plans to attend college. Eventually, Fannie recovered her health sufficiently to assist her mother in housekeeping. During that period, she developed such an interest in cooking that her family urged her to enter the Boston Cooking School. After her graduation from that institution in 1889, she was asked to remain as assistant to the director. Two years later she became the head of the school. It was while in the latter position that Fannie Farmer, age thirty-eight, wrote her cookbook. Originally, the book was privately printed, and its sale was confined to Miss Farmer's pupils. Publication in 1896 soon made its author so famous and wealthy that she proceeded to organize a school of her own, Miss Farmer's School of Cookery, which has flourished down to the present day.

In the Boston Cooking School the courses were designed for the training of teachers, but in Miss Farmer's own school the courses were planned for the training of housewives. The director's main interest was in practice not theory. Her school specialized in invalid cookery, supplied lecturers on that subject to training classes for nurses, and Miss Farmer herself gave a course on invalid cookery one year at the Harvard Medical School. A book in which she took particular pride, *Food and Cookery for the Sick and Convalescent,* never attained the popularity of her original masterpiece.

In her School of Cookery, Miss Farmer taught twice a week, dramatizing her lectures as she limped briskly about the demonstration platform. The classes were largely attended, usually by about two hundred students, and were reported at length in the Boston *Transcript.* In addition, Miss Farmer was much in demand for addresses to women's clubs, and for ten years, assisted by her sister, she conducted a popular page on cookery in the *Woman's Home Companion.*

Meanwhile, Miss Farmer's health, never completely normal after her teen-age illness, grew worse. In 1907, when she was fifty, she suffered another stroke which completely paralyzed her legs. Thereafter, she moved about on crutches or spoke to her students and other audiences from a wheelchair. Her last lecture was delivered only ten days before her death, in 1915 at the age of fifty-eight. Succeeding editions of the *Cook Book* have remained in the family, edited first by Fannie's sister, Cora D. Perkins, and next by Mrs. Dexter Perkins, Miss Farmer's niece by marriage.

It is not surprising that *The Boston Cooking-School Cook Book* has been the target of criticism by epicureans, gourmets, and gourmands, with their widely individual notions about what constitutes good food. Culinary savants, with a background in foreign cuisines, especially French, are practically unanimous in turning up their noses at "Fannie." Their attitude is expressed by Bill Rhode, an editor of *Gourmet Magazine*:

> The bride who goes into the kitchen for the first time with perspiration on her brow, desperation in her eye and a frying pan in her hand couldn't ask for a wiser counseler than Miss Farmer. She will teach her all the basic things—how to boil and broil and so on. But if, after the novice becomes mistress of the fundamentals, she yearns to achieve the nuances and subtleties of really great cooking, she will have to find another instructor.

"Fannie" is a good guide on the foothills but not on the mountains.

Another critic who savored the best in food and drink was H. L. Mencken, who reviewed the *Cook Book* in typical Menckenesque language. Mencken first commends the book for its "clarity, comprehensiveness and common sense," and recognizes that it is planned to serve ordinary housekeepers in kitchens with limited equipment, not "professional chefs with hordes of potato-peelers, beef-steak-beaters and fish-flayers to help them." "The weaknesses of the work," as seen by Mencken, "lie in two directions. First, it is written by a woman and addressed to women, and hence a certain tea-table preciosity gets into some of its récipés. What male with a normal respect for his pylorus, even in America, would actually eat a rasher of celery fritters? Or one of cherry fritters? Or one of sponge fritters? Clam fritters, yes, and apple and banana fritters perhaps, but who could imagine peach, apricot, pear or orange fritters?"

Mencken continues:

> The other defect of the book apparently flows out of the fact that it was hatched in Boston, where lower middle class British notions of cookery still prevail. Thus it deals very badly with the great dishes of more cultured regions. The récipé for terrapin à la Maryland, with its use of flour, cream and eggs, would make a true Marylander howl and so would the récipé for fried soft crabs . . . an obscenity almost beyond belief.

Nevertheless, though Mencken holds that the Farmer opus is "too feminine" and "a shade too Yankee," it is "a very worthy work" and if followed closely would improve American cookery —"not a great deal perhaps, but still some."

28 | PREDATORY MAN

Thorstein Veblen's *The Theory of the Leisure Class,* 1899

Social criticism was approached by Thorstein Veblen, remarked one commentator, "as if he were some expert envoy-extraordinary sent from a distant planet to report on human behavior." His *Theory of the Leisure Class* (1899) is one of the most scathing criticisms of the American social order—indeed of the social behavior of mankind in general—ever penned by an American writer. His ruthless dissection of the actions of the wealthy and powerful and their emulators has been compared to the scientific objectivity of a zoologist examining a cageful of monkeys. To Veblen, human behavior was the most fascinating spectacle in the universe.

Veblen, the child of Norwegian immigrants, was congenitally a nonconformist, a rugged individualist, always the square peg in a round hole. Throughout his life he was plagued by poverty— doubtless a factor reflected in his caustic literary style. Veblen's cross-grained personality led him into continual conflict with his environment. Nevertheless, there is little dissent from the view that he was one of the most remarkable intellects produced by America. "The last man who knew everything," he wrote freely upon such diverse fields as economics, political science, history, anthropology, sociology, technology, biology, and the physical sciences.

Veblen's aim in the first of his dozen books, *The Theory of the Leisure Class,* was "to discuss the place and value of the leisure class as an economic factor in modern life." He begins with a simple definition of the leisure class: "This class emerged gradually during the transition from primitive savagery to barbarism, during the transition from a peaceable to a consistently warlike habit of life." The economic history of mankind is traced from the primitive caveman to the social elite of our own time.

In the beginning was the "peaceful savage," living in a "Golden New Stone Age," non-warlike, lazy, with few material needs or desires, and lacking any urge to compete with his neighbors for the ownership of property.

This Eden was followed by the "predatory barbarian," as population grew, and hunting grounds were extended. Conflicts occurred with members of strange tribes, and enemy women were captured and brought home. With the coming of handicrafts and agriculture, women—being the weaker sex—were assigned the drudgery of preparing food and clothing. Establishment of the marriage custom resulted in households with male heads. Since strength, bravery, and warlike ability were needed to conquer enemy men and to take their women, the possession of multiple wives won prestige for their owner among his fellows.

Here was Veblen's theory of the origin of individual ownership, of the idea that all useful work, except hunting, should be assigned to women and other inferiors and that therefore all productive labor is beneath the dignity of the lordly male. "Conspicuous leisure," as Veblen calls it, was a mark of the idler's superiority, setting him apart from persons forced to work for a living. In feudal Europe and old Japan, for example, the upper classes were by custom exempt or excluded from industrial occupations. "Chief among the honourable employments in any feudal community," notes Veblen, "is warfare; and priestly service is commonly second to warfare." Manual labor, industry, whatever has to do directly with the everyday work of getting a livelihood, is the exclusive occupation of the inferior class. The inferior class includes slaves and other dependents and ordinarily also all the women. Acceptable occupations for the leisure class, in addition to warfare and religious observances are government and sports. Lower grades of the leisure class may be employed in subsidiary roles, such as "the manufacture and care of arms and accoutrements and of war canoes, the dressing and handling of horses, dogs, and hawks, the preparation of sacred apparatus, etc."

The emergence of a leisure class from primitive savagery to barbarism and beyond is a gradual process, as described by Veblen:

The conditions apparently necessary to its emergence in a consistent form are: (1) the community must be of a predatory habit of life (war or the hunting of large game or both); that is to say, the men, who constitute the inchoate leisure class in these cases, must be habituated to the infliction of injury by force and stratagem; (2) subsistence must be obtainable on sufficiently easy terms to admit of the exemption of a considerable portion of the community from steady application to a routine of labour.

According to the barbarian code of relative values, "the taking of life—the killing of formidable competitors, whether brute or human—is honourable in the highest degree."

Veblen points out, in a key chapter on conspicuous leisure, that it is not sufficient merely to possess wealth or power in order to obtain the admiration and esteem of one's peers: "The wealth or power must be put in evidence, for esteem is awarded only on evidence." In earlier stages of society, the accepted evidence of wealth was "the possession of many women, and presently also of other slaves engaged in attendance on their master's person and in producing goods for him." After a while, as the master's affluence increases, the wife or the chief wife may be exempted from industrial employment, as are servants whose duties are primarily concerned with personal service. There is a vital difference, however, between the master's leisure and any leisure granted to women and servants, for "the duties performed by the lady, or by the household or domestic servants, are frequently arduous enough, and they are also frequently directed to ends which are considered extremely necessary to the comfort of the entire household." The principal reasons for maintaining a staff of servants today, Veblen judges, is to free their masters for such demonstrations of conspicuous leisure as "calls, drives, clubs, sewing-circles, sports, charity organizations, and other like social functions," and to care for the accumulation of goods represented by conspicuous consumption: dwellings, furniture, bric-a-brac, wardrobe, and meals.

Teaming up with conspicuous leisure is conspicuous consumption. "In the nature of things," remarks Veblen, "luxuries and the comforts of life belong to the leisure class." Certain victuals and beverages illustrate the point:

The ceremonial differentiation of the dietary is best seen in the use of intoxicating beverages and narcotics. If these articles of consumption are costly, they are felt to be noble and honorific. Drunkenness and the other pathological consequences of the free use of stimulants therefore tend in their turn to be honorific, as being a mark, at the second remove, of the superior status of those who are able to afford the indulgence.

Conspicuous consumption, Veblen's analysis continues, is represented also by the accumulation of material things, not for need, but to impress one's neighbors. Chiefs, kings, and nobles competed for more servants, more elegant palaces and castles, and more expensive and showy clothes and jewels. "Conspicuous waste" was believed by Veblen to be the ruling canon of leisure-class life. The more useless an activity, service, or article, the greater the consumer's prestige. Fox hunting, for example, is superior to deer hunting, because the deer can be eaten; a butler or footman ranks ahead of a cook; and handicrafts are preferred to the machine-made product because they are scarcer and cost more. Maintenance of servants who produce nothing, says Veblen, evidences greater wealth, position, and prowess than the possession of slaves who produce goods, for useless servants are proof of the great captain's or chieftain's ability "to sustain large pecuniary damage without impairing his superior opulence."

The principle of conspicuous waste is illustrated also by domestic pets, such as caged birds, cats, dogs, and fast horses. The cat is the least reputable because "she may even serve a useful end" and in any event "lives with man on terms of equality." The dog is the favorite among the pets, for he is not only useless but has "special gifts of temperament" which feed the human ego. The dog, asserts Veblen, "is the filthiest of the domestic animals in his person and the nastiest in his habits. For this he makes up in a servile, fawning attitude towards his master, and a readiness to inflict damage and discomfort on all else." Further, "The dog is at the same time associated in our imagination with the chase—a meritorious employment and an expression of the honourable predatory impulse." The case of the fast horse is much like that of the dog—expensive, wasteful, and useless for any industrial purpose.

In contrast, the domestic animals that are industrially useful to a community—barnyard fowl, hogs, cattle, sheep, goats, and draft horses—are held in low repute and possess no social status.

Fashions in clothes are a perfect representation of conspicuous consumption and waste. The preference is for the unesthetic, ostentatious, and nonfunctional. Forms of dress which will give evidence of material wealth are of ever-increasing grotesqueness and wastefulness. Women's fashions are primarily designed to show that the wearer cannot engage in any productive activity while wearing them: the corset, the long skirt, the bustle, the hoop skirt, the high heel, the towering coiffure. In the same category are the bound feet of Chinese women and the old Russian aristocratic custom of allowing nails to grow so long and curved that all work with the hands was impossible. Styles must be continually changed to provide fresh opportunities for conspicuous waste.

The predatory traits characteristic of the leisure class Veblen sees as evidence of arrested moral development: "ferocity, self-seeking, clannishness, disingenuousness, a free resort to force and fraud," all "traits highly serviceable for individual expediency in a life looking to invidious success." Such a character is the modern captain of industry, dominating financial operations, a man of "no economic value to the community." Ranking slightly lower are employments immediately subservient to ownership, such as banking, and law, to which "no taint of usefulness attaches." Indeed, "The lawyer is exclusively occupied with the details of predatory fraud." The wealthy class is almost inevitably conservative, "to such an extent that an adherence to conservative views is comprised as a matter of course in our notions of respectability."

Sportsmanship, "the predatory and animistic habit of mind," is a typical characteristic of Veblen's leisure class. Athletics and sports contain within them elements of patriotism and the martial spirit, symbols of leisure-class status. They encourage habits of adventuresome exploit, exotic ferocity, cunning and strategy, all of which make the athletic struggle seem like actual war. Veblen continues:

> Chicane, falsehood, brow-beating, hold a well-secured place in the method of procedure of any athletic contest and in games generally. The habitual employment of an umpire, and the

minute technical regulations governing the limits and details of permissible fraud and strategic advantage, sufficiently attest the fact that fraudulent practices and attempts to overreach one's opponents are not adventious features of the game.

Veblen reserves some of his most critical and satirical comments for his long chapter, "Devout Observances." The sporting or gambling temperament which the author had discussed earlier "comprises some of the substantial psychological elements that go to make a believer in creeds and an observer of devout forms." Further, "The religious zeal which pervades much of the college sporting element is especially prone to express itself in an unquestioning devoutness and a naive and complacent submission to an inscrutable Providence." The modern conception of "the fatherhood of God" has softened somewhat the barbarian view of the divinity as "a warlike chieftain inclined to an overbearing manner of government," but in the popular mind there remains "a very substantial residue of the barbarian conception."

Carried over from barbarian cultures, too, is the rule that the priestly class must abstain from labor contributing to the general material welfare. On the contrary, devout observances are heavy consumers of goods and services. "The consumption of ceremonial paraphernalia required by any cult," Veblen comments, "in the way of shrines, temples, churches, vestments, sacrifices, sacraments, holiday attire, etc., serves no immediate material end," and may therefore properly be described as conspicuous waste. The same principle applies to sacred holidays: "The characteristic feature of all such seasons of devout vicarious leisure is a more or less rigid tabu on all activity that is of human use." Among the superior wealthy class, weddings, funerals, and like events "are solemnised with some especial degree of religious observance, as in barbarian cultures, and ritualistic features are accented at the cost of the intellectual." Veblen concludes that all the apparatus and services in devout observances may be attributed to the great pecuniary law of conspicuous waste of life, effort, and goods, lowering the vitality of the community and serving as obstacles to needed social change.

The final chapter of *The Theory of the Leisure Class* gives Veblen (for most of his career a university faculty member) an opportunity to pay his respects to "The Higher Learning as an

Expression of the Pecuniary Culture." In the past, he holds, institutions of higher education have exhibited some of the worst characteristics of the leisure class. They have been conservative, reactionary, and addicted to devout observances, with much ceremonial ritual and practice. A hierarchy of ranks prevails, comparable to an apostolic succession. The modern practitioners of higher education are the logical descendants of ancient medicine men, attempting to impress the community with their esoteric and occult knowledge. The principle of conspicuous waste is exemplified in the fact that "the higher learning comprises such knowledge as is primarily of no economic or industrial effect." It is education for leisure-class membership, not for service to the community. The classical studies are particularly esteemed, for they are obsolete, of no practical utility, and fit their students for no useful occupation. Next to the classics, Veblen observes, the social sciences are of highest repute. "These so-called sciences are substantially bodies of maxims of expediency for guidance in the leisure-class office of government as conducted on a proprietary basis."

Veblen derives some encouragement, however, from recent changes in the scope of college and university teaching, specifically in the partial displacement of the humanities by scientific subjects and "those more matter-of-fact branches which make for civic and industrial efficiency." The higher learning traditionally "is a by-product of the priestly office and the life of leisure," but modern science "is a by-product of the industrial process." Scientists have not been welcomed with open arms by institutions of higher education: "Men who have occupied themselves [with] new views, new departures in scientific theory, especially new departures which touch the theory of human relations at any point, have found a place in the scheme of the university tardily and by a reluctant tolerance, rather than by a cordial welcome."

Examining society as a whole, Veblen detects gleams of hope for the future. The predatory life of the leisure class is beginning to lose its appeal and dominant position, and an attitude of disapproval toward futile activity is growing. The ideal character in modern industrial communities, according to "the average dispassionate sense of men," is one "which makes for peace, good-will, and economic efficiency, rather than a life of self-seeking, force, fraud, and mastery."

Veblen's influence on later economists and social thinkers has been pervasive and far-reaching. A review of his career in *Fortune* concluded, "Every American who is skeptical of business glories, suspicious of great enrichment, contemptuous of social climbing and wealthy ostentation, dubious of the merits of keeping up with the Joneses, probably owes something to Thorstein Veblen's intellectual adventuring." Using the weapon of satire effectively, Veblen attacked such enemies of a good society as class pride and distinctions, the unsocial behavior of the wealthy, the parade of material possessions, and the placing of property and privilege ahead of humanity.

29 | BLACK MESSIAH
Booker T. Washington's *Up from Slavery:*
An Autobiography, 1901

At the height of his career, from 1895 until his death in 1915, no other black man, and probably no white man except Theodore Roosevelt, in America possessed the prestige or exerted the influence of Booker Taliaferro Washington, born a slave in Virginia about four years prior to the outbreak of the Civil War. Even during his lifetime, Washington was a controversial figure, bitterly attacked by more militant contemporaries, such as W. E. B. DuBois and Monroe Trotter, and over the past fifty-five years persistent efforts have been made to downgrade him as an "Uncle Tom" and a traitor to his race. Nevertheless, Washington represents a definite and important stage in American Negro history and culture.

Almost every conceivable handicap was overcome by Booker T. Washington in his climb upward. His father was believed to have been a white man from a neighboring plantation, whom it is doubtful that the son ever saw. The name Washington was adopted. As a child, Booker slept on filthy rags and foraged for his food. When he was ten, the family moved to West Virginia, where for several years he worked in salt and coal mines. The entire family endured dire poverty, and Booker's formal education was limited to no more than two or three months a year. Meanwhile, rumors reached him of a new school for colored people in Virginia, Hampton Institute, founded by General Samuel C. Armstrong. Driven by ambition and an eagerness for education, the seventeen-year-old Booker traveled the 500 miles to Hampton, and after some hesitation, because of his meager background, he was admitted.

General Armstrong, a remarkable personality in his own right, was convinced that the South's hope for the future depended upon "a vigorous attempt to lift the colored race by a practical education that shall fit them for life." At Hampton he trained

selected colored youth to go out and lead their people by showing them how to acquire land and homes, vocations and skills,
by teaching respect for labor, especially skilled labor, and the
molding of character. This was the philosophy which was absorbed by young Washington in his three years at the school
and which he subsequently applied as head of the newly established Tuskegee Institute in Alabama.

The era during which Booker T. Washington reached maturity was in some respects more difficult for Negroes than pre–Civil
War slavery. By a series of repressive measures, the Southern
whites were avenging their defeat in the war, the Reconstruction
years, and the brief time of Negro dominance in Southern state
governments. The South was in bankruptcy. A secret society, the
Ku Klux Klan, terrorized the Negroes; a system of peonage grew
up, under which the newly freed slaves were arrested for
vagrancy and on other pretexts and their convict labor leased to
farmers and business men; lynching became a common practice
(3,500 persons, nearly all Southern black men, were lynched
between 1885 and 1915); and the Negro was severely discrimi-
nated against in travel accommodations, education, public facilities, and police protection. Further, direct legislation in the
Southern states disfranchised a great majority of black voters.

This was the prevailing situation when in 1881 Booker T.
Washington, then only twenty-five years of age, was invited to
become the principal of a school for Negroes in Tuskegee,
Alabama. The school's prospects were bleak. The Alabama
legislature had appropriated 2,000 dollars to pay instructors, but
nothing for land or buildings. Undismayed, young Washington
opened his school in an old church and a shanty, with thirty
students on hand. In the years that followed, he traveled widely
to solicit support. Due almost entirely to his missionary zeal and
genius as a fund raiser, by the time of Washington's death
thirty-five years later, Tuskegee had more than 100 buildings—
for the most part erected and furnished by the students themselves; owned 2,000 acres of local land and had been granted by
Congress an additional 25,000 acres in northern Alabama; possessed an endowment of 2 million dollars; enrolled 1,500 students,
taught by 200 faculty members (all Negroes); and offered training in thirty-eight trades and professions.

From the outset Tuskegee emphasized practical training, the ideal which had been the chief motivation for Hampton Institute. As expressed by Booker T. Washington:

> We found that most of our students came from the country districts, where agriculture in some form or other was the main dependence of the people. We learned that about eighty-five per cent of the colored people in the Gulf states depended upon agriculture for their living. Since this was true, we wanted to be careful not to educate our students out of sympathy with agricultural life, so that they would be attracted from the country to the cities, and yield to the temptation of trying to live by their wits. We wanted to give them such an education as would fit a large proportion of them to be teachers, and at the same time cause them to return to the plantation districts and show the people there how to put new energy and new ideas into farming, as well as into the intellectual and moral and religious life of the people.

Such a philosophy of education was opposed or at best accepted with reluctance by many Negro students and their elders. Hard physical labor under slavery had turned them against work with their hands. They believed that the mystic power of education, especially acquiring the ability to read and write, would lift the hated burden of physical toil from their backs. One of Washington's tasks was to dispel the fetish that book learning alone provided salvation for the race. His travels through the Southern states had persuaded him that practice as well as theory were indispensable to a race whose opportunities in the foreseeable future would be mainly in agriculture or other forms of manual labor.

The Tuskegee plan was simple. The student worked to pay part of his expenses; he learned how to work most effectively, and was taught the dignity of labor. Negro youth was trained to be teachers, nurses, mechanics, and dietitians and to become skilled in many other practical fields. "We must admit the stern fact," stated Washington, "that at present the Negro, through no choice of his own, is living among another race which is far ahead of him in education, property, experience, and favorable condition; further, that the Negro's present condition makes him dependent upon white people for most of the things necessary to sustain life, as well as for his common school education." It was Washington's belief that through practical education, the Negro could make himself such a valuable factor in the economic life of the South "that he will not have to seek privileges, they will be freely conferred upon him."

Washington conceded that Negroes should produce teachers, ministers, doctors, lawyers, and statesmen and not confine themselves to agriculture, mechanics, and domestic arts; but he saw the latter areas as offering the most immediate opportunities for the race's advancement.

As the fame of the Tuskegee experiment spread, Washington realized that in a sense the eyes of the nation were upon him. "I knew," he wrote in his autobiography, "that the presumption was against us . . . that, in the case of white people beginning such an enterprise, it would be taken for granted that they would succeed, but in our case I felt that people would be surprised if we succeeded. All this made a burden which pressed down on us sometimes, it seemed, at the rate of a thousand pounds to the square inch." Years later, John Dewey was to popularize the concept of fusing practical and intellectual training, teaching his doctrine of the educational value of learning by doing useful and cooperative tasks, but when Booker T. Washington began, Hampton was the only institution with a comparable program.

Washington's appeal to the white community was strictly pragmatic, a fact which doubtless accounted for its success and wide popular acceptance. He warned the white race that if it kept blacks in the gutter, they themselves would have to remain in the gutter, also. He felt that the Negro could not be neglected or degraded without holding down both races.

An invitation to speak to the National Educational Association at a meeting in Madison, Wisconsin, provided Washington with a national audience to whom he could express his views on race relations. There he insisted that the whole future of the Negro rested on the question of whether or not he could, through his skill, intelligence, and character, make himself of such value to his community that it could not get along without him.

Another opportunity to expound his philosophy of education and race relations came to Booker T. Washington in 1895, when he was invited to speak at the Cotton States Exposition in Atlanta, as a representative of the Negro people. Washington was deeply moved by the invitation, recollecting that he had been born a slave, that his early years had been spent in poverty and ignorance, and this was the first time in history that a member of his race had been asked to speak from the same platform with Southern white leaders on any important national occasion.

Washington began the speech, his most famous, with a statement of fact: "One-third of the population of the South is of the Negro race." He made it plain that nothing affecting the material or moral welfare of the region could afford to overlook such a large element in the population. In comments addressed to his own people, he continued, "No race can prosper till it learns that there is as much dignity in tilling a field as in writing a poem. It is at the bottom of life we must begin, and not at the top. Nor should we permit our grievances to overshadow our opportunities." He pleaded with the whites to appreciate the abilities and loyalty of his race and to intertwine the industrial, commercial, and religious life of the two races.

In another aspect of race relations, however, Washington retreated, by declaring, "In all things that are purely social we can be as separate as the fingers, yet one as the hand in all things essential to mutual progress."

The speech was received with tremendous enthusiasm by Southern white leaders, who thereafter viewed Washington as the chief spokesman for the Negro people. In effect, he was willing to accept the status quo, which was exactly what the whites wanted to hear. Less conservative and less patient Negro leaders reacted with dismay; they felt that in the "Atlanta Compromise" Washington had conceded too much. It was apparent that he was willing to forgo political and social rights in exchange for economic opportunity. Critics held that Washington's policies would reduce Negroes as a whole to the status of laborers, barred from the higher walks of life; his emphasis on industrial training, they maintained, would keep the Negro in virtual bondage. A group of Boston intellectuals declared that the upper 10 percent of the graduating class of every Negro high school should be given a chance to pursue advanced studies.

Among the most outspoken and influential black leaders who condemned Booker T. Washington, for meekly submitting to injustice and committing treason against his race, was W. E. B.

DuBois, a graduate of Fisk and Harvard and a sociologist at Atlanta University. "There is among educated and thoughtful colored men in all parts of the nation," wrote DuBois, "a feeling of deep regret, sorrow, and apprehension at the wide currency and ascendancy which some of Mr. Washington's theories have gained." DuBois especially resented Washington's almost exclusive emphasis on industrial education, because he saw it as standing in the way of Negro ambitions for professional, literary, and artistic distinction. Further, DuBois believed that Washington was asking the black people to give up political power, their insistence on civil rights, and higher education of Negro youth. He concluded with a declaration that "so far as Mr. Washington apologizes for injustice, North or South, does not rightly value the privilege and duty of voting, belittles the emasculating effects of caste distinctions, and opposes the higher training and ambition of our brighter minds,—so far as he, the South, or the Nation, does this,—we must unceasingly and firmly oppose them."

Certainly, Booker T. Washington was not unaware of the injustices and restrictions which severely handicapped his people. "I do not overlook," he said, "the wrongs that often perplex us in this country." He was especially irked by discrimination in public education, arguing that no color line should be drawn in the operation of the legal system or "in the opportunity to get an education in the public schools." Writing for the *New Republic,* Washington came out strongly against segregation laws which were being passed in the South, though he insisted that amalgamation did not offer an acceptable solution to the race problem.

Is there convincing evidence that Washington's ideas achieved any large measure of success? Critics pointed out that stopping the agitation for civil liberties did not change the attitude of the Southern white man toward the Negro, lynchings reached their peak during the period of Washington's leadership, segregation on the basis of race and color increased, occupational opportunities in skilled trades diminished, farm ownership decreased and farm tenancy increased, and the Southern press, by and large, remained racist in its attitudes. Furthermore, as Merle Curti observed in his *Social Ideas of American Educators,* "At the very time when the crusade for industrial training was being launched, the technological basis of industry was rapidly shifting from that of the skilled artisan to machine production." Even on the farm, the machine was already pushing the established farmer to the wall.

Booker T. Washington's story was effectively told in his autobiography *Up from Slavery* (1901), a simple but dramatic account of his career. The book first appeared in serial form in the *Outlook.* Its reception far exceeded the author's expectations. Hundreds of thousands of copies were sold in all parts of the English speaking world, and numerous translations were issued in Western and Eastern languages. The style was obviously influenced by constant reading of the Bible and of Shakespeare, and the narrative bears some resemblance to *Pilgrim's Progress.* Unfortunately, there is a gap in the record; the last fifteen years of Washington's life were never covered.

Samuel R. Spencer, Jr., author of *Booker T. Washington and the Negro's Place in American Life,* sums up Washington's principles and philosophy in these words: "That Washington looked forward to the day of liberty and justice for all cannot be doubted. He accepted half a loaf, not as a permanent settlement, but as a means to a whole loaf later. He did what was possible, given the time and place in which he lived, and did it to the utmost."

Another writer, Howard Brotz, in his *Negro Social and Political Thought, 1850–1920,* suggests that Washington was fifty years ahead of his time, because the fundamental problems of the Negro are "beyond civil rights." That is, the Negro may have achieved full legal equality, but remains unequal in a number of important economic and social respects. Without the capacity to earn a good living, as advocated by Booker T. Washington, legal equalization falls far short of meeting the Negro's needs. This was the essence of Washington's teachings.

| BIRTH OF THE WESTERN
Owen Wister's *The Virginian: A Horseman
of the Plains*, 1902

The lead character in Owen Wister's *The Virginian* was the progenitor of every cowboy-hero who has drawn a gun since the turn of the century. *The Virginian* is the most popular "western" ever published and established the master design for all subsequent fiction with a Wild West setting. Since Wister created the literary form for "horse opera," his formula has been applied in innumerable instances to novels, short stories, stage plays, moving pictures, radio and television scripts. The conventions or clichés prescribe the cowboy as a kind of nineteenth-century descendant of the Knights of the Round Table, a virile hero intolerant of pretense, who defends justice and a lady's honor, shoots it out with the villain, and goes around subduing sin in the world.

A standardized scene in horse opera is the "walkdown." As described by Bernard DeVoto, "A sun god in leather pants, The Hero, and his adversary, who represents Evil, approach each other across an open space. The guns speak and The Hero, who has or has not suffered a flesh wound, steps sideward into a girl's expectant arms." The scene is a vital part of the tradition invented by Owen Wister, inserted by him into a series of short stories published in *Harper's Magazine* in the 1890s and subsequently incorporated in *The Virginian* (1902). In the opinion of various critics, as expressed by one, Cary Grayson, "This necessity for sanctioning murder and the romanticizing of the cowboy as a gentleman prohibited *The Virginian* and the genre it created from becoming serious fiction, or even an authentic product of the western experience. Instead, Wister gave us a sort of American folk epic, the cowboy story."

To understand the phenomenal popularity of *The Virginian*, one needs to place the novel in its proper setting, both of time and place. At the beginning of the twentieth century the virtues of an earlier, simpler agrarian society had vanished, replaced by crowded cities, an industrial economy, and a mad scramble for wealth and position. In sharp contrast, the Western cattle country symbolized space, beautiful scenery, independence, and individual opportunity. Too, partly as a carry-over from the Spanish American War, there was a revival of national pride and national consciousness, and the West was a reminder of America's infinite color and variety. Its people began to realize that America also had its folk heroes and heroines, fully as appealing and as interesting as those of the Old World. Another factor not to be overlooked is the American frontier tradition, so graphically described by Frederick Jackson Turner a decade prior to the advent of *The Virginian.*

Struthers Burt focused the matter with this comment: "Practically every American male has at one time or another thought of himself as a cowboy or rancher and practically every American woman has at one time or another envisioned herself as being wooed by something tall, sunburned, lithe and lean-hipped, with spurs and chaps, and the deed to a ranch in his hand." The development of Wister's ideas may be seen in his article "The Evolution of the Cow-puncher," published in *Harper's* in 1895, several years before *The Virginian* appeared on the scene.

Owen Wister was born in Philadelphia in 1860, and grew up in a refined circle, where he was taught to speak French fluently and to play the piano well enough to win praise from Franz Liszt; he met many interesting people, including Henry James, and traveled widely in Europe. His mother was the daughter of Fanny Kemble, noted actress. Befitting the scion of a wealthy, cultured family, young Owen entered Harvard College, studied law, and spent a year at a conservatory in Paris. In brief, he was a most unlikely prospect to enjoy the arduous, dangerous, harsh nature of Wyoming ranch life of the last quarter of the nineteenth century. But as a matter of fact he delighted in it.

Altogether, Wister made fifteen long Western journeys, at first for his health, later as an escape from the practice of law, and finally in search of literary materials. For him, Wyoming was the West, and Wister was devoted to the forty-fourth state of the Union. "Nobody, nobody who lives on the Atlantic strip," he wrote in his journals, "has a notion of what a sunrise and sunset and moonlight can be in his native land till he has come here to see."

The locale of *The Virginian* is Wyoming between 1874 and 1890, the end of an era according to Wister's preface, for "the horseman, the cow-puncher, the last romantic figure upon our soil" had virtually disappeared before the end of the century Wister viewed his work therefore as a historical novel.

In the beginning, the Virginian (who is always anonymous) has been sent to Medicine Bow to escort a guest, an Easterner, the 263 miles to Sunk Creek Ranch. While awaiting the arrival of the guest's trunk, the Virginian enters a poker game. One of the players is a cowboy named Trampas, the novel's prime villain. During the game there occurs one of the book's most famous scenes. Trampas decides that the Virginian is too deliberate and speaks up, "Your bet, you son-of-a————." At this point, "the Virginian's pistol came out, and his hand lay on the table, holding it unaimed. And with a voice as gentle as ever, the voice that sounded almost like a caress, but drawling a very little more than usual, so that there was almost a space between each word, he issued his orders to the man Trampas: 'When you call me that, *smile!*' And he looked at Trampas across the table." Trampas has his choice between backing down or of drawing his gun, and he retreats, but the Virginian has made an implacable enemy.

The next high spot in the plot is the coming of Mary Stark Wood of Bennington, Vermont, to teach in the new school at Bear Creek. Her arrival has been eagerly awaited by all the single men in the territory, including the Virginian. The latter has the good fortune to be able to play the hero in his first meeting with "Molly." A drunken stage-coach driver has tried to cross a stream in high water and succeeds in marooning himself and his passenger. The Virginian, happening to be passing by, rides to the stage, lifts out the girl, and carries her safely to dry land. A number of horsemen with ropes right the vehicle, pull it to the bank of the stream, and the journey proceeds. During the encounter, the Virginian has managed to steal Molly's flowered handkerchief.

The next time the Virginian meets Molly, they are guests at a ranch barbecue. The cowboy has ridden for two days to see her, but Molly coquettishly refuses to notice him. Provoked by her attitude, the Virginian proceeds to get drunk, and with the aid of a friend plays a practical joke on the people who had brought their children to the party. They switch places and clothing on the twelve babies whose parents have deposited them asleep in an adjoining room. When the barbecue is over, the mothers take the wrong infants home with them. A merry mixup results.

Molly sends back to Vermont for a collection of books—Shakespeare, Tennyson, Browning, Longfellow, Scott, Thackeray, Emerson, and others. A week later, the Virginian who had dropped out of school in the sixth grade, resumes his education. Serious discussions of literature with Molly follow.

The Virginian's character and personality have meanwhile raised him high in the estimation of his employer, Judge Henry, and he is placed in charge of a group of cowboys escorting two trainloads of steers to the Chicago stockyards. Trampas, a member of the gang, attempts to persuade the men to desert and to go prospecting for gold in the Black Hills. He comes near succeeding before the Virginian makes him look foolish with a tall tale about eating frog legs. Back at Sunk Creek after his successful mission, the Virginian is promoted by the judge to be foreman of the ranch. Trampas expects to be discharged, but the new foreman is not vengeful and allows him to stay on.

Cattle begin to disappear from the Sunk Creek and neighboring ranches, and at about the same time Trampas quits, after persuading another cowboy, Shorty, a weak-willed malcontent, to accompany him.

Returning from a neighboring ranch, the Virginian is ambushed by Indians and severely wounded. He manages to escape alive and is able to ride to a nearby spring before falling off his horse. There Molly finds him, half dead, and stays with him at the risk of her own life, for the Indians are still prowling in the area. She binds up the Virginian's wounds and manages to get him back to her cottage while a doctor is being called.

Molly has packed her possessions preparatory to returning East, but by the time the Virginian recovers his health, she has decided that she is in love with him and will not leave Wyoming.

Meantime, the cattlemen are continuing to suffer from the depredations of rustlers and organize a posse to track down the thieves. Two of the rustlers, including an old friend of the Virginian, Steve, are caught and hanged. It is a terrible shock to the Virginian to realize that he has aided in the execution of his long-time friend, an episode made more painful by the fact that Steve had refused to speak to his former boon companion—but justice must be done.

On the way back to Sunk Creek, the Virginian comes across the trail of two other rustlers, Trampas and Shorty; they have only one horse between them, and Trampas murders Shorty to make possible his own escape.

When Molly hears of the Virginian's part in the lynching of Steve and the second rustler, she changes her mind about marrying a man she now considers a murderer. Judge Henry convinces her, however, that his foreman was only doing his duty, and she relents. The date for the wedding is set.

Riding into Medicine Bow for the ceremony, Molly and the Virginian are passed by Trampas. In Medicine Bow, a drunken Trampas comes raging into a saloon where the Virginian is meeting with friends and gives the latter until sundown to leave town. The Virginian's honor is at stake, and he has no choice except to fight Trampas. A meddlesome informer at once carries the news back to Molly, waiting in the hotel. Molly, extremely upset, declares that she will not marry the Virginian if he fights and kills Trampas. Undeterred, the Virginian goes out and in the ensuing gun battle Trampas dies.

So great is Molly's relief when the Virginian returns to inform her of the fight's outcome that she surrenders: "Thus did her New England conscience battle to the end," writes Wister, "and, in the end, capitulate to love. And the next day, with the bishop's blessing, and Mrs. Taylor's broadest smile, and the ring on her finger, the Virginian departed with his bride into the mountains."

The happy ending is rounded out with Judge Henry taking the Virginian into partnership. Coal needed by the new railroad is discovered on land owned by the Virginian, who has become "an important man, with a strong grip on many various enterprises, and able to give his wife all and more than she asked or desired."

The character of the Virginian became the apotheosis of the heroic cowboy in later fiction. He is tall, strong, handsome, shrewd, gentle in all ways except formal breeding, courageous, incapable of meanness, polite to and considerate of women; he is taciturn and uncommunicative; he minds his own business; he is proficient at roping, handling horses, tracking down thieves, and managing men; he has a fondness for the practical joke and is sentimental about his favorite mount.

In one important respect subsequent "horse operas" departed from the pattern set by *The Virginian*, which is in part a love story. The latter-day cowboy story is typified by "Gunsmoke," most popular and enduring of television's westerns, whose Marshal Dillon is impervious to feminine charms and blandishments.

George Thomas Watkins, in his *Owen Wister and the American West*—the only full-length study of Wister's life and work—notes the large folklore element in *The Virginian*, pointing out that the book "overflows with tall tales, rough crude humor, practical joking, folk sayings and folk songs." All of chapter sixteen, for example, is taken up with a battle of tall tales between Trampas and the Virginian, a contest won by the latter with a long yarn about frog ranching in California and the large profits to be made therefrom. The tale is on a par with Mark Twain's story, "Jim Smiley and His Jumping Frog."

It has been stated that *The Virginian* has probably been read by more readers of American fiction than any other American novel. The claim might be disputed by Harriet Beecher Stowe's *Uncle Tom's Cabin*. In any case, the publisher had to reprint the book fourteen times before the end of its first year. Probably 2 million copies have been sold in hard-bound editions. A dramatic version was a stage hit which ran for years, and at least five moving pictures based on the book have appeared, both in the silent and sound eras. No accurate count of the number of copies sold in paperback editions and foreign translations is available.

Bernard DeVoto asserts that *The Virginian* was "put together, with the joints left visible, from short stories Wister had published in *Harper's* during the 1890s." Actually, a large portion of *The Virginian* was totally new work, not a mere assembling of short stories into a series of chapters. As Watkins points out, "It was the labor that Wister expended on *The Virginian* that made it a more unified work, that gave it superior coherence, that made it artistically superior, not the application of some mechanical formula."

At the beginning of the twentieth century the knightly warrior type, represented by the Virginian and Theodore Roosevelt's Rough Riders, was the national ideal—not the effete intellectuals and fancy talkers, Larzer Ziff, in *The American 1890s,* concludes that *The Virginian* "provided the archetype of escape fantasy for the new century. As commerce, politics, and art, as even war increasingly became abstract, how necessary was the Western, the constant reminder that there really is such a thing as being overcivilized, and the constant proclamation that Americans were bred to be warriors and that after all at a certain point a punch in the nose beats talk." Another critic, G. Edward White, holds similar views: "Wister was fortunate enough to dramatize the full acceptance of the cowboy as one of America's own; as his novel climbed to the top of the best-seller lists, he must have realized how many Americans had come to identify with the rude yet romantic life of his horseman of the plains."

31 | BLACK MAN IN A WHITE MAN'S WORLD

W. E. Burghardt DuBois's *The Souls of Black Folk*, 1903

A noted Negro poet and educator, James Weldon Johnson, concluded that W. E. B. DuBois's *Souls of Black Folk* is "a work which, I think, has had a greater effect upon and within the Negro race in America than any other single book published in this country since *Uncle Tom's Cabin*." The immense popularity of the book is shown by the fact that since its publication in 1903 *The Souls of Black Folk* has passed through more than thirty editions.

The impact of the most famous of DuBois's numerous books upon young Negro intellectuals has been particularly striking. As the Nashville *Banner* predicted in reviewing the original edition, it turned out to be "dangerous for the Negro to read, for it will only excite discontent and fill his imagination with things that do not exist, or things that should not bear upon his mind."

Essentially, *The Souls of Black Folk* is an impassioned black nationalist document, consciously directed toward the Negro people, and identifying with Africa, blackness, and the rural Negro. In the same fashion that Booker T. Washington's *Up from Slavery* is designed to gain the goodwill of the white race, *The Souls of Black Folk* is directed to the black consciousness of the Negro masses. The problem was defined by DuBois in these words:

> The history of the American Negro is the history of this strife,— this longing to attain self-conscious manhood, to merge his double self into a better and truer self. In this merging he wishes neither of the older selves to be lost. He would not Africanize America, for America has too much to teach the world and Africa. He would not bleach his Negro soul in a flood of white Americanism, for he knows that Negro blood has a message

for the world. He simply wishes to make it possible for a man to be both a Negro and an American, without being cursed and spit upon by his fellows, without having the doors of Opportunity closed roughly in his face.

Thus, in DuBois's view, the American Negro has had an inferiority complex imposed upon him by the whites, and suffers a kind of schizophrenia. He has an overwhelming need therefore to identify himself: Who is he and what role should he play in American society? "It is a peculiar sensation," remarks the author, "this double-consciousness, this sense of always looking at one's self through the eyes of others, of measuring one's soul by the tape of a world that looks on in amused contempt and pity. One ever feels his two-ness,—an American, a Negro; two souls, two thoughts, two unreconciled strivings; two warring ideals in one dark body, whose dogged strength alone keeps it from being torn asunder."

The backgrounds of Booker T. Washington, born to slavery on a Virginia plantation, and the man destined to contest his leadership of the Negro race, W. E. B. DuBois, could hardly have been more dissimilar. The latter conceived of himself as an aristocrat, and his personal history is untypical of a black man. DuBois was born in 1868 in Great Barrington, Massachusetts, at a time when few Negroes lived there. On his mother's side, he was descended from Tom Burghardt, who was brought by Dutch slave traders to the Hudson valley about 1740 and whose service in the Army during the Revolutionary War won freedom for himself and his family. On his father's side, DuBois was a descendant of French Huguenots who migrated to America three centuries ago. Young DuBois graduated with distinction from the Great Barrington public schools in 1884, was the class orator, and appeared to have suffered none of the traumatic experiences common to Negroes in a white society. Then it was decided that he should go to Fisk University, a Negro school in Nashville, an experience that changed his life forever. "Henceforward I was a Negro," writes DuBois. Subsequently, DuBois was awarded a Ph.D. degree by Harvard University and studied at the University of Berlin. In short, he received the best education that America could provide, and he always considered himself as belonging to the "Talented Tenth" (DuBois's phrase), the small group of educated and hard-working Negroes who were to serve as an example to the Negro mass and to uplift it.

Highlights in DuBois's later career were a professorship of economics and history at Atlanta University from 1896 to 1910, and head of the same institution's department of sociology from 1932 to 1944; editorship of *The Crisis*, a dynamic and forceful organ of the NAACP, from 1910 to 1932; and, from 1952 on, a full-time worker for world peace, for socialism, and Pan-Africanism. DuBois died in Ghana, at the age of ninety-five, after renouncing his American citizenship.

The initial chapter of *The Souls of Black Folk* describes the spiritual strivings of the Negro—how to be a Negro and at the same time an American—"to be a co-worker in the Kingdom of culture, to excape both death and isolation; to use his best powers and his latent genius," up to now so wasted, dispersed, and ignored. The second chapter, "Of the Dawn of Freedom," tells the story of emancipation, what it meant to the blacks, and reviews the events of the carpetbagger and Reconstruction period; the emphasis is on the Freedmen's Bureau, its strength and failings. DuBois pays eloquent tribute to "the crusade of the New England schoolma'am" in the South, which in one year gave instruction to more than 100,000 blacks.

The work of the Freedmen's Bureau is sympathetically viewed by DuBois. An act pased by Congress in 1866, over President Johnson's veto, established the organization, charged largely with the government of the unreconstructed South, granting it authority to make and enforce laws, levy and collect taxes, punish crime, maintain a military force, and to exercise such other powers as might seem necessary for the social regeneration of 4 million former slaves. The bureau's agents, DuBois notes, "varied all the way from unselfish philanthropists to narrow-minded busybodies and thieves." "Amid all crouched the freed slave, bewildered between friend and foe." On one side were arrayed the North, the government, the carpetbaggers, and the ex-slave. On the other stood the solid South, "whether gentleman or vagabond, honest man or rascal, lawless murderer or martyr to duty." Upon the bureau fell the responsibility for the relief of physical suffering, overseeing the beginnings of free labor, the buying and selling of land, the establishment of schools, the paying of bounties, the administration of justice, and the financing of all those activities.

Such an institution as the bureau, DuBois comments, "from its wide powers, great responsibilities, large control of moneys, and generally conspicuous position, was naturally open to repeated and bitter attack." The crowning blow was the bankruptcy of the Freemen's Bank, carrying down with it the hard-earned dollars of the freedmen. Officially the bureau ended in 1872, leaving, according to DuBois, much of its task unfinished, including Negro suffrage. As a consequence, when DuBois was writing in 1903, "despite compromise, war, and struggle, the Negro is not free." He continues:

> In the backwoods of the Gulf States, for miles and miles, he may not leave the plantation of his birth; in well-nigh the whole rural South the black farmers are peons, bound by law and custom to South the Negroes are a segregated servile caste, with restricted an economic slavery, from which the only escape is death or the penitentiary. In the most cultured sections and cities of the rights and privileges. Before the courts, both in law and custom, they stand on a different and peculiar basis. Taxation without representation is the rule of their political life.

The chapter of *The Souls of Black Folk* which created most controversy was the third, "Of Mr. Booker T. Washington and Others." Washington's rise to power, states DuBois, is easily "the most striking thing in the history of the American Negro since 1876." The Tuskegee Institute head's "program of industrial education, conciliation of the South, and submission and silence as to civil and political rights . . . startled and won the applause of the South, it interested and won the admiration of the North; and after a confused murmur of protest, it silenced if it did not convert the Negroes themselves." DuBois saw Washington as offering the white world contented Negro workers who would raise no claim to social and political equality. By following Washington's policy, the Negro was giving up political power, civil rights, and the higher education of Negro youth. The consequences of Washington's ideas, which had been actively promoted for ten or fifteen years before publication of *The Souls of Black Folk*, are summarized by DuBois: "(1) The disfranchisement of the Negro. (2) The legal creation of a distinct status of civil inferiority for the Negro. (3) The steady withdrawal of aid from institutions for the higher training of the Negro." Concerning the last point, DuBois insisted that good common-school and industrial training could not exist without institutions of higher learning: "Tuskegee itself could not remain open a day were it not for teachers trained in Negro colleges, or trained by their graduates."

In an interview with Ralph McGill a few months before he died, DuBois looked back on the extended debate with Washington:

> As I came to see it, Washington bartered away much that was not his to barter. Certainly I did not believe that the skills of an artisan bricklayer, plasterer, or shoemaker, and the good farmer would cause the white South, grimly busy with disfranchisement and separation, to change the direction of things. I realized the need for what Washington was doing. Yet it seemed to me that he was giving up essential ground that would be hard to win back.

DuBois was a brilliant intellectual who insisted that enlightened Negroes should accept only unconditional equality, and that there was an immediate need for the training of a Negro elite, "The Talented Tenth," who would lead the black masses. He believed in political action and that the black world should fight for equality with "the weapons of Truth, with the sword of the intrepid, uncompromising Spirit." In contrast, the politically passive Washington was a compromiser and gradualist, who believed that his economic program would yield more immediate and visible benefits to his race than constant agitation for equal rights.

Closely related to the differences with Booker T. Washington on the proper nature of Negro education is DuBois's sixth chapter, "On the Training of Black Men." Education is regarded by the author as a panacea for many of the problems of race relations: "such human training as will best use the labor of all men without enslaving or brutalizing; such training as will give us poise to encourage the prejudices that bulwark society, and to stamp out those that in sheer barbarity deafen us to the wail of prisoned souls within the Veil, and the mounting fury of shackled men."

But what kind of education? Following the Civil War, there

were army schools, mission schools, and Freedmen's Bureau schools, the whole lacking systematic planning and cooperation. There next ensued a decade of constructive effort toward building complete school systems in the South. Meanwhile, starting about 1885, the Southern industrial revolution was beginning, and industrial schools sprang up. While recognizing the value and importance of such schools for the training of the Negro race, DuBois poses "the broader question of the permanent uplifting and civilization of black men in America" and wonders "if after all the industrial school is the final and sufficient answer in the training of the Negro race." The greatest need as seen by DuBois is schools to train Negro teachers, and it was in response to the urgent need that such institutions as Fisk, Hampton, Howard, Atlanta, Shaw, Spelman, Wilberforce, and Lincoln University were established. "In a single generation," DuBois notes, "they put thirty thousand black teachers in the South; they wiped out the illiteracy of the majority of the black people of the land, and they made Tuskegee possible." The aim of the Negro colleges, invariably, was to give "teachers and leaders the best practicable training; and above all, to furnish the black world with adequate standards of human culture and lofty ideals of life." In addition, several hundred Negroes had graduated from Harvard, Yale, Oberlin, and other leading colleges, thus demonstrating their ability and talent for higher education. DuBois sees the Negro college as having four functions: It must maintain standards of popular education, seek the social regeneration of the Negro, aid in the solution of problems of race contact and cooperation, and "finally, beyond all this, it must develop men."

Chapter nine of *The Souls of Black Folk*, "Of the Sons of Master and Man," is a powerful indictment of the evils of racial discrimination and prejudice in the Southern states, a society marked by segregated housing; economic hardships for the Negro, imposed by custom and law; a ban on political activity, including disfranchisement of the Negro; inferior public schools for the black race; and the effectual elimination of social contacts between the races. "There is almost no community of intellectual life or point of transference," DuBois asserts, "where the thoughts and feelings of one race can come into direct contact and sympathy with the thoughts and feelings of the other." The author continues, "It is not enough for the Negroes to declare that color-prejudice is the sole cause of their social condition, nor for the white South to reply that their social condition is the main cause of prejudice. They both act as reciprocal cause and effect. Both must change, or neither can improve to any great extent."

The changing nature of the Negro church and of Negro religious attitudes is reviewed by DuBois in his discussion, "Of the Faith of the Fathers." In the early days, slave masters encouraged religious activity, for nothing suited the slaves' condition better than "the doctrines of passive submission embodied in the newly learned Christianity." At the turn of the century, when DuBois was writing, the Negro church was still the social center of Negro life in the United States, "and the most characteristic expression of African character." But the Negro faced a dilemma: "Conscious of his impotence, and pessimistic, he often becomes bitter and vindictive; and his religion, instead of a worship, is a complaint and a curse, a wail rather than a hope, a sneer rather than a faith." DuBois observed two "divergent ethical tendencies among Negroes. In the North the trend was toward radicalism, in the South toward "hypocritical compromise." Between the two extreme types of ethical attitudes waver millions of Negroes, North and South, while their religious life and activity reflect the social conflict within their ranks.

In *The Souls of Black Folk* and other writings, DuBois prefigured recent directions of Negro thought: the need for racial solidarity, an identification with Africa, a stress on the distinctive qualities and achievements of Negro culture, and the Negro's duty to maintain his racial integrity in order that he might fulfill his special mission to humanity. For fifty years, DuBois was a passionate fighter for full civil rights and equality of citizenship for the Negro. By the time of his death in the 1960s, DuBois's concept of the Negro's proper status in America had gone far toward realization. His vision of the future is contained in an eloquent and touching prophecy:

> Some day the Awakening will come, when the pent-up vigor of ten million souls shall sweep irresistibly toward the Goal, out of the Valley of the Shadow of Death, where all that makes life worth living—Liberty, Justice, and Right—is marked "For White People Only."

32 | BIRTH OF AN OCTOPUS

Ida M. Tarbell's *The History of the Standard Oil Company*, 1904

The post–Civil War period in the United States witnessed the rise of large-scale business and industrial activity, accompanied by rampant individualism and rugged competition. Unfettered by federal or state regulation, giant corporations or "trusts" emerged to engage in cutthroat rivalry with each other. Through monopolistic practices, corruption, bribery, and strong-arm methods, weak firms were eliminated, and a handful of companies began to fasten an economic stranglehold on the nation. In the forefront —a prime example of the success of such tactics—was the Standard Oil Company of Ohio. The graphic story of the corporation's meteoric rise is set forth in minute detail in Ida M. Tarbell's classic *History of the Standard Oil Company* (1904), probably the most enduring work of the early-twentieth-century "muckraking" school.

In her opening chapter, "The Birth of an Industry," Miss Tarbell traces the beginnings of commercial interest in petroleum. The dark-green, evil-smelling oil had been long known to travelers and settlers. It was believed by the Indians to possess marvelous healing properties. Enterprising Americans, always with an eye to business opportunities, started skimming the oil from the surface of creeks, bottling and labeling it, and merchandising it as a remedy for all the ills of mankind. As "Seneca Oil" and under other fancy names, hundreds of thousands of bottles were sold at home and abroad, for internal and external consumption. Later the greater value of the oil for purposes of illumination was discovered—vastly increasing the potential market. Until then, whale oil had been the main source for lighting fuel, and whales were becoming scarce.

Drilling for oil and the opening up of great petroleum fields in northwestern Pennsylvania and Kentucky brought problems of storage and transportation, refining and manufacturing, and of course marketing. As early as 1865 there were factories in Pennsylvania making naptha, gasoline, and benzene, several grades of illuminating oil, paraffin, and lubricating oils. According to Ida Tarbell's account, the oil industry in its early stages "had workers in great numbers with plenty of capital, who were meeting every difficulty and overcoming them," thereby providing "the normal unfolding of a new and wonderful opportunity for individual endeavor." By 1872 these entrepreneurs had produced 40 million barrels of oil; in the year 1871 alone, 152 million gallons of refined oil were exported to Europe, the Far East, Latin America, and elsewhere.

Just when victory had crowned the labors of the oil pioneers, the wilderness had been transformed, and rude camps had grown into thriving towns and cities, came John D. Rockefeller. It was an era of great expectations. "But suddenly, at the very heyday of this confidence," writes Miss Tarbell, "a big hand reached out from nobody knew where, to steal their conquest and throttle their future. The suddenness and the blackness of the assault on their business stirred to the bottom their manhood and their sense of fair play, and the whole region rose in a revolt which is scarcely paralleled in the commercial history of the United States."

S. S. McClure showed the instincts of a great editor when he chose Ida Tarbell to prepare a series of articles for *McClure's Magazine* on the complex and devious career of the Standard Oil Company. The four or five articles planned originally grew into two volumes.

Miss Tarbell had been born and bred in oil country, in Erie County, Pennsylvania, surrounded as she puts it, by "oil derricks, oil tanks, pipe lines, refineries, oil exchanges." The year of her birth, 1857, coincided with oil discoveries in the area. Franklin S. Tarbell, her father, had been one of the independent oil men who stood in the way of the Rockefeller juggernaut, had been run over, and thereby suffered financial ruin. Miss Tarbell had previously demonstrated her ability as a biographer and editor. Her exceptional educational background included three years' study at the Sorbonne. Despite any personal animus she may have felt, Miss Tarbell approached her study of the Standard Oil Company with complete objectivity—an attitude maintained through-out. As a scholar by inclination and a research historian by train-ing, she set out to write a factual, carefully documented account of the most gigantic of American business enterprises, carefully avoiding becoming a crusader for social justice.

The star actor in the drama presented by Ida Tarbell, John D. Rockefeller, bore none of the outward signs of being a deep-dyed villain. He has been described as thrifty, frugal, hard-working, pious, abstemious, charitable, a model of domestic propriety, in-different to social prestige, and averse to personal luxury and extravagance. But he worshipped success and money. Rockefeller grew up in Cleveland, Ohio, a city then in the thick of the fight to become a center for the transportation and refining of petro-leum. Young Rockefeller early recognized the potential wealth in oil and by 1863 had acquired sufficient investment capital to enter the petroleum refining business, in association with a tech-nical expert, Samuel Andrews, and others. Rockefeller was uniquely qualified by mind and temperament for his new career —he was shrewd, taciturn, scheming, acutely intelligent, a superb organizer, and absolutely ruthless.

Rockefeller's first goal was to obtain a monopoly of the oil industry in Cleveland. The strategy was to make a combination with a few firms on the most favorable terms possible and then to compel, under penalty of the destruction of their business, the others to come into the company on *his* terms. The success of his maneuvers is attested to by Miss Tarbell: "Under the com-bined threat and persuasion of the Standard, armed with the South Improvement Company scheme [a trust established to gain control of the oil business] almost the entire independent oil in-terest of Cleveland collapsed in three months' time. Of the twenty-six refineries, at least twenty-one sold out." Standard Oil was now master of more than one-fifth of the refining capacity of the United States.

Congressional investigations, state legislative enactments, court decisions, and violent opposition from independent producers elsewhere temporarily hampered Rockefeller's plans to expand his empire to take in the remainder of the country and eventually the world. There was never any deviation, however, in his central purpose—an aim which he considered for the "good of all." As he saw it, important savings could be achieved by the elimination of competition, and the consolidation of companies would ensure a minimum of waste.

The key to killing off Standard's rivals was transportation. To obtain a monopoly it was all-important to gain special privileges through concealed rebates from the railroads—an illegal, but highly effective device. In addition, under a secret scheme, the railroads turned over to Standard a considerable proportion of the rate charged competing oil men. This system of "drawbacks," in combination with rebates, assured the ruin of competitors. Bribery, bulldozing, price-cutting, influencing legislation, intimidation, and like methods did the rest. The independent refiners were given an opportunity to stand and deliver, if they were willing to accept a fraction of what their business was worth. If they refused, they were crushed. Inevitably, the Standard Oil Company within a short period became paramount in its field. As Miss Tarbell observes:

> The Standard had a greater capacity than the entire Oil Creek Regions, greater than the combined New York refiners. The transaction by which it acquired this power was so stealthy that not even the best informed newspaper men of Cleveland knew what went on. It had all been accomplished in accordance with one of Mr. Rockefeller's chief business principles—"Silence is golden."

Typical of Rockefeller's tactics was his practice of underselling his rivals. "Indeed," notes Ida Tarbell, "he had long used his freedom to sell at any price he wished for the sake of driving a competitor out of the market with calculation and infinite patience. Other refiners burst into the market and undersold for a day; but when Mr. Rockefeller began to undersell, he kept it up day in and day out, week in and week out, month in and month out, until there was literally nothing left of his competitor."

In time, Standard came to produce one-third and to control all except 10 percent of the supply of petroleum. The company's huge profits were invested in railroads, and its officials served as directors of nearly all the great railway lines, as well as such powerful organizations as the Steel Trust, Amalgamated Copper, and the National City Bank of New York. By 1878 the Standard Oil Company had driven out most of its rivals and held an effective monopoly over the vast business of transporting, refining, and marketing petroleum in the United States.

For a short time the independent producers saw a ray of hope when the pipeline method of transporting crude oil to the refineries was invented. It was thought that competition between refiners would again have fair play, but the hope was a delusion. Standard Oil was able to control the pipelines. The producers then pumped the oil over the Alleghenies and piped it to the seaboard. But when it reached the Atlantic, Standard was there waiting, for the independent refineries of New York, Philadelphia, and Baltimore had been bought up by the trust.

Meanwhile tremendous opposition had developed to Standard's practices—to the guile, chicanery, and illegal behavior which had enabled it to achieve its monopolistic position. A constant warfare was waged against Standard in the courts and in the legislatures of the various states in which it operated. Almost continuously after 1870 the company was under investigation by committees of the United States Congress. The mass of testimony, findings, and decisions which emerged from these bodies is thoroughly analyzed by Miss Tarbell to validate her story. Not all the documents were readily accessible; Standard had managed to have destroyed or suppressed a number of key items.

All the furor was deeply distressing to John D. Rockefeller, "for all he asked of the world by the year 1887 was to be let alone." Miss Tarbell continues:

> He had completed one of the most perfect business organizations the world has ever seen, an organization which handled practically all of a great natural product. His factories were the most perfect and were managed with the strictest economy. He owned outright the pipe-lines which transported the crude oil. His knowledge of the consuming power of the world was accurate, and he kept his output strictly within the limit. At the same time the great marketing machinery he had put in operation carried on an aggressive campaign for new markets. The Standard Oil Company had been organized to do business, and if ever a company did business it was this one.

To be a symbol of efficiency and perfect organization, however, was insufficient. Running counter to these virtues was Standard's long record of bribery, fraud, coercion, double-dealing, and even violence, giving rise to the question of whether such an enterprise should be permitted to exist. Ida Tarbell wondered about the influence on American business morality. "One of the most depressing features of the ethical side of the matter," she observed "is that instead of such methods arousing contempt they are more or less openly admired. And this is logical. Canonize 'business success,' and men who make a success like that of the Standard Oil Trust become national heroes." In Miss Tarbell's view, "blackmail and every other business vice is the natural result of the peculiar business practices of the Standard."

Reform and regulation were slow in coming. Establishment by Congress of the Interstate Commerce Commission in 1887 and passage of the Sherman Antitrust Act in 1890, coming in response to widespread public agitation, were designed to curb such abuses as those perpetrated by Standard Oil. The acts were largely circumvented, however, by Rockefeller and his associates, aided by limited interpretations handed down in judicial decisions. Not until 1911, seven years after the appearance of Ida Tarbell's book, was there a successful prosecution of Standard Oil under the Sherman act. Through prodding from President Theodore Roosevelt, whose trust-busting activities were influenced by reading the Tarbell history, the Standard Oil and American Tobacco trusts were ordered broken up. The U.S. Supreme Court held the Standard Oil Company to be in violation of the Sherman Antitrust Act and directed it to distribute among its stockholders its shares in more than thirty companies in California, Kansas, Nebraska, New York, and Ohio.

Publication of *The History of the Standard Oil Company* brought Ida Tarbell into the national limelight. Everybody was talking about trusts, and thus the Tarbell work was extremely topical. Reviewers were generally laudatory. An exception was an anonymous review in *The Nation* which indicted the author on the grounds of sensationalism, ignorance, and misrepresentation—a striking contrast in editorial policy with that of the present-day *Nation*. The *Nation* review was reprinted by Standard Oil and distributed in hundreds of thousands of copies over the country, as was a brochure written by Elbert Hubbard in 1910, praising the company and attacking Miss Tarbell's scholarship and manner of presentation. None of the criticisms altered a widespread public acceptance of the principal Tarbell thesis: that huge monopolistic trusts were inimical to the general welfare, their business practices were despicable, and for the good of the nation they should be dissolved.

Ida Tarbell concludes the *History* with a statement of her personal creed:

> As for the ethical side, there is no cure but in an increasing scorn of unfair play—an increasing sense that a thing won by breaking the rules of the game is not worth the winning. When the business man who fights to secure special privileges, to crowd his competitor off the track by other than fair competitive methods, receives the same summary disdainful ostracism by his fellows that the doctor or lawyer who is "unprofessional," the athlete who abuses the rules, receives, we shall have gone a long way toward making commerce a fit pursuit for our young men.

33 | EXPLAINING THE UNIVERSE

Henry Adams's *The Education of Henry Adams*, 1906

Few Americans have ever begun life as well endowed, by heredity and environment, to achieve greatness as Henry Adams. He was the son of Charles Francis Adams, grandson of President John Quincy Adams and great-grandson of the second President of the United States; a graduate of Harvard University; a person of moderate wealth and a world traveler; and he was intimately acquainted, from the inside, with the workings of the American and British governments. Yet, looking back upon his life, at the age of seventy, Henry Adams judged himself a failure, "a broken arch."

In his *Great Biographers,* Albert Britt sums up different viewpoints of Adams's autobiography, *The Education of Henry Adams:* "To some it was the dreary moan of a misanthrope who sought from life a special satisfaction which life can not and should not offer. To others it seemed more the measured, calculated sneer of a super-developed New England intellect which felt itself superior to a world which was not designed to recognize its superiority." More charitably and more accurately, the book is an account of Henry Adams's struggle for an education.

It has been remarked that Adams wrote 500 pages called *Education* and never defined the word. Obviously he did not use the term in the narrow sense of formal education. Succinctly expressed, to Henry Adams education and life were identical. The basic task of education, he says, is to resolve the problem "of running order through chaos, direction through space, discipline through freedom, unity through multiplicity." The ultimate aim of education is to attain a philosophy which will solve the mystery of life. For Henry Adams, the kind of education which he sought throughout the seventy years covered by his autobiography ought to provide not only personal enlightenment but a rational explanation of the world. It is scarcely a matter for wonder that the quest ended in less than complete success.

Henry's great-grandfather, John Adams, writing to his wife Abigail, stated the purpose of his own career in these words: "I must study war and politics that my sons may have liberty to study mathematics and philosophy, geography, natural history and naval architecture, navigation and commerce and agriculture, in order to give their children a right to study painting, poetry, music, architecture, statuary, tapestry and porcelain." The prediction was remarkable, for the latter are the subjects which Henry Adams studied—but not happily or with any sense of great personal fulfillment; evidently he would have preferred to follow in his great-grandfather's and grandfather's footsteps, with a career in government and politics. The opportunity never came his way.

The process of disillusionment for Adams began early. He seems to have regarded the schoolmaster as his natural enemy. Looking back on his undergraduate days at Harvard, he commented:

> The four years passed at college were for his [the *Education* is written throughout in the third person] purposes, wasted. Harvard College was a good school, but at bottom what the boy disliked most was any school at all. He did not want to be one in a hundred—one per cent of an education. He regarded himself as the only person for whom his education had value, and he wanted the whole of it. He got barely half of an average. He never knew what other students thought of it, or what they thought they gained from it; nor would their opinion have much affected his. From the first, he wanted to be done with it.

The Harvard faculty at the time included such notable names as Alexander Agassiz, Phillips Brooks, H. H. Richardson, and Oliver Wendell Holmes, but Adams claims to have gained nothing from them. "The chief wonder of education," he remarked, "is that it does not ruin everybody connected with it, teachers and taught."

Still seeking, however, Adams decided to go to Germany, hoping vaguely to find an education at the University of Berlin. One lecture was enough to convince him otherwise. "The shock that upset him was the discovery of the university itself. He had thought Harvard College a torpid school, but it was instinct with life compared with all he could see of the University of Berlin."

Resolved to learn the German language, in any case, Adams entered a public school which from an educational point of view he found equally hopeless. "No other faculty than the memory seemed to be recognized. Least of all was any use made of reason, either analytic, synthetic, or dogmatic. The German government did not encourage reasoning."

For the next two years, Adams wandered somewhat aimlessly around Europe, chiefly in Italy, and then returned home to enter the next stage in his education—serving as private secretary to his father, Charles Francis Adams, who had been appointed Minister to England in 1861. More than a third of the *Education* is devoted to the seven years in London, during and immediately after the American Civil War. Here Henry Adams had an opportunity to study international politics at first hand. Even before the arrival of the Adamses, the British government had extended recognition to Jefferson Davis's Confederacy, convinced that the rebels would succeed in establishing a separate and independent nation. Few English politicians escape unscathed in Adams's characterizations. Gladstone is represented as plotting against the American Union while pretending neutrality. Lord John Russell, Foreign Secretary, is described as "thoroughly dishonest." Young Henry even feared that, because of various provocations, war was imminent, but as the military tide turned against the South, that peril, if it existed, vanished. In any event, the English experience confirmed Adams's growing cynicism about politics and politicians.

His skepticism was increased further upon his return home, with the inauguration of U. S. Grant as President. The episodes and scandals that characterized the Grant administration were attributed by Adams to the President's "lapses of intelligence." To him, Grant represented "a type that was pre-intellectual, archaic, and would have seemed so even to the cave dwellers." From the point of view of evolution, "He had no right to exist. He should have been extinct long ago."

Viewing the elements which assumed power under Grant, Adams was convinced that he himself had no future in government circles, and henceforth for the next fifty years he remained on the sidelines, a disillusioned and embittered observer and commentator—an uncharacteristic end to an Adams career.

Adams's education was furthered, after a fashion, by his seven years from 1870 to 1877 as professor of medieval history at Harvard University, a position which he accepted unwillingly at the urging of President Charles Eliot. In the eyes of his students and colleagues, he was a success, discarding the use of textbooks and introducing the seminar method of teaching. But, asked Adams, "What was the use of training an active mind to waste its energy? The experiments might in time train Adams as a professor, but this result was still less to his taste." And so, Adams shook the dust of Cambridge from his feet and returned to Washington to live. His chief preoccupation for the remainder of his career was historical and biographical writing.

In tracing Adams's intellectual development as it related to his "education," religion played a strange role. By his time, the Calvinism of his ancestors has evolved into Unitarianism and in the case of many individuals into free thinking and agnosticism. Adams's personal response to the change was stated as follows:

> Of all the conditions of his youth which afterwards puzzled the grown-up man, this disappearance of religion puzzled him most. The boy went to church twice every Sunday; he was taught to read his Bible, and he learned religious poetry by heart; he believed a mild deism; he prayed; he went through all the forms; but neither to him nor to his brothers and sisters was religion real. Even the mild discipline of the Unitarian church was so irksome that they all threw it off at the first possible moment, and never afterward entered a church. The religious instinct had vanished, and could not be revived, although one made in later life many efforts to recover it. That the most powerful emotion of man, next to the sexual, should disappear, might be a personal defect of his own; but that the most intelligent society, led by the most intelligent clergy, in the most moral conditions he ever knew, should have solved all the problems of the universe so thoroughly as to have quite ceased making itself anxious about past or future, and should have persuaded itself that all the problems which had convulsed human thought from earliest recorded time, were not worth discussing, seemed to him the most curious social phenomenon he had to account for in a long life.

At one period, Adams glimpsed the possibility of a satisfying philosophy of life based on the theory of evolution. During his sojourn in London, Darwinism was convulsing society, and

Adams became well acquainted with Sir Charles Lyell, Darwin's geological champion, though he never met Darwin himself. Adams thus meditated on the new theory:

> Natural Selection seemed a dogma to be put in the place of the Athanasian creed; it was a form of religious hope; a promise of ultimate perfection. Adams wished no better; he warmly sympathized in the object; but when he came to ask himself what he truly thought, he felt that he had no Faith; that whenever the next new hobby should be brought out, he should surely drop off from Darwinism like a monkey from a perch; that the idea of one Form, Law, Order, or Sequence had no more value for him than the idea of none; that what he valued most was Motion, and that what attracted his mind was Change.

Hence, Adams found evolution to be a no more persuasive answer to the enigma of existence than religion because "he was conscious that in geology, as in theology, he could prove only Evolution that did not evolve; Uniformity that was not uniform; and Selection that did not select." To illustrate the point, he cited U. S. Grant: "That, two thousand years after Alexander the Great and Julius Caesar, a man like Grant should be called—and should actually and truly be—the highest product of the most advanced evolution, made evolution ludicrous."

Adams frequently referred to himself as an eighteenth-century man, out of tune and incapable of coping with more recent times. To him the dynamo was the genius of the modern age while the Virgin symbolized the past. Adams's old-world, old-fashioned education taught him to understand languages, diplomacy, and the Virgin, but to comprehend nothing of the dynamo except its mysterious force and to be generally unfit for the world of machines.

Even more remote, Adams profoundly admired thirteenth-century Europe as a magnificent era in world culture. The *Education* was intended to be a complementary work to his *Mont-Saint-Michel and Chartres* (1904), a study of medieval art and architecture, during a period when man and society were unified—or so Adams holds—in contrast to twentieth-century multiplicity. Now medieval unity had given way to modern multiplicity in all its complex manifestations. The acceleration of physical forces and the march of invention had made the old unity of mind impossible. "The struggle is not of men, but of forces," Adams asserts. "The men become every year more and more creatures of force, massed about a central power house. The conflict is no longer between men but between the motors that drive the men."

Adams's final conclusion was that there were no answers to the questions which life asked of him or which he asked of life. The *Education* is in fact the record of the defeat of great aspirations and of commendable ambitions. "The tragedy of Adams's education," in Paul Elmer More's discerning view, "is that of a man who could not rest easy in negation, yet could find no positive faith to take its place." At the same time, More continued, "If we regard Adams's scholarship, his imagination, his verbal dexterity, his cynical vivacity, his range of reflection, we must give him a high place in the American literature of the past generation." In the opinion of another acute critic, Louis Kronenberger,

> The *Education* is a perfectly *conscious* study of frustration and deflected purpose; of the failure of a superior man to find the right place, or any tolerable place, in a civilization growing ever more corrupt, rapacious, and vulgar. . . . Confronted by the greed of a banking civilization, the crookedness of boss-rule politics, the vulgarity of a parvenu culture, the cynicism of an exploitative ruling class, the middle-class intellectual was pretty well doomed either to suffer or succumb or escape.

Adams was never a crusader determined to reform society or to correct the evils by which he was surrounded; he was more the cynical bystander convinced that the world is being ruined and has gone beyond any possibility of reclamation. He never attained the kind of education, in a large sense, which would have enabled him to control and guide his future, or even to decide what sort of education would have given him such power. It appears that whatever he did or accomplished in life, he did by accident instead of by design. He felt that he had never made more than a negligible impression upon his time, despite outstanding ability and first-rate mental qualities.

The Education of Henry Adams was privately printed in 100 copies in 1906 for distribution to a few of the author's friends. Publication did not take place until Adams's death, in 1918.

34 | SCIENCE OF SOCIETY

William Graham Sumner's *Folkways*, 1907

When Franklin Delano Roosevelt used the term "the Forgotten Man" as a political slogan during the Depression years of the 1930s, there was revived interest in the writings of the man who coined the phrase, William Graham Sumner. But Roosevelt had either misread Sumner or chose to redefine the symbolic figure. To Roosevelt, the forgotten man was the man "at the bottom of the economic pyramid." To Sumner, he was a typical member of the middle class, "delving away in patient industry, supporting his family, paying his taxes, casting his vote, supporting the church and the school, reading his newspaper, and cheering for the politician of his admiration, but he is the only one for whom there is no provision in the great scramble and the big divide."

Sumner, born in 1840, was the offspring of English immigrants. Following periods of study at Yale, Geneva, Göttingen, and Oxford, and a few years as an Episcopal minister, Sumner became the first professor of political and social science at Yale, from 1872 to 1909. Harry Elmer Barnes, in his *Introduction to the History of Sociology*, states that Sumner "was probably the most inspiring and popular teacher that either Yale University or American social science has ever produced," and through his contacts with thousands of students exerted a major influence on the development of sociology in the United States.

Sumner's career as teacher, writer, and public figure may be divided into two phases. In the beginning years he was vigorously involved, as writer and popular lecturer, in support of economic individualism in its most extreme form—for free trade and sound money, in defense of the sacredness of private property, and against socialism, trade unionism, social legislation, and governmental efforts to control monopoly—a rigid social-Darwinism philosophy favoring the survival of the fittest, with no concession to humanitarian sentiments. His social theories appear to have been shaped largely by those of Herbert Spencer, particularly as presented in the latter's *Study of Sociology*.

Phase two of Sumner's career bore slight resemblance to the controversial early years. The study and teaching of political science were largely abandoned, as he devoted himself almost exclusively to sociology. Three years before his death in 1910, there was published his classic work, *Folkways*, a vast compilation of anthropological data on the origin and evolution of social institutions, a work characterized by Barnes as "unquestionably the most important objective treatment of a very essential portion of social psychology that has ever been written. . . . Of this work it is not inaccurate to say that it is unsurpassed as a sociological achievement by any single volume in any language and that it has made the sociological treatment of usages, manners, customs, mores, and morals essentially a completed task."

Folkways added to the vocabulary of sociology such terms as folkways, mores, in-group and out-group, and ethnocentrism. Sumner was the first American to treat the customs, folk beliefs, superstitions, religion, morals, and "fundamental notions" of the folk of all nations from a genetic point of view—a contribution that entitles him to be called "the father of American sociology." There is scarcely any conceivable topic relating to human behavior not illuminated by Sumner, as he brings a rich storehouse of information to bear on the field. A common theme running throughout *Folkways* is the significance and operation of custom and conduct in the evolution of society. The facts are presented with reasonable objectivity, but the total effect is like a tragic epic, as irresistible exterior forces coerce man's action, destroy his liberty, and frustrate his aspirations.

At the outset, Sumner states that anthropology and ethnography as applied to primitive men and primitive society show that "the first task of life is to live." Men doubtless inherited some guiding instincts from their beast ancestry, through trial-and-error methods which produced either pleasure or pain. The struggle to exist may be carried on in-groups, and out of their experience fixed customs or folkways develop. As time goes on, "the folkways become more and more arbitrary, positive, and imperative." Thus primitive people act the way they do "because they and their ancestors always have done so." Ghost fear also enters in—ancestors' ghosts would be angry if the living should change ancient folkways.

Folkways are seen by Sumner as "one of the chief forces by which a society is made to be what it is." The folkways may eventually add philosophical and ethical elements, converting them into mores and thereby "become the source of the science and the art of living." Folkways are made unconsciously, are not noticed until they have long existed, and therefore can not be regarded as creations of human purpose. The end result, in any event, Sumner points out, is

> that all the life of human beings, in all ages and stages of culture, is primarily controlled by a vast mass of folkways handed down from the earliest existence of the race, having the nature of the ways of other animals, only the topmost layers of which are subject to change and control, and have been somewhat modified by human philosophy, ethics, and religion, or by other acts of intelligent reflection.

The factor of risk and loss, good or bad fortune, is a primary force in shaping folkways. "The element of luck is always present in the struggle for existence," notes Sumner, a fact which gives rise to a dependence on superstitions and religion. But the origins of folkways are lost in mystery. All have antecedents which we can never hope to discover.

From an early stage in primitive society the folk are divided between a "we-group," or in-group, combining for peace, order, law, government, and trade, and an out-group, to which the relationship of the in-group is one of war and plunder. A consequence is the development of ethnocentrism, defined as "a view of things in which one's own group is the center of everything, and all others are scaled and rated with reference to it." Virtue consists in killing, plundering, and enslaving outsiders, out of which grow the modern concepts of patriotism and its degenerate offspring chauvinism.

Sumner's view is that there are four great motives of human action which directly influence the behavior of individuals in society: hunger, sex passion, vanity, and superstitious fear. The process of making folkways is continuous. Among the causal elements are the "mystic power" of the crowd, that is, the mass psychology which leads one to "a thrill of enthusiasm in the sense of moving with a great number." Folkways have also been formed by accident; that is on the basis of pseudo-knowledge, such as the notion of the evil eye and ritual notions of uncleanliness, irrational and incongruous folkways may originate. Thus are born many harmful folkways, among which Sumner lists the destruction of a man's goods at his death; the expenditure of labor and capital on graves, temples, pyramids, rites, sacrifices, and support of priests; the prohibition of numerous wholesome foods; taboos against killing certain animals harmful to men, such as crocodiles and cobras; and caste rules.

As folkways grow, especially in more advanced societies, they may assume philosophical and ethical aspects relating to the welfare of society and then become "mores," according to Sumner's definition. The mores consist largely of negative taboos, divided into two classes, protective and destructive. Out of the mores "are produced faiths, ideas, doctrines, religions, and philosophies, according to the stage of civilization and the fashions of reflection and generalization." The fundamental importance of the mores is emphasized by Sumner in these statements: "The life of society consists in making folkways and applying them. The science of society might be construed as the study of them."

Sumner dwells at length on the theme of classes and masses. Classes are rated according to their value to society, from the infinitely small number of men of genius at the top to the masses of mediocre people in the middle to the dependent, defective, and delinquent groups at the bottom. Historically, the elite or selected classes control society, and their ways are imitated by the masses. Any variations in customs are produced by the classes, while the masses, by habit highly conservative, carry forward the traditional mores. Sumner takes a skeptical view of the romantic notion that profound wisdom resides in the masses or the common man, concluding that the great central section of the masses is "shallow, narrow-minded, and prejudiced. . . . Patriotic emotions and faiths are its favorite psychological exercises."

Mores are developed and established by ritual in which everyone participates subconsciously. For example, Sumner asserts that social ritual determines "current habits as to hours of labor, meal hours, family life, the social intercourse of the sexes, propriety, amusements, travel, holidays, education, the use of periodicals and libraries, and innumerable other details of life."

Sumner reviews and summarizes his viewpoint on "status in the folkways" as follows:

> If now we form a conception of the folkways as a great mass of usages, of all degrees of importance, covering all the interests of life, constituting an outfit of instruction for the young, embodying a life policy, forming character, containing a world philosophy, albeit most vague and unformulated, and sanctioned by ghost fear so that variation is impossible, we see with what coercive and inhibitive force the folkways have always grasped the members of a society. The folkways create status.

The force of convention is a strong instrument for the preservation of folkways. Even when rational examination shows traditional folkways to be "gross, absurd, or inexpedient," Sumner finds that "they may still be preserved by conventionalization."

Following his exposition of "fundamental notions" relating to folkways, Sumner explores the characteristics of the mores. He finds that the mores are accepted as facts. "They have nothing to do with what ought to be, will be, may be, or once was, if it is not now." Blacks and whites in Southern society, in their habits of action and feeling toward each other, are cited as an example of the way in which popular mores develop and become fixed. A society does not record its mores formally because they are unnoticed and unconscious. The mores are persistent, inert, and rigid, presenting themselves as final and unchangeable. Nevertheless, mores change almost imperceptibly from generation to generation as conditions and interests change. An instance is the Puritan code of early New England, modified by time, but still exerting a strong influence. Revolutions and drastic governmental intervention may change or at least modify mores, as in the cases of the French Revolution and the emancipation of the serfs in Russia and the slaves in the United States, but even the variations brought about by such violent upheavals may affect only surface changes in the mores.

Since it appears, according to Sumner, that old mores may be mischievous and in some instances evil and vicious, what devices are available for alterations? "It is not to be inferred that reform and correction are hopeless." It must be recognized, however, that "the mores are a phenomenon of the society and not of the state," and statesmen and social philosophers must act with great intelligence, understanding, and circumspection to set the mores moving in new directions. Group pressure may also be effective; historical examples are the activities of the Quakers and Puritans in America and missionary and other religious enterprises. It is our duty, Sumner declares, "by education and will, with intelligent purpose, to criticise and judge even the most established ways of our time, and to put courage and labor into resistance to the current mores where we judge them wrong."

Having established his basic premises, Sumner proceeds in the remainder of *Folkways* to range over the historical background and current status, worldwide, of popular "usages, manners, customs, mores, and morals." In specific detail he describes, analyzes, and criticizes folkways concerned with such matters as the struggle for existence, labor and wealth, slavery, abortion and infanticide, cannibalism, sex, marriage, incest, blood revenge, uncleanliness and the evil eye, sacral harlotry and child sacrifice, sports and drama, and asceticism. Sumner's almost encyclopedic treatment of the field precludes more than a cursory view here of some of his principal topics.

Under the heading, "The Struggle for Existence"—obviously a phrase inspired by Charles Darwin—Sumner deals with tools, arts, language, and money, from their origins among prehistoric men to the modern era. "The processes and the artifacts which are connected with food supply offer us the purest and simplest illustrations of the development of folkways," Sumner states, as he traces methods of fishing, religion and industry, stone axes and other stone instruments, arrowheads, and fire-making tools. Language is a product of folkways, growing out of the need of cooperative understanding in war, hunting, and industry. Every group produces its own language, but regardless of the origin of language, "it owes its form and development to usage." Each great family of languages represents a different way of thinking. Money is another primitive device which is produced by folkways, from the earliest—shells and beads, stone money, wampumpeag, etc.—to sophisticated modern forms. All the foregoing, plus weights and measures, the measurement of time, communication of intelligence, and trade, have their origins in primary folkways and bear upon the struggle for existence.

Sex mores and related topics are regarded by Sumner as "one of the greatest and most important divisions of the mores," and receive corresponding attention. Among phases emphasized are sex differences, marriage (a universal custom), the family as an institution, inbreeding and outbreeding, polygamy and polyandry, monogamy, matriarchal and patriarchal societies, feminine virtue, virginity, divorce, child marriage, the status of widows in various societies, and celibacy.

Closely related is his extended treatment called "The Social Codes," concerned with definitions of chastity, decency, and propriety, conceptions of modesty and shame in various societies, taboos pertaining to the body, the relation of dress to decency, bathing and customs of nudity, the evolution of the idea of obscenity, the seclusion of women in certain societies, eating, kissing, and the development of good manners, morals, and behavior—among other themes.

Sumner devotes separate chapters to the folkways and mores, ancient and modern, dealing with incest, and to the influence of kinship on family and marriage, procreation, and blood revenge—the latter gradually superseded by the "king's peace" and the beginning of criminal law.

Notions of uncleanliness and the evil eye are prolific sources of folkways. Belief is universal among primitive peoples in demonism, called by Sumner "the broadest and most primitive form of religion." Closely akin is "demonism in the second stage" from which evolve notions of uncleanliness (especially of women during menstruation and childbirth), and the evil eye, bringing bad luck to the happy and prosperous.

An entirely different subject is taken up by Sumner near the conclusion of *Folkways* in his discussion, "Popular Sports, Exhibitions, and Drama." The principal divisions of the broad area are consideration of public amusements among the uncivilized; origins of Athenian, Roman, and other drama; relationships between drama and religion; gladitorial exhibitions; ancient popular festivals; dancing and public sports; and women in the theater and on the stage.

Critics have objected that Sumner simply brought *Folkways*

to an end, with no attempt to pull the multiple strands together or to draw any overall deductions or inferences. But Sumner was not of philosophical temperament, and instead of engaging in theory and flights of fancy, he appears to have been content to let his massive array of facts speak for themselves. In actuality, however, he not infrequently interpolates his personal judgment on specific issues.

The fundamental lesson which *Folkways* teaches is that all effective rules for human guidance come out of the mores, which are brought into existence by human beings pursuing what they assume, often erroneously, to be their best interests.

35 | DUTCH BOY MAKES GOOD

Edward Bok's *The Americanization of Edward Bok,* 1920

Except for the American Indians (and anthropologists find strong evidence that they originated in Asia 18,000 years ago), all Americans are of foreign descent. In a special category are the immigrants—from the Roanoke, Jamestown, Plymouth, and Massachusetts Bay Colonies forward—who had their beginning in the Old World and later decided to cast their lot with the New.

The individual contributions of millions of foreign-born citizens to American culture and civilization are largely unchronicled, but certain names stand out, among them: Alexander Graham Bell, inventor of the telephone; great industrialists such as Andrew Carnegie and James Jerome Hill; the scientists Louis Agassiz, John James Audubon, Albert A. Michelson, Michael Pupin, and Charles P. Steinmetz; the medical investigator Alexis Carrell; the journalists Edward Bok, James Gordon Bennett, S. S. McClure, and Joseph Pulitzer; and the musicians Percy Grainger and Theodore Thomas. Without them, the American scene would have been vastly different.

An eminent representative of the group was brought to the United States at the age of six. Edward Bok was born in 1863 in the Dutch seaport, den Helder, a descendant of a distinguished line of public officials. Severe financial reverses persuaded his parents to emigrate to New York in 1870, in hopes of bettering their condition. Edward entered public school in Brooklyn without knowing a word of English. From here on out, Bok's career was another Horatio Alger epic.

Bok's genius as an entrepreneur was exhibited at a tender age, beginning with window cleaning for a baker at 50 cents a week, delivering papers, and working at odd jobs. His first journalistic venture was reporting children's parties (being certain that the name of every person present was included) for the Brooklyn

Daily Eagle. At thirteen, Edward quit school to become an office boy for the Western Union Telegraph Company, where his father was employed as a translator. More money-making schemes were developed on the side, including a profitable one writing or editing 100-word biographical sketches of well-known actors and actresses and famous Americans to be printed on the backs of pictures enclosed in cigarette packages.

Now thoroughly bitten by the journalistic bug, young Bok proceeded to report public speeches for the local paper, edit a church paper entitled the *Brooklyn Magazine,* write theater news for the *Daily Eagle,* publish theater programs (which he designed), and to serve successively as stenographer in two publishing firms, Henry Holt and Charles Scribner.

Bok soon observed that few women read newspapers and the concomitant fact that the papers of the time paid slight attention to women's interests. Thus was born an embryo idea which was to lead to the young journalist's greatest success. He began to gather material designed to appeal to women and to influence their reading habits. Ella Wheeler Wilcox and others were engaged to write on women's topics, and shortly, through his syndicate, Bok was supplying newspapers with a full page of women's features.

Another void to be filled, in Bok's view, was news about books and authors. This feature, known as "Bok's Literary Leaves," soon had a following of readers in more than forty newspapers. In 1887 Bok was placed in charge of advertising for the newly established *Scribner's Magazine,* and in that capacity a year later helped to make famous Edward Bellamy's utopian novel, *Looking Backward.*

The foregoing accomplishments were all crowded into the first two decades after Bok came to America. In April 1889 Cyrus H. K. Curtis, who had been impressed by Bok's book reviews in the Philadelphia *Times,* invited him, at the age of twenty-six, to become editor of the *Ladies' Home Journal,* then a six-year-old magazine. After considerable hesitation and against the advice of his friends and relatives, Bok accepted the post. Thus began the career which was to make him an internationally known figure. Under his guidance, the *Ladies' Home Journal* became a national institution to a degree which no other magazine had ever achieved. By the time Bok retired, after thirty years in the editorship, two records had been set: the magazine's circulation had reached 2 million, and each issue carried advertising in excess of a million dollars.

The story of Bok's amazing life, from his earliest recollections until he left the *Ladies Home Journal,* is recounted in *The Americanization of Edward Bok* (1920), an autobiography told in the third person.

An important element in Bok's success was his self-confidence and complete lack of false modesty, as demonstrated by the ease with which he dealt with celebrities. Apparently, even as a youth, he never stood in awe of famous personages. At the age of about thirteen, Bok started to assemble an autograph collection, beginning with a letter from James A. Garfield. In pursuit of this hobby, and later through his editorial activities, he became personally acquainted—in some cases on intimate terms—with every president from U. S. Grant to Woodrow Wilson, and he met Mrs. Abraham Lincoln. In addition, he developed close and friendly relations with most of the prominent American and English authors of the time: Dr. Oliver Wendell Holmes, Emerson, Longfellow, Robert Louis Stevenson, Rudyard Kipling, Mark Twain, Harriet Beecher Stowe, Eugene Field, William Dean Howells, James Whitcomb Riley, and others. Quite legitimately, therefore, *The Americanization of Edward Bok* is a record of name-dropping par excellence..

For a mere man, furthermore an unmarried one, to undertake editorship of a woman's magazine exposed Bok to a great deal of jocular comment and even ridicule. As a first step, to compensate for his own want of intimate knowledge of the gentler sex, Bok offered prizes for the best suggestions for improving the contents of the magazine. Thousands of answers poured in, and combining them with his own ideas Bok proceeded to establish departments to advise girls on their personal problems, young mothers on infant and child care, and mature women on their spiritual needs. As Bok saw his function, he should not only "give the people what they want," but "give the people what they ought to have and don't know they want." He was unwilling to stop with trivia, as he explained in a forthright statement:

There are undoubtedly acute problems which concern themselves with the proper ingredients in cooking recipes, the correct stitch in crocheting or knitting, the most desirable and daintiest kinds of lingerie, and the momentous question whether a skirt should escape the ground by six or eight inches. These are vital points in the lives of thousands of women, and their wisest solutions should be given by the best authorities. But is it too much to say that they are hardly of a nature to develop and satisfy the mental and spiritual nature of a man? At least, not for a lifetime!

Guided by such principles in editing a magazine for women, Bok inaugurated a series of crusades, using the *Ladies' Home Journal* as a forum or pulpit. Some campaigns ended in splendid victories, others in ignominious defeats.

Bok soon learned that the average American girl was quite unprepared for motherhood, and a department was set up to distribute information about prenatal and postnatal care. After several years of successfully raising babies by mail, the editorial decision was made to deal with a less savory subject. At the turn of the century even the mention of venereal disease was banned in polite society and in every decent periodical and newspaper. With considerable courage, in 1906 Bok broke the conspiracy of silence in his magazine. Seventy-five thousand readers of the *Ladies' Home Journal* canceled their subscriptions when the first articles on the subject appeared. Gradually, as understanding and education grew, the matter became accepted as suitable for public debate and discussion.

Theodore Roosevelt once declared that Bok was the only man who ever changed the architecture of an entire nation. The editor had a keen desire to improve the architecture of the small American home. To that end, for years he published small-house plans by the country's foremost architects, and the plans were extensively used throughout the United States. All of them eliminated the useless parlor, previously a proud feature of the American home.

A similarly successful attempt was made to upgrade the interior appearance of homes. The *Ladies' Home Journal* carried pictorial representations of what were considered the best and most tastefully furnished rooms, as a result of which the physical appearance of domestic furniture completely changed within a few years. The next problem was to improve the pictures on the walls of the American home. After the invention of four-color presses, Bok obtained permission to reproduce art masterpieces from the greatest American private collections. More than 70 million copies were distributed through the magazine.

Beautiful homes were out of place in ugly cities, and Bok's next target was to get rid of the unsightly spots disgracing residential and business areas. A photographic campaign stirred the municipalities represented to initiate clean-up measures. A parallel drive to abolish offensive billboards was fought by vested interests and ended largely in failure—in the same fashion that the industry has resisted reform ever since.

One of Bok's most notable journalistic triumphs followed an announcement in the *Ladies' Home Journal* that no more patent medicine advertisements would be accepted—at the time a chief source of revenue for magazines and newspapers. The profits of the patent medicine business in the United States, almost totally unregulated, ran into hundreds of millions of dollars annually. The *Ladies' Home Journal* showed the actual contents of the most popular medicines, to demonstrate their worthlessness. Some contained as high as 40 percent alcohol. Next to an advertisement representing Lydia Pinkham in her laboratory, Bok placed a photograph of Mrs. Pinkham's tombstone showing that she had been dead twenty-two years. Mark Sullivan, later to achieve distinction as a journalist, was assigned to write a series of muckraking articles on the unethical practices prevailing in the business. Out of the ensuing fights with the nostrum makers, several lawsuits, and general public acclaim finally emerged the Food and Drugs Act of 1906.

Among Bok's "failures," to use his own word, was an attack on Parisian couturiers, protesting their lack of taste and questionable morals, their "deceit and misrepresentation." American women of refinement and position were actually dressing like Parisian streetwalkers. Bok employed the most expert designers in women's wear to create American designs, but the American woman ignored them. She continued to be a slave to Parisian styles, with absolutely no patriotic instincts. After a year, Bok abandoned any hope of reform and dropped the matter.

In another area involving women's fashions, Bok first lost and then won a campaign. A national mania for egret feathers used for decoration was threatening the extinction of the beautiful birds. An article with photographs and texts exposing the cruelty of the craze made no impact on the readers of the *Ladies' Home Journal*. Instead, the demand for the feather more than quadrupled. Having failed to enlist feminine support, Bok carried his case to the state legislatures and persuaded them to pass laws banning the butchery of the birds and making it a misdemeanor to import, sell, purchase, or wear an egret. Later a federal law came into existence, prohibiting the importation of bird feathers into the country.

Around the period of the beginning of World War I, America was dance mad, and in Bok's view the dances were becoming increasingly offensive. Vernon and Irene Castle were appointed to introduce to *Ladies' Home Journal* readers more decorous and dignified dances. The Castles attempted to revive the gavotte, the polka, and the waltz—all to no avail, as the public continued to turkey trot and bunny hug.

More success was achieved in promoting the spread of interest in music. The *Ladies Home Journal* presented the popular new marches by John Philip Sousa and new compositions by Reginald de Koven, Sir Arthur Sullivan, Tosti, Moscowski, Richard Strauss, Paderewski, Josef Hoffmann, Edouard Strauss, and Mascagni. Piano and vocal music lessons were given in the magazine, and for a number of years Josef Hoffmann was a regular contributor of articles on music.

A hornet's nest was deliberately stirred up by Bok in a series of attacks against women's clubs—in particular against the puerility and superficiality of their programs. He saw the clubs as a potential power for good in the civic life of the nation; instead, he felt that their energies were being wasted on pseudo-culture. The clubs were urged by Bok to place less emphasis on cultural subjects and to pay attention to numerous questions dealing with the life of their communities. Again there were widespread protests against Bok's criticisms and cancellations of subscriptions, but the end results appear to have been wholesome, for under the prodding many clubs began to broaden their interests.

During the period of Bok's editorship, the question of women's suffrage became a burning issue. Bok interviewed such leaders in the movement as Susan B. Anthony, Julia Ward Howe, Anna Howard Shaw, and Jane Addams. The editor claimed that "he was ready to have the magazine, for whose editorial policy he was responsible, advocate that side of the issue which seemed for the best interests of the American woman." But when Bok made up his mind, he came down on the unpopular side: "He felt that American women were not ready to exercise the privilege intelligently and that their mental attitude was against it."

Publication of an editorial stating Bok's position stirred up the greatest storm of all. As he wrote, "The denunciation brought down upon him by his attitude toward woman's clubs was as nothing compared to what was now let loose." President Cleveland, President Eliot of Harvard, Lyman Abbott, and a few women rallied to Bok's defense, but the final outcome was inevitable. The year after Bok retired from the editorship of the *Ladies' Home Journal*, the Nineteenth Amendment extended the franchise to women in all states of the Union..

In his *Postscript to Yesterday*, Lloyd Morris suggests something of the impact which Bok made on the feminine half of the nation:

> One needed only to look at the American woman to appreciate his influence on her existence. During the hour before dinner, for example. Her Bok-designed home was in a Bok-tidied city. Her Bok-raised children were upstairs, quietly imbibing the Bok-explained facts of natural life. In her Bok-furnished living room, hung with Bok-chosen pictures, she had no anxiety about the coming meal; it was being prepared according to directions by Bok.

But despite the preeminent position which he had attained in his field and the great material success which came to him, Bok was unhappy when he reached the end of his thirty years of editorial service. In short, he was disillusioned with women, and to some extent with his adopted homeland. In a chapter of *The Americanization of Edward Bok*, "Where America Fell Short with Me," the author condemned American wastefulness and failure to provide for the future; the emphasis on quantity rather than quality, with a resulting sloppiness in work produced and a general lack of thoroughness; the inadequacy of public school education, characterized by incompetent methods of teaching; lack of respect for and poor enforcement of laws; and the meager preparation which Americans receive for exercising the privileges of citizenship.

On the other hand, in discussing "What I Owe to America," Bok concluded that no other nation in the world offered the foreign-born the opportunities they had in the United States; he commended the "wonderful idealism" of the American people, a trait in the American character not generally realized abroad; and he found that the true American plays fair and is generally honest, despite the fact that some men succeed by unscrupulous behavior.

Concerning his views on women, Bok was discreet and even reticent. After thirty years of association, he had reached the conclusion that women had revealed their least attractive side to him through the magazine, and his ideal of womanhood had been virtually destroyed—for him, woman had fallen off her pedestal. As far as possible he avoided women, not because he disliked them, but because they did not interest him. (Bok did not marry until age twenty-nine and then to the boss's daughter, Mary Louise Curtis). When he accepted the editorial post with the *Ladies' Home Journal,* his mother had warned him: "I am sorry you are going to take this position. It will cost you the high ideal you have always held of your mother's sex. But a nature, as is the feminine nature, wholly swayed inwardly by emotion, and outwardly influenced by the insatiate love for personal adornment, will never stand the analysis you will give it."

Among the reasons for Bok's disillusionment were his experiences with the Parisian dress designers, failure to obtain the support of women in stopping the killing of the egrets, the shallow nature of activities in women's clubs, the lack of genuine intellectual interests among women, and clashes with militant feminists or suffragettes. It is not surprising therefore that upon his retirement, when the newspapers were clamoring for his opinions of women, Bok should have decided that discretion is the better part of valor and replied, "No, thank you, not a word," without ever giving his reasons.

The Americanization of Edward Bok was awarded the Pulitzer Prize in 1921 and went on to become a best-seller, with sales in the hundreds of thousands.

36 | REVOLT FROM THE VILLAGE
Sinclair Lewis's *Main Street,* 1920

In older American literature the small town was traditionally, in Sinclair Lewis's words, "the one sure abode of friendship, honesty, and clean-sweet marriageable girls." A more detailed portrait is painted by Carl Van Doren, quoting from an anonymous observer:

> the white church with tapering spire, the sober schoolhouse, the smithy of the ringing anvil, the corner grocery, the cluster of friendly houses; the venerable parson, the wise physician, the canny squire, the grasping landlord softened or outwitted in the end; the village belle, gossip, idiot; jovial fathers, gentle mothers, merry children; cool parlors, shining kitchens, spacious barns, lavish gardens, fragrant summer dawns, and comfortable winter evenings.

This euphoric scene had been disturbed occasionally before Sinclair Lewis's *Main Street*—by Mark Twain, Hamlin Garland, Edward Eggleston, E. W. Howe, Zona Gale, Edgar Lee Masters, Theodore Dreiser, and Sherwood Anderson—but the image of the ideal small town remained, for the most part, firmly fixed in the mind of the great American public until Lewis exploded a bomb to blast away the delusions.

The theme of *Main Street* had been gestating in Lewis's mind for some fifteen years before the birth of the book. He, too, had grown up in the belief that the village, such as Sauk Centre, Minnesota, in which he was born, was paradise, but in early youth Lewis changed his mind, for he had no nostalgic memories of his home town. Sauk Centre became the prototype for Gopher Prairie in his novel. The theme and purpose of *Main Street* is announced in a kind of preamble:

> This is America—a town of a few thousand, in a region of wheat and corn and dairies and little groves.
> The town is, in our tale, called "Gopher Prairie, Minnesota."

But its Main Street is the continuation of Main Streets everywhere. The story would be the same in Ohio or Montana, in Kansas or Kentucky or Illinois, and not very differently would it be told Up York State or in the Carolina Hills.

Main Street is the climax of civilization. That this Ford car might stand in front of the Bon Ton Store, Hannibal invaded Rome and Erasmus wrote in Oxford cloisters. What Ole Jenson the grocer says to Ezra Stowbody the banker is the new law for London, Prague, and the unprofitable isles of the sea; whatsoever Ezra does not know and sanction, that thing is heresy, worthless for knowing and wicked to consider.

Our railway station is the final aspiration of architecture. Sam Clark's annual hardware turnover is the envy of the four counties which constitute God's Country. In the sensitive art of the Rosebud Movie Palace there is a Message, and humor strictly moral.

Such is our comfortable tradition and sure faith. Would he not betray himself an alien cynic who should otherwise portray Main Street, or distress the citizens by speculating whether there may not be other faiths?

Main Street is not primarily a novel of plot or of complicated happenings. The tale itself could be readily condensed to a few pages. The reader's interest is held by the cast of characters and by the setting. Two principal actors stand out: Carol Milford, who has been an active city girl, a former librarian, and Will Kennicott, a country physician, her husband. Carol's disillusionment begins even before she arrives in Gopher Prairie, as she and Dr. Kennicott ride through the Midwestern flatlands, immediately after their marriage en route to their new home in Gopher Prairie. Carol is appalled by the smells, dirt, and squalidness of the train and its passengers, the unshaven drab farmers, and the ugliness of the towns through which they pass. Her husband accepts the communities matter of factly as "good, hustling burgs."

When Carol has a chance to view Gopher Prairie at first hand her original impressions are confirmed. In a walk through the village, she is struck by its complete "planlessness," by "the flimsy temporariness of the buildings, their faded unpleasant colors. Each man had built with the most valiant disregard for all others." Only thirty-two minutes are required to cover the town, east and west, north and south. Among the highlights of the stroll are the hotel, Minniemashie House, "a tall lean shabby structure, three stories of yellow-streaked wood, the corners covered with sanded pine slabs purporting to symbolize stone"; Dyer's Drug Store, "a corner building of regular and unreal blocks of artificial stone," inside of which are "a greasy marble soda-fountain" and "pawed-over heaps of tooth-brushes and combs and packages of shaving soap, shelves of soap-cartons, teething rings, garden-seeds, and patent medicines in yellow packages"; a small wooden motion-picture theater called the Rosebud Movie Palace; Howland & Gould's Grocery, in the display window of which are "black, overripe bananas and lettuce on which a cat is sleeping"; Dahl & Oleson's Meat Market—"a reek of blood"; "a fly-buzzing saloon with a brilliant gold and enamel whisky sign across the front"; a tobacco shop, the Snake House, "filled with young men shaking dice for cigarettes, racks of magazines, and pictures of coy fat prostitutes in striped bathing-suits"; Axl Egge's General Store, "frequented by Scandinavian farmers"; Chester Dashaway's House Furnishing Emporium, "a vista of heavy oak rockers with leather seats, asleep in a dismal row"; Ye Arte Shoppe, "a touching fumble at beauty"; "the damp, yellow-brick schoolbuilding in its cindery grounds"; and the Farmers' National Bank, "an Ionic temple of marble." The street is cluttered with electric light poles, telephone poles, gasoline pumps for motorcars, and boxes of merchandise.

The minds of people in Carol's small town are preoccupied with "cheap motor cars, telephones, ready-made clothes, silos, alfalfa, kodaks, phonographs, leather-upholstered Morris chairs, bridge-prizes, oil-stocks, motion-pictures, land-deals, unread sets of Mark Twain, and a chaste version of national politics." Such towns, thinks Carol, are populated by "a savorless people, gulping tasteless food, and sitting afterward, coatless and thoughtless, in rocking-chairs prickly with inane decorations, listening to mechanical music, saying mechanical things about the excellence of Ford automobiles, and viewing themselves as the greatest race in the world."

With such a life of unmitigated dullness, hundreds of thousands of women and young men are discontented, and the more intelligent young people flee to the cities, never to return. Even the most vociferous patriots of the towns pull up stakes in their old age, if they can afford it, to go live in California or in the cities.

When Carol comes to Gopher Prairie, she is keenly interested in sociology and fired up with ambition to reform villages and small towns. "I'll get my hands on one of those prairie towns and make it beautiful," she declares, before she ever sees Gopher Prairie. "Nobody has done anything with the ugly towns here in the Northwest except hold revivals and build libraries to contain the Elsie books. I'll make 'em put in a village green, and darling cottages, and a quaint Main Street!"

Carol's idealism is dealt a series of hard blows. She learns that Gopher Prairie's social habits and behavior are as depressing as its architecture and physical appearance. The men talk about motorcars and train schedules and boast of their town as God's own country. The women are mainly interested in gossip, sewing, and cooking. Most of the latter sex are members of the two women's clubs, the Jolly Seventeen and the Thanatopsis Club. Among men and women, the elements of a successful party are to invite the same people each time, to serve the same refreshments, talk about the same subjects, never to deviate from reactionary views about farmers, labor, and politics, and to arrive and depart at set times. Carol's attempts to make parties more fun are met with embarrassment and ridicule. Everyone wants to have things remain as they are. At the first meeting of the Jolly Seventeen, Carol stirs up controversy when she states her belief that it is the librarian's duty to stimulate people to read. The town librarian insists on the contrary, that her chief responsibility is to preserve the books.

The townspeople disapprove of many other things done by Carol. She hires a maid and pays her the overgenerous sum of 6 dollars a week, as well as treating her as a friend. A party with an Oriental setting which she gives is considered pretentious. Even worse, she redecorates the old Kennicott house and gets rid of the ancient bric-a-brac, the dark wallpaper, heavy furniture, and mildew—a move which upsets Will. Attempts to arouse interest in social reform through the Thanatopsis Club are rejected by the women, who insist that no real poverty exists in Gopher Prairie. A campaign to replace the ugly old building serving as the city hall is voted down. Private interests are paramount: The wife of the school superintendent thinks that reform should begin with a new school building, and the minister's wife wants a new and larger church. Carol can persuade no one to sympathize with her desire to beautify the town and to improve its entertainments. Furthermore, she is deeply distressed to learn from one of her few friends, Vida Sherwin, that the villagers are watching her and gossiping about her and criticizing her every movement, and even the town's adolescent boys are discussing her in overfamiliar language. The people's appearance of cordiality and friendliness is all on the surface. Carol never fully recovers from this traumatic revelation or completely forgives Gopher Prairie for it.

Other incidents bring out the provincialism, hypocrisy, narrowness, and cruelty of village life—all building up a case to demonstrate that small towns produce small people. The town's professional men are filled with petty jealousies and resentments toward each other. A young teacher is discharged from her job and forced to leave town, even though the school board does not believe in a charge of misconduct against her; she has been guilty only of youth and high spirits. Carol's fellow rebellious spirit, an atheist, socialist, and a thoroughly decent human being, Miles Bjornstam, leaves town a broken man when his wife and child die of typhoid and it is rumored that he has killed them with mistreatment.

Sinclair Lewis's later celebrated character, Babbitt, is foreshadowed in a speech by the "Booster and Hustler," Jim Blausser, who has been invited by the Commercial Club to launch its campaign to attract industry to Gopher Prairie and incidentally to boost real estate values. Jim begins his rip-snorting talk:

> I want to tell you good people, and it's just as sure as God made little apples, the thing that distinguishes our American commonwealth from the pikers and tinhorns in other countries is our punch. You take a genuine, honest-to-God homo Americanibus and there ain't anything he's afraid to tackle. Snap and speed are his middle name! He'll put her across if he has to ride from hell to breakfast, and believe me, I'm mighty good and sorry for the boob that's so unlucky as to get in his way, because that poor slob is going to wonder where he was at when Old Mr. Cyclone hit town.

After three years of marriage, Carol becomes pregnant, and the birth of her son Hugh diverts her attention from the unpleasant side of life in Gopher Prairie. She wants a new house, but she and Will cannot agree on the style of architecture: he is satisfied with a square frame structure, while Carol dreams of a Georgian mansion with columns and wide lawn or a white Cape Cod cottage.

Then Carol meets an artistic young aesthete, a bohemian, with whom for a time she imagines herself in love. She visits his shop often to talk about art, and Will warns her that the town is beginning to gossip about them. Carol stops seeing the young man, who eventually sells his soul to Hollywood and leaves town. No immorality is involved, and Carol is simply trying to brighten up a drab existence and to retain as much of her romantic youth as possible; but Gopher Prairie is prudish, gossiping, and censorious.

Only two of the character studies in *Main Street* are well rounded, those of Carol and Will. One critic, Daniel Aaron, calls Carol "a romantic ninny, after all, dreaming of medieval castles, bearded Frenchmen, nymphs and satyrs, jeweled elephants. Her vision of a remodeled Gopher Prairie as a New England village nestling in a Swinburnian landscape was as pathetic as it was ridiculous." Lewis's principal biographer, Mark Schorer, concurs: "Her values, her yearning for a free and gracious life, had only the vaguest shape, and when she tried to put them into action in Gopher Prairie, Minnesota, she found only the most artificial and sentimental means." Even Lewis shares these views, for while Carol is still in college he depicts her as a capricious, illogical reformer: "She wanted, just now, to have a cell in a settlement-house, like a nun without the bother of the black robe, and be kind, and read Bernard Shaw, and enormously improve a horde of grateful poor." She brings the same attitude to Gopher Prairie, where she wants to plant seeds of beauty and intelligence, but she is impulsive, undiplomatic, naïve, and unable to foresee inevitable complications. Another commentator, Percy H. Boynton, concludes that Carol is a take-off on the advanced young woman. Nevertheless, even though the author makes Carol seem somewhat ridiculous at times, he shares her dislike for Gopher Prairie's complacency and hypocrisy and sympathizes with her efforts to escape what Lewis calls "the village virus." There is nothing silly about her when she condemns the town's ugliness and narrowness.

Dr. Will is represented as a very competent physician and surgeon, fully at home with the civic boosters, enjoying their humor, and in complete accord with their reactionary politics. He is scornful of the artistic and esthetic, has deep prejudices about caste, class, and nationality, and is intolerant of social dissenters. In a revealing passage, he declares:

> Tell you, Carrie, there's just three classes of people: folks that haven't got any ideas at all; and cranks that kick about everything; and Regular Guys, the fellows with sticktuitiveness, that boost and get the world's work done.

This may be nonsense, at least in Carol's eyes, but one cannot disregard the values for which "Doc" Kennicott stands: honesty, hardwork, kindness, thriftiness, and common sense—good middle-class virtues.

The remaining characters in *Main Street* are chiefly two-dimensional, or "types," such as the town gossip, the town atheist, the frustrated schoolteacher, the lawyers and clergymen, and the rebellious young artist. Old Ezra Stowbody, the banker, "a distinguished bird of prey," bewails the fact that he no longer runs the town. A spokesman for the women in the Jolly Seventeen is Juanita Haycock, declaiming about hired girls:

> They're ungrateful, all that class of people. I do think the domestic problem is simply becoming awful. I don't know what the country's coming to, with these Scandahoofian clodhoppers demanding every cent you can save, and so ignorant and impertinent, and on my word, demanding bath-tubs and everything —as if they weren't mighty good and lucky at home if they got a bath in the wash-tub.

The climax for Carol and Will comes when Carol decides that she must get away from her husband and Gopher Prairie. After a long argument she takes little Hugh and goes off to Washington, where she plans to do war work. The new freedom, however, is empty and as disillusioning as life in Gopher Prairie. The people of Washington are discovered to be simply a congregation of those in thousands of Gopher Prairies. Washington, too, is

Main Street. After nearly two years, Will persuades her to return home, and Hugh is happy to be with his father again. Carol is reluctant to go back, but she no longer hates Gopher Prairie. She sees it now as "a toiling new settlement," and more or less accepts Will's judgment that its citizens are "a lot of pretty good folks, working hard and trying to bring up their families the best they can." Carol participates in a number of civic reforms and is finally accepted by the town.

Nevertheless, Carol Kennicott remains something of a rebel. She decides that society rather than the villagers are to blame for the existing state of affairs. Why should she rage at individuals?:

> Not individuals but institutions are the enemies, and they most afflict the disciples who the most generously serve them. They insinuate their tyranny under a hundred guises and pompous names, such as Polite Society, the Family, the Church, Sound Business, the Party, the Country, the Superior White Race; and the only defense against them, Carol beheld, is unembittered laughter.

The questioning attitude emerges again at *Main Street*'s conclusion when Carol points to the head of her sleeping daughter, her second child, and declares to Will: "Do you see that object on the pillow? Do you know what it is? It's a bomb to blow up smugness. If you Tories were wise, you wouldn't arrest anarchists; you'd arrest all these children while they're asleep in their cribs. Think what that baby will see and meddle with before she dies in the year 2000! She may see an industrial union of the whole world, she may see aeroplanes going to Mars."

The impact of *Main Street* was tremendous. The publication date, 1920, was a psychological moment. World War I and the Treaty of Versailles had left a bitter taste in the mouths of the younger generation and turned them against everything represented by their elders. Mark Schorer calls *Main Street* "the most sensational event in twentieth-century American publishing history." Two years after its appearance, John Farrar wrote in *The Bookman:* "Lewis' friends all bought the book, then the cognoscenti, then the literati, then the literate, a paltry thousand or so. Then the sleeping beast turned over, rubbed its eyes, and woke up. Fifty thousand. It howled in an ecstasy of self-torture.

One hundred thousand. His publishers estimate that it has beyond doubt reached two million readers. And people are still buying and reading it for the first time."

Mark Schorer, author of a monumental biography of Sinclair Lewis, concludes that "in any strict literary sense, he was not a great writer, but without his writing one cannot imagine modern American literature. No more, without his writing, could Americans today imagine themselves. His epitaph should be: *He did us good.*

37 | SOCIAL ARBITER

Emily Post's *Etiquette: The Blue Book of Social Usage*, 1922

Since colonial days Americans have been concerned with matters of social behavior. Breaches of right conduct—scandalmongering, cursing, lying, name calling, flirting, and drinking to excess—might be punished by ducking, flogging, being placed in the stocks, or other unpleasant chastisement. George Washington, at the age of fifteen, composed his own rules, including such precepts as "Contradict not at every turn what others say"; when dining, "Put not another bit into your mouth until the former be swallowed"; "Cleanse not your teeth with the table cloth, napkin, fork or knife"; "Spit not in the fire"; "Kill no vermin as fleas, lice ticks, etc. in the sight of others"; and "Reprehend not the imperfections of others for that belongs to parents, masters and superiours."

Considerable room for improvement remained in the young American republic after Washington's time. In her *Domestic Manners of the Americans,* based on a visit to this country in 1831, Mrs. Frances Trollope observed that a typical theater audience was like nothing that she had ever experienced back in England: "The noises were perpetual, and of the most unpleasant kind," she wrote. "Men came into the lower tier of boxes without their coats. . . . The spitting was incessant," and "the mixed smell of onions and whiskey" made her regret ever having come. Other travelers from abroad, notably Charles Dickens (in his *American Notes* and *Martin Chuzzlewit*), drew equally unflattering pictures of nineteenth-century American society and its behavior. And even as late as 1922 Emily Post had to remind her readers that in the theater it is "very inconsiderate to giggle and talk" or to drag your coat "across the heads of those sitting in front of you."

Made self-conscious and ill at ease by such comments from

foreign and domestic critics, the Americans provided a ready market for a large home-grown literature of etiquette and improvement books, which began to flourish in the nineteenth and early twentieth centuries. The mass of such writings was pretty dreadful.

To fill the breach came Mrs. Post's *Etiquette: In Society, In Business, In Politics, and At Home.* The first edition, issued in 1922, in a modest printing of 5,000 copies, immediately caught the public fancy, and in successive versions the work attained a position of commanding authority in its field. By 1970, there had been published twelve editions and ninety-nine printings, and more than a million copies had been sold. Generations of brides have arranged their wedding plans by Mrs. Post's rules, thousands of teen-age swains have followed her advice about corsages, and countless American matrons have placed the fish forks where Emily Post said they belonged.

Mrs. Post's qualifications for the job of regulating American social life were impeccable. Her family could be traced back to the seventeenth century, and she was ten times great-granddaughter of John and Priscilla Alden. Her father was a famous architect, and Emily grew up in New York, with summers in Bar Harbor or Tuxedo Park and frequent trips to Europe. A celebrated beauty, there were many candidates for her hand, from whom she chose a handsome young banker, Edwin Main Post. Within a few years, unfortunately, both her father and husband lost their money, and the Posts' marriage went on the rocks, leaving Emily with two sons to support. At that point she turned to writing. Her first literary efforts consisted of five novels with high-society backgrounds.

Mrs. Post's venture into the etiquette field came about by chance. Not without considerable persuasion, Richard Duffy, a Funk and Wagnalls editor, convinced her that existing books on etiquette were of miserable quality and that she should undertake to write a better one. The rest is history. Within a year, Post's *Etiquette* was at the top of the nonfiction, best-seller list. "No social climber should be without one," suggested one critic.

Since she was writing about the kind of society she had known so intimately, Mrs. Post inevitably filled the first edition with advice concerning the right livery for footmen, the order of precedence at formal dinners, the duties of a kitchenmaid in a staff of twelve servants, and other problems of the fashionable life. Edmund Wilson, in his *Classics and Commercials,* reports that he "fell under the book's spell and read it almost through," adding that "Mrs. Post is not merely the author of a comprehensive textbook on manners: she is a considerable imaginative writer, and her book has some of the excitement of a novel. It has also the snob-appeal which is evidently an important factor in the success of a Marquard or a Galsworthy." Wilson was reading the first edition.

The fictional atmosphere of *Etiquette* is enhanced by the creation of a cast of characters personifying various traits, who move in and out of the several editions. In a tradition that goes back to the medieval morality play *Everyman* and John Bunyan's *Pilgrim's Progress,* a group of abstract characters carries on the action for Mrs. Post. Undesirable and not to be emulated players include the Richan Vulgars, the Upstarts, Mr. and Mrs. Unsuitable, Mr. Parvenu, Mr. and Mrs. Gotta Crust, rich young people like the Lovejoys and the Gailys, newly rich such as Bobo and Lucy Gilding (she "smokes like a furnace and is miserable unless she can play bridge for high stakes"), "that odious Hector Newman," and, worst of all, "The Guest No One Invites Again."

Occupying the summit of Mrs. Post's social world, from the point of view of wealth and "social credentials" are the Worldlys of Great Estates and the Gildings of Golden Hall. Of Golden Hall, the author writes ecstatically:

> The house is a palace, the grounds are a park. There is not only a long wing of magnificent guest rooms in the house, occupied by young girls or important older people, but there is also a guest annex, a separate building designed and run like the most luxurious country club. . . . Perfectly equipped Turkish and Russian baths in charge of the best Swedish masseur and masseuse procurable . . . a glass-roofed and enclosed riding ring—not big enough for games of polo, but big enough to practice in winter.

Other memorable members of Mrs. Post's cast of characters are Mr. and Mrs. Kindheart, the Toploftys, the Oldnames, the Wellborns, the Eminents, the Notquites, the Spendeasy Westerns, Professor Bugge (the one intellectual admitted to the charmed circle), the Newlyweds, Mr. Stocksan Bonds, Miss Nobackground, the Greatlakes (representing the Midwest), the Littlehouses, and a clutch of eligible young bachelors or men-about-town: Frederick Bachelor, John Hunter Titherington Smith, and Clubwin Doe. The one artist we meet in the best society has a derisive name, Frederick Dauber.

Mrs. Post's own hero and heroine among this motley assemblage are undoubtedly Mr. and Mrs. Oldname, who dwell in "The Small House of Distinction." Mrs. Oldname knows how to dress to "express the individuality of beautiful taste combined with personal dignity and grace which gives to a perfect costume an inimitable air of distinction." Her tact is unfailing, equal to any occasion, and her home is furnished to perfection. Even her walk is a thing of beauty, resembling Pavlova dancing: "Her body is perfectly balanced, she holds herself straight, and yet nothing suggests a ramrod. She takes steps of medium length, and like all people who move and dance well, walks from the hip, not the knee. On no account does she swing her arms, nor does she rest a hand on her hip! Nor, when walking, does she wave her hands about in gesticulation."

All of Mrs. Post's actors are based upon real people. She dedicates *Etiquette* "To you my friends whose identity in these pages is veiled in fictional disguise." It would appear that her years in the upper reaches of society may have left her with grudges to settle.

As a literary device, however, the imaginary characters were useful for illustrating points of etiquette. An instance is a disastrous dinner party given by the Newlyweds, and attended by such distinguished guests as the Gildings, Mrs. Toplofty, the Kindhearts, and Mr. Clubwin Doe. The guests enter a smoke-filled drawing room where "everyone begins to cough and blink. They are very polite, but the smoke, growing each moment denser, is not to be overlooked. Mrs. Toplofty takes matters into her own hands and makes Mr. Doe and the husband carry the logs, smoke and all, and throw them into the yard." After an interminable delay, the cook shouts from the dining room, "Dinner's all ready." The meal begins with a "greasy-looking brown" soup served at room temperature. What might have been salvaged from the remainder of the menu is torpedoed by the waitress Delia (so named because she had a habit of dealing plates around the table "like a pack of cards"). Delia punctuates the already strained conversation by her clash and rattle of dishes, as she clears, stacks, drops, and spills. The deeply-distressed Mrs. Newlywed realizes that her guests "without malice, but in truth and frankness" would advise everyone, "Whatever you do, don't dine with the Newlyweds unless you eat your dinner before you go, and wear black glasses so no sight can offend you."

Not until after publication of *Etiquette* did Mrs. Post discover the true nature of her mass audience, when letters began pouring in from all over the country. Desperate people wanted answers to simple questions: "Is it true that bread, before being eaten, must be broken into pieces exactly one inch in diameter?" "When passing your plate for a second helping, must you hold your knife and fork in your hand?" "Should a widow sign her letters Mrs. John Jones or Mrs. Mary Jones?" "How can I give a formal dinner for eight people and cook and serve it myself?" "How many butlers should a really elegant house have?" (From the wife of a postwar millionaire—the answer was one).

Responsive to obvious lacks in her book, Mrs. Post endeavored to clarify such matters in later editions. A chapter entitled "American Neighborhood Customs" was added dealing with showers, sewing circles, and other suburban activities, and a new character was born: Mrs. Three-in-One. Here was a wife who had no servant, but who managed to be an efficient cook, waitress, and charming hostess all at once. Nine pages of *Etiquette* came to be devoted to Mrs. Three-in-One, and only 2½ pages to butlers.

From the first to the twelfth editions a series of revisions have kept *Etiquette* in tune with changing social mores. An example is a chapter in the original edition called "The Chaperon and Other Conventions," wherein the author stated: "A young girl unprotected by a chaperon is in the position of an unarmed traveler walking alone among wolves." Subsequently the chapter was retitled "The Vanishing Chaperon and Other New Conventions," and still later "The Vanished Chaperon and Other Lost Conventions." Mrs. Post states that "The Chaperon has largely become a lost convention," but she leaves herself an escape clause: "Parental *training* has largely taken the place of the chaperon's *protection.*" Under the relaxed rules, an unmarried girl over eighteen may go unchaperoned to the theater with a man, and even to dinner in his apartment, "if it will not stir comment in her circle." To the question, "How late may you stay?" the answer is, "If you dine alone, you should leave before ten, at which hour 'early evening' changes to 'night.'" There is a firm line drawn, however, to govern another situation: "An unmarried girl should not go alone on overnight trips with any young man, even with her fiancé."

The latest edition of *Etiquette* deletes, as noted by the author, "certain non-essential customs and old-fashioned ideas," as it seeks to accommodate itself to a new generation which has rejected many once generally accepted formalities. Flexibility has been maintained by following the precept that manners are simply "a sensible awareness of the needs of others," and each generation has a right to interpret social law to suit itself.

Mrs. Post is presently adamant on some aspects of social behavior and yielding a bit on other fronts. Illustrative of her conservative-liberal approach are the following excerpts:

Going steady: A fact of American teen-age life. . . . This is for several reasons an unfortunate practice, and it is the wise young person who widens instead of narrowing his circle of friends.

Plastic tablecloths: They fill a very real need in today's living. . . . Paper napkins complement the plastics and are so attractively made today that they solve one household problem.

Silverware: The supposedly essential silver tea service is no longer the central feature of the bride's silver equipment that it once was.

TV: If you are invited to watch a television show and you are not interested in seeing 'Billy Bruiser' try to knock out 'Tommy Tough,' or the horse show, or the dog show, or listen to an opera, it is not discourteous to say, "Thank you, no."

Mourning: During the past 25 years no other changes in etiquette have been so great as those of the conventions of mourning. . . . A greater and ever greater number of persons today do not believe in going into mourning at all. . . . The normal routine of children should not be curtailed—more than ever they need to romp and play.

One point on which Mrs. Post has steadfastly refused to make any concession is the practice of serving the hostess first, a custom that she brands as "the Great American Rudeness." There is no excuse for it, she maintains, unless the food is possibly poisoned or unless the guests are ignorant of how to serve themselves from a dish presented to them and need to be shown—both unlikely contingencies. Mrs. Post appears to be losing the battle, because hostesses and servants refuse to accept her dictum.

Mrs. Post holds a hostess' guiding rule always should be to make her guests feel at ease. On one occasion, her tact was put to a severe test. A shy representative of her newspaper syndicate was invited to lunch. To fortify himself, he stopped en route for several double martinis. When he arrived, Mrs. Post had prepared cocktails and to be polite the reporter drank them and lurched in to lunch. Somewhat befuddled, the next thing he knew he had pushed his lamb chop off his plate and it was skidding across the dining-room table. Completely shaken, he looked at Mrs. Post and said, "You wrote the book. What do I do now?" "If I were you," Mrs. Post answered gravely, "I would pick it up and start all over again."

In turn, guests should avoid under any circumstances embarrassing their hostess. An example is a technique used by Mrs. Toplofty in dealing with a repugnant dinner partner:

> At dinner once, Mrs. Toplofty, finding herself next to a man she quite openly despised, said to him with apparent placidity, "I shall not talk to you—because I don't care to. But for the sake of my hostess I shall say my multiplication tables. Twice one are two, twice two are four—" and she continued on through the tables, making him alternate them with her. As soon as she politely could, she turned again to her other companion.

The phenomenal success of Emily Post's *Etiquette* naturally encouraged the rise of competitors and emulators. In the early years, Lillian Eichler's *Book of Etiquette* was the chief rival, attracting sales comparable to Mrs. Post's. More recently, Amy Vanderbilt's *Complete Book of Social Etiquette,* first published in 1952, has had a great vogue. Some young moderns believe that Mrs. Vanderbilt is more in tune with the times because of her extended attention to such topics as servantless entertaining, gossip columnists, baby sitters, buying an automobile, and divorce. Critics of strict etiquette and social conformity who question the need for guides on the subject are answered by Amy Vanderbilt in these words: "You can't be a social maverick today except on a Texas ranch. I don't advocate intellectual conformity, but rules of etiquette are for everybody's protection."

In an attempt to explain the popularity of Mrs. Post's *Etiquette,* Edmund Wilson asserts: "What you get in Emily Post, for all her concessions to the age's vulgarization, is a crude version of the social ideal to which the mass of Americans aspired after the Civil War: an ideal that was costly and glossy, smart, self-conscious and a little disgusting. . . . Today this ideal must be fading with the money that kept it up, but, such as it is, a great many people must still enjoy reading about it." A more recent commentator, Justin Kaplan, points out that the concept of the book has changed over the years from "a guide to forms and etiquette to a general encyclopedia of modern living which now gives practical and for the most part sensible advice on how to conduct yourself" in virtually any situation. In any event the remarkable staying powers of Emily Post and her *Etiquette* show little sign of weakening.

38 | LABOR LEADER

Samuel Gompers's *Seventy Years of Life and Labor*, 1925

For nearly fifty years Samuel Gompers personified the American labor movement, but for practically his entire career, ending in 1924, he remained a controversial figure.

Diametrically opposite appraisals are reflected in such comments as these: "Samuel Gompers was, in my opinion, one of the ten or twelve greatest Americans" (John R. Commons, economist and labor historian); "No single individual in American industrial history has exercised an influence on the labor movement even remotely comparable to that of Samuel Gompers" (John A. Fitch, labor economist); "Taken all in all, he was incomparably the greatest leader that the trade-union movement of any country has yet produced" (John Spargo, Socialist leader); "The arch-reactionary, the idol of all the holdbacks in the labor movement . . . considered as a labor organizer, he is a first-class failure" (William Z. Foster, United States Communist Party leader); "Nowhere in the annals of labor history, on this continent or across the water, has there been such complete and such childish domination of trade unionism as Sam Gompers exercised in the years 1881–1924" (George Simpson, sociologist).

An extended self-portrait of Gompers is to be found in his two-volume autobiography, *Seventy Years of Life and Labor* (1925). The author was born in London in 1850, of a Jewish family that had found its way through Portugal and Holland to England. When Samuel was fourteen, the parents emigrated to New York, exchanging the slums of one city for a ghetto in another. Immediately after his arrival, young Sam joined the Cigar Makers' Union, a union with which he remained affiliated, for sentimental reasons, for the rest of his life. Even in his early youth he showed unusual organizing ability, starting up new athletic and fraternal clubs and throwing himself with tremendous energy into neigh-

borhood activities. His personal appearance in later years is color-
fully described by a close acquaintance, Benjamin Stolberg:

> Gompers had the physical spell of the personal leader. When
> seated, the powerful, long-armed torso and the enormous head
> seemed to belong to a six-footer. But when he arose, his hefty,
> absurd little legs kept him from soaring above five feet four and
> gave a touch of anthropoid strength to his chronic restlessness.
> The head was magnificent. It looked like an animated boulder,
> on which the weathers of a rich and dangerous life had carved
> large and rugged yet tremulously sensitive features.

Another contemporary, M. A. DeWolfe Howe, concluded, "In
his powerful carrying voice and cocksure manner, untroubled by
subtleties, his hail-fellow-well-met manner of dealing with men
of every kind [Gompers] possessed invaluable attributes for a
labor leader."

During the period when Gompers was beginning to work at
his trade as a cigar maker in New York, the American labor movement, though not a new phenomenon, was still in a rudimentary
state. As far back as the eighteenth century, workmen in various
trades and communities had joined together to improve working
conditions. In 1827 carpenters in Philadelphia struck for a ten-
hour day, and shoemakers, printers, and other organized laborers
went out in sympathy.

The workmen had more than sufficient cause for strong resentment against prevailing conditions. The labor of women and children was being mercilessly exploited. Free pubic schools scarcely
existed in many communities. Wages were unbelievably low and
imprisonment for debt was a common practice.

An industrial revival following the Civil War brought with it
an upsurge of labor union activity. By 1870 there were more than
thirty national unions of workers in various trades. Over a six-
year period an annual conference of the National Labor Union
attempted, without success, to persuade the diverse groups to
consolidate their interests and activities into a national federation. Among the abortive efforts in that direction were the Industrial Brotherhood, the Order of Sovereigns of Industry, and the
Noble Order of Knights of Labor.

As early as the 1870s, a dispute—which led in the 1930s to a
major schism between the American Federation of Labor and the

Congress of Industrial Organizations—erupted over the issue of craft versus industrial unions. Gompers was a lifelong fighter for the craft, or trade, union made up of the workers in a single craft, and for a federation uniting these workers on the basis of their individual forms of labor. He adamantly opposed the principle of the industrial union which would join all the workers in a single industry, regardless of crafts. Thus, one of Gompers's early battles was against the Knights of Labor, an organization which welcomed all types and levels of workmen, skilled and unskilled, including farm hands, women, and Negroes.

Union involvement for Samuel Gompers began almost as soon as he landed in America. He was notably successful as president of Local 144 of the Cigar Workers International Union, gaining a solid reputation for courageous and realistic leadership. From this base, he became one of the principal founders and an officer of the newly organized Federation of Organized Trades and Labor Unions of the United States and Canada. But the federation was weak and ineffectual, split by dissention, and after five years, in 1886, was succeeded by the American Federation of Labor, with Gompers as president. Meanwhile, the chief rival, the Knights of Labor, was gradually disappearing from the scene because of weak organization, a series of unsuccessful strikes, and too much direct political action. Under Gompers's shrewd direction the AFL prospered by avoiding the mistakes made by the Knights of Labor. In later years, it was remarked that "if Gompers was the American Federation of Labor, the Federation was in the main also Gompers."

As a measure of Gompers's remarkable achievements, it should be noted that in 1886 the federation existed only on paper. There were no traditions nor any feeling of solidarity to guide the members. The federation was loose, and the constituent unions were jealous of their individual sovereignties. The tasks that lay before Gompers, when he assumed the presidency, are well summarized by Louis S. Reed in *The Labor Philosophy of Samuel Gompers:* "To build up this organization, to get the unions to affiliate and to stay affiliated, to get them to cooperate with one another, to cultivate a sense of unity, to make the Federation count for something." In addition, Gompers was busy organizing local unions, bringing the locals together into national organizations, and the national unions into the federation. For this monumental assignment, the presidency of the federation carried with it a salary of 1,000 dollars a year plus expenses.

By 1890 the federation counted about 250,000 members. At the end of the Gompers era thirty-five years later the membership had risen to 3,000,000.

Gompers and his associates were little concerned about organizing the unskilled. In his autobiography, *Seventy Years of Life and Labor*, Gompers looked back on the beginnings of the federation and defended its establishment on the ground that such an organization was needed so that "work could go forward daily for the organization of all workers of America, skilled as well as unskilled." Nevertheless, as long as Gompers lived, the AFL was primarily a federation of craft unions. The skilled workmen, in his view, were the dependable men, the core of industry, without whom no permanent, stable trade unions could be created. It was this attitude on the part of the AFL leaders that delayed efforts to organize the great mass-production industries, with their preponderance of semiskilled and unskilled workers. In his report to the AFL convention in 1903, President Gompers stubbornly maintained the federation's position:

> Industrial organization is perversive of the history of the labor movement, runs counter to the best conceptions of the toilers' interest now and is sure to lead to the confusion which precedes dissolution and disruption. It is time for our fellow unionists to help stem the tide of expansion madness lest their organizations will be drawn into the vortex that will engulf them to their possible dismemberment and destruction.

Gompers's social philosophy, insofar as he possessed one, was dominated by his belief in laissez faire or individualism, or, as he called it, "voluntarism." This creed grew out of his hatred of socialism and opposition to any interference by government in the labor movement. Gompers's premise was that unions are voluntary organizations, which must not be coerced by government or by each other. The federation "had to win men by authority of sound logic and results. Its continuous existence depended upon mutual service and welfare. It was at once a rope of sand and yet the strongest human force—a voluntary association united by common need and held together by mutual self-interest." As Gompers viewed their relationships, groups of workers had something to sell and employers something to buy, and each tried to drive the hardest bargain. The bargaining process, Gompers held, should be carried on outside the jurisdiction of the state. Labor should never try to attain its economic aims through legislation but through collective bargaining. Voluntarism, Gompers insisted, was "the corner stone upon which labor's structure has been builded."

At the 1906 convention, Gompers clarified certain aspects of the AFL's policy of no government interference. "We are asking from Congress and from our legislatures," he said, "only the things we cannot secure ourselves." Thus he was willing to accept protective legislation for children and women, because they lacked enough economic power for self-protection, and for public employees. Legislation was approved also for areas not susceptible to collective bargaining, such as control of immigration and a ban on the power of courts to issue injunctions in labor disputes. Anticipating the Norris-LaGuardia Act by thirteen years, the AFL Executive Council in 1919 recommended legislation to "make it a criminal offense for any employer to interfere with or hamper the exercise" of the right to organize.

Concerning other social legislation, Gompers favored accident compensation and pensions for the aged, but strongly opposed unemployment insurance and health insurance on the assumption that they would make all activities relating to labor and employment subject to the regulation, discipline, and decision of government, with "every petty or high official of the government intermeddling and guiding and commanding." In opposing minimum wage and hour legislation, Gompers again voiced his fear of the lawmakers: "If the legislature should once fix the minimum wage it would have the opportunity to use the machinery of the state to enforce work at that rate whether the workers desired to render service or not"; and further, "I have some apprehension that if the legislature were allowed to establish a maximum work day it might also compel workmen to work up to the maximum allowed." In his autobiography, Gompers states that it was "foremost in my mind to tell the politicians to keep their hands off and thus to preserve voluntary institutions and opportunity for individual and group initiative."

Gompers's negative attitude toward government as an instrument of economic reform was described by Gus Tyler in the *New Republic* as "a strange admixture of Old World revolutionary dogma on the class character of the state (Gompers was certain that the Sherman Act would become an anti-union act—as it did); of Jeffersonian and Jacksonian notions on the evils of leviathan government; of a native rugged-individualist attitude applied to the collective efforts of a working class to improve its status."

The courts gave Gompers ample cause to look on governmental meddling with a jaundiced eye. The judges, federal and state, were, with rare exceptions, allied to the industrialists and manufacturers and were seldom impartial in handing down decisions affecting labor. They themselves were usually members of the upper classes and reverent toward past precedents; consequently, they were convinced that property and wealth were sacred and must be protected. The Sherman Antitrust Act, passed in 1890 to prohibit "any combination in restraint of trade," was immediately interpreted by the judiciary to apply to labor unions, to ban the combination of workers for mutual protection. An infamous case involved the Hatters' Union and the Loewe Manufacturing Company in Danbury, Connecticut. The manufacturers sued the strikers for damages incurred as a result of the workers' refusal to make hats; the U.S. Supreme Court found in favor of the company, on the basis of the Sherman act, and held the workers liable for a quarter of a million dollars damage. The homes and savings of the workers were seized to satisfy the judgment. Under Gompers's leadership, the American Federation came to the rescue and raised sufficient funds to save the hat-workers' homes and savings.

Actually, Gompers was not antipolitical or politically neutral. When he was convinced that positive benefits to labor could result from legislation, he did not hesitate to make use of the state. He thought, however, that it would be unwise for labor to commit itself to any one party. Candidates should be endorsed or opposed on a nonpartisan basis. The official policy of the AFL is to "reward your friends and punish your enemies"—a strategy followed by the federation throughout its history.

Socialism and its doctrines were emphatically rejected by Gompers in these words: "Economically they are unsound; socially they are wrong; industrially they are an impossibility." Thus for over forty years he fought the different socialist schools, from anarchism to communism. Gompers disapproved of force or violence, as, for example, in a declaration to the Chicago federation concerning strikes: "We cannot win by thuggery or violence. Brutality only grows. If we had to win by that method, it would be better to lose. Violence and thuggery only hurt our movement. When compulsion is used, only resentment is aroused and the end is not gained. Only through moral suasion and appeal to men's reason can a movement succeed."

On the other hand, Gompers viewed the trade union movement as a militant force, with the wage earners engaged in a constant warfare against their employers, for the purpose of obtaining higher wages, shorter working hours, and better working conditions. The union's chief weapon was seen to be the power to strike or at least to hold the strike as a threat over the heads of recalcitrant employers. In practice, Gompers frequently prevented strikes and discouraged those who wished to strike. The "right to strike," however, was a sacred canon to him, and he condemned in no uncertain terms everyone who held that the right was not absolute, even for public employees.

Labor historians assessing Gompers's career see both negative and positive factors. Among the areas in which his leadership was highly constructive were the fight for the eight-hour day and the long-drawn-out battle against labor injunctions and against government's intervention on the side of capital in labor disputes. Gompers also paved the way for child-labor legislation, for better sanitary conditions in shops and factories, for compensation for on-the-job injuries, and for sickness, death, and old-age benefits. In response to union pressure, the Department of Labor was established in 1913 in the President's Cabinet.

Countering the positive accomplishments, critics frequently picture Gompers as a dyed-in-the-wool conservative and reactionary. By preaching individualism and resisting legislation on wages, hours, and social insurance, he doubtless harmed the labor movement. The void left by the lack of governmentally sponsored social insurance was filled in part by employers' paternalism, in the form of group insurance, old-age pensions, and other welfare measures. The effect was to strengthen the employers and to weaken the unions. Further, the craft union, so obstinately defended by Gompers, was an inadequate type of organization to cope with what Louis S. Reed describes as "larger and larger aggregations of capital, consolidation among the ranks of the employers, the increasing mechanization of industry, obliteration of craft skills, continuous technical innovation, and employers' welfarism." Reed continues: "Gompers came to the labor movement at the beginning of an epoch. He helped discover the policies and principles that were right and good for that epoch, and led in building the movement upon these policies and principles. Then the movement passed into a new epoch. But Gompers never recognized that the new epoch had arrived."

The "new epoch" referred to by Reed was the overwhelming demand of the great mass of unskilled and unorganized workers for unions. These workers distrusted the American Federation of Labor, viewing it as an aggregation of snobbish aristocrats who cared nothing for their less fortunate fellows in the labor force. The AFL consequently began to lose ground. From the end of World War I to 1924, its membership fell from 4 to 3 million. But Gompers stubbornly held to the principles which had guided him throughout his career, failing to keep pace with the times. In effect, he was a nineteenth-century performer in a twentieth-century role.

The extensive body of federal legislation which was to revolutionize the American labor movement, it should be noted, postdated Gompers. The Railway Labor Act was passed in 1936, two years after Gompers's death; the Norris-LaGuardia Act against injunctions was enacted in 1932; the Wagner Act, protecting the right of working people to organize, became law in 1935; the Social Security Act was passed in the same year (with complete AFL support); and a variety of subsequent legislation dealt with minimum wages, working hours, safety, strike breaking, prison labor, health insurance, fair employment practice, unemployment compensation, working conditions for women and children, etc.

On the basis of his record and written statements, one must assume that Gompers would have been hostile to such governmental interference in labor-management relations.

Unquestionably, Gompers was a pioneer in American labor organization from about 1890 to 1910, and his constructive efforts entitle him to a claim to greatness. He lived a long and significant life, and his influence continues to permeate numerous aspects of organized labor in America.

39 | MASTER BUILDER

Frank Lloyd Wright's *Autobiography*, 1932

When Frank Lloyd Wright died at the age of ninety, he left as his monument 700 completed structures and plans for at least 300 more, including homes, hotels, factories, office buildings, museums, and churches. Wright had achieved fame beyond any American artist and was as renowned abroad as at home. Throughout much of his career, however, he was at odds with society for refusing to become a conformist and for his irrepressible desire to reform the manners and morals of his countrymen. Wright's flamboyant personality, articulateness in expressing his ideas, opinions, and feelings, and distinguished appearance kept him in the limelight for seventy years.

Frank Lloyd Wright began his career under one of the most remarkable figures in the history of American architecture, Louis Sullivan, of Chicago, always referred to by Wright as "The Master." From Sullivan, Wright learned fundamental principles which he never forgot: the desirability of fitting the structure to the environment, using appropriate materials usually indigenous to the region, avoiding superfluous ornamentation, and working closely with engineers and skilled technicians.

In reviewing Wright's many achievements, a fellow architect and friend, Edward Durrell Stone took a backward look:

> Great ideas in architecture are rare. Throughout history, beginning with the Greeks or even with earlier civilizations, there have been scarcely half a dozen structural innovations. The Greeks perfected the use of the lintel. The Romans added the arch, the vault, and the dome, and Byzantine culture added the square surmounted by the dome. The great Gothic contribution was the flying buttress, designed to counter the thrust of huge vaults. From the Gothic period until Mr. Wright's time no new principle was added to our architectural vocabulary.

The revolutionary changes which have occurred in the twentieth century, Mr. Stone points out, were made possible by the development of reinforced concrete, the steel frame, and the elevator. Pioneers in the utilization of the new materials and technology were H. H. Richardson and Wright's mentor Louis Sullivan, but "it remained for Frank Lloyd Wright to become the creative inspiration and the prophet who established the still-unexploited principles of twentieth-century architecture."

Wright was the first to employ the use of the cantilever on a large scale. The cantilever is a beam supported near its midpoint with one end held down and the other end free to support a load. It had been previously used for balconies and in other minor ways, but the cantilever as developed by Wright revolutionized architecture by freeing the exterior walls from any requirement that they support additional stories or a roof.

When Wright began his architectural practice, American habitations were, as Lewis Mumford called them, "uniquely hideous." Mid-Victorianism had descended on America like a blanket of fall leaves. Everything was derivative from European, especially English, models, and the situation was aggravated by the pseudo-classic revival stemming from the Chicago World's Fair of 1893. The Beaux Arts movement emanating from the fair cluttered the country with Greek temple banks, Renaissance hotels, Gothic department stores, and government buildings surmounted by fake domes. In Wright's opinion, the fair set American architecture back for generations. Thomas Craven, in his *Modern Art*, notes that the houses of the period "were indeed so hideous in their high-storied pretentiousness, their dislocated gables and dormers and their scroll saw embroidery, that our painters, of late, have been putting them on canvas as records of a barbaric culture." Wright was twenty years old when he entered this chamber of horrors. Before he had reached the age of thirty he had developed a new type of building, highly original in form.

In his *Autobiography* (1932) and other writings, Wright traces the growth of his imaginative concepts. The basic motives and principles governing his designs were stated as follows, in a series of lectures at Princeton University:

1. To reduce the number of necessary parts of the house and the separate rooms to the minimum, and make all come together as enclosed space—so divided that light, air, and vista permeated the whole with a sense of unity.

2. To associate the building as a whole with its site by extension and emphasis of the planes parallel to the ground.
3. To eliminate the room as a box and the house as another by making the walls enclosing screens, the ceilings and floors and enclosing screens to flow into each other, To make the proportions more liberally human, and the structure appropriate to the material. Extended straight lines or stream-lines were useful in this.
4. To harmonize all necessary openings to the outside or inside with good human proportions and make them occur naturally —singly or in a series.
5. To eliminate combinations of different materials in favor of mono-material so far as possible; to use no ornament that does not come out of the nature of the materials.
6. To incorporate all heating, lighting, and plumbing so that these systems become constituent parts of the building itself. These service features become architectural and in this the ideal of an organic architecture is at work.
7. To incorporate as organic architecture—so far as possible— furnishings, making them all one with the building and designing them in simple terms, again straight lines and rectilinear forms.
8. To eliminate the decorator. He is all curves and efflorescence, if not all period.

If there was any single principle which lay at the root of Wright's ideas it was what he called "organic" or "natural" architecture. By this he meant that an architect designs a building for a specific function, and its function or purpose must be visible in the structure. In brief, form must follow function. Furthermore, the structure itself must be integrated with its surroundings. Wright describes in his *Autobiography* the planning and building of his famous home, Taliesin, at Spring Green, Wisconsin. "I knew well by now," he writes, "that no house should ever be on any hill or on anything. It should be *of* the hill, belonging to it, so hill and house could live together each the happier for the other." Later, when Wright built Taliesin West in Arizona, it did not look the same as Taliesin East, because the areas in which they were placed were entirely different. Thus, if a building truly reflects its purpose and is integrated with its surroundings, it meets Wright's criteria for organic architecture.

Much of Wright's theory was applied in his "prairie architecture"—low, spacious, well-lighted homes. The characteristics of the prairie style are universally known among architects: low block forms of brick, or wood and stucco, emphasizing horizontal masses; a long roof-line; a low-pitched, or flat overhanging roof; windows grouped as compositional units; sparse but appropriate use of ornament; and the entire structure in perfect harmony with the surrounding landscape. The Wright houses constructed on inclines seem to be part of the hills on which they are built. Wright was the first modern architect to view the house as a whole, blending it with its site; bringing harmony among its style, materials, and furnishings; letting in air and light; utilizing the latest technology for plumbing and heating.

Frank Lloyd Wright was the first architect, also, to use freely all the materials available for modern construction. He believed that each climate dictated its own form of architecture. As a principle, therefore, he used materials locally available as much as possible. For example, in his houses in California, where brick, stone, and wood were in limited supply, he devised a decorated concrete block, poured at the building site. In Arizona, where rocks in the desert were plentiful, walls were made of piled-up stones. In the interior of Wright houses, brick or stone piers were never plastered over, and the grain of wood was part of the decorative motif. Wright rejected imitations: plaster must look like plaster and not fake marble, and brick, wood, and stone should appear to be exactly what they are. The beauty comes in fitting the material to its purpose.

Most revolutionary of all Wright's methods of utilizing materials was his architectural use of glass. A window was no longer a hole in the wall, but a continuous band or wall of glass running to the ceiling. A typical Wright technique was to build walls of block units from floor to ceiling with glass inserts, giving the interior cheerful lightness without undue exposure. Rainbow tinted, subtly colored glass was sometimes set into the wall blocks along with clear panels—the combination creating a soft mellow glow inside to replace the outside glare.

Ornament was considered desirable and necessary by Wright, though he was fully aware of the absurd excesses of many earlier architects and protested against them. One commentator suggested that to Wright, "a building without its complement of ornament was like a face stripped of its features, an anonymous skull. To him, ornament on a building was as natural as plumage to a bird, blossoms to a plant, or music and poetry to the human spirit." Ornament, however, must be an integral part of the building and not an excrescence applied from another era, another form of material, or a different style of architecture. Wright's influence had a part in eliminating useless cornices, Renaissance façades, and medieval ornament from twentieth-century skyscrapers. He led the movement, too, for the wholesale scrapping of filigree, bridal-cake curlicues, pseudo-classical veneer, and any other designs that were still being employed by architects simply because of tradition, regardless of their lack of suitability for modern structures. To Wright, ornament that appeared stuck-on or applied in extraneous fashion and unrelated to the total scheme should be omitted.

Frank Lloyd Wright designed a variety of buildings, but his prime interest was the house. His earliest and most continuous success was achieved with suburban dwellings, and the range was from simple summer cottages to large expensive homes for the wealthy. To Wright, the typical house was a box with holes cut in it to permit air and people to go in and out. Such houses were built anywhere, with no thought about the nature of the ground or of the surroundings. Wright's organic architecture concept changed all that by blending homes into their environments. The modern home, he insisted, must provide its owners with freedom, space, and light, as well as with style and dignity. Among the important features of what Wright called the "Usonian" house were a large living room, letting in sunlight and giving a good view of the surrounding land, with bookshelves, a fireplace, and dining area; a kitchen area close to but not a part of the living and dining areas; no basement nor attic; heating by steam or hot-water pipes beneath the concrete floor without radiators; a small room housing the heat and laundry units; the outside shell of precast concrete blocks; plumbing, wiring, and heating units prefabricated; simple roof-lines; carport instead of a garage; indirect lighting to reduce the number of lighting fixtures; the use of wood, glass, brick, cement, and paper for con-

struction materials. The interior of the house is far more important than the exterior, in Wright's view, for that is where people
live.

The ugliness of the modern city repelled Wright. "The architect's immediate problem," he wrote, "is how to mitigate the
horror of human life caught helpless or unaware in the machinery
that is the city? How easiest and soonest to assist the social unit
in escaping the gradual paralysis of individual independence that
is characteristic of the Machine-made moron, a paralysis of the
emotional nature necessary to the triumph of the Machine over
man, instead of the quickening of his humanity necessary to
Man's triumph over the machine?" Wright's answer—probably
impracticable because of land costs and poor transportation—
was to decentralize the city, giving each family an acre of ground,
providing luxurious motorbuses traveling over magnificent land-
scaped highways, and landing fields for safe, noiseless airplanes;
setting up rural factories and power plants; and building tall
cooperative apartment houses in the center of natural parks. The
entire concept appears visionary and utopian.

In his commercial and institutional structures, Wright was concerned most of all with the uses to which a building would be
put. His first important project of this nature was the Larkin
Building in Buffalo, New York, constructed in 1904. It was the
first completely air-conditioned office building and the first to use
plate-glass doors and metal furniture, designed by Wright himself. Unity Church in Oak Park, Illinois, 1906, was the world's
first poured-concrete building. The Imperial Hotel in Tokyo,
1922, brought international fame to Wright when, with its floating
foundations and cantilevered floors, it was one of the few
undamaged buildings left standing after the catastrophic
earthquake of 1923. Another celebrated building is the Johnson
Laboratory, 1939, at Racine, Wisconsin, essentially a tube of
glass, with floors cantilevered from a central shaft in which the
mechanics of the building are enclosed.

Wright's buildings often inspired violent controversy. An instance is the six-story Guggenheim Art Museum in New York
City, completed in 1959. The gallery is a continuous spiraling
ramp, along which, as one commentator noted, "the paintings
seem to float in space." The Guggenheim building was highly

praised by some critics and condemned by others; the latter called it a washing machine, a marshmallow, a cupcake, a corkscrew, an imitation beehive, and an inverted oatmeal dish.

Although Frank Lloyd Wright became recognized as one of the first geniuses of world art, he was never asked by the federal government to plan a building for the national capital, nor did his own state of Wisconsin ever commission him to design or build any kind of public structure. Considering the enormous number of governmental buildings erected during Wright's long career, the fact is astonishing. On the other hand, the neglect or indifference may be explained by Wright's well-known hostility to the Greco-Roman tradition which for decades has dominated official governmental structures in America. At the end of his career, Wright was finally given an opportunity to plan a county office building—the Marin County Civic Center in San Rafael, California.

Frank Lloyd Wright's writings are prolific. His published works include *Organic Architecture, When Democracy Builds, Genius and the Mobocracy, The Future of Architecture, The Natural House, Modern Architecture: A Testament, An American Architecture,* and *Drawings for a Living Architecture.* The best single source for Wright's ideas is *An Autobiography,* which covers all the years of his life up to about 1942. Included in it are virtually all his major statements on the nature of organic architecture, of materials, of the site, and of structure. In the *Autobiography* Wright dwells at length, also, on his incredibly complicated domestic affairs, marked by tragedies and tangled finances that would doubtless have brought an end to the career of a less courageous and determined spirit.

Though a sharp critic of society and of his contemporaries in the architectural world, Wright won more official honors at home and abroad and erected more structures than any other individual architect of the twentieth century. His permanent impact on the history and development of architecture is conceded even by his sharpest critics.

40 | SOCIETY VERSUS THE INDIVIDUAL

Ruth Benedict's *Patterns of Culture,* 1934

For a serious and scholarly anthropological study to achieve sales in excess of a million copies was unheard of until the publication in 1934 of Ruth Benedict's *Patterns of Culture.* In hardback and paperback editions this extraordinary work has made publishing history by reaching best-sellerdom in the English language and in numerous translations.

There may be significance in the fact, too, that Ruth Benedict's student and close friend Margaret Mead is also the author of several extraordinarily popular and successful studies of primitive societies. The two writers broke away from traditional approaches to anthropology and started new trends, which continue to dominate the field. Conceivably, the feminine viewpoint brought a warmth and understanding of human beings that was lacking in the dry, technical reports of their male confreres.

The older anthropologists were generally theorists who relied upon materials gathered by others—such as travelers' and missionaries' accounts. Attempts were made to reconstruct human history historically, using methods developed for the study of archaeology, linguistics, and biological evolution. Attention was centered on the diffusion of cultural traits, with the aim of tracing the spread of the human species, the history of inventions and technologies, etc. A leading early-twentieth-century anthropologist and Ruth Benedict's teacher, Franz Boas, emphasized exact descriptions. The case for the old anthropology is well stated in an introductory passage in *Patterns of Culture:*

> Anthropological work has been overwhelmingly devoted to the analysis of culture traits, rather than to the study of cultures as articulated wholes. This has been due in great measure to the nature of earlier ethnological descriptions. The classical anthro-

pologists did not write out of first-hand knowledge of primitive people. They were armchair students who had at their disposal the anecdotes of travelers and missionaries and the formal and schematic accounts of the early ethnologists. It was possible to trace from these details the distribution of the custom of knocking out teeth, or of divination by entrails, but it was not possible to see how these traits were embedded in different tribes in characteristic configurations that gave form and meaning to the procedures.

Nevertheless, Ruth Benedict did not reject the types of sources utilized by her predecessors. She found of value, for example, old eyewitness accounts of American Indians, such as those recorded in the *Jesuit Relations*. But the documentary sources were extensively and intensively complemented by field work among the Indians for first-hand observation of their cultures.

Attempts to study the customs of various cultures and then to draw overall deductions from them, for example, in mating or death practices, were compared by Mrs. Benedict to the building up of "a kind of mechanical Frankenstein's monster with a right eye from Fiji, a left from Europe, one leg from Tierra del Fuego, and one from Tahiti, and all the fingers and toes from still different regions. Such a figure corresponds to no reality in the past or present."

A definition of anthropology preferred by Ruth Bennett, and exemplified in *Patterns of Culture,* as stated by the author, is "the study of human beings as creatures of society. It fastens its attention upon those physical characteristics and industrial techniques, those conventions and values, which distinguish one community from all others that belong to a different tradition." The premise is that every culture has individual features, that is, practices, beliefs, and institutions, which distinguish it from every other culture. A society must be viewed as a whole, in all its facets, and should not be judged in terms of isolated details. As a corollary, the individuals who go to make up a given society are molded by the culture into which they have been born. Man's life is lived according to the traditions of his group, and it is a rare individual who tries to break out of the mold.

The diversity of cultures is a paramount fact in the study of anthropology, and the range of differences is infinite. Further, cultural differences are only partially, if at all, explained by race, or by the accidents of geography, climate, or other features of the physical environment. The rate of change in a culture is far slower than in an individual member of a society. The latter, of course, is limited at best to a few score years, whereas a culture is "time binding," perhaps perpetuating itself for thousands of years.

For illustrative purposes, Ruth Benedict selected three radically different cultures. Two are American Indian and the other is that of a Melanesian people who live on the island of Dobu off the northern shore of Eastern New Guinea. Reasons for the decision to treat these three primitive civilizations in detail are thus stated by the author:

> A few cultures understood as coherent organizations of behaviour are more enlightening than many touched upon only at their high spots. The relation of motivations and purposes to the separate items of cultural behavior at birth, at death, at puberty, and at marriage can never be made clear by a comprehensive survey of the world. We must hold ourselves to the less ambitious task, the many-sided understanding of a few cultures.

Certainly, a worldwide search could scarcely have found three more diverse societies than those treated in depth in *Patterns of Culture*. The first is the Pueblo Indians of the Southwest, one of the most widely known tribes of aborigines in Western civilization. Despite the fact that they live in mid-America and are much visited by outsiders, their culture is relatively unspoiled, and they continue to live after the old native fashion. The ancient dances of the gods are performed in their stone villages, life follows traditional routines, and anything taken from the white-man's civilization is adapted to their attitudes and requirements. The individual person is subordinated to the group. It is social values that count, and personalities must give way to the needs of the larger society.

Several Indian tribes lived in the Pueblos of the Southwest United States. *Patterns of Culture* concentrates principal attention on the Zuñi, who belong to the great western Pueblos. Pueblo culture, with a long homogeneous history behind it, is oddly a culture at wide variance with those surrounding it and indeed different from the rest of North America. The Zuñi are a ceremonious people, sober and inoffensive, their lives filled with cults of masked gods, healing, the sun, and sacred fetishes concerning war and the dead. "Probably most grown men among the western Pueblos," Mrs. Benedict observes, give to ritual "the greater part of their waking life," and the daily conversation of all the people in the Pueblo centers about it. The reason for the preoccupation is that Zuñi religious practices are believed to be supernaturally powerful.

The Zuñi place great reliance upon imitative magic. Their prayers are traditional formulas that ask for orderly life, pleasant days, and shelter from violence. Religious observances have one primary purpose: to bring rain and to increase fertility, both in the gardens and in the tribe. Given the culture's religious foundation, the priesthoods naturally stand on the highest level of sanctity. The heads of the major priesthoods make up the ruling body of the Zuñi, constituting a theocracy. The cult of the masked gods is popular; more than a hundred different masked gods exist in the Zuñi pantheon. The dances of the masked gods are conducted by a tribal society of all adult males, organized in six groups, each with its "kiva," or ceremonial chamber. When boys reach the proper age, they are initiated into a kiva.

Another great division of the Zuñi ceremonial structure is that of the medicine societies, whose supernatural patrons are the beast gods, chief of whom is the bear. The societies have amassed great stores of esoteric knowledge, imparted to the members, both men and women, throughout their lives. The Zuñi group war and hunting and clowning cults with the medicine societies.

Domestic affairs like marriage and divorce are casually arranged among the Zuñi. Marriages take place almost without courtship. Divorce is easy, though most marriages are permanent and peaceful. Economic wealth is comparatively unimportant, outweighed by membership in a clan with numerous ceremonial prerogatives.

In contrasting the Pueblo Indians with other North American Indians, Mrs. Benedict emphasizes a fundamental difference. The Indians of North America outside the Pueblos have what she characterizes as a "Dionysian" culture, the most conspicuous feature of which is the practice of obtaining supernatural power in a dream or vision, induced by hideous tortures, drugs, alcohol, fasting, or the frenzy of marathon dancing. The Pueblos, whose culture is described as "Apollonian," do not seek or tolerate any experiences outside of ordinary sensory sources. They "will have nothing to do with disruptive individual experiences of this type," notes Mrs. Benedict. "The love of moderation to which their civilization is committed has no place for them."

Individual authority is strictly subordinated among the Zuñi. Both in domestic and religious situations, the group is most important, and responsibility and power are always distributed. In their economic life, too, all activity is on a community basis: the planting, harvesting, and storing of crops; the building of houses; the herding of sheep, etc. Anger, marital jealousy, grief, and violent emotions of any kind are suppressed. Suicides are virtually unknown. The Zuñi priests and medicine men engage in supernatural practices, but not in malicious sorcery. Mrs. Benedict sums up the prevailing mores with the statement: "In the Pueblos, therefore, there is no courting of excess in any form, no tolerance of violence, no indulgence in the exercise of authority, or delight in any situation in which the individual stands alone."

The natives of Dobu Island provide a vivid contrast to the Zuñi. The Dobuans exist on rocky volcanic upcroppings with scanty pockets of soil. They are one of the most southerly of the peoples of northwestern Melanesia, and the population presses hard upon limited resources. Their barren environment is reflected in their reputations, for *Patterns of Culture* describes them as "the feared and distrusted savages of the islands surrounding them. . . . They are noted for their dangerousness. They are said to be magicians who have diabolic power and warriors who halt at no treachery." Until stopped by white men, they were cannibals. In short, the Dobuans are lawless and treacherous, and every man's hand is against every other man. All is suspicion, and a pleasant person is regarded as foolish, if not actually insane.

The Dobuan culture is classified as "Dionysian"; it includes the desire, in personal experience or in ritual, to attain a certain psychological state, to achieve excess. Such an emotion may be gained by drunkenness or working oneself into a state of frenzy.

The Dobuans function in groups of villages in a particular locality. Every grouping is a war unit and is on terms of permanent hostility with every other similar locality. There is also internecine warfare: "People with whom one associates daily are the witches and sorcerers who threaten one's affairs." It is believed that individuals within one's own locality "play havoc with one's harvest, they bring confusion upon one's economic exchanges, they cause disease and death." The only persons from whom one may expect any backing or for whom any affinity is felt are those in the mother's line. Within this line inheritance passes and cooperation exists.

Marriage is surrounded by elaborate customs. Husband and wife remain mutually antagonistic, and the illness or death of either is assumed to have been caused by evil sorcery on the part of the other. The jealousy, the suspicion, the fierce exclusiveness of ownership characteristic of all Dobu culture are strongly evident in Dobuan marriage. A sort of mania runs through the society, convincing the Dobuan that "all existence is cut-throat competition, and every advantage is gained at the expense of a defeated rival."

Religion among the Dobu is primarily concerned with magic:

> Yams cannot grow without incantations, sex desire does not arise without love magic, exchanges of valuables in economic transactions are magically brought about, no trees are protected from theft unless malevolent charms have been placed upon them, no wind blows unless it is magically called, no disease or death occurs without the machinations of sorcery or witchcraft.

In summary, Mrs. Benedict characterizes the Dobuan as dour, prudish, and passionate, consumed with jealousy, suspicion, and resentment, and certain that any prosperity he has achieved has been wrung from a hostile world. "Suspicion and cruelty are his trusted weapons in the strife and he gives no mercy, as he asks none."

For her treatment of a third primitive society, Mrs. Benedict turns again to America, but to a culture vastly different from the Pueblos: that of the Kwakiutl Indians of the Northwest Coast, a culture which fell into ruin during the latter part of the nineteenth century. The Kwakiutl lived on a narrow strip of Pacific seacoast from Alaska to Puget Sound. The economic basis of their society was fish, obtainable in great quantities with a minimum of effort. Practically all transportation, commerce, and intercommunication were by water, by seagoing canoes. Aside from fishing and hunting, the men's chief occupation was woodworking.

The tribes of the Northwest Coast were Dionysian in their culture, like most American Indians—except those of the Southwest Pueblos. In their religious ceremonies, the aim was to achieve states of ecstasy. Their dancers would work themselves into frenzies, during which they lost all self-control and were capable of doing irreparable harm, unless severely restrained. Among the Kwakiutl, one group, the Cannibal Society, whose members had a passion for human flesh, outranked all others. The Cannibal would even attack onlookers and bite flesh from their arms. But unlike the cannibals of Africa and Oceania, the Kwakiutl abhorred the actual eating of human flesh, and the Cannibal spat out or voided that which he took into his mouth. Many weird customs and ceremonies were associated with the cannibalistic rituals.

Extensive possessions were held by the tribes of the Northwest Coast: areas of the land and sea, fishing territories, such material things as houseposts, spoons, and heraldic crests, and such immaterial possessions as names, myths, songs, and special privileges. The women made great quantities of mats, baskets, and cedar-bark blankets, while the men accumulated canoes and the shells, or "dentalia," used for money.

Other striking features of the Kwakiutl culture included the acquisition of status by marriage; that is, a man transferred his privileges to his son-in-law. Further prerogatives and property were bestowed upon the son-in-law upon the birth of children. Both secular and religious organizations existed; that is, the tribes were organized in lineages, and there were also societies with supernatural powers—the Cannibals, the Bears, the Fools, etc. Behavior was dominated at every point by attempts to demonstrate the greatness of the individual and the inferiority of his rivals.

The culture of the Northwest Coast, Ruth Benedict observes, "is recognized as abnormal in our civilization," but "the megalomaniac paranoid trend is a definite danger in our society." In further defense of her detailed analyses of all three societies dealt with in *Patterns of Culture,* the author asserts:

> It is one of the philosophical justifications for the study of primitive peoples that the facts of simpler cultures may make clear social facts that are otherwise baffling and not open to demonstration. . . . The whole problem of the formation of the individual's habit-patterns under the influence of traditional custom can best be understood at the present time through the study of simpler peoples.

41 | LIBERTY VERSUS SECURITY

Walter Lippmann's *An Inquiry into the
Principles of the Good Society*, 1937

Walter Lippmann's dominant theme in *The Good Society* (1937)
is a passage from Milton's *Samson Agonistes*, cited by the author
on the book's title page:

> But what more oft, in nations grown corrupt,
> And by their vices brought to servitude,
> Than to love bondage more than liberty—
> Bondage with ease than strenuous liberty.

The Good Society was published only two years prior to the
outbreak of World War II. Fascism, communism, and other
forms of totalitarianism had reached a crest and were threatening
to take over the world. Lippmann's premise is that socialism, or
any other centrally controlled economic system, must necessarily
abandon democracy, establish strict controls over industry, labor,
and agriculture, and eventually become a coercive dictatorship.
Latter-day liberals, he holds, have been seduced by a "heresy,"
a belief that only through collectivist principles and planning
by a powerful state can the excesses of capitalism be regulated
and restrained. The primrose path has been followed of applying
collective knowledge, collective planning, and collective action
as the most feasible solution to society's problems. In the process,
individual liberty and law are sacrificed. As described by the
author,

> Everywhere two movements which bid for men's allegiance are
> hostile to the movements in which men struggled to be free.
> The programs of reform are everywhere at odds with the liberal
> tradition. Men are asked to choose between security and liberty.
> To improve their fortunes they are told that they must renounce
> their rights. To escape from want they must enter a prison. To
> regularize their work they must be regimented. To obtain greater
> equality they must have less freedom. To have national solidarity

they must oppress the dissenters. To enhance their dignity they must lick the boots of tyrants. To realize the promise of science they must destroy free inquiry. To promote the truth they must not let it be examined.

In reviewing *The Good Society,* Max Eastman concludes:

The whole mood of the book is that of the Hebrew prophets. It begins with a devasting attack upon the collectivisms of the day as the Sodom and Gomorrah that have brought mankind to its present pass. It continues with a passionate defense of the older liberalism. And it ends in an apocalyptic vision of a future society in which men are once more free.

Unfortunately, in the view of most commentators, Lippmann does not differentiate or discriminate among forms of collective action, lumping together, for example, such violent manifestations as Russian communism and Adolf Hitler's Nazi state and the comparatively mild socialistic experiments of Franklin D. Roosevelt's New Deal, then in its heyday.

The alternative to big government, economic planning, and their concomitant centralization of power and collective control, as seen by Lippmann, is a return to Adam Smith's style of laissez faire capitalism. The principles of human freedom are equated with a free market, as it prevailed in the late eighteenth and early nineteenth centuries.

Lippmann's prime argument against strong central government and socialistic action is that modern society is far too complex for any human being or group of human beings to grasp. No one person can see a huge government or all society whole. Therefore, instead of submitting to the coercions of political power with its limited understanding of governmental complexities, Lippmann advocates a regime of individualist capitalism and the free market—without adequate recognition of the social abuses and even chaos that have usually resulted from unregulated and unrestrained laissez faire policies.

Lippmann does concede, however, that it was a popular revolt against capitalism's inflexibility and resistance to change which brought about governmental regulation and social controls. "The period from, say, 1776 to 1870," writes Lippmann, "was the golden age of free trade and of political emancipation throughout the world. It was an age when the reforming passion of men was centered upon the abolition of privileges, the removal of restraints, the restricting of the authority of the state." But then, liberalism became sterile and the economic and social system as it had developed was unresponsive to the hopes and grievances of mankind. A kind of counterrevolution turned to collectivism for solutions. This is a false trail in Lippmann's view, for "There is only one purpose to which a whole society can be directed by a deliberate plan. That purpose is war, and there is no other." An authoritarian society can be made to work, it is contended, only in a military state.

Rather than proceeding down the road advocated by the collectivists, "to an abyss of tyranny, impoverishment, and general war," or to the old liberalism which has lost its drive and effectiveness, Lippmann proposes a third choice—to resume "the process of liberation." The powers of government must be used, but social controls should be exercised through stronger laws. A model law "defines the reciprocal rights and duties of persons and invites them to enforce the law by proving their case in a court of law." The truly liberal state, Lippmann maintains, "does not administer the affairs of men. It administers justice among men who conduct their own affairs." Thus changes in human relations would be determined not by "commands from on high," but "by amending the laws under which men deal with one another."

In short, Lippmann distrusts men's ability to plan their society, and at the same time he is willing to place in their hands a vast and complex system of legal controls through litigation. The question is, Would it work? Max Lerner offers a strong negative answer: "I can only assume that Mr. Lippmann, in his proposal for stripping away all governmental controls except those of the common law, is writing with a naive innocence of legal history. It was because the jury and the writs and the injunctions were a complete failure that we have had to build up our complex body of administrative law." A British writer, R. H. S. Crossman, attacks the concept in even more outspoken terms:

> The rule of law for the protection of natural rights—this is the splendid vision offered to the sharecropper, the Negro and the striker! If a factory sweats its workers, government shall not intervene till the workers have got Judge and Co. on their side.

Judge and Co. shall smash the trusts, the rackets and the big bosses, and put through the agenda of liberalism. Could any proposal be more fantastic? British Trade unions fought the law for a hundred years and only obtained freedom by political action. Law and order defends the natural rights of those in possession: for the exploited they are opponents to be conquered by one power alone, the State.

Nevertheless, Lippmann argues that man is capable of administering justice but not of ordering and planning human affairs in general. "To the liberal mind," he writes, "the notion that men can authoritatively plan and impose a good life upon a great society is ignorant, impertinent, and pretentious."

Corporations are no more immune to law, Lippmann asserts, than are individuals. A state can specify the conditions under which a charter is granted to a business, and if the corporation violates the terms of its charter, a court of law can withdraw its franchise. According to Lippmann, "there is no such thing as an absolute, illimitable, and indefeasable system of property rights." He makes a distinction between "big" business and "collectivist" business. There is no objection to bigness as such, if an enterprise is operating under fair competitive conditions with other companies in its field; but holding companies and all other "artificial" combinations aiming to eliminate competition violate the principles of the free market and should be restrained by law. If such combinations rest on a legal basis, Lippmann maintains that "monopoly can be destroyed and prevented by changing the law." His biographer, David E. Weingast, points out that Lippmann's approach to this problem "was ignoring the whole tortuous history of governmental efforts to make monopolies conform to existing laws." Also highly unrealistic, critics generally agree, is Lippmann's proposal to replace regulatory commissions by "law."

Much of Lippmann's indictment of collectivism is aimed directly or indirectly at the New Deal. He arrives at his point of view, as previously noted, by grouping the New Deal with fascism, communism, and other totalitarian schemes of government. The author concedes that there are differences, but they are like the differences between "African and Indian lions," both of which are equally predatory in the eyes of the lamb. The moderate collectivists of democratic countries, it is stated, cannot distinguish their aims and policies in principle from the absolute authoritarianism of the dictatorships. No matter how good the intentions of democratic socialists and New Dealers, Lippmann argues, a collectivist society is in essence authoritarian and ultimately leads to absolutism.

The force of Lippmann's criticisms of Roosevelt's New Deal is considerably weakened, however, when he ends up accepting much of its program. In what he terms his "conservative program of a liberal reformer" Lippmann commends the relief of unemployment, monetary and banking reform, the control of credit to prevent speculative excesses, conservation and reclamation, relocation of populations, public housing, prohibition of child labor, prevention of unfair trade practices, the regulation of water power to prevent floods and soil erosion and to provide irrigation and electricity, reduction of tariffs by reciprocal trade agreements, the increase of the bargaining power of labor and the purchasing power of agriculture, the Food and Drug Act, the supervision of the issue of securities, the taxation of wealth by a steeply graduated income tax, the attempt by various methods to improve the condition of the less privileged and to reduce the disparity of incomes, and reform of the Supreme Court to make it more responsive to changed economic conditions and to prevent it from usurping legislative functions—all of which in one form or another were embodied in the New Deal.

Thus, though Lippmann distrusted government bureaus and their administrators, he perceived the need for government administration of certain social services. He repudiates the philosophy of laissez faire because it contains too many inherent potentialities for evil in a capitalist system. Lippmann calls his program of needed reforms, to mitigate the hardships of a free economy, the "Agenda of Liberalism." He proposes to take measures to protect and to improve the economic condition of the worker, the farmer, and the consumer; and to extend and improve education, to provide recreational facilities, and to conserve the country's natural resources. Appropriate government enterprises, Lippmann believes, would be great public works designed to improve waterways, ensure the fertility of the soil, control floods and erosion, and preserve our forests and parks. To pay for the social reforms he advocated, Lippmann urges a taxation system that would bear most heavily on "unearned" income, striking "not at the profits of successful competition but at the tolls of monopoly."

The principal difference between Roosevelt's New Deal and Lippmann's "Agenda of Liberalism" appears to be in the method of administration. Lippmann's proposals were to be carried out under the conditions of a free market in a society where the "law" was supreme. Any official required for superintending the operation should possess a "judicial" temperament, and there would be no top-heavy, sinister bureaucracy. The essence of Lippmann's argument is that our form of government (democracy) and our method of enterprise (capitalism) when combined, and protected from privilege and monopoly, form a far more effective system than collectivism for increasing the national well-being.

Weingast concludes:

> Surely Lippmann was asking here for the impossible—a "free market" and a New Dealish "Agenda of Liberalism." . . . Lippmann's lumping of New Deal reformism with Communism and Fascism can hardly have enlightened his readers. And his exaltation of a puristic society under "law," governed by men with the "judicial" temperament can only have stirred discontent with the human efforts of Mr. Roosevelt to preserve republican institutions while mastering a shattering economic crisis.

In the same vein, Lewis Mumford objects strongly to

> Mr. Lippmann's many attempts to equate planning with dictatorship and to show that planning inevitably brings with it coercion, militarism, poverty, no less than a general loss of liberty. If that were so, Denmark, which collectively promotes, regulates, standardizes, and markets its main agricultural products, should be the most belligerent and dictator-ridden and impoverished nation in Europe. . . . Everyone knows that this is not true: so does Mr. Lippmann: hence he is careful not to mention Denmark as an example of the evils of collectivist regimentation.

Lippmann's thesis that America had to make a choice between fascism or communism on one hand and an unplanned democracy on the other is rejected by various critics, who point out that there is an infinite number of other possibilities between the extremes. "Actually," as Max Lerner comments, "man's fate lies with a whole variety of socialism and partial collectivisms that are yet unexplored." Lerner accuses Lippmann of branding "with the fascist stigma every attempt of mankind to carve out a good society for itself by conscious social action."

Other critics come to Lippmann's defense and insist that his heart is in the right place, even though his methods may be faulty. Few democrats, they suggest, would disagree with such principles enunciated by Lippmann as the idea that all legislation should advance the interest of liberalism; that we want to live in a free society, where maximum individual initiative, consistent with the freedom of others, is permitted; that we wish to keep in check the arbitrary control of our affairs by any man or group of men; and that the population as a whole should stand on their own feet, free to express their own opinions, and to act according to their own consciences. These concepts apparently are the main constituents of Lippmann's notion of the "Good Society."

42 | MEDIEVAL VILLAGE TO MODERN MEGALOPOLIS

Lewis Mumford's *The Culture of Cities*, 1938

One of the most indefatigable writers of our time, Lewis Mumford, has interests which have taken him off in varied directions: architecture, city planning, painting, belles lettres, regional planning, cultural evolution, and industrial history. Despite the seeming dispersal of talents, however, Mumford's *Culture of Cities* makes clear that all his studies are focused on one subject: the past, present, and future of the city in the civilization and progress of the race. In this book, which established the author's international reputation, is traced the drama of the city for the past 1,000 years, presenting an exhaustive record of its technology, economics, architecture, fashions, greeds, evils, and blind folly.

Mumford's epic story starts with the medieval city. The notion is immediately rejected that the period from the tenth century to the sixteenth "was a compound of ignorance, filth, brutality, and superstition," for which defamers from the Renaissance on damned it. Indeed, Mumford finds in the medieval town a nearly ideal organization. Its form was well integrated: surrounded by a protective wall, centered in an open space where the church or cathedral, the town hall, the guild hall, and the market represented the religious, political, and economic life of the people. The towns were usually small and set against a background of nature. Everyone shared a feeling of physical, economic, and spiritual security. Mumford stresses the civilizing influence of the monasteries and the monastic orders, not only in the preservation and transmission of the intellectual heritage, but in the management of everyday life and in the specialized field of agriculture. To exist in the Middle Ages one had to belong to an association, a manor, a monastery, a guild, or a household. There was no room for the unsocial individualist. Narrow limits of wealth and power existed, and the towns were comparatively democratic. Sanitary conditions were bad by modern standards, but were somewhat redeemed by the availability of "usable open spaces." The medieval house possessed little or no separation of space by function—the kitchen was likely to serve also as dining room, living room, bedroom, and workshop (the workshop was in the home because the organization of industry was simple).

By the sixteenth century the medieval town had practically ceased to exist as a viable unit. "Its economic and its social basis had disintegrated," Mumford comments, "and its organic pattern of life had been broken up. Slowly, the form itself became dilapidated, and even when it continued to stand, its walls enclosed a hollow shell, harboring institutions that were also hollow shells." The cannon of royal armies battered down the walls, heretics were breaking away from the church, and a rising middle class had destroyed feudalism.

Mumford is critical of the Renaissance and the claims made for its advancement of culture. He points out, for example, that the fifteenth century generally accepted a belief in witchcraft rejected in the eighth century, and the thirteenth century had bathhouses and baths where the later centuries had none. During this era began the rise of what Mumford calls "the baroque city" which became increasingly ugly, overcrowded, smelly, and unsanitary with the rise of artillery, Protestant capitalism, Renaissance princely despotism, and utilitarian economics. The baroque city began to arrange its avenues and streets for wheeled traffic and marching men, because military considerations demanded wide, straight avenues for columns of troops during periods of war or insurrection and for the fashion parade of the rich in periods of peace. The city became a symbol of wealth and power, centering in the palace and the court and sucking the life out of the countryside. The old freedom and the old free spaces vanished altogether. "For the mass of people in the baroque city," states Mumford, "the result of its political absolutism, its mercantile enterprise, and its ruthless system of taxation was deterioration of environment and a depression of the standard of living." Only the rich enjoyed space and comfort.

The third major phase in the growth of cities is described by Mumford as "the insensate industrial town," which emerged in full-blown form in the nineteenth century. The principal characteristics are poverty, lack of sunlight, pure air, and good food, and a minimum of life, cleanliness, rest, and shelter. The mammoth industrial cities which grew up in the nineteenth century were totally unplanned, chaotic, without center or boundary, a hodge-podge of manufacturing, commercial, and residential districts jammed together with great blighted areas of slums. Such municipal government as existed was in the hands of corrupt political rings and bosses. The industrial city was a noisy, smoke-begrimed wilderness of brick and stone far removed from the pleasant countryside. The cities became progressively less fit places for the happiness and well-being of those who had to live in them. Population increased by leaps and bounds and pushed into already overcrowded centers. Powerful and ruthless industrialists rose to the top in these "coketown" jungles and mercilessly exploited their fellow men. As Mumford describes the deplorable conditions:

> The brakes of tradition and custom were lifted from the exploitation of land; there was no limit to congestion, no limit to rent raising; there was no standard of order or decency or beauty to dictate the division and layout and building up of urban structures. Only one controlling agent remained: profit. The two main elements in the new urban complex were the factory and the slum. Never before in recorded history had such vast masses of people lived in such a savagely deteriorated environment.

"The insensate industrial town" in Mumford's view represents the triumph of our "machine civilization." The labor-saving machine seemed to damn the laborer. Those who could afford to do so saved their health and sanity by running away, escaping to the suburbs, where they could find space, fresh air, natural beauty, and privacy.

But the industrial city was not totally lacking in commendable features and hopeful developments. Despite existing in an age of rugged individualism, dominated by the callous-hearted rich, and despite the totally inadequate physical organization, the new towns were beginning to pay some attention to the social side of life. It was during the nineteenth century, Mumford points out, that "new organs for social co-operation and social thought were defining themselves: the trade union, the scientific society, the public library: means whereby the military-capitalistic regime could be eventually transformed into a social commonwealth."

Finally in *The Culture of Cities* we encounter the most inhuman monster of all, the megalopolis—"the maximum possible assault upon the processes of civilization," the huge, shapeless, bloblike excrescence which occurs all over the world. Notable examples are New York, London, Tokyo, Berlin, Chicago, and Los Angeles. Mumford's indictment of the megalopolis is scathing. An example is a paragraph on urban transportation:

> The cost of all the urban transportation systems in a big city is equally massive: certain factors elude exact calculation. The initial capital cost, particularly for the underground systems, with their difficult tunneling and boring, is necessarily high: but this is only a part of the total expenses . . . above all, one must add on the human cost, the physiological wear and tear, the psychological boredom and harassment and depression brought about by this daily shuttling between dormitory and workhouse. Consider the number of man-hours reckoned in multiples of a million stupidly expended in the daily transportation of the human body . . . add to this the depression of the uncomfortable journey, the exposure to infectious diseases in the overcrowded car, the disturbance to the gastro-intestinal functions caused by the strain and anxiety of having to reach the office or factory on time.

The basis for the megalopolis was laid in the tremendous increase of population that began in the nineteenth century and continued at an accelerated rate in the twentieth. Other influential factors were the constant migration from rural to urban areas; the growth of continental railroad lines, super highways, and worldwide lanes of ocean commerce, bringing an endless flow of raw materials and foods into the metropolises; and the concentration of government, economic, and industrial resources, and financial power in the great population centers. In its all-devouring growth the big city absorbs smaller communities, which then proceed to lose their identities. The city continues to grow, writes Mumford, "by breaking through the edges and accepting its sprawl and shapelessness as an inevitable by-product of its physical immensity."

The megalopolis under the influence of the capitalistic system concentrates upon bigness and power. Belief in size dominates every department of life: "the biggest monuments, the highest buildings, the most expensive materials, the largest food supply, the greatest number of worshippers, the biggest population."

But every city contains the seeds of its own decay. Inevitably, blight sets in, marked, Mumford notes, by the inability of the inhabitants or the owners of buildings to pay their taxes, the street-cleaning department's neglect of run-down neighborhoods, the failure to keep properties repaired, and eventually the conversion of what may have been once streets of fine mansions, for example, on the South Side in Chicago, "into low quarters, boarding houses and tenements, usually crowded, often filthy." The last stage is depopulation: "deserted houses, in ruins: no rents: no taxes: a vast economic and civic liability."

The imminent decline of the megalopolis unable to meet the ever-rising costs of congestion was thus foreseen by Mumford in the 1930s. His dire predictions have come to pass in the 1970s. Confronted by the almost insurmountable problems of New York, for example, many experts in municipal affairs have thrown up their hands in despair and concluded that the large city is virtually ungovernable. Among the most aggravated symptoms are density of population, particularly in ghetto districts; the flow of population from the soil to the city, which in the past decade has become a flood; the violent ethnic conflicts; the rapid growth of suburbs at the expense of the central city; the killing of mass transit by automobiles (which in turn poison the atmosphere); housing decay and destruction without replacement; and acute financial problems, pointing toward eventual bankruptcy.

Mumford paints a gloomy picture of the city, but he is optimistic about the future and devotes the second half of *The Culture of Cities* to presenting possible solutions for the chronic dilemmas in which cities are caught. The answer, he believes, is a long-time process of decentralization and regionalism. The overgrown city will be gradually dispersed, replaced by self-sustaining regions which in turn would be divided into cities with not more than 50,000 inhabitants each. The author does not propose to scrap the machine or to start a back-to-the-country movement or to demolish the city. We must accept the city, but not megalopolis. Mumford describes an appealing, possibly utopian, scheme of regional planning, made possible by electric power lines, automobiles, more light, air, and contact with nature for all the people, and industry decentralized and scattered efficiently over the landscape. He takes full account of economic and industrial progress, but is somewhat vague about the future disposition of the old metropolitan areas.

There are striking similarities between Lewis Mumford's and Frank Lloyd Wright's visions of the ideal city of the future. Neither faces up to the many hard realities of life, but anyone seeking a better world will doubtless find inspiration in one of Mumford's concluding statements: "Man is at last in a position to transcend the machine, and to create a new biological and social environment, in which the highest possibilities of human existence will be realized, not for the strong and the lucky alone, but for all co-operating and understanding groups, associations, and communities."

43 | OKIES AND ARKIES

John Steinbeck's *The Grapes of Wrath*, 1939

The Great Depression years of the 1930s saw the rise of the pro-
letarian novel, the novel of social protest. With one notable exception—John Steinbeck's *Grapes of Wrath*—a great majority of
such propagandistic efforts vanished with no more than literary
footnotes to remind us of their former existence. The survival of
The Grapes of Wrath can be attributed to two factors: Steinbeck's
concern for people rather than with political ideology, and the
philosophical breadth, the imaginative power, and narrative skill
which mark his major work. Clifton Fadiman compares *The
Grapes of Wrath*, in its impact on the Depression, to *Uncle Tom's
Cabin*, in the latter's bearing on the Civil War, and adds that
The Grapes of Wrath is directly in the tradition of such celebrated humanitarian novels as *Les Misérables* and *Oliver Twist*.

The theme of *The Grapes of Wrath* developed slowly in Steinbeck's mind. The novel had been foreshadowed in his earlier *In
Dubious Battle*, the story of a strike of the depressed, poverty-
stricken migratory fruit harvesters in the Torgas Valley orchards.
In preparation for a larger, more ambitious work, Steinbeck
made a tour of "Hoovervilles," the itinerant laborers' camps, in
the Salinas and San Joaquin Valleys. He picked fruit and cotton
beside the field workers and wrote a series of articles for the San
Francisco *News* reporting his observations on living and working
conditions among "the harvest Gypsies." The fruit and vegetable
crops of California, formerly harvested by Mexicans and Ori-
entals, were being picked by Okies and Arkies—tenant farmers
and sharecroppers and their families forced off the land in Oklahoma, Arkansas, Texas, and neighboring states.

For further background, Steinbeck visited the Oklahoma dustbowl, which was sending so many homeless families to California.
He saw at first hand the natural and economic forces that were
bringing ruin to the small farmer: heavy mortgages, land exhausted by erosion, greedy banks and agricultural corporations

combining many farms into one plantation which could be planted to cotton and cheaply cultivated with tractors. Hundreds of thousands of dustbowl migrants went west to California in the 1930s, responding to advertisements for men to harvest the crops. It was perhaps the greatest exodus of farm families in American history. Steinbeck, returning from the East, drove through Oklahoma, joined migrants who were going west and worked with them in the fields after they reached California. The stark realism of *The Grapes of Wrath* is thus based on the author's own direct experience and observation of conditions.

The story of *The Grapes of Wrath* is simple and straightforward, though involving many characters. A family of tenant farmers in Oklahoma, the Joads, occupy the center of the stage. The great dust storms have ruined their crops, they are forced to give up their land to a bankers' syndicate, huge tractors are plowing up the land for miles around and pushing the poor shacks of the farmers out of the way. The Joads sell their furniture at a fraction of its value and buy an old car at twice its worth. The last pig is killed and salted, all the family is bundled onto the jalopy, with the tent and saucepans, clothes and tools, and dogs, ready to make the 2,000-mile odyssey across desert and over mountains to the Pacific. The Joads had read the handbills urging agricultural workers to come to California, the promised land.

At the beginning of the westward trek, the Joad family numbers twelve, self-respecting people of old American stock, whose ancestors for decades have lived and died on their home farm. The patriarchs are Grampa Joad, senile and bawdy, and Granma Joad, senile and highly religious. The other members are Pa and Ma Joad, the former losing his grip because of worry over the loss of his farm, and the latter a true heroine who governs the family and holds it together; a son-in-law, Uncle John, who suffers from a sense of sin because he had mistaken his wife's acute appendicitis for a stomach-ache and let her die without calling a doctor; three sons: Tom, just released from the Oklahoma state prison, where he had served a sentence for killing a man in self-defense; Noah, mentally backward; and Al, an adolescent younger brother; a daughter, Rose of Sharon or Rosasharn, pregnant and crazy for love of her young husband Connie Rivers; and the Joad children, Ruthie and Winfield. A friend of Tom's, Jim Casy, an ex-preacher, is invited to join the caravan.

There is little money for gasoline and nothing to spare for food above a bare minimum. They camp by the roadside, and Grampa dies of a stroke during their first overnight stop. There is no money to bury him properly, and it is a crime to bury him without telling the law; but the Joads proceed to inter him beside a creek and write on a scrap of paper torn from the end of a Bible, in case he is found and thought to be murdered:

> This here is William James Joad, dyed of a stroke, old old man. His fokes buried him becaws they got no money to pay for funerls. Nobody kilt him, jus a stroke and he dyed.

The journey is a long one, for the old car cannot be pushed too fast; even so, there is a long delay when the vehicle breaks down. It is a desperate race against time, to reach California before their money and supplies run out. A friendly couple, the Wilsons, join the Joads for a time, and they meet others headed in the same direction. More disheartening are the families they meet returning from California who report that there is no work, the Californians call them Okies—a synonym for tramps—the police mistreat them, and if work is found, the wages are at the starvation level. But the Joads refuse to believe such gloomy tales and push on.

Along the highway, historic 66, small-business people regard the migrants with contempt and distrust. Close to the California line, the group stops to bathe in the Colorado River, and Noah, Tom's retarded older brother, feeling that he is a hindrance to the family, wanders off, never to be seen again. Granma dies during the night trip across the desert, and the family crosses the California border with her lying dead under a tarpaulin in the back. A great moment of joy is experienced as they reach the top of the mountains and see the rich valleys spread out below.

> They stood, silent and awestruck, embarrassed before the great valley. The distance was thinned with haze and the land grew softer and softer in the distance. A windmill flashed in the sun, and its turning blades were like a little heliograph far away. Ruthie and Winfield looked at it and Ruthie whispered: "It's California."

The cruel realities lie ahead of them. In the promised land, the Joads find that they are unwelcome and despised, and work is nearly impossible to find. They go into a camp for migrants, popularly known as a Hooverville, later destroyed by local vigilantes, where they see the misery and hunger of the migrant workers and the arrogance and cruelty of deputy sheriffs. Connie Rivers deserts his wife, and Jim Casy is arrested for striking a police officer.

The Joads move on to a federal government camp for farm workers, where they stay for a month, happy and comfortable in a clean, friendly, self-governing little community. No work is available, however, except for a temporary job found by Tom. Out of food and money, they move north and find work picking peaches on the Hooper ranch, where they find that they are being used as strikebreakers. The lodgings provided are miserable, and the entire family earns in a day barely enough money to buy one meal at the company store. Tom discovers that Casy is one of the strike leaders. During the night, vigilantes invade the strike-committee's tent, one of them kills Casy with a club, and Tom in turn seizes the club and kills the attacker. Tom escapes, but not until after receiving a severe blow on his head from another vigilante; he has to go into hiding to avoid having anyone see his swollen face.

Wages for picking peaches are cut in two after the strike is broken, and the Joads move on to the cotton fields. Tom remains hidden until his young sister Ruth boasts to other children that her brother has killed a man. Ma realizes the danger of Tom's being discovered and captured and sends him away. Before he departs, Tom promises to carry on Casy's work for unionization of the farm workers and to obtain justice for the downtrodden everywhere.

After the cotton picking, there is no more work for three months. The Joads are living in an abandoned boxcar along a creek. The heavy winter rains begin and swell the stream until the squatters' camp is flooded. Under these nearly impossible conditions, Rose of Sharon gives birth to a stillborn baby, who is placed in an empty apple box by Uncle John and set afloat in the creek, to be carried away by the swift stream. Forced from the boxcar by the rising water, the Joads find refuge in an old barn on higher ground, sharing the barn with a boy and his starving father. Rose of Sharon, bereft of her baby, feeds the starving man with milk from her breasts.

The final incident is melodramatic but symbolic: only if the poor nourish and sustain each other will they survive. The Joads' strong sense of family loyalty has now been expanded to encompass all mankind. One Steinbeck critic, Joseph Warren Beach, states the case:

> It is a type of the life-instinct, the vital persistence of the common people who are represented by the Joads. Their sufferings and humiliations are overwhelming; but these people are never entirely overwhelmed. They have something in them that is more than stoical endurance. It is the will to live, and the faith in life.

Rose of Sharon's self-sacrificing gesture in the barn is matched by another symbolic happening at the beginning of *The Grapes of Wrath*. A chapter is devoted to a land turtle crossing the highway, an act made perilous by heavy trucks and cars thundering by, and in one or two instances making a deliberate attempt to run over the turtle. But the turtle's persistence and obstinacy win out, and he finally makes the dangerous crossing successfully. The story sets the keynote for the later heroism of men and women.

In *The Grapes of Wrath*, Steinbeck developed an effective literary device to place his characters in a larger setting. In addition to telling the adventures of the Joads, their experience is given universal meaning by a series of short interchapters that show what is happening to people like the Joads all over America. Of the novel's thirty chapters, fourteen are specifically concerned with the Joad story; the remaining sixteen are essays or sketches of typical situations in the great migration, telling the story of all the migrants from economic, historical, and social points of view. The interchapters make no reference to the Joads.

The interchapters are powerful aids for background purposes and to carry the dramatic narrative forward. At the outset, there is an account of a dust storm over the gray and red lands of Oklahoma, and the response of men, women, and children to the catastrophe. In chapter five the banks and land companies, and the men behind them, are characterized as inhuman monsters which "don't breathe air, don't eat side meat;" instead "they breathe profits; they eat the interest on money. If they don't get it, they die the way you die without air, without side meat. . . . The bank is something else than men. It happens that every man in a bank hates what the bank does, and yet the bank does it." The giant tractors are devils incarnate: "Snub-nosed monsters, raising the dust and sticking their snouts into it, straight down the country, across the country, through fences, through door-yards, in and out of gullies in straight lines," with inhuman creatures in the driver's seat.

As a rule, each of the interchapters has a particular theme. A famous one is chapter seven on second-hand automobile dealers —highly unscrupulous characters dedicated to covering up defects, buying cheap and selling dear. Later there is a graphic picture of the tenant farmers picking over their pathetic possessions preparatory to the western trek. Chapter fifteen contains an unflattering portrait of the rich:

> The big cars on the highway. Languid, heat-raddled ladies, small nucleuses about whom revolve a thousand accouterments: creams, ointments to grease themselves, coloring matter in phials—black, pink, red, white, green, silver—to change the color of hair, eyes, lips, nails, brows, lashes, lids. Oils, seeds, and pills to make the bowels move. A bag of bottles, syringes, pills, powders, fluids, jellies to make their sexual intercourse safe, odorless, and un-productive. And this apart from clothes. . . . Beside them, little pot-bellied men in light suits and panama hats; clean, pink men with puzzled, worried eyes, with restless eyes. Worried because formulas do not work out; hungry for security and yet sensing its disappearance from the earth.

Another interchapter, number seventeen, presents the basic Steinbeck theme—the interdependence of men, as separate families in roadside camps quickly become one community. At times, as many as twenty families would stop at one campsite. "In the evening a strange thing happened: the twenty families became one family, the children were the children of all. The loss of home became one loss, and the golden time in the West was one dream. . . . Thus they changed their social life—changed as in the whole universe only man can change. They were not farm men any more, but migrant men."

A bitter chapter deals with the California land syndicates who ruin the small owners; who allow cherries, prunes, pears, and grapes to rot on the ground to keep up the price; and who employ men with hoses to squirt kerosene on the fruit, while there are "a million men hungry, needing the fruit." The companies were blind not only to their own best interests, but to all humanitarian instincts: "The granaries were full and the children of the poor grew up rachitic, and the pustules of pellagra swelled on their sides. And money that might have gone for wages went for gas, for guns, for agents and spies, for blacklists, for drilling." Thus the companies and the banks were sealing their own doom without knowing it, as the anger of the hungry began to ferment.

Various critics have noted the close Biblical parallels in *The Grapes of Wrath*. The novel's title is taken from "The Battle Hymn of the Republic:" "He is trampling out the vintage where the grapes of wrath are stored," which in turn was inspired by several passages from the Bible, including Deuteronomy's "Their grapes are grapes of gall, their clusters are bitter. Their wine is the poison of serpents." Peter Lisca, in *The Wide World of John Steinbeck*, points out that

> The novel's three sections [drought, journey, and life in California] correspond to the oppression in Egypt, the exodus, and the sojourn in the land of Canaan, which in both accounts is first viewed from the mountains. This parallel is not worked out in detail, but the grand design is there: the plagues (erosion), the Egyptian (banks), the exodus (journey), and the hostile tribes of Canaan (Californians).

Expanding on this concept, Lisca views the drought and erosion as the plagues of Egypt; the banks and land companies as Pharaoh and the Egyptian oppressors; California as Canaan, a land flowing with milk and honey; and the Californians, like the Canaanites, as hostile to the immigrants. Further, Ma Joad's words, "We're the people—we go on," implies a chosen people, and in the roadside camps the migrants, like the Hebrews, formulated codes of law or of conduct to govern themselves. The final touch is the placing of Rose of Sharon's stillborn child afloat in an apple box, as the infant Moses was placed in a basket among the bulrushes in the river.

Numerous other parallels are suggested by Joseph Fontenrose

in *John Steinbeck: An Introduction and Interpretation.* For example, the name Joad may stand for Judah; the dust ruined the corn as hail ruined the Egyptians' flax and barley; the Joads slaughtered their pigs as the Hebrews sacrificed their lambs; the Colorado (Red) River is crossed; Grampa and Granma Joad, like the elder Israelites, died on the way; the hostile reception of the migrants in California corresponds to the efforts of the Edomites, Moabites, and Amorites to keep the Israelites from entering their countries; and Tom's killing of a murderous vigilante is comparable to Moses' killing of an Egyptian for beating a Hebrew laborer. Unlike the Book of Joshua, however, which ends in victory and conquest, *The Grapes of Wrath* concludes with defeat.

Indeed, Steinbeck appears to have stacked the cards against his characters. Like a Greek or Shakespearean tragedy, an inexorable fate carries the Joads and their kind to inevitable doom. No matter what they do, disaster lies ahead. Another critic, W. M. Frohock, in *The Novel of Violence in America*, concludes that Steinbeck "has put into *The Grapes of Wrath* most of the elements of tragedy: the driving forces, the swift rush of events, inevitability, mounting pity and terror, clash, violence. His characters react properly in the face of evil, and the foolish things they do are pieces of eternally human foolishness." Frohock compares the interpolated chapters, which explain events to the reader, to the choruses in Greek drama.

Publication of *The Grapes of Wrath* in 1939 aroused a storm of controversy. The book was attacked for its "vile language," for factual inaccuracies, as communistic propaganda, as "obscene sensationalism," as "propaganda in its vilest form," and "a black, infernal creation of a twisted, distorted mind." The book was banned in some libraries for obscenity. California farm owners claimed that Steinbeck had slandered them, and many Oklahomans considered the novel to be an outsider's malicious attempt to smear the state of Oklahoma with outrageous lies. Cardinal Spellman's denunciation of it was carried in all the Hearst papers. Several books of refutation or reverse propaganda appeared: *Grapes of Gladness: California's Refreshing and Inspiring Answer to John Steinbeck's "Grapes of Wrath," The Truth about John Steinbeck and the Migrants,* and *Plums of Plenty.*

But Steinbeck was not lacking in defenders. Professors of sociology, clergymen, and government officials investigated conditions for themselves and reported that Steinbeck's information was accurate.

Anger at social injustice was undoubtedly the motivating force behind the creation of *The Grapes of Wrath,* a fact which permeates the book with enormous sympathy and a pervading sense of humanity. As Lisca comments, Steinbeck was able to create an "emotionally compelling novel out of materials which in most hands have resulted in sentimental propaganda." To which another critic, Frederic I. Carpenter, adds:

For the first time in history, *The Grapes of Wrath* brings together and makes real three great skeins of American thought. It begins with the transcendental oversoul, Emerson's faith in the common man, and his Protestant self-reliance. To this it joins Whitman's religion of the love of all men and his mass democracy. And it combines these mystical and poetic ideas with the realistic philosophy of pragmatism and its emphasis on effective action. From this it develops a new kind of Christianity—not otherworldly and passive, but earthly and active.

44 | NATIONS UNITED

Wendell Willkie's *One World*, 1943

The travels described in Wendell Willkie's remarkable book, *One World,* were undertaken at the height of hostilities in World War II. *One World* is Willkie's account of his airplane trip around the globe, lasting forty-nine days and covering 31,000 miles, in the fall of 1942. The route followed took him to North Africa, Turkey, Iran, the Soviet Union, China, and Siberia, and enabled him to hold conferences with the principal wartime leaders, as well as with many lesser personalities.

To give official status to the mission, Willkie was designated as a personal representative of President Franklin D. Roosevelt, to whom he had lost the 1940 presidential election. In interviews, speeches, articles, and in *One World,* however, Willkie makes clear that, as he said, "I speak for no one else and no one else speaks for me."

Throughout *One World,* Willkie reiterates three main points: First, the smallness of the world which we now inhabit; second, the speed of social, political, and economic change in the Eastern half of that world; third, the obligation that all Western people had to learn these facts and to act magnanimously in international affairs. The net impression of his flight, Willkie wrote, "was not of distance from other peoples, but of closeness to them. . . . The world has become small not only on the map, but also in the minds of men. All around the world there are some ideas which millions and millions of men hold in common, almost as much as if they lived in the same town." What these ideas are and their implications for mankind, Willkie elaborates in his book. In essence, *One World* is a stirring appeal for self-government among the peoples of the Far and Middle East, for the end of white imperialism everywhere, and for the immediate creation of international machinery to keep the peace.

Willkie's circumnavigation of the globe in a world immersed

in war required great personal courage. His travels occurred before American troops had invaded Africa, when Hitler's armies dominated Central Europe, and Marshall Rommel held North Africa. The consensus among historians is that Willkie's flight performed a major service to the Allied cause, principally in favorable publicity, by showing that America and her Allies were united in their determination to defeat the Axis Powers.

The major stop of the Willkie party in Africa was at Cairo. The Nazi armies under Rommel's command were practically knocking at the gate but were being held and eventually were defeated by General Montgomery's forces. Economic and social conditions were distressing. Willkie comments, "Everywhere I went in the Middle East I found a kind of technological backwardness along with poverty and squalor . . . little has changed in two thousand years. Modern airlines, oil pipe lines, macadam streets, or even plumbing constitute a thin veneer on the surface of a life which in essence is as simple and as hard as it was before there was any West." Egypt's cultural sterility was blamed by Willkie on "the complete absence of a middle class" and the lack of social consciousness among wealthy landowners whose property was largely hereditary. "The great mass of the people, outside of the roaming tribes," Willkie notes, "are impoverished, own no property, are hideously ruled by the practices of ancient priestcraft, and are living in conditions of squalor."

An exception was the industrial, agricultural, and cultural progress made under the influence of the Zionist movement in Palestine. The Jewish viewpoint came out in an interview which Willkie held with Henrietta Szold, founder of Hadassah, who maintained that the Jews must have a national homeland and there was no other appropriate place in the world where the persecuted Jews of Europe could come. Furthermore, there was no "necessary antagonism between the hopes of the Jews and the rights of the Arabs." Willkie concluded, however: "It is probably unrealistic to believe that such a complex question as the Arab–Jewish one, founded in ancient history and religion, and involved as it is with high international policy and politics, can be solved by good will and simple honesty."

Willkie's comments on colonialism and imperialism, as he saw them functioning in Africa and Asia, are highly critical. Some of the leaders with whom he conferred in Egypt and Jerusalem, for example, told him that "the natives don't want anything better than what they have," to which Willkie retorted, "That is the argument that has been used everywhere for centuries against the advancement of the underprivileged, by those whose condition makes them satisfied with the *status quo*." Colonial officials of the Middle East, Willkie found, were derived from "Rudyard Kipling untainted even with the liberalism of Cecil Rhodes."

The colonial people of the Near, Middle, and Far East, Willkie discovered, were demanding social, political, and economic equality with the advanced nations of Europe and America—stirrings over a vast region which have since brought about profound changes in areas formerly administered as colonial empires by Britain, France, Belgium, Holland, Japan, and other outside powers. The awakening forces, Willkie predicted with remarkable foresight, "if they are flouted or ignored, will continue to disturb the world." He concedes that "there is much historical and even present-day justification for the current 'protective' colonial system," but adds:

Pragmatically, however, in view of the present ferment which is going on, it is a question whether that system can be maintained. Idealistically, we must face the fact that the system is completely antipathetic to all the principles for which we claim to fight. Furthermore, the more we preach those principles, the more we stimulate the ferment that endangers the system.

Willkie's criticisms of colonialism were favorably received by most Americans, but not generally by the British or by ruling groups in the colonies themselves. Winston Churchill was provoked into a belligerent rejoinder: "That there may be no mistake in any quarter, we intend to hold what we have. I have not become the King's First Minister to preside at the liquidation of the British Empire." On the other hand, the *Times* of London pointed out that the modern British Empire had "become in a certain sense a self-liquidating concern, dissolving itself by an orderly process into a commonwealth of peoples united by a common ideal of partnership in freedom."

The high-minded purposes for which the war was being fought must also be applied, Willkie insisted, to American society: "The

defense of our democracy against the forces that threaten it from
without has made some of its failures to function at home glar-
ingly apparent . . . we cannot fight the forces and ideas of imperialism abroad and maintain any form of imperialism at home."
Willkie goes on to assert that "we have practiced within our own
boundaries something that amounts to race imperialism. The
attitude of the white citizens of this country toward the Negroes
has undeniably had some of the unlovely characteristics of an
alien imperialism—a smug racial superiority, a willingness to exploit an unprotected people."

From Cairo, Willkie flew to Beirut, Ankara, Bagdad, Tehran,
and then Kuibyshev, Soviet Russia's wartime capital. In Beirut,
he met General Charles de Gaulle, and the two men talked far
into the night. Willkie found the Frenchman to be arrogant and
unbending, with a Joan of Arc complex. In the general's private
room, it was noted, "every corner, every wall held busts, statues
and pictures of Napoleon." De Gaulle stated dogmatically that
French territories must be maintained inviolate: "In no place in
this world can I yield a single French right"—an attitude of mind
which in later years led to the disasters of French Indo-China
and Algeria.

Willkie was in the Soviet Union only two weeks, during which
he met with Stalin for two extended sessions, both off the record.
Willkie's chief purpose in visiting Russia was to find an answer
"to the actual problems posed for our generation of Americans
by the simple fact that the Soviet Union, whether we like it or
not, exists." He concluded that "Russia is an effective society. It
works. It has survival value," and he found much to admire in
the U.S.S.R., whose dynamic spirit he compared with the pioneer
era of the American West. The most important consideration, in
Willkie's estimation, was that "we must work with Russia after
the war. At least it seems to me that there can be no continued
peace unless we learn to do so." Later, he adds:

Many among the democracies fear and mistrust Soviet Russia.
They dread the inroads of an economic order that would be
destructive of their own. Such fear is weakness. Russia is neither
going to eat us nor seduce us. That is, unless our democratic
institutions and our free economy become so frail through abuse
and failure in practice as to make us soft and vulnerable. The

best answer to Communism is a living, vibrant, fearless democracy—economic, social, and political.

When Willkie returned home, he was met with a barrage of questions about Russia: "What is Russia going to do? Is she going to be the new disturber of the peace? Is she going to demand conditions at the end of the war that will make it impossible to re-establish Europe on a decent peaceful road? Is she going to attempt to infiltrate other countries with her economic and social philosophy?" Willkie had no definitive answers, of course, to such queries, though he reiterated the conviction that "it is possible for Russia and America, perhaps the most powerful countries in the world, to work together for the economic welfare and the peace of the world," and further, "that there can be no enduring peace, no economic stability, unless the two work together."

The final stops on Willkie's itinerary, before flying back to America, were in China, which he entered "through the back door, the vast hinterland of China's northwest." Six days of his stay, from late September to mid-October, were spent in the company of Chiang Kai-shek and his family and associates. What Willkie saw in China impressed him with the country's tremendous potentialities. "The era in which 400,000,000 Chinese could be kicked around," he believed was ending. His great admiration for Chiang Kai-shek and his able and charming wife did not delude him into thinking that their regime was representative. In Chungking, one of the Chinese who impressed him most was a Communist leader, and he met and admired Chou En-lai, but did not meet Mao-Tse-Tung. Willkie's biographer, Ellsworth Barnard, makes a perceptive comment on the mission to China: "Reading between the lines, one can discover evidence of the autocracy, the incompetence, the corruption in high places, that eventually destroyed all popular support of Chiang's regime and made inevitable the triumph of the Communists."

On every possible occasion in *One World,* Willkie urges the importance of international organization to preserve future world peace. He was distressed to find in the Middle East, Russia, and China "everywhere a growing spirit of fervid nationalism, a disturbing thing to one who believes that the only hope of the world lies in the opposite trend." A fatal weakness of the Atlantic

Charter in his view was that it "forecast the recreation of western Europe in its old divisions of small nations, each with its own individual political, economic, and military sovereignty"—a system that had greatly facilitated Hitler's conquest. The proper solution, in Willkie's opinion, was: "The re-creation of the small countries of Europe as political units, *Yes;* their re-creation as economic and military units, *No,* if we really hope to bring stabilization to western Europe, both for its own benefit and for the peace and economic security of the world." These comments foreshadowed the establishment after World War II of the North Atlantic Treaty Organization (NATO), the European Community (Common Market), and the European Free Trade Association.

For America, when the war ended, Willkie foresaw three choices: narrow nationalism, which "means the ultimate loss of our own liberty"; international imperialism, which "means the sacrifice of some other nation's liberty"; or the creation of a world with "equality of opportunity for every race and every nation."

As a first step toward the last goal, Wilkie proposed to set up a common council of the United Nations. The United Nations had begun simply as a phrase, coined by President Roosevelt, to include all the nations at war with the Axis Powers. The phrase meant a united front in war, but with no commitments beyond. In *One World* and in numerous articles and speeches, Willkie urged that the United Nations make a firm commitment to establish a postwar world organization, "a new society of independent nations, free alike of the economic injustices of the West and the political malpractices of the East."

The United Nations organization, the concept of which Willkie had so actively promoted, began to become a reality in October 1943, when the American, British, and Russian foreign ministers, meeting in Moscow, drew up a statement pointing out "the necessity of establishing at the earliest practicable date a general international organization based on the principle of the sovereign equality of all peace-loving states . . . large and small, for the maintenance of peace and security." The proposal was endorsed by the United States Senate with a declaration that "the United States, acting through its Constitutional processes, join with free and sovereign nations in the establishment and maintenance of international authority with power to prevent aggression and maintain the peace of the world." Willkie urged that beyond such general principles the United Nations should be armed with "the machinery needed to enforce its decisions," in order to avoid becoming a "mere debating society," as in fact it has gradually degenerated into being.

In an introduction to a 1966 edition of *One World,* Donald Bruce Johnson comments: "The international organization about which Willkie dreamed came into existence, but the unified world of free and democratic people that was the foundation of the dreams disintegrated gradually as the forces of nationalism were resurrected over the earth." In any event, Willkie contributed immensely to the creation of public opinion and to the bipartisan political support which made the United Nations possible.

The reception of *One World* was phenomenal. The book came off the press on April 4, 1943, and within four days had sold 170,000 copies. By the end of the year, an estimated 3 million copies were in print, translations were appearing in numerous foreign languages, and underground editions were circulating in Nazi-controlled territories. No accurate record exists of the final sales of the most important and influential book published in America during the war. In addition to various hardback and paperback editions issued at home and abroad, several magazines published it in digest form, and a condensed version was syndicated in 107 daily newspapers.

The dramatic story told in *One World* gripped the popular imagination, making firm the latent sentiment for world cooperation and international organization. Even the title influenced people's thinking and helped to destroy any remaining support for isolationism. Great appeal lay in Willkie's basic premise: People are people, and regardless of race, language, religion, and nationality, all human beings have certain desires and needs in common, among them a degree of material comfort, some participation in their own governance, and a measure of individual freedom. As Donald Bruce Johnson points out, "Willkie's messages about liberty, domestic imperialism, and freedom of choice ring as freshly and as necessarily as ever "

45 | MOTHER'S CONSTANT COMPANION

Benjamin Spock's *The Common Sense Book of Baby and Child Care,* 1946

The latest edition of Alice Payne Hackett's *70 Years of Best Sellers, 1895–1965*, reports that Dr. Benjamin Spock's *Common Sense Book of Baby and Child Care* (1946) had reached the status of all-time champion seller in America (except for the Bible), going ahead of a long-time leader, Charles Sheldon's *In His Steps*. During its first twenty years, from 1945 to 1965, "Spock" sold 19,076,822 copies, all except 475,000 in paperback, and solidly established itself as the "baby's bible." The international impact was scarcely less resounding: at least sixteen foreign translations were in print.

In an autobiographical sketch, Alexander Woollcott claimed that when he was growing up one area of his home, reserved for the children, was labeled "The Infantry," and the remainder, exclusively for the elders, was called "The Adultery." Dr. Spock showed equal concern for both children and their parents.

Theories of child rearing have a long and changing history, dating back at least to Hippocrates, the "father of medicine." Beginning in the eighteenth century, efforts were made to learn about children's behavior and emotions by studies of the original source—the child himself. The famous Swiss educator Johann Heinrich Pestalozzi kept notes on his 3½-year-old son's development. His example was followed later by Charles Darwin, who in 1887 published *The Biographical Sketch of an Infant*, based on the "evolution" of his own child; and by Bronson Alcott, whose diary of the first years of his daughter, Louisa May Alcott, was published in 1832 under the title *Observations on the Vital Phenomenon of My Second Child*. A further advance occurred with the formation in 1888 of the Child Study Association of America, an organization that is still flourishing after more than eighty years.

The most popular (at least with the parents) and influential of Dr. Spock's predecessors in the field of child care was a New York pediatrician, Dr. L. Emmett Holt. For nearly half a century before Spock, the American infant world was dominated by Holt's stern dos and don'ts. The latter's *Care and Feeding of Children*, first published in 1894, sold more than a million copies in hardback editions in ninety printings prior to going out of print in the 1950s. There was no nonsense about Dr. Holt's book, which helped to shape the upbringing of countless Americans for two generations. The author frowned on hugging and kissing the baby and insisted that the clock must regulate the hours when he should be fed. If the infant was obstinate about thumb-sucking, Dr. Holt advised confining "the elbows by small pasteboard splints to prevent the child from bending the arm."

For generations before the advent of the child experts, a mother raised her child by instinct and traditions. There were few books to guide her, and practically nothing of a scientific nature available on the behavior problems of children. If possible, she breast-fed her baby, usually on demand, and when he cried, she picked him up and rocked him. Such methods began to be frowned upon about 1910, as Dr. Holt and his school of baby specialists condemned what they termed "smothering" and insisted on setting up rigid schedules for eating, sleeping, and playing. The prevailing practices of rocking the baby, or walking the floor with him when he cried, or changing feeding times to suit his appetite were considered detrimental to his physical and psychological development.

A short time later, in the 1920s, Dr. John B. Watson led the "behaviorists" to offer even more extreme advice. "Kissing and coddling infants is taboo," wrote Watson. "Learn not to talk to children in endearing terms lest dreadful neurotic conditions be initiated."

Dramatic changes in popular and scientific attitudes toward child rearing were brought about under the influence of Sigmund Freud's psychoanalytical writings. Freud convinced the experts that children as well as adults had minds, emotions, and reflexes, and further that serious adult psychological problems could be traced back to childhood experiences and frustrations which had scarred the child's psyche.

Benjamin Spock is a disciple of Freud. He, too, believed that the old-fashioned, strait-jacket type of child rearing was producing neurotics. His medical training had included a year's psychiatric residency and five years as a student in the New York Psychoanalytic Institute. In combination with some years of pediatric practice in New York, Spock possessed an ideal background for bridging the gap between pediatrics and child psychiatry, and furthermore, he was able to communicate his knowledge of the two fields in language that parents could understand. The teachings of Freud and his followers had already reached a wide audience. Practically every literate adult had become aware of the possibly lifelong effects of experiences in infancy and that each baby was as much of an individual as his parents. But how were parents who were untrained in psychoanalytic theories to interpret Freudian ideas in relation to their own offspring? It became Spock's mission to provide them with reassuring, common-sense advice, as though he were an old friend and trusted family doctor.

The writing of *Baby and Child Care* was carried on intermittently by Dr. Spock, with his wife's assistance, during the last years of World War II. Prior to publication, the original manuscript was sent to some twenty medical specialists for suggestions based upon their own work with children, and Spock drew extensively upon his own dozen years or more of practical experience at baby doctoring. Even the detailed index was prepared by the author himself, for, as he said, "I think I know how mothers will look things up." The index is complete from "abscess" to "Zwieback." The timing of the book's first appearance was perfect. The wartime baby boom was at its height. Thousands of young mothers were far from home, without help and in need of reassurance and sound advice.

"Trust Yourself," is the first subheading under "The Parents' Part" of *Baby and Child Care,* and the opening statement is "You know more than you think you do." Later, Spock adds, "Don't take too seriously all that the neighbors say. Don't be overawed by what the experts say. Don't be afraid to trust your own common sense. Bringing up your child won't be a complicated job if you take it easy, trust your own instincts, and follow the directions that your doctor gives you." And again, "All parents do their best when they have a natural, easy confidence in themselves. Better to make a few natural mistakes from being natural than to do everything letter-perfect out of a feeling of worry."

An analogy is drawn by Dr. Spock with parents in a primitive society: "Think of a mother in an uncivilized land. She has never heard of a schedule, or a pediatrician, or a cow. Her baby starts to cry. She puts him to breast, he nurses until he is satisfied, then falls asleep. She has followed her instinct and doesn't have to bite her nails waiting for the clock to say that it is feeding time."

Spock stresses deep understanding and love for the child. "Your baby is born to be a reasonable, friendly human being," he writes. "Don't be afraid to enjoy him. Every baby needs to be smiled at, talked to, fondled gently and lovingly, just as much as he needs vitamins and calories. That's what will make him a person who loves people and enjoys life."

The Common Sense Book of Baby and Child Care touches on practically every question likely to occur to parents from the time they expect a baby until they begin to worry about such matters as comic-book reading, television viewing, and progress in school. Spock deals with queries on spoiling, spanking, tantrums, thumb-sucking, and punishment; whether or not to pick up a baby when he cries; children's manners, fears, and jealousies. His comments are frequently interspersed with admonitions like "Take it easy" and "Don't take it too seriously." Following are some typical "Spockisms:"

> Don't sit around communing with your conscience, trying to make a perfect world for your children. No parent is going to do a perfect job. Don't feel guilty; you are probably doing the best job that you can. Don't be too dependent on child-guidance experts. Many doctors do not allow parents to develop self-assurance and teach them to make their own decisions. Don't feel that you must devote all your time to your children. Parents should have some fun of their own.

Dr. Spock's constant aim is reassurance. "I wanted," he said, "to offer parents the combination of psychological and physical care needed in child care. I wanted to write to a mother in a way that would *reassure* her. I didn't want to scold or lecture her." In a typical passage, Spock consoles the parents of head-bumping infants: "It's disturbing to a mother to have her baby take up the habit of bumping his head. It seems so senseless and painful that it makes her doubt if he's really bright, after all. She wonders if the repeated blows can injure his brain. Even if she doesn't have these worries, she finds it nerve-racking to sit in the next room and listen to the steady thud, thud, thud." Dr. Spock explains that the baby will not hurt himself, is not stupid, and is simply relieving tension and developing his sense of rhythm. Antidotes suggested are cuddling the child and padding the crib.

Within a few years, *Baby and Child Care* had become so well established that it was being called "The Gospel According to Spock," but the author had become increasingly dissatisfied with one aspect of the work—that treating discipline or "permissiveness." He notes:

> When I was writing the first edition, between 1943 and 1946, the attitude of a majority of people toward infant feeding, toilet training, and general child management was still fairly strict and inflexible. However, the need for greater understanding of children and for flexibility in their care had been made clear by educators, psychoanalysts, and pediatricians, and I was trying to encourage this. Since then a great change in attitude has occurred, and nowadays there seems to be more chance of a conscientious parent's getting into trouble with permissiveness than with strictness.

In the new edition of his book issued in 1957, therefore, Dr. Spock tried to give "a more balanced view."

Many parents had carried permissiveness to a point of allowing their children to become little tyrants—behavior for which Dr. Spock was blamed. He himself denied being a permissivist; instead, as he states his defense, "I was part of a movement that was saying, 'It isn't necessary to be so rigid.' We did not go too far before we could pull back on the reins, but that was inevitable." After all, he declared, "parents should not be slaves. They are entitled to good behavior from their children." Today, even the Freudians concede that children need wise guidance and that "discipline" is not a bad word. A Gallup poll showed that 74 out of every 100 parents approved of spanking. Some psychiatrists disagree, especially when the child does not understand why he is being punished, but most recommend spanking in preference to nagging.

Two of Spock's famous contemporaries who share his general philosophy are Dr. Arnold Gesell and Dr. Milton Senn, both associated with Yale University's Clinic of Child Development. Dr. Gesell, founder of the clinic, set up movie cameras behind one-way glass to photograph the actions of babies and growing children. From these records, Gesell and his associates were able to trace personality and physiological development in children. Their studies, *The First Five Years of Life* and *The Child From Five to Ten*, have been best-sellers for years and have been read by millions of parents. Gesell's emphasis is on the hereditary aspect of human behavior. His successor as director of the clinic, Dr. Senn, goes further, examining the child's environment, the physical, metabolic, and psychological forces that determine his growth, and why children behave as they do.

Dr. Spock is an idealist with faith in the future. He has been quoted as saying,

> We know enough now to begin making our world over, if we only had the vision. All studies in child development in the first half century point in the same direction. A child is born with a greater capacity to love than to hate, to build than to destroy, to profit from every chance to learn and mature. The greater part is done through the love and care of parents. Only second in importance are schools and teachers.

46 | THE PROPER STUDY OF MAN

Alfred C. Kinsey's *Sexual Behavior in the Human Male*, 1948

Prior to the investigations conducted by Alfred Kinsey and his associates at Indiana University's Institute for Sex Research, human sexual behavior was the least explored area of biology, psychology, and sociology. As Dr. Kinsey points out in a historical introduction to his pioneer work, *Sexual Behavior in the Human Male* (1948), "Scientifically more has been known about the sexual behavior of some of the farm and laboratory animals." The subject was largely taboo because of religious, legal, and social restrictions. A breakdown of Victorian conventions and interdictions in the twentieth century, however, led to an increasing demand for objective data among physicians, psychiatrists, and persons concerned with such matters as sexual adjustments in marriage, the sexual guidance of children, and sex education. The prevailing situation was described by Alan Gregg of the Rockefeller Foundation's Medical Sciences division, in a preface to the Kinsey work:

> Certainly no aspect of human biology in our current civilization stands in more need of scientific knowledge and courageous humility than that of sex. The history of medicine proves that in so far as man seeks to know himself and face his whole nature, he has become free from bewildered fear, despondent shame, or arrant hypocrisy. As long as sex is dealt with in the current confusion of ignorance and sophistication, denial and indulgence, suppression and stimulation, punishment and exploitation, secrecy and display, it will be associated with a duplicity and indecency that lead neither to intellectual honesty nor human dignity.

Years of strict scientific discipline had prepared Dr. Kinsey for his task. A biologist who had spent decades of research on a minute field of specialization, Dr. Kinsey's previous publications had borne such esoteric titles as *The Gall Wasp Genus Cynips,*

The Gall Wasp Genus Neuroterus, The Origin of Higher Categories in Cynips, and *Edible Wild Plants of Eastern North America.* (A report on a single species of gall wasp was based on 150,000 individual specimens.) His concern with studies of human sexual behavior began late and appears to have been inspired originally by inability to answer students' questions on the subject. Current research was practically nonexistent, and available publications had so little solid basis that they were almost worthless.

Ten years passed between the start of Dr. Kinsey's work in his new field of inquiry and the appearance of the first report, *Sexual Behavior in the Human Male.* During that period he was joined by Wardell B. Pomeroy, a clinical psychologist, and Clyde E. Martin, a specialist in statistical procedures, both of whom aided in perfecting the methodology for the investigation and participated in the thousands of interviews which form the foundation for the book. Various psychologists and scientists from other disciplines also took part in the project as full-time staff members or consultants. Financial support came from Indiana University and the Rockefeller Foundation's Division of Medical Sciences.

Throughout his researches, Kinsey had one objective: to study all aspects of human sexual behavior without "preconception of what is rare or what is common, what is moral or socially significant, or what is normal and what is abnormal." At the outset, Dr. Kinsey announces his intention strictly to avoid social or moral interpretations of facts discovered, though some critics question whether he is fully successful in that aim.

As the first in a projected series of reports, *Sexual Behavior in the Human Male* places specific limitations on its scope: the data are confined to information collected from 5,300 white American males (omitting Europeans and Negroes), chiefly from the northeastern quarter of the United States. Social groups represented includes inmates of penal institutions and the underworld in general, laborers, clerks, farmers, business executives, lawyers, physicians, high school students, college students and professors, and clergymen. The population is subdivided by race-cultural group, marital status, age, age at adolescence, educational level, occupational class (ten categories), occupational class of parents, rural-urban background, religion, degree of religious adherence, and geographic origin.

One reviewer commented that "Kinsey has studied the sex behavior of the American male as though the American male, too, were a gall wasp." His book is described by Kinsey himself as "a taxonomic study of the frequencies of sources and sexual outlets among American males." Data were obtained in intimate personal interviews in which each individual was asked between 300 and 500 questions. The interviews lasted from one to six hours, and elaborate care was exercised to make them valid, painless, and confidential.

Courage was required to gather data for the study and later to publish the findings. The mere news that the investigation was in progress aroused violent opposition in some quarters. Kinsey notes in his introduction that he and his associates were

> repeatedly warned of the dangers involved in the undertaking and were threatened with specific trouble . . . there were attempts by the medical association in one city to bring suit on the ground that we were practicing medicine without a license, police interference in two or three cities, investigation by a sheriff in one rural area, and attempts to persuade the University's administration to stop the study or to prevent the publication of the results, or to dismiss the senior author from his university connection, or to establish a censorship over all publications emanating from the study.

In one city the president of the school board, a physician, dismissed a teacher because he had assisted in getting histories outside of the school. A hotel manager refused to allow interviews under his roof. But for every individual or group that opposed the study, hundreds cooperated, ranging from Harvard and Columbia Universities to the Kansas state police and the Salvation Army's Home for Unwed Mothers.

Why should a report of a scientific investigation prepared by an Indiana University zoologist arouse so much antagonism and cause so many attempts at suppression even before publication? The primary reason, of course, was the fact that it dealt with a tabooed subject. Another factor doubtless was the fear of what the inquiry might disclose. Those who had reason to be nervous about the findings were justified, for when the book came off the press its revelations upset numerous popularly held opinions, prejudices, and superstitions.

Among the most important findings of the Kinsey report, in summary, are that the sex impulse exists in every individual, of whatever age, beginning in infancy; in nearly every person it is extremely powerful; and it has numerous forms of expression. Further, there is a vast difference between the moral pretensions of the community and actual behavior, that is between what we do and what the conventions say that we should do. There is a wide range in the sexual activity of individuals, sexual activity begins much earlier and continues longer than is commonly believed, and the period of highest activity in the male comes much earlier than is generally supposed.

Sexual Behavior in the Human Male includes findings about masturbation, petting, intercourse, prostitution, and homosexuality. The book is filled with such facts as these: 88 percent of single men between sixteen and twenty practice masturbation; 99 percent of American boys begin having a sexual life at adolescence; 37 percent of young married males and 22 percent of men aged sixty have extramarital relations; 27 percent of the youngest unmarried group have had some form of homosexual experience, and that figure increases to 39 percent among unmarried males over thirty-six years old; 70 percent of preadolescent boys report sex play with other children between the ages of five and fourteen; 75 percent of boys who go no further than high school have premarital heterosexual experiences, in contrast to those who go to college, of whom 42 percent have indulged in teen-age premarital sex relations.

Kinsey verifies Sigmund Freud's theories of infantile sexuality. The former's data show that sexual activity in the male is present from birth to death. The popular belief in "sex conservation" as a reason for continence is refuted by Kinsey, who finds that boys who attain early puberty and begin sex activity earlier have the highest rate of sex activity and continue such activity longer. The facts clearly makes nonsense of the oft-repeated warning that early indulgence will weaken the sexual powers in later life; the exact opposite appears to be true. Prior to Kinsey, it had not been recognized that maximum sexual activity occurs in the teens. Boys between sixteen and seventeen have more frequent sexual arousals than at any other period in their lives. By fifteen years of age, 95 percent of males were found to be regularly active. This is a fact of challenging significance in the light of the increasing lag between biological maturity and economic security and marriage. During the years when a boy's sexual drive is at its highest, no socially approved outlet is provided. The boy seeks his outlet in various forms, all of which are banned by society and give rise to much anxiety and conflict in the individual. Concerning the physical and psychological harm caused thereby, Kinsey remarks:

> Whether there should be sex instruction, and what sort of instruction it should be, are problems that lie outside the scope of an objective scientific study; but it is obvious that the development of any curriculum that faces the fact will be a much more complex undertaking than has been realized by those who think of the adolescent boy as a beginner, relatively inactive, and quite capable of ignoring his sexual development.

With advancing age, Kinsey's data show, there is a slow and steady decline in sexual activity, but no evidence was found of a sudden male climacteric. The indications are that even at seventy years of age only 30 percent are impotent.

Another unexpected finding of the Kinsey study is that sexual behavior is influenced in many significant and complex ways by social level, as measured by educational attainment, grade school, high school, or college graduation. Social levels are not supposed to exist in a democratic society, but realistically there are an "upper class" and a "lower class," and "most people do not in actuality move freely with those who belong to other levels." There are wide and consistent differences in the sphere of sexual behavior between educational and occupational classes. Single males with only grade school education practice only half as much masturbation as do the college group, and tend to be more ashamed of it, while their frequency of intercourse is, in the lower-age levels, almost three times as high. Lower-level groups are also inclined to frown on nudity, petting, oral eroticism, and unconventional poses in intercourse—all practices which the upper-level population indulges in frequently. Among the lower economic and sociological groups, intercourse with prostitutes is six times more frequent than in the upper.

Grade school graduates show considerable extramarital intercourse during the first years of marriage, but with time become
increasingly faithful to their wives, whereas the college population begins marriage with high fidelity and in time become
increasingly promiscuous. Dr. Kinsey comments, "Some persons
may interpret the data to mean that the lower level starts out by
trying promiscuity and as a result of that trial, finally decides
that strict monogamy is a better policy; but it would be equally
correct to say that the upper level starts out by trying monogamy
and ultimately decides that variety is worth having." Another
commentator suggests that the changing pattern may simply
be a matter of opportunity. Upper-level males are surrounded by
a surplus of unmarried, divorced, and widowed women and
also have more money and freedom to arrange liaisons with
such women, while the lower-level male has fewer women
available and less means to maintain his personal attractiveness.

The incidence of homosexuality among males is considerably
higher than was realized prior to the Kinsey investigation, which
indicates that "at least thirty-seven percent of the male population has some homosexual experience between the beginning
of adolescence and old age." Actually, the high percentage may
be misleading, as the author notes, for it applies to men who
have had any kind of homosexual experience in their lives; in
some instances this may have been a single experience. Nevertheless, the figure show that 10 percent of men between the ages
of sixteen and sixty-five are homosexuals for at least three years,
and 4 percent are entirely homosexual throughout their lives.

The legal implications of the Kinsey report are obvious.
Numerous commentators have suggested that important changes
in our laws and social customs are desirable to close the wide
gap between what we preach and what we practice. The
dimensions of the problem are startling: 85 percent of the total
male population have premarital intercourse, 37 percent have had
homosexual experience, 59 percent have experienced oral-genital
contacts (a criminal offense in a number of states), 30 to 45
percent have extramarital intercourse, nearly 70 percent have had
relations with prostitutes, and 17 percent of farm boys have intercourse with animals—altogether a total of 95 percent of the
entire male population involved in illicit activities. As Dr. Kinsey

remarks, the periodic call for a "clean-up of the sex offenders in a community is, in fine, a proposal that five percent of the population should support the other 95 percent in penal institutions," if strict legal penalties were enforced.

The psychological effects of the Kinsey findings are also significant. Millions of people, Kinsey points out, carry around with them feelings of guilt, believing that they belong to a small minority that has transgressed moral law. Some individuals are so conscience-smitten that they break down under the burden and end up in psychiatrists' offices or hospitals. Such people still regret their actions, but their feelings of remorse might be less acute knowing that they belong to 90 percent instead of 1 percent of the population.

A barrage of criticism greeted the Kinsey report on its appearance. It was argued, for example, that people will not answer questions of this nature honestly; either they will conceal important facts or lie about their sexual prowess. Kinsey and his fellow interviewers took great precautions to avoid such pitfalls. Other critics observe that the study's emphasis is too exclusively on the physical and mechanistic aspects of sexual activity, largely ignoring the influence of affection, tenderness, and human sentiment in sex behavior. The word "love" is scarcely mentioned. Similar in character is a point stressed by Lionel Trilling in a lengthy critique appearing in the *Partisan Review*, that is, Kinsey's equating of *much* sexuality with *good* sexuality; Trilling maintains that there is almost no relationship between sexual frequency and sexual satisfaction. On the contrary, an unusually high frequency may be a symptom of deep sexual disturbance.

Kinsey's sample of 5,300 males has been criticized, also, as unrepresentative of the total population: too high proportions of college students, professional psychologists and psychiatrists, and male prostitutes; too small a percentage of men over thirty and of residents of rural areas; and too limited geographic distribution.

A hostile comment on *Sexual Behavior in the Human Male,* heard not infrequently, is that it only proves what everyone already knows. The statement is misleading, for it is quite evident that the Kinsey report contains material that surprised everyone when it was revealed. Previous impressions and suspicions were confirmed or disproved with a mass of detailed facts useful to parents, teachers, psychiatrists, ministers, jurists, and legislators. The broad findings of the study present a picture of a people endowed with sexual drives of various intensities, whose sexual activities begin early in life and are often conditioned and modified by society. For a large proportion of the population sexual activity is not limited to the institution of marriage, and there is a higher degree of homosexuality than was previously realized. Finally, strong and insistent sexual drives are a basic biological element in everyday life.

Complementing the original Kinsey report, *Sexual Behavior in the Human Female* was published in 1953, followed by a series of more specialized studies. The path blazed by Kinsey was taken later by scores of other writers, popular and scientific. Probably most original and constructive, because it was based on extensive laboratory research, was William H. Masters's and Virginia E. Johnson's *Human Sexual Response* (1966), the work of a gynecologist and of a psychologist on the staff of the Reproductive Biology Research Foundation of St. Louis, supported by the Washington University School of Medicine.

47 | STUDIES IN INTEGRITY

John F. Kennedy's *Profiles in Courage*, 1956

A foremost commentator on American political institutions, James Bryce, decried the spinelessness of American legislative bodies, asserting that "the American statesman is apt to be timid in advocacy as well as infantile in suggestion." Even more caustic is a judgment on both politicians and voters from the pen of Walter Lippmann:

> With exceptions so rare they are regarded as miracles of nature, successful democratic politicians are insecure and intimidated men. They advance politically only as they placate, appease, bribe, seduce, bamboozle, or otherwise manage to manipulate the demanding threatening elements in their constituencies. The decisive consideration is not whether the proposition is good but whether it is popular—not whether it will work well and prove itself, but whether the active-talking constituents like it immediately.

That there has been no perceptible improvement in conditions since Bryce was writing in the 1880s and Lippmann in the 1950s would appear to be demonstrated by insistent, but unheeded, demands for congressional reform, the sinister power wielded by a small number of committee chairmen, the use of public office for personal aggrandizement, and innumerable charges of venality against individual senators and representatives.

In part to restore public faith in the democratic process and to defend the body of which he was then a member, Senator John F. Kennedy examined the historical record to find outstanding instances of political courage and integrity, primarily in the United States Senate. He was "convinced that the complication of public business and the competition for the public's attention have obscured innumerable acts of political courage—large and small—performed almost daily in the Senate Chamber." The fruits of Kennedy's researches are presented in his *Profiles in*

Courage (1956), written during a long period of hospitalization and convalescence following a serious spinal operation.

At the outset, Kennedy analyzes the pressures which discourage acts of political courage, prevent politicians from following their consciences, and persuade them to conform or to compromise principles. The principal types of pressure are three in number. The first pressure is the desire to be liked, to get along with fellow legislators, that is, the fellow members of the club, "to abide by the club-house rules and patterns, not to pursue a unique and independent course which would embarrass or irritate the other members. . . . The path of the conscientious insurgent must frequently be a lonely one."

A second pressure on the public-spirited senator is the desire to be re-elected. As Kennedy states, "Senators who go down to defeat in a vain defense of a single principle will not be on hand to fight for that or any other principle in the future." Defeat for re-election also hurts the candidate's party, the friends and supporters who have given him their whole-hearted backing, and his wife and children whose happiness and security are wrapped up in his. And why should so much be demanded of a congressman? "In no other occupation but politics," Kennedy notes, "is it expected that a man will sacrifice all—including his own career —for the national good." Thus, "The prospect of forced retirement from 'the most exclusive club in the world,' the possibilities of giving up the interesting work, the fascinating trappings and the impressive prerogative of Congressional office, can cause even the most courageous politician serious loss of sleep."

The third and perhaps most significant source of pressure discouraging political courage, even in the most conscientious senator or congressman, is his constituency, the special-interest groups, the economic blocs, and organized letter writers. Few have the nerve to respond to an obnoxious constituent as did one congressman quoted by Kennedy, John Steven McGroarty of California:

> One of the countless drawbacks of being in Congress is that I am compelled to receive impertinent letters from a jackass like you in which you say I promised to have the Sierra Madre mountains reforested and I have been in Congress two months and haven't done it. Will you please take two running jumps and go to hell.

Frequently the pressure groups represent diametrically opposite interests and points of view, for example, one group of businessmen will demand lower and another higher tariffs on imports, and organized labor will press for a higher minimum wage while industry is urging that the line be held.

The forgoing, then, are some of the pressures which a man of conscience in Congress must face, for he cannot disregard the pressure groups, his constitutents, his party, the friendship of his colleagues, his family, the practical necessity of compromise, and the importance of remaining in office. Nevertheless, some men resist the pressures and have the courage to stand steadfast in support of what they conceive to be the public good. The theme of *Profiles in Courage* is a study of the actions and motivations of a small group of such individuals—the lives of American legislators who in difficult situations showed notable courage, usually in opposition to the popular will. These were men who dared to pit their own best judgment against the wishes of their colleagues or their constituents or the weight of public opinion.

Kennedy draws from the history of the United States Senate eight examples of political courage, beginning with John Quincy Adams and ending with Robert A. Taft. In some, though not all, instances history has vindicated their judgments. However, Kennedy makes "no claim that all those who staked their careers to speak their minds were right." Two of the "men of courage," Thomas Hart Benton and Daniel Webster, for example, were on opposing sides of the same issue. In any event, each of the stirring tales told by Kennedy is packed with drama, suspense, high purpose, reward, and retribution. Their stands cost some of the principal actors their political heads, but raised them above their now-forgotten associates to a certain measure of immortality.

John Quincy Adams was one of the most talented men ever to serve his nation, but he was coldly intellectual, lacking color and charm of personality. Nevertheless he had the distinction of being the only man to succeed his father as President and to have a long and notable career after leaving the White House. Following a period of diplomatic service abroad, immediately subsequent to the Revolution, Adams was elected in 1803 to the Senate as a Federalist. The party label, however, meant little to him. His conscience, not party loyalty, was his guide. He was the only member of his party to support Jefferson's purchase of the Louisiana Territory. On two other major issues, the impeachment of Federalist judges and the embargo against British goods (for attacking American ships and shanghaiing American sailors), Adams allied himself with the Jeffersonian Republicans. For these rebellious acts, the Federalists bitterly denounced him, read him out of the party, and rejected him for reelection after his one term in the Senate. Adams's vindication came in 1824, when he was elected sixth President.

Next in Kennedy's hall of fame for courageous senators was Daniel Webster of Massachusetts. Webster's political career extended from about 1812 until his death in 1852. He was one of the great American orators, and immense crowds turned out to hear him whenever he spoke. His life was dominated by a ceaseless and never-successful pursuit of the presidency. As a member of the Senate, he supported Henry Clay's famous Compromise of 1850 on the issue of slavery—"not as a Massachusetts man, nor as a Northern man, but as an American"—and scolded the North for refusing to cooperate with the South in recovering fugitive slaves. Webster's "Oration of March the Seventh" on the issue was one of the greatest that even he ever delivered, from the viewpoint of rhetoric. The Massachusetts electorate, however, poured out its wrath on him for this speech in which Webster said that he had tried "to beat down the Northern and the Southern follies, now raging in equal extremes." One vitriolic attack came from the pen of the abolitionist poet John Greenleaf Whittier, who proclaimed in his *Ichabod* that "the glory has departed from Israel." Any prospect that Webster had for gaining the Whig nomination for the Presidency in 1852 vanished, and he died a broken, disappointed man.

Ranged on the opposite side from Webster was Senator Thomas Hart Benton of Missouri. Popularly known as "Old Bullion," because of his advocacy of hard money, and long the political leader of his state, it is probable that Benton opposed Clay's Compromise of 1850 out of a bitter and disinterested contempt for the slave power. He was not an abolitionist, but a determined battler to preserve the Union. In objecting to the 1850 Compromise, Benton urged a more clear-cut decision between nullification and submission. His defeat at home was inevitable. Missouri was a slave state, and its people looked with increasing suspicion upon her rebellious Senator whose first loyalty was neither to his party or section but to the Union. Benton's devotion to the Union was far greater than his devotion to the South or to the Democratic party. His uncompromising fight against the extension of slave territory alienated his Missouri constituents and finally cost him his seat in the Senate. But the battle was not in vain: Missouri refused to join her sister slave states in secession. Benton's political philosophy is revealed in his final speech as Senator:

> I value solid popularity—the esteem of good men for good action. I despise the bubble popularity that is won without merit and lost without crime. . . . I sometimes had to act against the preconceived opinions and first impressions of my constituents; but always with full reliance upon their intelligence to understand me and their equity to do me justice—*and I have never been disappointed.*

Another Southern leader, whose stand on secession drove him out of a governorship, was the frontier hero, soldier, and statesman from Texas, Sam Houston. As a Senator, Houston had strongly opposed the Kansas-Nebraska Bill which would have repealed the Missouri Compromise of 1820 and reopened the slavery extension issue thought settled in the Compromise of 1850, by permitting the residents of the territory from Iowa to the Rockies to decide the slavery question for themselves. Houston's opposing vote broke the solid front of Southerners supporting the Kansas-Nebraska Bill and subjected him to vicious attacks from his Texas constituency, many of whom were slaveholders. Sam Houston's reply to his traducers was: "I know neither North nor South; I know only the Union." On November 10, 1857, Houston was summarily dismissed from his Senate seat by the Texas Legislature and a more militant spokesman for the South was elected as his successor. Undaunted, the old warrior returned to the fray again in 1859, running as an independent candidate for Governor with no party, no newspaper, and no organization. Against heavy odds he was elected, but despite his strenuous campaign to save Texas for the Union, a Secession

Convention voted to take the state into the Confederacy. On March 18, 1861, Houston was deposed as Governor.

In 1868 a far more obscure figure performed what one historian described as "the most heroic act in American history, incomparably more difficult than any deed of valor upon the field of battle." The hero was Edmund G. Ross, United States Senator from Kansas, and the occasion was the impeachment trial of President Andrew Johnson. The President was determined to carry out Abraham Lincoln's policies of reconciliation with the defeated South. The more radical Republican leaders in Congress were equally determined to administer the downtrodden Southern states as conquered provinces which had forfeited their rights under the Constitution. A succession of Presidential vetoes were in part overturned by Congress, but not all, and the radicals decided that the only way to carry through their program of punishment for the South was to impeach the President. Articles of impeachment were voted by the House and there ensued a long and dramatic trial in the Senate. A two-thirds vote was required for impeachment. The division in the Senate was so close that the outcome depended upon one man, the newly elected Senator from Kansas. Ross did not reveal his decision until the actual balloting. Then, voting against instructions from Kansas, he took the stand that the President's opponents lacked the evidence for a fair conviction, and thus saved Johnson from removal. Ross's political career was ended by his action. Neither he nor any other Republican who had voted for Johnson's acquital was ever reelected to the Senate. When Ross and his family returned to Kansas in 1871, they had to endure social ostracism, physical attack, and near poverty. A degree of vindication came to Ross in later years when he served as Territorial Governor of New Mexico from 1885 to 1889.

The aftermath of the Civil War provided the background for Kennedy's next study in political courage—the career of Lucius Quintus Cincinnatus Lamar of Mississippi. Prior to the outbreak of the war, Lamar was an extreme sectionalist congressman who had resigned his seat to draft the Mississippi Ordinance of Secession. Following the end of hostilities, however, Lamar was the first Confederate officer to be elected to the Senate. In that chamber he outraged his unreconciled fellow Mississippians by advocating a policy of reconciliation with the North and the resumption of normal federal-state relations. Further antagonism was stirred up against Lamar at home by his support of the Electoral Commission which made Rutherford B. Hayes President of the United States and by his refusal to support the free-silver movement. Nevertheless, Lamar was reelected to the Senate and subsequently served as Secretary of the Interior in Cleveland's Cabinet and as a justice of the Supreme Court. Lamar's political convictions were expressed in a reply to a bitter attack made upon him in 1878:

> The liberty of this country and its great interests will never be secure if its public men become mere menials to do the bidding of their constituents instead of being representatives in the true sense of the word, looking to the lasting prosperity and future interests of the whole country.

The first of two twentieth-century examples offered by Kennedy was George W. Norris of Nebraska, "one of the most courageous figures in American political history." As a member of the House, Norris led the movement in 1910 to overthrow "Cannonism," the dictatorial power wielded by Speaker Joseph Cannon. Later, Norris was to win fame as an advocate of public power, finally winning a long fight to bring the benefits of low-cost electricity to the people of the Tennessee Valley. The struggle which came near resulting in political disaster by Norris, however, was his filibuster against the Armed Ship Bill in 1917. In response to unrestricted German submarine warfare, Woodrow Wilson had asked for legislation authorizing him to arm American merchant ships. The bill passed by an overwhelming margin in the House, but when it reached the Senate, Norris and a small band of other dissenters filibustered against it, convinced that it would drag the United States into war. The filibuster was temporarily successful, though eventually Norris's group lost in a special session of Congress. The Nebraska State Legislature and the press condemned Norris in strong terms, while expressing confidence in President Wilson and his policies. Norris returned to Nebraska, hired an auditorium and told his audience of 3,000: "I have come home to tell the truth." He survived in the Senate to win battles in later years for Muscle Shoals, the

TVA, the Lame Duck Amendment to the Constitution, and a unicameral legislature in Nebraska.

The last of Kennedy's profiles in courage deals with another Republican and another Midwesterner, Senator Robert A. Taft of Ohio. Taft's great ambition was to be President, and he was bitterly disappointed never to win his party's nomination. As a member of the Senate, he sponsored the Taft-Hartley Act, condemned by organized labor, and a number of enlightened education, housing, health, and other welfare measures. But the act of political courage for which Kennedy cites Senator Taft is his severe criticisms of the Nuremberg war crimes trials, condemned by Taft as "a blot on the American record which we shall long regret." Punishment for the German and Japanese wartime leaders, contrary to Taft's point of view, was enthusiastically acclaimed at home and abroad. Leading Republicans were quick to disassociate themselves from Taft's argument that the trials "violate the fundamental principle of American law that a man cannot be tried under an *ex post facto* statute." Attacks on Taft came from all quarters, Republican and Democratic, for his "defense of the Nazi murderers." Taft remained adamant, however, in support of what he regarded as the traditional American concepts of law and justice, regardless of public opinion.

In a supplementary chapter, "Additional Men of Courage," Kennedy makes clear that his select eight by no means exhaust the roster of senatorial and other political heroes. Further examples cited include Senator Albert Beveridge of Indiana, defeated for opposing the Payne-Aldrich Tariff Act; Senator Oscar W. Underwood of Alabama, denied reelection because of criticisms of the Ku Klux Klan; Senator Andrew Johnson of Tennessee, the only Southern Senator in 1860 to speak for the Union; Senator John Tyler of Virginia, who resisted a measure to expunge criticisms of Andrew Jackson from the *Senate Journal;* Senator Humphrey Marshall of Kentucky, who backed President Washington in approving the immensely unpopular Jay Treaty with England, thereby incurring defeat for reelection; Governor John Peter Altgeld of Illinois, who committed political suicide for pardoning three defendants in Chicago's Haymarket Square bombing of 1886; and Charles Evans Hughes, who defended five Socialists denied their seats in the New York State Assembly. A reviewer of Kennedy's list suggested that senators Flanders of Vermont and Benton of Connecticut should be added for daring to stand up against Senator Joseph R. McCarthy and McCarthyism when nearly every other member of the Senate remained silent or cowered in fear.

Of the eight senators singled out for commendation in *Profiles in Courage,* Kennedy comments: "Most of them, despite their differences, held much in common—the breath-taking talents of the orator, the brilliance of the scholar, the breadth of the man above party and section, and, above all, a deep-seated belief in themselves, their integrity and the rightness of their cause."

48 | THE DISMAL TRADE

Jessica Mitford's *The American Way of Death*, 1963

When Jessica Mitford opened up, in *The American Way of Death* (1963), the bizarre world of American funeral practices, she discovered death customs far more curious than those of ancient days or of remote tribes. The most nearly comparable usages, perhaps, were those of the ancient Egyptions, with their intense preoccupation with the preservation of bodies for the hereafter.

According to Mrs. Mitford's calculations, as of 1960, the nation's burial bill is in excess of 2 billion dollars per year, or a nationwide average of $1,450 for the disposition of the mortal remains of every adult American. The cost of burying a person is the third largest cash outlay by a family, exceeded only by the purchase of a house and an automobile. A variety of shady devices are utilized by the undertakers, Mrs. Mitford asserts, to raise the expense: false advertising claims, outright lies on matters of law, and withholding from the grief-stricken customers the information they need to arrange an inexpensive funeral.

A highly revealing insight into the funeral business was provided by a Washington, D.C., mortician, W. W. Chambers, testifying before a congressional committee in 1947. Chambers, who had built up a million-dollar mortuary empire, admitted: "It's the most highly specialized racket in the world. It has no standard prices; whatever can be charged and gotten away with is the guiding rule. My competitors don't like my habit of advertising prices in black and white, because they'd rather keep the right to charge six different prices for the same funeral to six different people, according to what they can pay."

What the undertakers describe as "the care and memorialization of the dead" is a complex business involving many agencies: funeral parlors; the transportation of the dead by train, plane, or other conveyance; the buying of graves and mausoleum crypts; funeral flowers which account for considerably more than half of the dollar volume of all sales by retail florists in the United States; the manufacturing of caskets and other funeral paraphernalia; and the sale of cemetery markers, monuments, or gravestones. Mrs. Mitford demonstrates that more is spent by Americans on death than is spent for conservation of natural resources, for fire or police protection, and for personal expenditures for higher education.

Funeral directors, or funeral "consultants," as they like to be called, maintain that the decision of how much to spend for a funeral always rests with the family. The exact truth is hardly so simple. There is constant pressure on the family to go beyond reasonable limits. The attitude of the industry is illustrated by the statement of a funeral director, quoted by Mrs. Mitford: "In keeping with our high standards of living there should be equally high standards of dying. The cost of a funeral varies according to individual taste and the niceties of living the family has been accustomed to." One commentator retorted, "All this means is that the undertaker will exact what the traffic will bear."

Psychological states of mind are heavily involved in funerals, a fact fully exploited by undertakers, in Mrs. Mitford's view. The customer who walks into the funeral home is usually filled with grief, lacks any knowledge of standards upon which to make a choice, and knows nothing of laws pertaining to death. In short, he is quite unprepared to meet the pressures which are unknown in any other type of business dealing. Further, he usually has insurance money readily available and cannot long delay a decision. As for the cost of the ritual, a trade journal points out that

> a funeral is not an occasion for a display of cheapness. It is, in fact, an opportunity for the display of a status symbol which, by bolstering family pride, does much to assuage grief. It seems highly probable that the most satisfactory funeral service for the average family is one in which the cost has necessitated some degree of sacrifice. This permits the survivors to atone for any real or fancied neglect of the deceased prior to his death.

On the basis of such remarks, Mrs. Mitford accuses the seller of funerals of having "a pre-conceived, stereotyped view of his customers," believing the bereaved person who enters his establishment is "a bundle of guilt feelings, a snob, and a status seeker." Holding such views, the undertaker feels justified in trying to sell his customer the top-priced casket for purposes of "grief therapy."

The casket display room is usually arranged so as to obscure or hide the few inexpensive coffins which may be available. Large funeral homes, in fact, may maintain three casket display rooms. The first one to which the customer is led contains caskets costing a thousand dollars or more. If no sale is made there, a second room holds slightly less ornate and less expensive coffins. Only the most persistent customer gains access to a well-concealed third room, perhaps in the garage, where a simple, cheap casket may be found.

Sometimes, to help protect a family against pressures to overspend, a clergyman is brought along—to the irritation of the undertaker. The trade's journal, *Mortuary Management,* offers a solution, however, to this situation:

> We tell the family to go ahead and look over the caskets in the display room, and that the minister, if he has to come with them, will join them later. We tell the minister that we have something we would like to talk to him about privately, and we've found that if we have some questions to ask him, he seems to be flattered that his advice is being sought, and we can keep him in the private office until the family has actually made its selection.

By then, the family may have been persuaded that they must have a casket richly lined in "600 Aqua Supreme Cheney Velvet, magnificently quilted and shirred, with matching jumbo bolster and coverlet," equipped with Sealy innerspring mattress, "soft and buoyant, but will hold firm without slipping." Décors offered by Cheney include a variety of "more than sixty color matched shades, magnificent and unique masterpieces." The Colonial Classic Beauty, an "18 gauge, lead coated steel, seamless top, lap-jointed welded body construction" casket is designed to endure for an eternity.

The cult of the prettied-up corpse is further promoted by fancy merchandise. In the "slumber room" of the modern "memorial chapel," the corpse models "handmade original

fashions—styles from the best in life for the last memory—
dresses, men's suits, negligees, accessories." One astounding
specialist is the Practical Burial Footwear Company of Columbus,
Ohio, which advertises Fit-a-Fut oxfords (in patent, calf, tan,
or oxblood) and Ko-Zee, with its "soft cushioned soles and warm
luxurious slipper comfort, but true shoe smartness." Another
firm, Courtesy Products, offers the "new Bra-Form, Post Mortem
Form Restoration," which "accomplish so much for so little."
Florence Gowns, Inc., of Cleveland, carries a line of "hostess
gowns and brunch coats" for the departed loved ones.

Prior to the development of intravenous embalming in the
mid-nineteenth century (probably by Thomas H. Holmes, who
made 400,000 dollars embalming Civil War dead), open displays
of corpses were exceptional. Embalming made possible conceal-
ment of some of the grimmer aspects of death. The successful
undertaker must persuade people to view bodies; otherwise, he
will lose most of his business, for his major function is the
preparation or "restoration" and display of cadavers. The professional mortician looks upon the embalmed body as a work of
art, providing a "Beautiful Memory Picture" of the deceased.
Mrs. Mitford comments that "foreigners are astonished to learn
that almost all Americans are embalmed and publicly displayed
after death. The practice is unheard of outside the United States
and Canada." An English jurist, Alfred Fellows, writes, "A public
exhibition of an embalmed body, as that of Lenin in Moscow,
would presumably be dealt with as a revolting spectacle and
therefore a public nuisance."

The actual process of embalming is simple. When the undertaker hauls the corpse back to his shop, he pumps out the blood
and fills it up with forty cents worth of formaldehyde; he sews
up the lips, gives the body a good coat of tint from an aerosol
bomb—"Cover-Up Spray Paint" has a choice of five colors:
Natural, Rachel, Flesh, Brunette, Suntan—and adds a touch of
rouge. The deceased is then placed in a casket propped up in
the most lifelike posture possible, ready for viewers to carry
away with them the final "Beautiful Memory Picture."

Aside from the possible aesthetic advantages of embalming
and the aid it furnishes the undertaker in selling more expensive
caskets, what justification is there for the practice of embalming?

The funeral industry has long argued that embalming is an essential hygienic measure; that is, it disinfects the body so that it is no longer a health menace. It is also held that embalming preserves the body from decay (whereas the truth is that embalming merely halts the decomposition of bodies long enough to permit them to be displayed). Some zealots in the trade even go as far as to attribute the falling death rate to embalming, though perhaps conceding, as one writer did, "a great deal of credit" to the medical profession, but adding that funeral directors are responsible for "about 50 percent of this wonderful work of sanitation which has so materially lowered the death rate." A more realistic appraisal comes from Dr. I. M. Feinberg, an instructor at the Worsham College of Mortuary Science: "Sanitation is probably the farthest thing from the mind of the modern embalmer. We must realize that the motives for embalming at the present time are economic and sentimental, with a slight religious overtone."

In any event, the medical profession is in general agreement that the public health virtues of embalming are practically nil. As for the efficacy of embalming as a means of preservation, it appears that few cadavers embalmed for funerals are actually preserved. Even the most expensive caskets soon disintegrate. An embalmed corpse fares no better in a sealed metal casket, for putrefactive bacteria thrive in an airless atmosphere.

A point of friction between medical men and funeral directors is postmortem medical examinations. The morticians dislike autopsies because they make embalming more difficult, and the family is less willing to buy an expensive casket if the body has been autopsied. A characteristic reaction comes from one undertaker quoted by Mrs. Mitford: "If a funeral director knows that an autopsy is going to work a hardship, and result in a body that would be difficult to show, or that couldn't be shown at all, then I think the funeral director has not only the right, but the duty, to advise the family against permitting an autopsy."

The legal aspects of the funeral business are explored at length in *The American Way of Death*. Despite the claims of the undertakers, embalming is not required by law in any state, except in such special circumstances as when the body is to be shipped by common carrier. Operators of crematoria assure clients that it is against the law to cremate without a coffin, although in most states no such law exists. Regardless of the law, privately owned crematoria usually have a rule that they will not cremate without a coffin; many are in the casket-selling business themselves, or their business depends upon undertakers who sell caskets. It is the law in most states that when a decedent bequeaths his body for use in medical research, his survivors are bound to carry out his wishes, but a standard embalming textbook advises ignoring such laws, holding that "No one owns or controls his own body to the extent that he may dispose of the same in a manner which would bring humiliation and grief to the immediate members of his family." A free-and-easy attitude toward the law is re-portedly found even in the colleges of mortuary science.

In a chapter entitled "God's Little Million-dollar Acre," Mrs. Mitford reveals the fabulous profits which can be realized when it is possible to sell space for 3,177 "plantings" in one, tax-free acre. Profits soar even higher in the community mausoleum, where an average crypt, 32 by 25 by 90 inches in diameter, sells for 720 dollars, and there is room for 10,000 spaces to an acre. High-pressure door-to-door salesmen have been sent out by the owners of "non-profit" private cemeteries to sell millions of plots on a "pre-need" basis. By exploiting their tax-free status, buying cheap land and subdividing it endlessly, and by investing their huge "perpetual care" resources, the owners of Foreverness Lawn Memory Gardens, Inc., and similar enterprises have become the new rich of the death business. They are frequently in competi-tion with the undertakers, selling vaults (outer casings to protect the coffin) and even supplying funeral chapels and mortuaries for "one-stop" funerals.

The efforts of the florist industry to fight a growing menace, "Please Omit Flowers," also come in for their share of Mrs. Mit-ford's attention. Florists' associations, aided and abetted by fu-neral directors, threaten to withdraw their advertising from news-papers that include the antiromantic words "Please Omit Flowers" in their funeral notices, and some newspapers have capitulated to the blackmail.

The buyers' financial standing is naturally a matter of keen concern to the undertaker. He makes it his business to know the death-benefit payments of every labor union in the community, the social security and workmen's compensation scale of death benefits, and veterans' and servicemen's death benefits. Thanks to the funeral lobby, under the law of virtually every state the funeral bill is entitled to preference in payment as the first charge against an estate. Mrs. Mitford notes that efforts in some states to pass legislation to limit the amount of the priority for burial costs to a fixed sum, say 500 dollars, are regularly frustrated by the lobby.

Poetically inclined undertakers have dreamed up some wonderful terminology. The funeral men have deleted the word "death" and all its connotations from their vocabulary. The morgue has been replaced by "preparation room"; coffin by "casket" and "eternity bed"; undertaker by "funeral director," "funeral consultant," or "mortician"; embalmer by "derma-surgeon"; laying-out room by "reposing room" or "slumber room"; showroom by "display room"; hearse by "casket coach"; flower truck by "flower car"; ashes by "cremains" or "cremated remains"; shroud by "clothing," "dress," or "suit"; parlor by "drawing room"; death certificate by "vital statistics form." A grave is "opened" and "closed," not dug and filled; a body is "interred" instead of buried; and the last rites take place in a "memorial park," not in a graveyard or cemetery. The deceased is beautified by "cosmetics," not makeup; he didn't die, but "expired"; and the cost of the casket is described as the "amount of investment in the service." A "pre-need memorial estate" is cemetery jargon for a grave bought for future occupancy.

Counterattacks on *The American Way of Death* began immediately after publication. Propagandists for the funeral industry were inclined to view the book as part of a vast Communist plot, designed to undermine the American way of life. For example, Frederick Llewellyn, executive vice-president of Forest Lawn Memorial-Park in Glendale, California, wrote a series of articles for *The American Funeral Director*, containing a dire warning:

> There is a great tide sweeping over America today, washing away at the foundations of decent memorialization. If the Communists can help undermine one of the most fundamental of religious rites, the way in which we care for our dead; if they

can get more people asking not, "Is it right?" but "Is it practical?" they can undermine religion and with it the laws of the land.

In the same vein was an advertisement in an Oakland, California, newspaper, sponsored by the Renowned Abbey Memorial Gardens of Vallejo. A well-dressed father is pictured talking to his young son, while the heads of both are bowed in profound sorrow. The father is saying solemnly:

> My dear son, I am so sorry you are going to have to live under Communism. It seemed to come so quickly. I didn't think their lies could win. No nation has ever turned to Communism, Socialism or Fascism until the leaders have first been able to destroy MEMORIALIZATION. The dignity of man, the freedom of life and the worship of God—these principles on which our nation was founded—throughout all ages and in all lands have never been any greater than the MEMORIALIZATION shown in death. Many so-called "memorial societies" are trying to destroy this MEMORIALIZATION. First, they would have you eliminate flowers—then the sacred burial rites—and finally, will it be the Church and the sermon?

The reader of *The American Way of Death* is shown several ways out, if confronted by the problem of having to make arrangements for a funeral: first, do not permit the undertaker to trade upon your distress, grief, and pride; ask questions and compare prices; second, remember that expense, display, and mumbo jumbo are unrelated to any Christian or Jewish tradition of respect for the dead; third, inform yourself about memorial societies and related organizations, whose business it is to provide simple, dignified, and inexpensive funerals. Mrs. Mitford appends a list of such organizations, whose number and membership have shown a large increase since publication of her book. The undertaking business tends to dismiss the societies as aggregations of "do-gooders and left-wingers," who are trying to wipe out beauty, sentiment, and religion. Some of the societies emphasize cremation, others are interested in educational programs advocating bequeathal of bodies to medical schools, and still others stress freedom of choice in the matter of burials. Regardless of their intents, they are described in the funeral trade press as "burial beatniks of America," "weasels sucking away at the life blood of our basic economy," and "alien to every principle of the American way of life."

But to the person who wishes to avoid being cosmetized, casketed, and transferred to repose in the slumber room of the mortuary chapel, the funeral societies or memorial associations appear to be the best solution.

49 | CONSUMERS' CRUSADER

Ralph Nader's *Unsafe at Any Speed,* 1965

Muckraking has been a favorite occupation of American reform-
ers and liberals since the 1890s. Nearly all the practitioners—
Upton Sinclair, Ida Tarbell, Lincoln Steffens, Ray Stannard Baker,
Mark Sullivan, and others—have been journalists. The tradition
has been maintained most successfully in recent years, however,
by a brilliant young Washington attorney, Ralph Nader, whose
devastating indictment of the automobile industry, of engineering
groups, governmental agencies, and traffic-safety organizations,
Unsafe at Any Speed (1965), achieved best-seller status. Some
450,000 copies were sold in hardback editions.

Nader, son of immigrant Lebanese parents, is reported to have
become obsessed with the subject of automobile safety while a
student in the Harvard Law School, where he carried on research
in automobile accident cases. Later he was appointed by Assistant
Secretary of Labor Daniel Patrick Moynihan to serve as a consultant to write a report on government policy in the field of
automobile safety. The following year, Nader was an unpaid assistant to Senator Abraham A. Ribicoff's Government Operations
Committee, then engaged in its celebrated hearings on highway
safety. Nader was thereby placed on his way to fame.

The accident rate involving automobiles has long been a matter
of national concern. Fatalities from auto accidents were 55,000
in 1969, a figure approximately equal to deaths from all other
types of accidents: falls, burns, drownings, firearms, machinery,
poison gases, and other poisons. In addition, nonfatal automobile
injuries are running at the rate of 2,000,000 annually, 170,000 of
them causing total and permanent impairments. The average age
at death by automobile is thirty-eight, in contrast with that in
other categories of accidents, which is sixty-two; the automobile
is the leading cause of death between ages five and thirty. "At
present rates," Nader writes, "one of every two Americans will
be injured or killed in an automobile accident."

Unsafe at Any Speed has a simple and direct theme: The automobile as presently designed is a death trap, though it has long been possible to mass-produce an automobile in which the occupants could not only survive, but were unlikely to be injured by collisions at speeds up to 40 miles per hour. Further, Nader maintains that in the design of automobiles safety has been regarded as much less important than styling, cheapness, and other factors which affect profits. The result is that the typical product turned out by Detroit has been far more dangerous to drivers and pedestrians than is necessary.

In the past, Nader points out, efforts to increase safety and reduce carnage on the highways have concentrated attention on the driver, the roadway, and speed laws, and little heed was paid to the automobile itself. The automobile manufacturers have obvious reasons for wishing to focus public concern elsewhere than on themselves. For decades the policy has been followed that greater automobile safety was to be achieved primarily by campaigns of driving legislation, law enforcement, technical education, and perhaps moral persuasion. While conceding the validity of these approaches, Nader turns the argument around and points an accusing finger at the automobile manufacturers, charging them with indifference, selfishness, and arrogance in failing to accept responsibility for producing safer cars. Instead of taking the usual adamant position, "It is the driver's fault," Nader insists that technology presently available, if utilized in the design of vehicles and traffic systems, could reduce accidents to less than one-fourth of the existing rate. The prevailing view in the industry, however, is contained in a statement from a prominent tire manufacturer: "Being inanimate, no car, truck or bus can by itself cause an accident any more than a street or highway can do so. A driver is needed to put it into motion—after which it becomes an extension of his will." Therefore, instead of making its product safer, the automobile industry places the blame for accidents on drivers, on drink, on highways—anywhere, in fact, but on the murder weapon itself.

Nader has no hesitation in naming names in his attack on the manufacturers, directing his chief fire at General Motors, which has long dominated the automotive industry. His first chapter is devoted to "the sporty Corvair" and its design weaknesses. The

Chevrolet Corvair from 1959 to 1963 was a faulty, dangerous vehicle, unstable and uncontrollable even under normal conditions. It had a unique trick on a turn at some speed to tuck its wheels under (camber) to the point of scraping the roadway with the wheel rim, after which the car would roll over. This idiosyncrasy was apparently due to the combination of its rear engine and rear swing-axle suspension. From the time the Corvair was introduced in 1959 until 1963, it is estimated that as many as 10,000 lives were lost in it because of its suspension and handling hazards, giving rise to numerous lawsuits. Nader writes, "It took General Motors four years of the model and 1,124,076 Corvairs before they decided to do something for all unsuspecting Corvair buyers by installing standard equipment to help control the car's handling hazards." The Corvair was withdrawn from production in 1969, when its sales had dropped by 93 percent, even though by then the earlier faults had been substantially corrected.

Another unsafe car was the 1963 Buick Roadmaster, which had a habit of sucking the fluid out of the power-brake unit and burning it up. Suddenly the driver would find himself with no brakes. After a year of pleading from dealers and mechanics, the Buick division issued a kit of replacements for the defective parts, but customers were never informed of the potential danger which they faced.

The 1964 Ford Mustang, a very popular car, had "inadequate brakes, poor handling, and marvelous promotion," a "stylist's dream," which ignored good engineering and the welfare of buyers. Eight good safety features on the operational model were eliminated in the production model. The regular Ford came on the market in 1965 lacking a bracket on the rear suspension arm, and the 1965 Plymouth Fury, Chrysler, and Dodge, went out with a steering-gear bracket that needed rewelding. The lethal razor-backed Cadillac tail fins were discontinued after a time, but for stylistic not safety reasons.

The high rate of fatalities and injuries on the highways is blamed by Nader on faulty design, specifically "pop-open doors, cardboard-like roof structures, uprootable seats, flying cushions, jutting metal dashboards, bone-crushing knobs, chisel-like rear-view mirrors, and above all, dangerous shafts and steering wheels." There are also serious obstructions to visibility, including "dash-board and panel reflections, wind-shield distortions, hood and chrome reflections, corner posts and sunshades."

Until the 1965 models, all mileage gauges were made to register up to 5 percent high. Thus, guarantees ran out 5 percent sooner, gas mileage appeared 5 percent better, insurance rates rose sooner, the trade-in value was less, and cars rented by mileage cost more.

Automobiles are conceded to be a major factor in air pollution —a problem of increasing national and international concern, to which Nader devotes a full chapter. Car exhausts add to the breathing atmosphere each year millions of tons of hydrocarbons, carbon monoxide, and oxides of nitrogen. Hydrocarbons have been known for the past twenty years to be leading contributors to photochemical smog, and carbon monoxide is highly toxic, perhaps bearing some responsibility for driver failure on crowded highways and undoubtedly advancing lung cancer, emphysema, and heart disease. California forced Detroit to reform its exhausts in 1966, and changes have since been made for the country as a whole, but air pollution is of such immense proportions that correction remains a long-term problem.

The automobile industry was not prepared to accept Nader's scathing criticisms without fighting back. General Motors, through a Washington law firm, put private detectives on Nader's trail to investigate his sex life, associations, and political attitudes, with the aim of discrediting his attacks on the industry. Nader's charge of harassment led to hearings before a Senate committee, where the president of General Motors publicly apologized for the company's investigation. The event turned out to be fortunate for Nader, whose book was thereby brought to the attention of millions who might otherwise never have heard of it.

If improvements are to be made in car and traffic safety, scientific and unbiased research is essential, but Nader finds that the traffic-safety establishment is both subsidized and run by the industry. The Society of Automotive Engineers is top-heavy with Detroit personnel, and the American Standards Association, Nader charges, is another Detroit rubber stamp. The National Safety Council is subsidized and ruled by Detroit, carries on no safety research, and invariably follows the party line that the driver is to blame for accidents. The Automotive Safety Foundation is a Detroit creation, substantially financed by the Automobile Manufacturers Association. The President's Committee for Traffic Safety, in turn, is dominated by the Automotive Safety Foundation.

Why have the stylists been permitted to supersede the engineers in automobile design? The probable answer comes from a General Motors vice-president, William Mitchell: "The motor car must be exciting and create a desire and not become mere transportation, or we will have just a utility and people will spend their money for other things, such as swimming pools, boats, hi-fi sets, or European vacations," to which Nader suggests as alternative expenditures "education, clothes, food, medical care, furniture, and housing." The stylists proceed on the principle that a car's only selling assets are the visible ones. The annual retooling for new models, which adds hundreds of dollars to the cost of each car, is strictly for looks, not for engineering or for safety. The stylists are responsible for maintaining a high annual volume of sales. "What words other than Madison Avenue's," Lewis Mumford asks, "can adequately describe these exciting confections, glittering with chrome, pillowed in comfort, sleepy-soft to ride in, equipped with mirrors, cigarette lighters, radios, telephones, floor carpeting; liquor bars and tape-recorders are still optional."

Nader charges that every device for increasing the safety of the motorcar has been resisted by the manufacturers. The industry fought long and hard against the introduction, for example, of such now commonly accepted features as the safety door catch, stop lights, windshield wipers, directional signals, and safety glass. Even when the automotive engineers have included safety measures in their designs, they have been removed in order to reduce cost, to emphasize some nonessential selling point, or to eliminate any worry about danger from the prospective buyer's mind.

In addition to his revelations on the derelictions and weaknesses of the automobile industry in the field of safety and social responsibility, Nader offers a series of constructive recommendations. Highly important is the principle of "the second collision," developed at length in the third chapter of *Unsafe at Any Speed*. This is a concept first evolved by a young air cadet, Hugh De Haven, who survived a collision 700 feet above a Texas airstrip because his cockpit remained relatively intact upon hitting the ground. De Haven proceeded to design restraining equipment to keep air passengers from hitting instruments and metal surfaces inside a plane. An air traveler is often killed because the interior of a plane cracks up around him and into him. If the structure of the plane were made "crashworthy," the human body could survive tremendous decelerative forces. Nader contends that automakers should build "crashworthy" cars that would not cause bodily injury in a "second collision" after the accident itself—a view now recognized by many courts.

Nader does not ask for new technological discoveries to improve safety, but rather for the application of what is known and technically feasible to establish common-sense safety standards. Illustrations are the elimination of sharp edges or projections from both interior and exterior designs; the steering-wheel column should not be rigid or extend so far forward that it forms a bayonet pointed at the driver's chest; the windshields need not be made of laminated glass which grips a jagged collar around any object breaking through it; optical distortion, glare from reflecting surfaces, obstructing corner posts, tinted windshields, and poor wiper, defroster, and mirror design should be eliminated; energy-absorbing bumpers can considerably reduce peak forces by lengthening the collision time; seat belts and even more obvious restraints are essential.

Lewis Mumford points out that the manufacturers, "as if to show their open contempt for the whole safety argument," have based their chief sales appeal on speed and then "underlined their incitement to calculated recklessness" by naming their cars Thunderbirds, Wildcats, Tempests, Furies, Javelins, Barracudas, Cougars, Firebirds, and Falcons, "while their allies in the oil industry, for good measure, offer to place a tiger in the tank."

Ralph Nader has been accused of fanaticism and of disregarding some factors relating to car safety. New leftists condemn him for wanting to improve the economic system rather than to tear it down, and businessmen complain that he is a publicity-seeking gadfly. But more enlightened businessmen agree that Nader is an important and often valuable critic. The impact of his research and writings, not only on the automobile industry but on needed reforms in other areas, is comparable to those achieved by Rachel

Carson's exposure of the evils of pesticides and herbicides, Senator Estes Kefauver's revelations on the pharmaceutical industry, and Jessica Mitford's shocking picture of the funeral business. Concerning the last, Nader commented facetiously that while Jessica Mitford only wrote a book criticizing the funeral industry, "I'm trying to reduce the number of their customers."

An engineer, J. Douglas Brown, is quoted as asking his engineering colleagues: "If engineers can design space ships to go to the moon, why can't they design a safer automobile? Who is to be the bridge between science and human fulfillment, the professional engineer or the Madison Avenue pollster?" In *Unsafe at Any Speed*, Ralph Nader made a notable contribution to finding proper answers to these questions.

50 | TOO MANY PEOPLE

Paul R. Ehrlich's *The Population Bomb*, 1968

Nearly two centuries ago, in his *Essay on the Principle of Population as It Affects the Future Improvement of Society*, Thomas R. Malthus warned the world of the perils of overpopulation. Malthus was convinced that population, if unchecked, inevitably increases at a much faster rate than the food supply. In time, therefore, if population growth is uncontrolled by either artificial or natural restraints, many must starve.

The rising standard of living in the nineteenth century, and greatly increased agricultural production since, persuaded many that Malthus was unduly pessimistic. But suddenly, beginning in the 1960s, the world awoke to the unpalatable fact that it faced problems of gigantic magnitude created by the population explosion (particularly acute in the "have-not" nations of Asia and Latin America), diminishing food supplies in relation to population, and the destruction of man's environment. Almost overnight, the word *ecology*, the branch of biology dealing with how each living plant and animal influences and is influenced by its environment, became common parlance. The crux of the problem, ecologists and environmentalists asserted, was too many people.

Of a flood of books, articles, and reports, popular and scientific, which appeared in response to wide public concern, probably none had greater impact than that of Paul R. Ehrlich, *The Population Bomb* (1968). Within two years after publication, a million copies were in print. The essence of the book is that mankind will perish from starvation because of inability or unwillingness to restrict population growth.

Salient arguments advanced by Ehrlich to support his thesis is that population has been increasing faster than the food supply since 1968; 10 to 20 million people are already starving to death each year; three-fourths of the world's people now go to bed hungry each night; the accumulation of DDT and similar poisons could bring the life-providing processes of photosynthesis to a stop and leave the oceans as dead as Lake Erie by 1979; even Americans will be subject to water rationing by 1974 and food rationing by the end of the decade; hepatitis and epidemic dysentery rates could easily climb by 500 percent in the United States within the next few years because of crowding of people and increasingly polluted water; and prospects of worldwide plague and thermonuclear war grow more likely as population pressures increase and natural resources diminish.

It took one million years, Ehrlich points out, to double the world's population, bringing it up from 2½ million to an estimated 5 million in 6,000 B.C. The population did not total 500 million until almost 8,000 years later—about A.D. 1650. The doubling rate was then once about every thousand years. The population reached a billion people around 1850, doubling in some two hundred years. Only eighty years were required for the next doubling, as the population reached 2 billion around 1930. Now the world's population exceeds 3 billion, and the doubling rate is down to thirty-seven years. Ehrlich has worked out a fantastic calculation showing that if the growth rate continued to double every thirty-seven years into the indefinite future, in 900 years there would be 60 million billion people on earth, or about 100 persons for each square yard of the earth's surface, land and sea.

Science-fiction fans propose to solve our terrestrial problem by exporting surplus population to the other planets of our solar system, a notion ridiculed by Ehrlich, first because of the virtual certainty that those planets are uninhabitable and second because of the incredible difficulties and expense of reaching and colonizing remote planets, assuming that life on them would be viable.

Population growth is not occurring uniformly over the face of the earth. Unfortunately, as Ehrlich emphasizes, the most rapid growth rates are to be found among about two-thirds of the world population occupying "undeveloped countries," that is, unindustrialized nations, tending to be inefficient agriculturally, having small gross national products, high illiteracy rates, and similar problems. Most Latin American, African, and Asian countries belong in this group. On the other hand, comparatively slow growth rates characterize the modern industrial nations, such as the United States, Canada, most European countries, Israel, the Soviet Union, Japan, and Australia. Even so, most of the "developed countries" are overpopulated if we apply the criterion of being able to produce enough food to feed their populations.

Why, after thousands of years of relatively slow increases in the earth's inhabitants, did the total population begin a precipitate rise about two centuries ago? The first step was the beginning of an agricultural revolution which greatly reduced the chances of dying by starvation in some human groups, followed by an improved standard of living due to industrialization. But the most dramatic change came with the development of medical science. Lower death rates resulted immediately in the developed countries and then "instant death control," as Ehrlich terms it, was exported to the undeveloped countries: "Medical science, with its efficient public health programs, has been able to depress the death rate with astonishing rapidity and at the same time drastically increase the birth rate; healthier people have more babies."

Very simply, Ehrlich maintains, the world's population will continue to grow as long as the birth rate exceeds the death rate. He sees only two possible solutions to the problem: one, to find ways to lower the birth rate; the other, a "death rate solution," in which war, famine, and pestilence wipe out great numbers of people.

Examining the matter of world food production, Ehrlich finds that only ten countries grow more food than they consume: the United States, Canada, Australia, Argentina, France, New Zealand, Burma, Thailand, Rumania, and South Africa. More than half of the surplus is produced by the United States, with Canada and Australia contributing most of the balance. All other countries, including the huge populations of China, India, and Russia, import more than they export. The United States ships nearly one-quarter of its wheat crop to India, but the Indian population is expected to add 200 million by 1980. Indeed, population is far outstripping food production throughout the "other world." Some of the most depressing situations are found in Latin America, where under the influence of the Catholic faith the birth rate is the highest in the world and where "the poverty, hunger, and misery of the people are equally spectacular." One demographer, Arthur Hopcraft, in his book *Born to Hunger*, reports that in

Colombia alone 100 infant deaths per day are caused by malnutrition.

From these facts, Ehrlich concludes that our vast agricultural surpluses are gone and it is impossible for the United States to save the world from famine with her food exports. There is not enough food today, and it is probable that massive famines will occur in the 1970s and certainly by the early 1980s.

Possibly of longer-range significance than the imbalance between food and population, in Ehrlich's view, is the progressive deterioration of our environment, which may cause even more death and misery. The United States is paying a high price for huge food production, including the loss of thousands of acres by erosion and many thousands of others by strip-mining, salinization of irrigated lands in the West from rising water tables, and lowered water tables in coastal regions, allowing salt water to seep in. Increased food production is almost invariably accompanied by modifications in the environment: clearing of forests, draining of swamps, the extensive use of chemical pesticides, and the extinction of wild animal life. Ehrlich is especially scathing in his comments on the misuse of pesticides and herbicides, such as DDT, which are responsible for serious problems of environmental pollution. Pesticides, however, are only one of many factors in the pollution of our planet. Lakes, rivers, streams, and oceans around the world are being steadily poisoned. Lake Erie is cited as a horrible example: "The once beautiful lake is now a septic tank—a stinking mess"—where even "the snakes are almost gone."

To summarize his discussion of environmental deterioration, Ehrlich states that "the causal chain of the deterioration is easily followed to its source. Too many cars, too many factories, too much detergent, too much pesticide, multiplying contrails, inadequate sewage treatment plants, too little water, too much carbon dioxide—all can be traced easily to *too many people*."

Ehrlich finds highly unsatisfactory practically all the existing efforts to control world population. The concept of family planning is rejected on the ground that people *want* too many children. We would still have a severe population problem, therefore, even if we prevented all unwanted children. "Family planning," says Ehrlich, "is a disaster because it is giving people a false sense of security. No one should have more than two children; anything beyond that is irresponsible, suicidal." The failure of family planning in India is cited as an example. At the start of the program the Indian population was 370 million and at the end over 500 million, and the growth rate had leaped 1.3 percent per year to nearly 3 percent. Our own government has been ineffective in disseminating birth-control information to the undeveloped nations of the world, preferring to spend funds on medical research to save lives and to prolong life.

Another fallacious assumption, according to Ehrlich, is the possibility of "multiplying bread." Great increases in food production cannot occur through placing more land under cultivation, since most uncultivated land is unsuitable for farming. The "unmeasurable riches" of the sea are mainly a myth. More hopeful are the development and distribution of new high-yield varieties of food grains, especially of rice, wheat, and corn. Increasing the yield on land already under cultivation is easiest and ecologically the most intelligent method of multiplying bread. "All of these new grains," writes Ehrlich, "have the potential for at least doubling yields under proper growing conditions."

Nevertheless, Ehrlich places little confidence in the "Green Revolution," which puts emphasis on vast and dense plantings of single types of grains. Without genetic variability in crops, "You can't stay ahead of the bugs and the pests." Further, "The cost of giving a new food to two million people without population control could be the ultimate deaths of four million people!"

In the direction of protecting our environment, Ehrlich reviews a variety of measures being tried or which are under consideration. Though highly serious, industrial-automotive air pollution, he believes, is perhaps most easily solved of our pollution problems; factories and automobiles can be forced to meet standards of pollutant production, and probably without much economic loss. Pesticide pollution in the air, water, and earth is more difficult to control, in good part because of the close ties between the petrochemical industry and powerful governmental agencies, such as the U.S. Department of Agriculture. Noise is another type of pollution receiving increasing attention from designers of dwellings, factories, and office buildings, but the principal sources of noise—motorcycles, power mowers, jet transports, TV sets, and trucks—"multiply merrily on with the population." Thus to the question of whether we are nursing our sick environment back to health and getting ahead of filth, corruption, and noise, Ehrlich's answer is "the palliatives are too few and too weak. The patient continues to get sicker."

Having examined in detail the nature of the dilemma facing humanity, Ehrlich asks "What Needs to Be Done?" His conclusion is

> Mankind may be facing its final crisis. No action that we can take at this late date can prevent a great deal of future misery from starvation and environmental deterioration. The dimensions of the programs that must be mounted if we are to survive are awe inspiring.

If today's trends continue, Ehrlich contends, there is likely to be further rapid deterioration of man's environment. He proposes four steps toward limiting population, "in full knowledge that they are socially unpalatable and politically unrealistic:" first, establish a Federal Population Commission with a large budget for propaganda and information; second, change our tax laws to discourage rather than to encourage reproduction; third, make instruction in birth-control methods mandatory in all public schools, and abolish laws against abortions approved by physicians; and, fourth, provide federal support for biomedical research in broad areas of population regulation, environmental sciences, and behavioral sciences, rather than for programs of "death control." If all these steps fail to reverse the population growth trend, some form of compulsory birth regulation must be faced.

Ehrlich ends by a "brief checklist" of sixteen points which those concerned with the population explosion and pollution of the environment should heed: Population is far outstripping food production; more than half of the world is hungry and many are dying of starvation; population growth must come to an end; our only choices are a lower birth rate or a bigger death rate; the long-term growth rate must be zero; it is necessary to plan for a stable population of optimum size; family planning alone does not lead to population control; change of attitudes is more important than contraceptive technology in population control; need for better contraceptive methods is great, notwithstanding; in the short term the only feasible way to increase food production greatly is by increasing yield on land already under production; research in tropical ecology and agriculture is badly needed; a firm agricultural base is prerequisite for industrialization; not all countries can be industrialized; developed nations cannot feed undeveloped; environmental deterioration poses a colossal threat to man's survival; governmental attention to this entire problem is less than insignificant.

Mankind should have certain "inalienable rights," Ehrlich continues: the right to limit our families, the right to eat, the right to eat meat, the right to drink pure water, the right to live uncrowded, the right to avoid regimentation, the right to hunt and fish, the right to view natural beauty, the right to breathe clean air, the right to silence, the right to avoid pesticide poisoning, the right to be free of thermonuclear war, the right to educate our children, the right to have grandchildren, and the right to have great-grandchildren.

"If the connection between growing population at home and abroad and the steady deterioration of the quality of life can be made apparent," states Ehrlich in a final plea, "then perhaps successful action can be instituted before our planet is irreversibly ruined."

BIBLIOGRAPHICAL NOTES

ADAMS, HENRY (1838–1918)
The Education of Henry Adams. Washington, D.C.: Privately printed in 100 copies, 1906. 453 pp. Revised edition: Boston: Houghton Mifflin, 1918. 519 pp.

ALGER, HORATIO, JR. (1832–1899)
Ragged Dick: Or, Street Life in New York with the Boot-Blacks. Boston: Loring, 1868. 296 pp. First published serially in Oliver Optic magazine *Student and Schoolmate,* 1867.

AUDUBON, JOHN JAMES (1785–1851)
The Birds of America: From Original Drawings. London: Published by the author, 1827–1838. 4 v.

BENEDICT, RUTH (1887–1948)
Patterns of Culture. Boston: Houghton Mifflin, 1934. 290 pp.

BOK, EDWARD WILLIAM (1863–1930)
The Americanization of Edward Bok: The Autobiography of a Dutch Boy Fifty Years After. New York: Scribner, 1920. 461 pp.

BOWDITCH, NATHANIEL (1773–1838)
The New American Practical Navigator: Being an Epitome of Navigation. Newburyport, Mass.: Edmund M. Blunt, 1802. 589 pp.

BRYCE, JAMES (1838–1922)
The American Commonwealth. London and New York: Macmillan, 1888. 2 v.

BURNETT, FRANCIS HODGSON (1849–1924)
Little Lord Fauntleroy. New York: Scribner, 1886. 209 pp.

BYRD, WILLIAM (1674–1744)
History of the Dividing Line Betwixt Virginia and North Carolina, first publication in *The Westover Manuscripts: Containing the History of the Dividing Line Betwixt Virginia and North Carolina; A Journey to the Land of Eden.* A.D. *1733; and A Progress to the Mines. Written from 1728 to 1736, and Now First Published*

373

Petersburg, Va.: Printed by E. and J. C. Ruffin, 1841. 143 pp. *Secret History of the Line*, first published in William Byrd's *Histories of the Dividing Line Betwixt Virginia and North Carolina*, edited by William K. Boyd. Raleigh: North Carolina Historical Commission, 1929. 341 pp.

CLEMENS, SAMUEL LANGHORNE (1835–1910)
The Adventures of Huckleberry Finn (Tom Sawyer's Comrade). London: Chatto and Windus, 1884. 438 pp.

COOPER, JAMES FENIMORE (1789–1851)
The Deerslayer: Or, the First War-path. Philadelphia: Lea and Blanchard, 1841. 2 v.; *The Last of the Mohicans: A Narrative of 1757*. Philadelphia: Carey and Lea, 1826. 2 v. *The Pathfinder: Or, the Inland Sea*. Philadelphia: Lea and Blanchard, 1840. 2 v. *The Pioneers: Or, the Sources of the Susquehanna*. Philadelphia: Carey and Lea, 1823. 2 v. *The Prairie: A Tale*. London: H. Colburn, 1827. 3 v.

CRÈVECOEUR, MICHEL GUILLAUME JEAN DE (1735–1813)
Letters from an American Farmer; Describing Certain Provincial Situations, Manners, and Customs, Not Generally Known; and Conveying Some Idea of the Late and Present Interior Circumstances of the British Colonies in North America. London: Davies and Davies, 1782. 318 pp.

DANA, RICHARD HENRY, JR. (1815–1882)
Two Years Before the Mast: A Personal Narrative of the Sea. New York: Harper, 1840. 483 pp.

DUBOIS, WILLIAM EDWARD BURGHARDT (1868–1963)
The Souls of Black Folk: Essays and Sketches. Chicago: A. C. McClurg, 1903. 264 pp.

EDDY, MARY BAKER (1821–1910)
Science and Health. Boston: Christian Scientist Publishing Co., 1875: 456 pp.

EHRLICH, PAUL RALPH (1932–   )
The Population Bomb. New York: Ballantine Books, 1968. 223 pp.

FARMER, FANNIE MERRITT (1857–1915)
The Boston Cooking-School Cook Book. Boston: Little, Brown, 1896. 567 pp.

FRANKLIN, BENJAMIN (1706–1790)
Experiments and Observations on Electricity, Made at Philadelphia, . . . Communicated in Several Letters to P. Collinson. London, 1751. 86 pp.

GOMPERS, SAMUEL (1850–1924)
Seventy Years of Life and Labor: An Autobiography. New York: Dutton, 1925. 2 v.

GRAY, ASA (1810–1888)
Elements of Botany. New York: G. and C. Carvill, 1836. 428 pp.

HOLMES, OLIVER WENDELL (1841–1935)
The Common Law. Boston: Little, Brown, 1881. 422 pp.

JAMES, WILLIAM (1842–1910)
The Principles of Psychology. New York: Holt, 1890. 2 v.

KENNEDY, JOHN FITZGERALD (1917–1963)
Profiles in Courage. New York: Harper, 1956. 266 pp.

KINSEY, ALFRED CHARLES (1894–1956)
Sexual Behavior in the Human Male. Philadelphia: W. B. Saunders, 1948. 804 pp.

LEWIS, SINCLAIR (1885–1951)
Main Street: The Story of Carol Kennicott. New York: Harcourt, Brace, 1920. 451 pp.

LIPPMANN, WALTER (1889–   )
An Inquiry into the Principles of the Good Society. Boston: Little, Brown, 1937. 402 pp.

MATHER, COTTON (1663–1728)
Magnalia Christi Americana: Or, the Ecclesiastical History of New-England, from Its First Planting in the Year 1620, unto the Year of Our Lord, 1698. London: Printed for T. Parkhurst, 1702. 7 pts. in 1 v.

MAURY, MATTHEW FONTAINE (1806–1873)
The Physical Geography of the Sea. New York: Harper, 1855. 274 pp.

MELVILLE, HERMAN (1819–1891)
Moby-Dick: Or, the Whale. New York: Harper, 1851. 634 pp

MITFORD, JESSICA (1917–   )
The American Way of Death. New York: Simon and Schuster, 1963. 333 pp.

MUMFORD, LEWIS (1895–   )
The Culture of Cities. New York: Harcourt, Brace, 1938. 586 pp.

NADER, RALPH (1934–   )
Unsafe at Any Speed: The Designed-in Dangers of the American Automobile. New York: Grossman, 1965. 365 pp.

PARKMAN, FRANCIS (1823–1893)
The California and Oregon Trail: Being Sketches of Prairie and Rocky Mountain Life. New York: Putnam, 1849. 448 pp.

POST, EMILY (1873–1960)
Etiquette in Society, in Business, in Politics and at Home. New York: Funk & Wagnalls, 1922. 627 pp.

SMITH, JOHN (1580–1631)
The Generall Historie of Virginia, New-England, and the Summer Isles with the names of the Adventurers, Planters, and Governours from their first beginning. Ano: 1584 to this present 1624. With the Procedings of those Severall Colonies and the Accidents that befell them in all their Journyes and Discoveries. Also the Maps and Descriptions of all those Countryes, their Commodities, People, Government, Customes, and Religion yet Knowne. London: Printed by I. D. and I. H. for Michael Sparkes, 1624. 248 pp.

SPOCK, BENJAMIN (1903–   )
The Common Sense Book of Baby and Child Care. New York: Duell, Sloan & Pearce, 1946. 527 pp.

STEINBECK, JOHN (1902–1968)
The Grapes of Wrath. New York: Viking Press, 1939. 619 pp.

SUMNER, WILLIAM GRAHAM (1840–1910)
Folkways: A Study of the Sociological Importance of Usages, Manners, Customs, Mores, and Morals. Boston: Ginn, 1907. 692 pp.

TARBELL, IDA (1857–1944)
The History of the Standard Oil Company. New York: McClure, Phillips, 1904. 2 v.

THOREAU, HENRY DAVID (1817–1862)
Walden: Or, Life in the Woods. Boston: Tichnor and Fields, 1854. 357 pp.

VEBLEN, THORSTEIN BUNDE (1857–1829)
The Theory of the Leisure Class. New York: Macmillan, 1899. 400 pp.

VESPUCCI, AMERIGO (1451–1512)
Lettera di Amerigo Vespucci delle Isole Nuouamente Trouate in Quattro Suoi Viaggi. Florence, Italy: Pietro Pacina da Pescia, 1505–1506. 32 pp. First edition, in Italian, of four voyages.

WASHINGTON, BOOKER TALIAFERRO (1859–1915)
Up from Slavery: An Autobiography. New York: A. L. Burt, 1901. 330 pp.

WEBSTER, NOAH (1758–1843)
A Grammatical Institute of the English Language. Part 1. Containing a New and Accurate Standard of Pronunciation. Hartford: Hudson and Goodwin, 1783. 120 pp. Title later changed to *The American Spelling Book.*

WEEMS, MASON LOCKE (1759–1825)
A History of the Life and Death, Virtues, and Exploits, of General George Washington; Dedicated to Mrs. Washington; and Containing a Great Many Curious and Valuable Anecdotes Tending to Throw Much Light on the Private as Well as Public Life and Character of That Very Extraordinary Man. George-Town: Printed by Green and English, 1800? 80 pp.

WHITMAN, WALT (1819–1892)
Leaves of Grass. Brooklyn, N.Y., 1855. 95 pp.

WIGGLESWORTH, MICHAEL (1631–1705)
The Day of Doom: Or a Description of the Great and Last Judgement, with a Short Discourse about Eternity. London: Printed by J. G. for P. C., 1662. 95 pp.

WILLKIE, WENDELL (1892–1944)
One World. New York: Simon and Schuster, 1943. 206 pp.

WISTER, OWEN (1860–1938)
The Virginian: A Horseman of the Plains. New York: Macmillan, 1902. 504 pp.

WRIGHT, FRANK LLOYD (1869–1959)
An Autobiography. London, New York: Longmans, 1932. 371 pp. Revised edition, 1943.